"INTO THE VERY MIDST OF THIS MOVING CIVILIZATION
THERE CAME THE METHODIST PREACHER"

THE STORY OF METHODISM

by

HALFORD E. LUCCOCK
and
PAUL HUTCHINSON

With illustrations by
HAROLD SPEAKMAN

THE METHODIST BOOK CONCERN
NEW YORK　　　　　　**CINCINNATI**

To
NAPHTALI LUCCOCK
AND
CHARLES X. HUTCHINSON
FAITHFUL MEMBERS OF THE METHODIST MINISTRY

CONTENTS

CONTENTS

LIST OF ILLUSTRATIONS

CHAPTER I

MEET JOHN WESLEY!

§ 1.   A London Crowd Two Hundred Years Ago

HAD you been in London one September Sunday in 1739 and followed the pushing crowds, as well you might, to Moorfields, that Coney Island of the eighteenth century, you might have found yourself a part of a throng milling about on Kennington Common. Standing on the edges, with some behind you trying to push in and some in front trying to push their way out, you might, for a time, have wondered what excitement had drawn this multitude together. But as you gradually worked your way toward the center, farther and farther into a circle of silence, at last your ear would have caught unhurried accents, falling with no sense of strain but with the subtle timbre of intense conviction, and drawing the eyes of those who heard toward a common focus.

Looking that way yourself, it might still have taken you a moment to discern the lips from which the words were issuing, for the head of their owner stood scarcely higher than that of many others. But as you craned your neck about, the better to see, you might have caught a fleeting glimpse of clerical garb upon the shoulders of the speaker, or seen a momentary gesture as one hand was lifted to impress a point or brush back a lock of long dark hair. Standing beside the speaker you might have noted the erect figure of an older woman, her eyes alight, partly with pride and partly with participation in the message. And if you had stood there long enough—which is likely, for once there it would not have been an easy matter to

13

leave—you would have felt a strong emotion pass through the crowd as, from time to time, the speaker repeated words which evidently formed his text: "Believe on the Lord Jesus Christ, and thou shalt be saved." For you would have been, whether you knew it or not, in the presence of the most powerful social force in the England of the eighteenth century.

If England to-day is not what England was then, if the

"THE TRUE CENTER OF A CENTURY"

Englis h - s p e a k i n g world of the twentieth c e n t u r y differs in thought and outlook from that of the eighteenth, it is to a large extent due to the fact that this little man turned his back on a career at Oxford or a comfortable benefice within the Established Church and went out to just such places as Moorfields to meet his fellows when all their guards were down and call them to a new kind of life. There was present in that crowd on Kennington Common that day, had your eyes been able to see, the true center of a century of English history, and that a century that was to contain such names as Marlborough and Wellington, Nelson, Clive and Wolfe, Swift and Addison, Johnson and Goldsmith, Pope and Gibbon, Byron and Burns, Coleridge and Wordsworth. For that little man who spoke that day was John Wesley; that woman at his side was his mother; that crowd that milled about you was the London, the England, of that time; and that text, echoed by that same man under like conditions a thousand times, was the word that was to make a new social order. Let us look at them all more closely.

§ 2.   On a Soap-Box

Perhaps no man ever ascended a soap-box with more hesitation than John Wesley. Perhaps no man ever stood on one

"THE WORD THAT WAS TO MAKE A NEW SOCIAL ORDER"

with more power. So short of stature that even when on a platform his head scarcely rose above the heads of his hearers, some electricity that filled his scant five feet and four inches of frame and snapped from his eyes compelled attention.

Wesley's slowness when his friend, George Whitefield, proposed preaching in the open is not to be wondered at. Whitefield seemed born for that sort of thing. Upstanding and muscular, Whitefield had been kicked and cuffed through life from the day when he first saw light as the son of a tapster in a Gloucester inn. But Wesley came of different stock. His father and his grandfathers before him had been clergymen— courageous enough, in all conscience, but hedged about with the protection that frequently is afforded men of the church. Wesley's own life had been that of a scholar, a university tutor. Even in Georgia, to which he had gone as the chaplain of a struggling colony, he had lived an ascetic. There was something almost fragile about him—the small hands, wrists and ankles, the pale face, the long and silken hair. Put him into the gown of an Oxford fellow, or the robes of a priest of the Church of England, and he seemed the last man to stand up before the impatience of the mob.

"THE COOL QUIET WITHIN AN AGE-OLD CHURCH"

But there was that about the face of John Wesley that belied his slight frame. Perhaps it was his nose, high-ridged, aquiline, the nose of a commander, the same nose to be seen in the portraits of his distant cousin, Arthur Wellesley, Duke of Wellington. More likely it was his eyes, dark, vivid, brooding and quiet during moments of repose, but flashing and compelling when aroused in public speech. The high forehead, coming down to the steep brows, seemed made to provide a curtain for those eyes when their owner wanted to be alone—and John Wesley could be much alone in the midst of a multitude. But when the instant for action arrived that curtain seemed to be lifted, and the eyes came blazing out to hold captive the attention of such as they might light upon.

Field preaching, in 1739, was still a new experience for John Wesley. He had begun it at Bristol, after the churches had closed their pulpits to him and his brother Charles and his friend, George Whitefield. He had hesitated a long time, for he was a child of the church in which he had been ordained, and that church, he well knew, set great store on the doing of all things in accord with custom and with as little fuss and excitement as possible. Charles Wesley, venturing to preach in the open air in London, had been called upon the carpet before the bishop and warned that if he did not leave off these unaccustomed ways excommunication might be his lot. And John Wesley, loving the cool quiet within an age-old church, the carved beams lost aloft in the gloom of the vaulted roof, the muted light filtering in through stained-glass windows, the calm security of the consecrated pulpit, could hardly bring himself to take his priest's white robes and stand to preach where mud was plentiful and jeers more likely than prayers. Yet, under the urging of bold Whitefield, he had done so.

He had shown the stuff within him by not only taking himself to the open air about Bristol, but by seeking out the most degraded, and consequently the most needy folk in all that region. Straight to the miners of Kingswood he had gone —men utterly without contact with religion, men who would have cursed the ordinary priest as fluently as they cursed every other incident of their besotted lives, desperate men, living like savages, and considered such by the rest of the community. Those were the men who comprised John Wesley's first outdoor congregations, who came, at first by tens and hundreds, to see what new sport this mad-brained parson had contrived, and who remained, to swell his audiences from one hundred to five, to a thousand, and finally to ten thousand—wild, riotous men, silent before the voice of this frail young priest, until at last the deeps of their beings were rent, and the cries of strong men broken sounded on the quiet evening air, and the tears flowed down the coal-grimed faces, leaving their telltale traces behind.

We may wonder, to-day, how such results could have come so quickly from such preaching. There was nothing eccentric about the preacher. He did not shout; he did not threaten. He later used to warn his preachers against both these things, saying, "No man can be bullied into heaven, and never was." He used few gestures—a single lift of the arm being enough to drive home the points of greatest moment. His words were not as ornate as those of most preachers of his time, nor was there anything bizarre about them. He never talked down to his audience. Instead, he used the simplest words that he could find to say exactly what he meant.

He kept as far away as possible from terms that sounded pious, but that he knew really meant nothing to the majority of hearers. "I am sick and tired of hearing some men preach Christ," he once exclaimed. "Let but a pert, self-sufficient animal, that hath neither sense nor grace, bawl out something about Christ or his blood, or justification by faith, and his hearers cry out, 'What a fine gospel sermon!'" John Wesley never indulged in that kind of claptrap. During all his life the First Epistle of Saint John was his model for style, and if you will read the simple but sun-clear sentences of that ancient letter, you will catch the note that marked this preaching.

This very simplicity and directness accounted for much of the response to Wesley's first outdoor preaching. But these qualities alone were not enough to produce such results. The real secret lay in the message itself. For so many years the Kingswood miners had been regarded as subhuman by the respectable people of Bristol that they had come to look upon themselves in that light, and lived accordingly. They distrusted their own hearing when the young preacher assured them that he believed in them, that he considered them fit to talk to, that he was sure they were capable of better things. And when he spoke of a God who loved them, personally, individually, intensely, so that He would make any sacrifice to bring them back into touch with Himself, the idea proved overwhelming. For a while they might hold off, certain that no such thing could be true. But when, persuaded by the preacher's clear sincerity, they finally gave the thought room in their minds, it was not long before the whole mass was moving forward toward the first recognition as decent, worthy members of society they had ever known. This little preacher did not threaten them; he pleaded and he loved and he pointed out a shining road ahead. And that was a call that could not be denied.

How the heart of John Wesley, that slender thirty-six-year-old preacher, must have pounded as he walked out to preach his first sermon in the open air! "I could scarce reconcile myself to this strange way," he told his friends, "and thought the saving of souls almost a sin if it had not been done in a church." But, the plunge once taken, the crowds gathered, the hearts stirred, the lives transformed, the little clergyman came to look upon his departure from custom in a far different manner. Clearly the hand of God was in this, for here were myriads—the word is Wesley's own—of people who never darkened a church door brought to hear a word that was again proving its ancient power. The testimony of such results could not be ignored. At once the preacher gave evidence of that clearness of judgment, that readiness to abide by the facts, which was to be one of the outstanding characteristics of his career. What if a bishop or curate condemned the meetings on the green? Obviously, in the light of what was happening, the Lord did not. Therefore Wesley was ready to go ahead, theorizers on church order to the contrary notwithstanding. He was committed to what worked—an enduring peculiarity of his true followers.

§ 3. A FAMILY REUNION

What an eager journey it must have been that the young preacher made back from Bristol to London in September, 1739! Three months before, he had spent a short period in the

FROM BRISTOL BACK TO LONDON

capital, preaching for Mr. Whitefield to several crowds of more than ten thousand. But the burden of the work he had under way at Bristol had been too heavy on him to give him any peace, and he had hastened away again almost before his friends knew he was in the city. Now he could see his way clear to several weeks in London, for he had left his brother, Charles, in charge at Bristol. His heart was all a-fire as he pushed homeward, for not only was there the tale of his wonderful experience with the colliers to tell, but there awaited him, at the end of the road, the person to whom his heart was always closest, his mother.

The last months had not been easy ones for Susannah Wesley. For four years now she had been a widow, forced to leave that Epworth where she had reared her family and entwined herself with the lives of her neighbors of thirty-nine years. None of her children were wealthy, so it was agreed that she should pass from one of their homes to that of another, thus distributing the burden of her support. At last, however, a woman of seventy, she had come back to the London where she was born, where lived her eldest son, Samuel, as a parish clergyman of the Church of England, and where her two other sons had been stirring up so much other interest. There she awaited the return from Bristol of her Jacky, the boy who always occupied a peculiar place in her affection.

Would that we had some record of that reunion! How eagerly the aged woman must have plied her boy with questions! How joyously he must have answered them! How her eyes must have begun to glow as he told of the new light that had shone amidst the darkness of the miners of Kingswood; of the great throngs which had covered the brickyard of Bristol; of the select bands with their unmistakable evidence of transformed lives! And how she must have kept thinking as she sat there, listening to the rushing story of such spiritual victories as England had not known for centuries, "If only his father could have lived to hear this! If only Samuel were here to-day!"

But it was not long before the keen eyes of the son had perceived that there was a change in his mother. And when he questioned her, the facts came out without hesitation. To his amazement he discovered that she was rejoicing in the same sense of spiritual satisfaction and assurance that he had been promising to the multitudes in his open-air meetings. It seemed impossible that this should have been a new experience for the woman who had always represented to him the very summit of human virtues, but, as she told the story, it all seemed very much in line with what he had known to happen in other lives.

"Until I learned what you and Charles and Mr. Whitefield were preaching," said his mother, "I had scarce heard such a thing mentioned as having forgiveness of sins now, or having God's Spirit bear witness with my spirit. Much less did I imagine that this was the common privilege of all be-lievers. For that reason, I never dared to ask for such an experience for myself. Then I read the paper which you wrote, explaining what you are trying to preach. And then, two or three weeks ago, while your brother-in-law Hall was pro-nouncing those words in delivering the cup to me, while I knelt at the communion rail, 'The blood of the Lord Jesus Christ, which was given for thee,' the words struck through my heart, and I knew God for Christ's sake had forgiven me all my sins."

It is not hard to imagine how much such a testimony must have cheered John Wesley. The opposition was piling up fast against him. His own older brother clearly showed that he felt that the two juniors had strayed far from the proper path of Christian ministers. Charles, indeed, had already been called on the bishop's carpet and threatened with punishment. Most of the friends of the Holy Club days had turned away for one reason or another. The young evangelist must have had many hours when he wondered whether the course he was following was the right one. But here was his mother, the one person whose advice and experience meant most to him, and she was telling him that she had just gone through an experience which was exactly like the experience he was promising those who would act on the urging of his preaching. No wonder that when John Wesley got off alone in his room, and pulled out the little book in which he jotted down the events of each day, the angular shorthand read, "I talked largely with my mother"!

It was the next Sunday that Susannah Wesley put her stamp of approval publicly on what her sons were doing. For when five o'clock came and John put on his clerical garb and went out to what was one of the favorite preaching places of Mr. Whitefield, Kennington Common, his mother insisted on coming along. Not that the son made any objection. He was only too glad to have such a source of inspiration at his side. What a thrill she must have had as she looked for the first time at a crowd of almost twenty thousand people, all gathered just to hear her boy preach! It was there we first caught sight of him as this chapter opened.

§ 4. LONDONERS ALL

But if John Wesley held our eyes as he preached on the common that day, how must we have looked to him— we folk from the alleys and mews, the streets and lanes, the stores and dwelling-houses, the dram shops and hovels of eighteenth century London? We were not the dandies, those scented and bewigged creatures in silks and ruffles who strolled in Hyde Park or were carried in their sedan chairs from coffee-house to theater. We were not the courtiers, bowing attendance on a German king who had small interest in his realm, save as a source of revenue for the support of his court and the royal mistresses. We were not the men of college nor of church, whose only religious interest was in disputing over points of theology about which nobody cared tuppence, the disputants included.

We were not, on the other hand, the pitiful wretches who festered in the debtors' prisons, nor the felons who, for crimes that ranged from highway robbery to the cutting of a cherry tree, were soon to be taken to Tyburn hill and hanged to make another public holiday. No, we were just the ordinary folk of London's streets, out for a day's sport. Perhaps we had started for a cock-fight or a bull-baiting. At any rate, here we were in a crowd listening to this strange apparition—a preacher in clerical robes, but without a pulpit.

We were not an attractive crowd. Our social lords might employ French hair-dressers and wear elaborate wigs, but our hair was likely to be matted, our scalps scrofulous, and one had only to come near us to know how seldom did we bathe. We were dirty, brutish. Most of our faces were pock-marked, for smallpox was an almost universal experience. Our clothes were ragged, made of cheap cloth and anything but in order.

The pinch of underfeeding showed on many of our faces, and a sniff of the surrounding atmosphere was enough to prove that many of us were trying to make cheap gin do the work that should have been done by expensive food. And why not? Every sixth house in our city was a licensed grog-shop, and when the misery of our existence flooded in on us we caught the promise of forgetfulness in those signs: "Drunk for a penny; dead-drunk for tuppence."

We lived, a large part of us, by our wits. Steady employment paid so little that it seemed better to trust to the luck of pickpockets, petty thievery, gambling, or an occasional trip to the coast to help land a boatload of liquor without benefit of excise. However, here and there among us might be seen the holiday finery of some clerk out from behind his counter, the threadbare coat of a young apprentice, or the sober garb of a servitor in some aristocratic family.

Our emotions were easily aroused. Unschooled, most of us, we believed firmly in spooks of all kinds; in wonders, such as the Godalming woman who gave birth to rabbits; in the satisfaction of all animal desires. Dick Turpin, hanged last year, was our hero. The constables were our villains. Let some leader tell us to shout, and we shouted. Let him tell us to hurl stones, and we hurled them. Let him tell us to kill, and we were perfectly ready to commit murder.

In the church we had no interest, for it had none in us. To politics, we were indifferent. Let the fine gentlemen wrangle as they would about Hanoverian George or "the king over the water." It meant little to us. Perhaps London would be gayer should the Stuarts return. But we would not lift a finger to bring them. London was gay enough as matters stood.

Many of us had come crowding into this city from other parts of the kingdom, for it was the time of the first shiftings away from the land to the urban centers. In all England there were scarce six million souls, but half a million of these were now to be found in the capital. Bristol, Newcastle, Liverpool, Manchester, Birmingham, Sheffield —all these, too, were experiencing the first stirrings of the great growth that was soon to come to them.

And who can blame us for having turned away from the bleak and lonely countryside? Vast tracts, now cultivated, lay waste and unenclosed. Sherwood Forest, for instance, still covered most of Nottinghamshire, as in the

"CROWDING INTO THE CITY"

days of Robin Hood. From one end of Derbyshire to the opposite extremity of Northumberland, a hundred and fifty miles, there was nothing but waste. Willows marked what were, by courtesy, called roads as they showed above the swamps; after dusk the village bells rang to guide belated travelers; land lighthouses were necessary to guide at night across the uncharted moor.

Within the farmsteads our life was appalling in its monotony. Food and clothing came from the work of our hands, fuel we gathered, all the implements of labor and of the table and kitchen we fashioned ourselves. Ours was a communal life, sharing the pasturage and the land for tillage with our neighbors, but communication with the outside world there was almost none, so that life rarely rose from its most drab levels. Can you wonder, then, that some of us have made our way, whether by foot or by the infrequent and slowly lumbering stage, to the city, so that we stand in the London crowd, listening to this preacher on Kennington Common?

§ 5.   A New Message

And what words we are hearing! "Believe on the Lord Jesus Christ, and thou shalt be saved!" But what does that mean? Why all this talk about repentance? I am to repent, am I? Yes, parson used to say that, back in the village church. But what do I do to repent? Ah, listen. The little man says that if I become thoroughly convinced of my sinfulness, my guilt, my helplessness, then I have repented. Well, I can understand that. I know I'm a sinner. No use trying to deceive myself or anyone else about that, particularly in this crowd. We're all sinners here! "Guilty?" Yes, to be sure, guilty. "Helpless?" God knows how helpless. I'm with the little man to this point, surely.

But what's to be done? I'm what I am—repentant as may be, but will that help me when I go back to the old crowd? Not a bit, little preacher; not a bit. Then what's to be done by the likes o' me? I'm to have faith in Christ? Tosh! what does that mean? More parson talk. More pious twaddle. More empty words. Come, let's be pushing along.

But pause. What's that? What's that he's saying? "Faith in Christ is a conviction that Christ has loved *me* and given himself for *me*"? Is that it? Is it true? Has he loved me? Has he given himself for me? Me? *Me?* Why, do you know the sort I am? Do you know the kind of a life I lead? Loved *me?* Given himself for *me?* Given himself . . . crucified . . . stabbed by that cruel spear . . . killed . . . for *me!* Me, that's out here lost in the rough London crowd? Me, that's besotted with this filthy liquor on which I live? Me, that's not been in a church this many a year? It's something for me! For me! For me! . . .

Had you been in London one September holiday in 1739 and followed the pushing crowds, as well you might, to Moorfields, that Coney Island of the eighteenth century, you might have found yourself a part of a throng milling about on Kennington Common. There you might have seen a masterful, gray-haired woman standing beside her son. And the words that came from that son's lips might have captured you, for the first time, with the thought that the great God had some interest in you. That might well have happened to you, for it did happen to hundreds of persons. And because it happened there spread in England a movement known to history as the Methodist Revival that still exerts a mighty influence on human affairs.

CHAPTER II

A TALE OF TWO VILLAGES

§ 1. IN NOTTINGHAMSHIRE AND LINCOLNSHIRE

FOURTEEN miles from each other in north central England lie two villages which gave to the English-speaking world the most transforming spiritual forces of the seventeenth and eighteenth centuries. One of them, in Nottinghamshire, stands on the great north post road that long linked Scotland with London. The other, across the river Trent, on a little island formed by three small rivers and a canal, is almost lost in one of the most lonely parts of Lincolnshire. The Nottingham village, when it had made its gift to humanity's progress, fell back into a profound anonymity that was not to be broken until, not much more than fifty years ago, persistent dabblers in ancient affairs discovered it and made it a center of world pilgrimage. The little town in Lincolnshire, never quite forgotten, still remains so far off the beaten routes of travel that only the traveler in love with the out-of-the-way comes to know its charm.

It may be hard, sitting in the cool stillness of the little parish church in Nottinghamshire, or cycling across to that other church in the neighboring county, to conceive that here were ever cradles for world events. But the post road town in Nottinghamshire is Scrooby, from which went forth the Pilgrim Fathers. And the island town in Lincolnshire is Epworth, where Samuel and Susannah Wesley reared their family. There the two lie, almost, in clear weather, within sight of each other. And perhaps, in that pride of little villages of which the poets tell, one says, "I nurtured the spiritual force that planted a new world!" To which the other

28

replies, "I saw the unfolding of the life that launched the mightiest religious awakening of modern times!"

§ 2. King and Commoner

What pranks history plays upon us! In the year 1603 Elizabeth, England's virgin queen, died and James VI of Scotland, son of that Mary Stuart whom Elizabeth had beheaded, became James I of England. There is no evidence that James ever suffered from overmodesty. Sometimes we stumble on that introduction to the King James version of the Bible that the bishops who knew the monarch felt it wise to insert: "To the Most High and Mighty Prince, James, by the Grace of God king of Great Britain, France, and Ireland, Defender of the Faith, &c. Great and mani-

"JAMES, BY THE GRACE OF GOD"

fold were the blessings, most dread Sovereign, which Almighty God, the Father of all mercies, bestowed upon us the people of England, when first he sent Your Majesty's Royal Person to rule and reign over us. . . . The Lord of heaven and earth bless Your Majesty with many and happy days, that, as His heavenly hand hath enriched Your Highness with many singular and extraordinary graces, so You may be the wonder of the world in this latter age for happiness and true felicity, to the honor of the Great God, and the good of His Church, through Jesus Christ our Lord and only Saviour." We read that and exclaim, "What abject nonsense!" But it didn't sound that way to James. To that "wonder of the world" it is probable that, on the whole, it seemed a very conservative and most inadequate putting of the case.

Regard, then, James, having heard that he is king of England, setting out upon the state journey from Scotland southward, and undoubtedly feeling that the focus of history moves with him from Edinburgh to London. On the way his royal majesty goes hunting in Sherwood Forest, glad, doubtless, that no Robin Hood remains within that storied wood. When he reaches Nottingham, just to show the people of the county who is who, he has a man hanged out of hand. And, in the heat of the day, he stops at a post village called Scrooby where, while the horses are being rested, he graciously deigns to accept refreshments from the keeper of the post.

Perhaps he notes some of the great carved beams of the manor house in which the post keeper receives him. Perhaps his insatiable curiosity moves him to ask enough questions to discover that this had once been an establishment connected with the archbishopric of York. Perhaps he is told how, seventy years before, the great Wolsey came here to hide his disgrace at court, spending in this retirement three of the short months that were to intervene before he died with a broken heart.

Perhaps he notes the firm, keen bearing of his post keeper, the mark of a man who has long been familiar with men and affairs of high import. Perhaps he does. But more likely he merely drinks too much and eats too much and goes to sleep and snores until his lackeys come on tiptoe to tell him that the royal mounts are ready. And so royal Jamie goes on his self-satisfied way southward, never giving another thought to the little village or its keeper of the post.

What would he think could he guess the smile with which history writes now about him and his preposterous pretensions? Or the anxiety with which it traces down the very last fact about that post keeper who was none other than William Brewster, one day to be, thanks to the bigotry of this same king, Elder Brewster of Plymouth Colony?

§ 3. PATRON AND PARSON

Again, who in London paid much attention to that country parson who came to the gay capital in the early years of the century that followed, trying to peddle verses lauding Marlborough and the victory of Blenheim? Fair enough verses, but London was overrun with just such petty rimesters. Really, it was an act of condescension on the part of the great Swift to write the line in *The Battle of the Books* that dispatches the country parson with a kick from the steed of Homer. What could Epworth mean to an Addison or Steele, or any of the throng of wits in the coffee houses of London during the brave days of Queen Anne?

Here and there a nobleman, here and there a man in the upper ranks of the clergy, paused to give a moment to this man who wrote fulsome verses and tiresome commentaries. Perhaps they felt a momentary glow of self-satisfaction at the evident joy they gave the humble parson when they nominated one of his sons to be a student at the Charterhouse or assured him of a patronage to be extended later. For this was London in an exalted period, a London perfectly sure that the victories of Marlborough's armies in the Low Countries had made it the center of the world.

And again history looks at all this fuss and pomp and smiles its twisted smile as Southey perfectly expresses its mood:

> "And everybody praised the Duke,
>   Who this great fight did win."
> "But what good came of it at last?"
>   Quoth little Peterkin.
> "Why, that I cannot tell," said he,
> "But 'twas a famous victory."

Yet every line that can be discovered about what went on in

that country rectory is treasured, because the nursery of that rectory contained, among a good many others, a little boy whose name was John Wesley.

§ 4. HISTORY SPRINGS A SURPRISE

History is like that. Nero was certain that the most important happenings in Rome were the words he said, the laws

EPWORTH AND ITS NEIGHBORS

he enacted, the things he did, even down to the tunes he fiddled. But history looks past Nero to a secret prayer meeting being held in the catacombs.

The family of the Medici were certain that the most important happenings in Europe during those years of the Renaissance were the palaces they built, the art galleries they filled, the cities they governed. But history looks past even Lorenzo the Magnificent to a little boy playing about on the docks of Genoa, looking out across the Mediterranean waters and dreaming of a time when men might sail beyond those pillars of Hercules to the lands of spices and gold.

Napoleon was certain that the biggest fact in the world was the march of his grenadiers to command of the kingdoms of Europe. But history looks past Napoleon to a lad sitting in a Scotch cottage watching the cover of a tea-kettle bob up and down; wondering what giant's hand was working there.

To-day we name glibly Wilson, Lloyd George, or Foch, and we like to think these the mighty figures of our time. But the chances are that history is again preparing to play its old ironic game, and to point future generations to those two boys

"THAT COUNTRY RECTORY"

puttering about in the bicycle shop back of the Ohio parsonage, and bringing to birth plans which will make men masters of the air. And if not there, then almost certainly to some other hidden and inconspicuous spot that imperious finger will point. For history is like that.

Surely, however, it is worthy of comment that the person who tramps about England to-day can stand on that low hill-side in Nottinghamshire, looking away across the level, well-kept farms, with here and there the spire of a parish church thrusting up from a clump of trees and thatched roofs, and then, in an afternoon, can cross the Trent, penetrate that boggy district called the isle of Axholme, and then write a post-card, saying, "I have stood this afternoon in two little villages where two centuries found their souls." Scrooby and Epworth! From the first, in truth if not in actual chronicle, the May-flower set sail to plant a new world. From the second, John Wesley went out to save an old one.

CHAPTER III

A NURSERY EPIC

§ 1. Nineteen Children!

IF EPWORTH was the spot from which came the spiritual awakening of England, then the nursery on the second floor of the three-storied building of timber and plaster was the center of Epworth. Not the old stone church, so dark and damp within. Not even the rector's study, from which issued those poems and commentaries we have already mentioned, as well as the sermons that frequently roused the black resentment of Epworth's inhabitants. But the room in which the children of the rectory sat for six hours each day at the feet of their mother—that was the place where world events were forming.

A casual visitor would have found it hard to believe that there was such a room in the parsonage. Place nineteen children in a building—any building, no matter how large—and the result is fairly certain to be bedlam. To be sure, there were never nineteen children in this nursery at one time. Ten of the Wesley children died in infancy (a reminder of the sacrifice of infants that in those days was thought inevitable) but the whole company of them were born within the space of twenty-one years, so that there never was a time, for the first fifteen years of the century, when the house was not filled to overflowing. Yet the troop of young Wesleys seemed to pass about the halls, up and down the stairs, or melt behind that nursery door with never a sound.

The secret, of course, of that quietness lay in a system of training that began before the child was out of the cradle, and continuously regulated the most minute details of daily life.

There are those in this day who say that the proper way in which to bring up a child is to let him do as he pleases. The more vociferous and irritating his behavior, the better, for that is the best means of developing his personality. Self-develop-

"WHERE WORLD EVENTS WERE FORMING"

ment, for such folks, means an entire absence of reins. They would be scandalized by the methods of the Wesley nursery, where every child, before his first birthday, was taught to cry q u i e t l y, and where the slightest d e v i a t i o n from modes of language and deportment that might have provided the model for some book of etiquette brought down instant reproof. But, even in the face of our supposed advance in knowledge of child nature and educational methods, the chances are that the Wesleys, both father and mother, would be willing to put up the products of their system for comparison with the products of our "modern" homes.

A system so Spartan as that employed in the Epworth rectory would not work with every child. It did not work with all the children in that family. Of the six girls who survived to maturity, several of them, in later life, gave evidence that their spirits had been more warped than developed. It would not have worked with any of them had it not been for the remarkable nature of the woman who employed it.

In the hands of any lesser person, such a rigid discipline must have been little better than a tyranny, with the youngsters only waiting for the moment of freedom to let go the resentment that the years had distilled within them. In the hands of Susannah Wesley, it was a means whereby the innate powers of several remarkable children were given a chance to develop without being imposed upon by other children almost equally remarkable, at a time when all were forced to live together in a restricted space.

The stern rule of the Epworth nursery protected one child from another, and at the same time gave each a chance for self-development. The sons, at least, never ceased to give thanks that the rules had been enforced. Many years after, one of them, having by that time a good many thousand families looking to him for advice in all matters, attempted to tell them how to bring up their children. The rules he laid down were almost a copy of the Epworth rules. But the results were not the same, for there were not many Epworth mothers to administer the Epworth discipline.

§ 2. SUSANNAH WESLEY

By all tests, Susannah Wesley must have been one of the world's most wonderful women. Her idea of parental discipline may not have been that of this first part of the twentieth century, but there is no certainty that it will not be that of the next part. And many of the other circumstances of her life show her to have been, in the best sense of that much-abused term, a modernist.

She used to call her husband "My master," but that was

merely a deference to the customs of her period, and perhaps a means of keeping the good parson from realizing just how independent she was. " 'Tis a misfortune peculiar to our family that your father and I seldom think alike," she once wrote her most famous son. But if it was a misfortune, there is no sign that it greatly worried her. She had come of an independent line, her father and her grandfather before her having given up their positions for conscience' sake. And she preserved that same independence.

Her first evidence of her ability to stand on her own feet and control her own life came when, as a girl of thirteen, she, the youngest of the twenty-five children of the famous Dr. Samuel Annesley, deliberately rejected the nonconformity of her father and reentered the church which had cast him forth. Later, when her husband, in accord with the rule of the *Prayer Book,* asked for the divine blessing on King William, come from Holland to sit on the throne James II had brought to such low repute, Mrs. Wesley shut her lips in a firm line, and kept them shut, even when her husband, to bring her to terms, went off to London and left her to shift as best she might with her extensive brood. But for all of Susannah Wesley her Samuel might have died in the capital without a sign of repentance on her part, had not King William obligingly broken his neck the next year and so allowed her husband to come home with his "face" saved.

A better mark of her independence was shown when the war of the Spanish succession broke out and England, under the Duke of Marlborough, swept to glory at Blenheim. We have already seen how Mr. Wesley, bursting with patriotic fervor, dashed off his poem called "Victory" and hastened to London to celebrate the national hero. Probably there never was a war that more completely swept the popular imagination. But Susannah Wesley was not stampeded—not she. A day having been appointed for fasting and prayer for the success of English arms, the rector's wife again refused to have any part in the proceedings, for, said she, "Since I am not satisfied of the lawfulness of the war, I cannot beg a blessing on our arms till I can have the opinion of one wiser and a more competent judge than myself in this point, namely, whether a private person that had no hand in the beginning of the war but did always disapprove of it may, notwithstanding, implore God's blessing upon it, and pray for the good success of those arms which were taken up, I think, unlawfully."

Another mark of the spirit of Susannah Wesley was found in her refusal to be bound by the customs that so severely restricted the interests of women. In a day when the education of a girl, even of the upper classes, included no more than a little rudimentary reading and writing and enough acquaintance with figures to make it possible to keep score at cards, Susannah Wesley was well educated herself, and she saw to it that her daughters were likewise. And when her husband went off to London, leaving the parish for a long stretch without what seemed to her fit ministerial attention, she gathered the people in the rectory and there led them in their devotions.

The rector, when he heard about it, was horrified. Why, a religious meeting in a private house was no better than a nonconformist conventicle! And a woman leading such a meeting was a defiance of Saint Paul! Susannah Wesley knew all about conventicles and she knew all about Saint Paul, and she accordingly told her husband, after explaining why the meetings had been held and how much good they were doing, that she would not stop them unless he positively commanded that she do so. Probably she knew him well enough to know that no such command would be forthcoming. Nor was there.

§ 3. ON THE FIFTH BIRTHDAY

But it was as an educator that she did her greatest work. She made education a wonderful adventure, to which the children came with unflagging zest and from which they took an eagerness of mind that was to mark them through all their years. The coming of the fifth birthday, that great day upon which the child was to be inducted into the fellowship of learn-

"SHE MADE EDUCATION AN ADVENTURE"

ing by mastering the alphabet in a single day, was made the great event of childhood, the day of days, to be looked forward to with greater anticipation than any Christmas. The Wesley children thus went into their education with the swing of victory. From the first day they lived in an atmosphere of triumph, and that enthusiasm of achievement did much to carry them on to the triumphs of later years.

They were never, in the classroom, allowed to become familiar with the disenchantment of defeat. "Sukey," exclaimed the rector one day, "you have told that child twenty times the same thing." "Had I satisfied myself with only nineteen," she calmly replied, "I should have lost all my labor. It was the twentieth time that crowned the whole."

Susannah Wesley was as careful in the nurture of the reli-

gious life of her children as in the other aspects of their training. Once a week she took each one aside for an hour of private
conversation concerning the deepest things of the Spirit. She
went to great lengths to make clear to them the tenets of the
church, so that John, at least, had been admitted by his exacting
father to the communion by the time he was eight years of age.

She so formed in her children the habit of coming to her,
rather than to their ordained father, with their inner problems
and difficulties that the earliest Wesley correspondence we have
is largely the record of a boy away from home writing to his
mother for guidance. Even when he had reached the proud distinction of being a Fellow in Lincoln College, Oxford, one of
the sons was not ashamed to ask this mother to keep for him
the hour that had been especially his during his boyhood, so that
he might know that, at that sacred time, he was still peculiarly
in her prayers. It is probable that he voiced a request which
was unnecessary.

We have spoken of Susannah Wesley as a modern woman,
free to think as she would, to teach as she would, and to act as
she would. The modern woman demands for herself an increasing sphere of action. She will not be held within old boundaries; constantly she is pressing into new professions.
Susannah Wesley was really a pioneer in a new profession. She
was—although she never suspected it—a pioneer electrical
engineer. She had the magic gift of harnessing the mysterious
energy that she found in her nursery and using it to propel a
thousand messengers to every hamlet of her land, to light the
slums of every city with a shining light, and to make a hundred
thousand lives that had seemed cold and lifeless glow with the
warmth of a new fire.

§ 4. SAMUEL WESLEY

In centering our attention thus upon Mrs. Wesley we
must not altogether overlook the other parent in this Epworth

household, the Rev. Samuel Wesley, M.A. In his own way Samuel was quite as much an individual as was his wife. Like her the offspring of two generations of Puritan nonconformist preachers, he like her had for himself decided to go back into the old church. To carry out that decision he had enough strength of character to enroll as a servitor in one of the Oxford colleges. It is not unusual for an American boy to work his way through college by waiting on table. In Oxford such a course required courage of the first order.

After ordination and marriage, when the responsibilities of his fast-increasing family were beginning to settle upon him, Samuel Wesley did not hesitate to resign the living at South Ormsby, which he had been lucky enough to obtain, rather than wink at the loose life of the nobleman who had bestowed it.

If he was not afraid of the patron above him, neither was he of the crowd about him. Sometimes that takes the greater bravery. The people of Epworth were an ignorant, godless lot. He told them so. Indeed, he impressed the fact with so much vigor and so little tact that they burned his rectory about his ears. But that only stirred him up to renewed zeal. Finally, the very ardor of his ministry won them. They came to grant him, at least grudgingly, a hearing, and most of them made at least enough show of the forms of religion to rejoice their rector's churchly soul.

Samuel Wesley was a man of some vision and of a great deal of true piety. As a young man he had served as chaplain on a man-o'-war, which released him so completely from the narrow parochialism which cursed the church of his day that he later became the advocate of a broad and comprehensive scheme for foreign missions. In this he was just about a century ahead of his time, but the foreign missionary enthusiasm that finally swept the churches as the eighteenth century was closing really owed much of its power to the work that Samuel Wesley's sons had done in preparing the hearts of men.

When he went to London the rector seems to have had no difficulty in joining at least the outer rim of the company of the social and literary leaders of his day. It is said that he loved to sit in the circle when talk of books or of political affairs was passing; that he knew how to tell a story; that he attracted friends easily. It is to be suspected that, when he had a bit of money, he was not always over-careful about his method of spending it.

The fashion of speaking of the Epworth living as a poor one is not, there is reason for believing, well founded. The parish paid its rector one hundred and fifty pounds a year. In a day when money was at least four times as valuable as it now is, in a little village where living expenses must have been low (for the rector had his own herds and gardens) one hundred and fifty pounds a year was not at all a poor wage. It was one hundred and twenty pounds more than John Wesley ever allowed himself! Yet the rector at least once knew what it felt like to languish in a debtor's prison. And his letters to his sons away at school were largely a recital of financial troubles.

With it all, however, there went a spirit of deep religious concern that had more to do with the molding of the character of the sons of the rectory than some writers have admitted. Without in the least detracting from the honor due Susannah Wesley for what she gave her famous sons, it is clear that her teachings had powerful emphasis placed behind them by her husband. To his son John the old man said, as the final shadows closed about him, "The inward witness, son, the inward witness—this is the proof, the strongest proof, of Christianity." Who but hears there the note which was to echo in after years in that son's preaching? And to his youngest son, Charles, the rector, struggling back up out of the mists of unconsciousness, roused himself enough to whisper: "Charles, be steady; the Christian faith will surely revive in these kingdoms. You shall see it, though I shall not." Who but catches there that optimism which carried the movement begun by those sons to glorious victory?

§ 5. JOHN WESLEY'S BIRTH

It was to parents such as these, and into a family such as this, that John Wesley was born on June 17, 1703. Fifteenth in the line of nineteen children, some reaching back of the mother's heart to two of the babies who had failed to survive their infancy made her name him, after them, John Benjamin. Where the Benjamin disappeared we do not know. John Wesley was always in too much of a hurry to trouble himself with a middle name.

The boy who was to make a new England was one more example, as we have already suggested, of the fact that men are, to a large extent, but the lengthened shadows of their forebears. He once wrote his brother Charles that he had never known another person whose immediate ancestors, on both the paternal and maternal sides, had all been preachers. Not only were they preachers; in the annals of those days they ranked as outstanding preachers.

One of John Wesley's great-grandfathers was one of the original patentees of the Massachusetts colony, and all of them were Puritans of the kind who supplied the moral dynamic for Cromwell's revolution. With the return of the Stuart kings, as we have told, these rugged men gave up their churches and gladly accepted the privations of nonconformity. When John Wesley, years later, drifted almost unconsciously so far away from the church in which he had been reared and ordained, some part of the reason was to be sought in the heritage of four dissenting grandfathers and twice that many great-grandfathers at work within him. As a study in heredity, there are few families to equal in interest the Wesleys.

What must it have been like to have been one of nineteen children! And that in a family where there never seemed money enough to hold off the bill collector! To be sure, but three of the sons lived to grow up, and so, with the long gaps between them, they may not have tread very much on each other's toes. But with the girls it must have been different.

How chequered must have been the career of a gingham dress in the Wesley family! Brought down from London by the rector, and worn by Susannah until it could serve her no longer, then how it must have been divided between Emilia and Susannah, and when it had been outworn by them passed down, in its much-mended condition, to Hetty and Anne, to Martha and Mary, until finally what remained was brought together again to do final duty by little Keziah!

In the midst of this highly individualized group John Wesley grew up, a quiet, reflective sort of a boy, whose natural inclinations helped him to fit easily into the almost military regime his mother required. Perhaps he was inclined to ponder too long and to question too easily. "I profess, sweetheart," the rector one day exclaimed to his wife, "I think our Jack would not attend to the necessities of nature unless he could give a reason for it." And in the attempt to change the ways of the boy he declared: "Child, you think to carry everything by dint of argument; but you will find how very little is ever done in the world by close reason." The time was to come when the son would admit the force of his father's contention, but the day never came when he did not delight in the most closely wrought debate.

The family was bound together by an affection which nothing ever shook. In later years the eldest brother, Samuel, lost patience with John and Charles, and even with his mother for encouraging them, but the family ties held fast. And when the sisters, one after another, married themselves to about as worthless a collection of men as could have been gathered in the British Isles the bonds still held, and the two surviving brothers —for Samuel died at about the time the public career of John and Charles was opening—managed in one way or another to help care for their sisters. All of them had an attitude of mingled affection and reverence for their parents that flooded the declining years of both father and mother with light.

§ 6. Boyhood's Highest Hours

For John the outstanding events of boyhood were the hours at the knee of his teacher-mother; the days when he underwent his ordeal by smallpox; and most of all the night when, a lad of six, he was caught from the burning rectory at the moment just before the roof crashed in. In all the years which followed John Wesley never forgot that night of terror, brought upon the family by ruffians who had been more than usually roused by one of the rector's uncompromising sermons. He thought of himself as "a brand plucked from the burning," and desired the phrase to be carved upon his tomb. And his mother impressed upon him the belief that such a deliverance could only mean that God had in store for him some great destiny. In her own heart she vowed that she would take the greater care to see that he was ready for that destiny when it came.

When he was ten years old the day came on which John Wesley left that nursery. With what a pumping of heart he must have mounted up behind his father to start that long ride to London! And how large the lump in his throat must have been when he found himself alone within the cloisters of the great Charterhouse school in the metropolis! But there he settled down into the routine of the school so acceptably that, by the time he was seventeen, although he still looked much the infant, he was ready for Oxford.

Charterhouse, that treasures on its rolls such names as Lovelace, Barrow, Roger Williams, Addison, Steele, Blackstone, Havelock, and Thackeray, has few traditions of John Wesley. His masters remembered him as a studious boy, who made his way through Greek and Hebrew with great thoroughness, and who participated in the ordinary religious exercises of the school in a spirit of earnestness.

Because of the rough customs of the school life of his day Wesley, in later years, recalled that the bigger boys grabbed most of the meat at meal time, so that he was forced to live largely on a vegetable diet. But he considered that one reason for his later health. Never a strong lad, his father, suspecting the pulmonary trouble which, twenty years later, almost carried him off, ordered the youngster to run about the quadrangle three times every morning, and this he religiously did.

Perhaps the only real bit of excitement that came to him in those years was in the letters from Epworth which told of the visits of "old Jeffrey," the ghost who took to pounding about the rectory whenever the rector started praying for the Hanoverian house by then reigning in England. The Wesleys seem none of them to have been particularly affrighted by this apparition, who banged doors and tipped tables and went through all the other maneuvers that mediums generally produce. The family rather turned in to hunt down the cause of the spook's appearance. And John, by mail, shared in the family excitement. All his life he was a great spook-hunter, and, it must be confessed, a good deal of an easy mark for those with ghost-stories to tell.

§ 7. DAVID LOOKS AT GOLIATH

Finally the days of his preparatory schooling neared their end. His Brother Samuel, now a teacher in Westminster school, London, where the younger, Charles, had fought his way to the captaincy of the student body, reported to the father that John was fully ready for Oxford. Accordingly, an interview was arranged with the great Doctor Sacheverell, the High Church, Tory preacher whose power was enough to bring a ministry to ruin.

Wesley has told us the story of what happened. "I found him alone," he told his friends in later years, "as tall as a may-

"I DESPISED HIM IN MY HEART"

pole and as proud as an archbishop. I was a very little fellow. He said, 'You are too young to go to the university—you cannot know Greek and Latin yet; go back to school.' I looked at him as David looked at Goliath, and despised him in my heart. I thought, if I do not know Greek and Latin better than you, I ought to go back to school indeed. I left him, and neither entreaties nor commands could have again brought me back to him."

All of which goes to show that the John Wesley of Epworth and Charterhouse was the same John Wesley who changed England. All his life he was looking at conditions "as David looked at Goliath," and all his life he was forging ahead as triumphantly as the shepherd-hero of ancient Judah. Now, failing help from one source, Wesley obtained a scholarship on the strength of his scholastic record in the preparatory school and entered Christ Church College, Oxford, anyway.

CHAPTER IV

STUDENT AND MISSIONARY

§ 1. The Oxford Undergraduate

FROM the time he left the Charterhouse school until the night, eighteen years later, when he had a spiritual experience that fixed the course of his career, John Wesley was a young man trying to find his place in the world. Every ambitious young man knows the strain of the years while he is asking himself, What shall I do? And, when that is answered, Where can I find a chance to do it? Young Wesley went through the same unsettled period. He made several false starts before he found himself in the place where he was to win a deathless renown.

He started, as we have said, a young fellow of seventeen as an undergraduate in Christ Church College, Oxford. In all probability he had slight notion what his life-work was to be when he went to the university. As a student at Charterhouse he had won a scholarship worth forty pounds a year, which was enough to make his course possible, and, coming from a long line of educated men, college was the natural thing to undertake next. As undergraduate, postgraduate and faculty member, Wesley was at Oxford, save for two leaves of absence, for fifteen years.

Oxford, in John Wesley's day, had reached a low ebb. It was the seat of a political reaction which expressed itself in glorifying the exiled Stuarts and drinking confusion to the reigning Hanoverians. It was the seat of a religious reaction which expressed itself in the glorification of that wishy-washy, lifeless type of ecclesiasticism that came in after the Puritan decline, hating nothing quite so much as zeal, no matter where applied. And it was the seat of an educational reaction, having no interest in the wider realms of knowledge that had begun to beckon with Sir Isaac Newton, Halley, and their like, but being content to mumble along about the old dry-as-dust academic matters that had been the interests of the monks of the Middle Ages.

Edward Gibbon, the historian, was a student at Oxford not long after Wesley left there, and he assures us that the place had fallen to such depths that it was scarcely fit to rank as a school. And Mark Pattison, a famous rector of the college with which Wesley was most intimately associated, admitted that the university, in those days, gave scarcely any education at all. It was a place for roistering on the part of the undergraduates and loafing on the part of the men who were supposed to be teaching. Years later, John Wesley preached a sermon to the undergraduates, and when he described the shiftless sort of life most Oxford men were leading he made a much more thorough job of blistering their hides than any outsider could have done.

But if Oxford, as such, had sunk to the point where it offered little in the way of education, John Wesley had already risen to the point where he was capable of securing an education for himself. Here was where the years of training in doing things methodically, begun at Epworth under his mother's direction and continued at Charterhouse at the behest of letters from home, came to the front. Already at home in classical literature, Wesley pushed into the library with enthusiasm, and began to pile up for himself that reputation as a student that was to bring him, when only twenty-three, to a place on the faculty of the college whose scholastic standards were then the highest at Oxford.

But he was not at all a recluse. He spent what money he had much more freely than his parents thought proper, and he had time to carry on a mild flirtation with the sister of one of his college-mates. All in all, he must have presented the picture of a young man with great mental powers, keen to enjoy the passing hour, yet living a wholesome, clean life.

Years later, in that sort of self-examination that exacting saints sometimes thrust upon themselves, he wrote disparagingly about his spiritual condition during those undergraduate days. The truth seems to have been that he was a wholly normal young man, not too good to live with, but infinitely superior, both in mind and spirit, to nine tenths of the men who were in the Oxford of his day.

In fact, if there was anything to be worried about in connection with John Wesley during his undergraduate career, it was his physical and not his spiritual condition. For while he was at Oxford the tubercular condition which was to threaten him during all his early years, and even bring him so low that his own brother, Charles, mourned his supposed death, reached a serious state. Hemorrhages became so frequent and so severe that at one time, to stop the bleeding, Wesley had to strip off his clothes and leap into a stream.

It has been the custom to exclaim at the hardships that Wesley underwent in traveling his thousands of miles a year, speaking in the open air, and in general carrying through one of the most strenuous careers known to history. It is probable, however, that it was just this sort of a career which saved Wesley's life. Had he remained a recluse at Oxford or in some village church, he might never have lived to be as old as his brother Samuel. Wesley himself felt that way about it, for he always attributed his long life and continuing vigor to the demanding regime under which he lived. He did not believe that Methodist preachers could be worked to death, for he knew that, in his own case, he had been worked to life.

§ 2. CHOICE OF A LIFE-WORK

After five years at Oxford Wesley began seriously to face

that bugaboo of the undergraduate, What am I going to do? With his ancestry, it was inevitable that he should seriously consider the ministry. In truth, his father seems to have feared that, when he made up his mind to become a minister, John was being a bit too much influenced by heredity and environment.

His mother was not deceived. Even though her rector-husband might have forgotten during the years while the boy had been away at school, Susannah Wesley did not forget the lad who would do nothing until he had a good reason for it. So, when he wrote that he had made up his mind to be ordained, his mother encouraged him. At the age of twenty-two he became a deacon in the Church of England.

Some of those who have written about John Wesley have

CHRIST CHURCH COLLEGE, OXFORD

told the story of this period of his life as though, just at this point, there came a sharp change in his behavior. They evidently think he was more or less of an irresponsible undergraduate up to the time of his ordination; after that they have him a very pious young man, reading Bishop Taylor's *Rules for Holy Living and Dying, The Imitation of Christ,* by Thomas à Kempis, and other books of that kind. Certainly, Wesley began to read many such books, but that is not reason enough to believe that he suddenly became awesomely pious.

It was just another sample of Wesley. He had a career now. He was going to be a minister. What would Wesley do under such circumstances? Why, he would read every book, hunt out every mind that he could discover which offered any help toward the making of a good minister. He would do whatever it was humanly possible to do to make himself in every respect a first-class member of his profession. It would have been the same had he chosen to be a lawyer, a teacher, or some other sort of worker, for that was the sort of person he was.

A few months after his ordination there came to Wesley the distinction that he was proud to claim during all the rest of his days. In 1726, when still only twenty-three years old, he was elected a Fellow of Lincoln College, Oxford. The joy of that stanch old Oxford man, his father, knew no bounds. Letters from home had been, for months, largely concerned with the financial troubles of the Epworth rector. He started another note in much the same vein. But he could not continue it. From the discouraging plaint that he might not have five pounds to keep the family until harvest, the old man suddenly broke over: "What will be my own fate God only knows. *Sed passi graviora.* Wherever I am, my Jack is Fellow of Lincoln!"

§ 3. "Leisure and I Have Said Good-by"

It was as Fellow of Lincoln, a member of the faculty of that college, that John Wesley first began to show clearly the stuff that was in him. "Leisure and I have taken leave of each

other," he wrote his brother, a promise that he was to keep
literally during all the long years that followed. Harking back
to those old days in the Epworth nursery when his mother had
insisted upon a regular order for living, he gave the first day
of every week, Sunday, to the study of divinity, the next two
to Greek and Latin, the next to logic and ethics, Thursday to
Hebrew and Arabic, Friday to metaphysics and natural philosophy, and Saturday to oratory and poetry. And, better than
all else, he had to preside daily at the debates of the undergraduates, point out the fallacies of argument, and decide the
outcome. Six years of that sort of training made him, in his
later days, a debater not lightly to be challenged to combat.

The second of youth's great questions remained to be
settled for Wesley. Granted that he was to be a minister, was
he to spend his life teaching or as the pastor of a congregation?
Plainly, his father, an old man at sixty-five, hoped the latter.
He urged his son to secure a leave of absence from his teaching
duties and, when that was arranged, made him his curate. As
such, most of his duties concerned the oversight of the little
church at Wroote, a hamlet about five miles from Epworth,
from which it was separated by almost impassable bogs. Here
John lived with a sister for housekeeper, occasionally making
the trip back to Epworth, and once narrowly escaping death
by drowning while attempting to do so.

It cannot be said that he was much of a success as a pastor.
In later years he diagnosed his failure as having been due to
preaching as though his hearers did not need to repent of their
sins. A good deal of fruitless preaching has doubtless been due
to that same cause. At any rate, when, at the end of two years,
the rector of his college informed Wesley that he must either
provide a substitute or return to teach if he meant to retain his
fellowship, Wesley went back to Lincoln with few regrets at
leaving Wroote.

Five years later, when his father wanted him to apply for

the pulpit at Epworth, he brought forward all sorts of poor reasons why he should not do so. The chances are that the real reason why a settled pastorate had so few attractions to him was his unlucky experience at Wroote.

§ 4. THE HOLY CLUB

Coming back to Oxford from Wroote, Wesley found himself in a situation that quickly called forth the latent powers of leadership that were later to distinguish him. His younger brother, Charles, had come up from Westminster school, and was now an undergraduate at Christ Church. John, with perhaps some of that anxiety of an elder for a junior's spiritual welfare which makes the elder so exasperating, tried to point out to Charles the way in which he should go, but Charles proved reluctant to pay much attention to the admonitions of his brother.

However, while John had been preaching over the heads of the people of Wroote, Charles had been finding himself. His interests had grown more and more sober. He had discovered some friends with similar interests. John Wesley, on his return, was glad to find such a little group of serious thinkers. As a faculty member he naturally became its leader. The fact that he was a faculty member may not have had much to do with it. He was John Wesley; that was enough to make him the leader.

The little group which the Wesley brothers gathered about them at Oxford was formed, at first, for the purpose of discussing the classics. The real interests that bound the men together, however, were religious rather than intellectual. They never, during all the years of their fellowship, gave up their mental pursuits. But the religious aspects grew to be the all-important ones.

In a period when college life was usually synonymous with the sowing of an extensive and luxuriant crop of wild oats, here came together a few young fellows who were interested in something else. And even to-day when lovers of Oxford are forced

to admit that the wonderful university touched low-water mark
in the early decades of the eighteenth century, they will counter
with, "But you must remember that even then there was a
Holy Club there."

Of course Wesley and his friends were mercilessly pilloried
by the Oxford of their day. Even outside the university
preachers were spending their time expounding those two comfortable texts, "Be not righteous overmuch," and "Let your

"METHODIST!"

moderation be known to all men." In college, what were sure
to be the comments on young men who gave all they possessed,
save just the amount required to keep body and soul together,
to the needy; who spent their time visiting the sick and imprisoned and conducting schools for the poor; who prayed three
times aloud during the day and stopped for silent prayer every
hour; who practiced all the ordinances of the church in the most
meticulous fashion? They might draw up lists of questions
that would reduce to absurdity the complaints of their fellow
students, and, under Wesley's direction, they did. But the
ridicule, and worse, would not down.

"Methodists" was almost the mildest name applied to this
group of campus cranks. Wesley tried to detect an aristo-
cratic-sounding source for that name in the name by which a

certain school of physicians went in the days of Nero. It would be of interest to think that the largest of Protestant groups drew its name from the activities of men who were relieving human ills centuries ago, but the inference is farfetched. The origin of the name—it was almost an epithet to those who first used it—is more clearly indicated by the doggerel of that time:

> "By rule they eat, by rule they drink,
> Do all things else by rule, but think—
> Accuse their priests of loose behavior,
> To get more in the laymen's favor;
> Method alone must guide 'em all,
> Whence Methodists themselves they call."

For a time the Wesley brothers seem to have been disturbed by the outburst of opposition that greeted their efforts to live as they thought Christian students ought to live. But John came at last to see that the real root of the trouble lay in the fact that they were daring to be different from those about them, and an issue of that kind never worried him. And from the old rector at Epworth there came words of good cheer that strengthened their determination to go ahead in the acts of philanthropy and personal devotion that had caused the storm.

The old rector probably knew that just such groups of odd dicks are appearing on college campuses from generation to generation, and that they form the salvation of the colleges. Colleges tend to turn out machine-made goods; folks who dress alike, think alike, talk alike, act alike, and all on a dead level of mediocrity. But, every so often, there come men and women who refuse to wear the clothes, either physical or mental, that are the mode of the moment. They lead a lonely existence. But, after they are safely dead and gone, sleek young undergraduates with that season's brand of stacomb on their brains will point out the ivy circling about a window and demand, "Do you see that room? That's where the Holy Club used to meet."

At that, it is easy to look back at Wesley's club in a fashion which gives a false idea of the men who composed it.   There were in it three giants, the Wesley brothers and George White-field, a student who was working his way through Pembroke

"THE IVY CIRCLING ABOUT A WINDOW"

College by waiting on tables.   Then there was a man who was later to write the best seller of the eighteenth century, James Hervey.   The name of his book was *Meditations Among the Tombs,* which in itself tells quite a lot about the eighteenth century.   And there were two or three men who, as pastors in the Anglican Church, had faithful if undistinguished careers.

But the rest were rather a poor lot.   One of them, who married a sister of Wesley's, is pronounced by the historian of the club "an unmitigated scamp," and two or three others failed conspicuously to live up to the promise of their student days. Even while the club was in existence there were violent fluctuations. When the Wesleys were invigorating it with their presence the number willing to undergo the Spartan regime and the undergraduate taunts might mount almost to thirty; when they were absent the group shrank to five. Looked at candidly, it will be seen that this group was, in the main, made up of just such young fellows as are to be found on any campus in any college generation. Only, it must be admitted, you cannot always find two Wesleys and a Whitefield there at the same time.

§ 5. GEORGIA

Six happy years John Wesley had in active service as Fellow of Lincoln, lecturing once a week on the Greek Testament, presiding every day at the undergraduate disputations, and living the exacting life that he and his companions had determined would properly become a Christian. Then, as old age came creeping rapidly over his father, the question came to the front again as to what the son was to do. The father, who feared that the effects of his years of ministration might be dissipated if some fox-hunting parson were appointed to succeed him at Epworth, urged his boy to apply for the living. The son evaded the issue, raising objections which showed how prone he was, at that time, to look at religion from the standpoint of the satisfaction of his own personal desires. The father brushed his equivocations aside. Finally the son gave in. But it was too late. The fox-hunter had the living. And the old rector was sleeping his last long sleep in Epworth churchyard.

Hardly was his father dead, and his way clear to remain in Oxford if he so desired, when Wesley swung to the other extreme and volunteered to go as a missionary to the Indians of Georgia. It was at the time when General James Oglethorpe was organizing his colony recruited largely from the debtors' prisons of London. The general felt the need of a chaplain for his colonists, and, having been a friend of the father, offered the place to the son. Initial hesitation seems to have been swept aside by the answer of his mother, when he laid the matter before her. "Had I twenty sons," she replied, "I should rejoice that they were all so employed, though I never saw them more." So, with a salary of fifty pounds involved, John Wesley accepted a place as missionary of the Society for the Propagation of the Gospel to the Indians.

There is no use in trying to tell in detail about Wesley's one piece of personal experience in America. He does not seem to have understood the people with whom he tried to work, and they certainly did not understand him. He went out filled with romantic notions of the Indians which showed how careful a reader of the novels of his time he had been. To him the noble red man was waiting with open heart and mind for the coming of the gospel.

WHAT AN EIGHT-EENTH - CENTURY PARSON'S CREST MIGHT HAVE BEEN '

"They have no comments to construe away the text," the outgoing missionary wrote, "no vain philosophy to corrupt it, no luxurious, sensual, covetous, ambitious expounders to soften its unpleasing truths. They are as little children, humble, willing to learn, and eager to do, the will of God." A year later he knew better. "They are all," he then testified, "except perhaps the Choctaws, gluttons, thieves, dissemblers, liars. They are implacable, murderers of fathers, murderers of mothers, murderers of their own children."

With the colonists Wesley had little better success than with the Indians. At that time the young missionary was obsessed with many High Church notions which hardly fitted in with conditions in the young and struggling community.

Various biographers of Wesley have tried to make plain what a rough lot the Georgia colonists were. Doubtless they were. But our sympathies in this particular matter are inclined toward them.

They were dealing with a young man just out of a collegiate atmosphere, who lived in the most ascetic fashion, going barefoot a large part of the time, held to the requirements of the most unbending sacerdotalism, tried to introduce the confessional, penance, and similar practices, and refused both the sacraments and Christian burial to nonconformists.

What would have happened had such a preacher come, in the name of Methodism, into the new communities of Ohio and Kentucky? Exactly what happened to Wesley in Georgia. "We are Protestants," one of the disgusted colonists told the young priest, "but as for you we cannot tell what religion you are of. We never heard of such a religion before; we know not what to make of it."

On top of all this misunderstanding, Wesley complicated his trouble with a love affair. We do not intend, in this story, to give all the details of John Wesley's love affairs, much less to try to justify him in all of them. The truth is that he was never very wise where women were concerned. His experience in Georgia with Miss Sophia Hopkey was merely one of the occasions on which he displayed the truth of that statement.

He loved Miss Hopkey; he should have married her. He didn't. But when he didn't, and she married someone else, he was foolish enough, not long after, to subject her to a bit of ecclesiastical discipline by excluding her from communion. Naturally, tongues wagged, and Miss Hopkey's husband brought suit against Wesley for defamation of character.

It was in the midst of the teapot tempest stirred up by this suit that Wesley concluded that his usefulness in Georgia was at an end and sailed back to England. He was to have an enormous influence on America, but it was not to be as a High Church missionary.

§ 6.   THE MORAVIAN INFLUENCE

However, the Georgia trip was not all loss.   For while on it he first met the Moravians, those simple-hearted believers who, after long vicissitudes in central Europe, were beginning to go in little bands to the New World.

John Wesley first fell in with them on shipboard while Georgia bound.   In the little colony he constantly sought their company.   And when he came back to England he was seldom long separated from some of them, for they had something that he knew he lacked and desperately wanted.   He was in a fever, in those days, over the state of his own soul.   He told himself that he had "a fair-weather religion," but a reading of his diary suggests that generally the weather reports read, "Cloudy, with increasing winds and rain."

The poor chap seems to have been almost in a frenzy, most of the time, because he could not be sure whether or not he was saved.   The Moravians were the first people he had met who seemed to understand what the anxiety was that was tearing at his soul, and yet to have won complete serenity themselves.   They had no fears either for soul or body.   In the midst of storms at sea and in all the other hours when young Wesley's whole being was shaken, the Moravians were calm.

The world knows no more rare or envied person than the man who holds the secret of inner spiritual content.   Wesley haunted the company of these Moravians, determined that he would discover their secret if such discovery was humanly possible.   One young preacher among them, Peter Böhler, a German who had stopped over in England for a few weeks on his way to America, became his particular companion.   If it had not been for Böhler, Wesley might never have come out from the clouds of depression that he had been under ever since, in defeat, he turned away from Georgia. But Böhler and the other Moravians began to show him how little forms of worship had to do with his spiritual condition. And at last they brought him to the place of self-distrust where he was ready for that Aldersgate Street experience which was to change his life.

CHAPTER V

A PRAYER MEETING AND WHAT CAME OF IT

EARLY in the evening of May 24, 1738, a little group of people gathered in a secluded room in Aldersgate Street, London, to conduct a prayer meeting. Outside, it was not yet dark, for the light lasts long in England in May. Inside there was an atmosphere of cheerfulness and of earnestness. These people were members of the Church of England who had failed to find in the stately services of that church all that they sought in the way of spiritual help. So they gathered, week after week, to seek additional strength in an informal meeting of this kind.

In the company there sat a slight young man in the habit of an Anglican clergyman. He had come, as he later testified, "very unwillingly." But for three months he had been passing through a period of intense inner struggle. For the last two weeks this struggle had seemed to be coming to a crisis. All through this day there had been signs that some decisive point was about to be reached.

When he had waked at five o'clock that morning he had opened his New Testament and found these words confronting him: "Whereby are given unto us exceeding great and precious promises; that by these ye might be partakers of the divine nature." "Partakers of the divine nature"—he had closed the book to meditate for a while on a promise of that kind.

Then he had opened the book again. This time it was another verse which seemed to leap from the page: "Thou art not far from the kingdom of God." All morning the two promises had filled his mind. When the afternoon came he had been one of the congregation in vast Saint Paul's cathedral. All the familiar ritual came to him with new meaning. Especially was his music-loving soul moved when there came from the choir the first words of the anthem: "Out of the deep have I called unto thee, O Lord; Lord, hear my voice." Church music probably never rendered a greater service than during the minutes while that anthem continued, until the young minister found himself repeating its final words: "O Israel, trust in the Lord; for with the Lord there is mercy, and with him is plenteous redemption. And he shall deliver Israel from all his sins."

After a day of that kind bare lodgings could not hold the young man. Just what he wanted to do he was not sure. He felt that he did not want to attend another religious meeting. He may have wanted to walk. Whatever his wishes, once in the streets his feet took him unerringly to the gathering of the little society in Aldersgate Street.

What hymns were sung, what prayers said, we do not know. All we know is that the young man continued to sit there quietly, until, at about a quarter of nine, his attention was riveted by the words of a speaker. We do not know who the speaker was. In fact, he was not rightly a speaker at all. He was a reader. Probably a layman, he would not presume to speak or to preach to these good Anglicans. But it was perfectly in order for him to read, and this he was doing. He was reading the preface which Martin Luther had written, two hundred years before, to explain to the original Protestants of Germany the ends which Saint Paul had in mind when he wrote his Epistle to the Romans.

Now, listen to what happened as this young man sat there that May evening, not yet two hundred years ago. We had better let him tell it in his own words: "While he [Luther, he means] was describing the change which God works in the heart through faith in Christ, I felt my heart strangely warmed. I felt I did trust in Christ, Christ alone, for salvation; and an assurance was given me that he had taken away *my* sins, even *mine,* and saved *me* from the law of sin and death."

Then notice the characteristic next act: "I began to pray with all my might for those who had in a more especial manner despitefully used me and persecuted me. I then testified openly to all there what I now first felt in my heart." And after the testimony the young man, thrilling with this wonderful experience which had come to him, rushed to tell the good news to his brother, Charles, sick in a house near by.

Some of those who had been in the prayer meeting went along. In a moment the brother's sick room was transformed into a place of holy joy. And as the little group knelt about the bed the man lying there led them all in singing a hymn which he had himself composed only the day before:

"Where shall my wondering soul begin?
How shall I all to heaven aspire?
A slave redeemed from death and sin,
A brand plucked from eternal fire.
How shall I equal triumphs raise,
Or sing my great Deliverer's praise?"

"It is," wrote the great historian, Lecky, when he came to his monumental work on *England in the Eighteenth Century,* "it is scarcely an exaggeration to say that the scene which took place at that humble meeting in Aldersgate Street forms an epoch in English history." The historian had good reason for his verdict. The young minister who felt his heart strangely warmed that night was John Wesley. And the fire then lit in his heart was destined not to be put out until it had "kindled a land into flame with its heat."

§ 2. DAYS OF SPIRITUAL CONFLICT

The steps by which John Wesley approached his transforming experience in Aldersgate Street were curious ones.

He had landed in England on the first day in February, after more than a month on the wintry Atlantic. All through the stormy voyage home he had been trying to find out what was the matter with his religious life. For twenty-five years he had been trying to serve God. For the last half-dozen years his efforts had been almost desperate. Yet he was retreating from what had been a disastrous failure, so far as his own hopes had been concerned. What was the matter?

Only one clear light seems to have come to him during that voyage. He saw that religious content was not a necessary result of withdrawing from the world or of ascetic living. He had been tempted with that idea ever since his Oxford days. But he had a chance to test it out on the lonely high seas, and it did not work. He was just as miserable alone as he had been among the turbulent colonists of Savannah. Religious health, he saw, must be found in some other way than by cutting oneself off from one's fellows.

When he reached London, two days after his landing, Wesley found General Oglethorpe and the other leaders of the Georgia enterprise unprepared for his coming. His report of the condition of affairs in Savannah disturbed them, but they felt that it needed careful checking in the light of the report on Wesley himself that the colonists had sent. Doubtless they were right. It would hardly have been possible for Wesley to have given a dispassionate or unprejudiced account of the conditions under which he had undergone such torments. The upshot of the whole matter seems to have been that Wesley was allowed to resign, and that his charges were taken "under consideration." It was not the last time that a missionary who "didn't fit" has been disposed of in that manner.

On his first Sunday at home Wesley preached in two London churches. There seems to have been great eagerness to hear the returned missionary. Doubtless the fashionable congregations expected a tale of converted Indians and adventurous pioneering in the American wilderness. What they got was something very different.

Wesley had come home concerned, not with the conversion of the Indians, but with the conversion of himself and of the other white men of his homeland who, he knew, were like himself. So he preached of the necessity of a new birth, not in Georgia, but in London. And the result was that he was told that he could not preach any more in the pulpits of these two churches.

It must have proved a blow for the young preacher. But while the disappointment was still fresh, on the Tuesday after his sermons, he called at the house of a Dutch merchant and found there four German Moravians on their way to Carolina as missionaries. One of the four was the young graduate of the University of Jena of whom we have already spoken, Peter Böhler.

What John Wesley got from Böhler more than made up for the sting of his exclusion from the London pulpits. For three months he shadowed the young German. At the first the two university men had to carry on their conversation in Latin, for Wesley's German was meager and Böhler's English was nonexistent. But it was not long before the young Englishman was using the other's native tongue with fluency.

Carlyle once exclaimed that the course of English church history might have been changed had John Henry Newman known enough German to read the first scientific studies of church history produced by the German scholars of the nineteenth century. How enormously the course of church history *was* changed because John Wesley mastered enough German to come quickly and confidently to an understanding of what Böhler had to teach him!

The main thing that Böhler did for Wesley was to teach him that religious certainty is not a matter of the mind but of the heart. It was the old lesson of the Epworth rectory all

over again: "Our Jack must have a reason for everything."
Böhler and the Moravians were saying, "Be at peace inwardly
just by giving yourself in faith to Christ." Wesley saw that
they had experienced what they preached. But he could not
help saying, "Yes, but how?" That was the stumbling-block
with the Oxford philosopher: How? "My brother," said
Böhler to him one day, "that philosophy of yours must be
purged away." As long as the "how" loomed so large he knew
that there was little chance for the fact itself to occur.

A letter written by Böhler to his Moravian chief, Count
Zinzendorf, back in Germany, gives us the situation in a nut-
shell: "I traveled with the two brothers from London to Oxford," he says. "The elder, John, is a good-natured man; he
knew that he did not properly believe in the Saviour, and was
willing to be taught. His brother is at present very much dis-
tressed in his mind, but does not know how he shall begin to be
acquainted with the Saviour." Then the young Moravian
made this significant comment: "Our mode of believing in the
Saviour is so easy to Englishmen that they cannot reconcile
themselves to it; if it were a little more artful, they would
sooner find their way into it. Of faith in Jesus they have no
other idea than the generality of people have. They justify
themselves; and, therefore, they always take it for granted,
that they believe already, and try to prove their faith by their
works, and thus so plague and torment themselves that they are
at heart very miserable."

All this is reprinted here, not only because it shows the
slow, hard way by which John Wesley came to his great hour
in Aldersgate Street, but because it is so much like the experience of many of the rest of us. There are so few of us who
do not feel that the sure basis of religious satisfaction must be
in our *doing* something! If we only *do* enough good things—
and keep from doing enough bad things—we feel that we are
bound to be inwardly at peace. The thing Böhler had to do was

to teach Wesley that religious satisfaction comes not from doing something but from *being* something.

Böhler did his work well. On May 4 he sailed for his mission field in the New World. On May 22 Charles Wesley, after a gradual approach to the experience of inward assurance which had lasted over several days, went to sleep feeling that he was about to realize his desires. The next morning, as he himself says, he "waked under the protection of Christ, and gave himself up, soul and body, to him."

Charles had been the first at Oxford to be called a Methodist; so now he was the first to have the experience of religious sureness which was to be the outstanding characteristic of the Methodist Revival. What a day May 23 must have been for John, as he watched his brother, sick in body, but radiant in spirit because of his new satisfaction! The story of what May 24 brought to the elder brother has already been told.

There is one word of caution which needs to be said at this point. The inner blessing which came to Charles Wesley on May 23, 1738, and to his brother a day later, was not to be the end of all spiritual struggle for them. Charles, with his mercurial temperament, was to know ups and downs of religious happiness all his life. John was to have months of further torment. His diary shows frequent recurrences of periods when he felt spiritually morose.

As late as January of the next year he bursts out like this: "My friends affirm I am mad, because I said I was not a Christian a year ago. I affirm, I am not a Christian now." This is strange, bitter language, yet obviously genuine. Soon after the beginning of this year, 1739, it disappears. There is no more inner torment of that kind to the very end. Why not?

The simplest answer seems to be that, from that time on, John Wesley was too busy to be tormented. It took Wesley almost a year after his heart-warming in Aldersgate Street to find the work to which he was to give his life. But once he got into the full current of his career, there was no more worrying about saving his soul.

§ 3. AFTER THE GREAT CHANGE

The two things that John Wesley did immediately after the transforming prayer meeting were characteristic. The first was a trip to his old university, Oxford, always the center of his affection. There he preached on, "By grace are ye saved through faith." It was an echo of the words from Luther which had been so effective in his own case, but it did not fit the mood of the proud university.

The scholars did not especially like the idea of being saved at all. And if there were any salvation needed for persons of their distinguished position, they had an idea that it would come by knowledge through learning, rather than by grace through faith. Other men have made that same mistake. But the Fellow of Lincoln who stood in the pulpit of Saint Mary's that day was by this time forever protected from such an error.

After he had taken his new message to Oxford, John Wesley turned his steps toward Germany. This new light had come to him largely at the hands of a young German; he wanted to see for himself the shrine at which Böhler had kindled his torch. So, afoot, Wesley spent the summer crossing Europe, until he came into Bohemia, and found there, on the estates of Count Zinzendorf, that Herrnhut—"the house of the Lord"—which was the headquarters of Moravianism.

With the kindly Moravians Wesley had a summer of content. Their whole colony he acknowledged to be nearer to the sort of a Christian community the New Testament had in mind than anything he had ever seen or heard of elsewhere. It was, in fact, an expression of Christian communism, in which the welding force was the love and service of God. Wesley would have been glad to have settled down as a part of the community. But he had a sense of responsibility for the spiritual condition of his homeland, and when September came he was back in England again.

§ 4. THE HOUR OF DESTINY

Whether he realized it or not, John Wesley returned to his great task in England at the moment when the movement of world forces had marked that "tight little island" for a spiritual shaking. Ten years before, the preaching of Jonathan Edwards and others had led to the breaking out of what the historians still call the Great Awakening in New England. Five years before, the revival among the Moravians had given birth to the pietistic movement in Germany, and the real beginning of Protestant foreign missions. In the year Wesley was preaching in Georgia there began

"IT WAS TIME SOMETHING BURST LOOSE"

what was to prove the greatest of all revivals in Wales, under the preaching of another young Oxford man named Howel Harris. Even in dour Scotland there were remarkable outbursts of religious interest.

England was ringed round with revival. It was time something burst loose.

Within England there were discernible two points of view. Most of the clergy, whether in the Church of England or in the various nonconforming bodies, were against anything that savored of religious excitement. England had just gone through two centuries of strife, when the land had been bloodied with the battles of Puritans and Cavaliers, and, as one writer has well put it, "Men were still sore with the wounds of the strife." Religious enthusiasm was credited with having been the cause of the recent troubles; the majority were desperately afraid of what more such enthusiasm might do. "Moderation" might well have served as the motto of their crests, which must have been an easy-chair rampant on a pipe and a tankard of ale quartered.

Against these easy-going parsons, whom we have previously said much about, there must be set the sort of people who made up the religious society in Aldersgate Street. If there were hundreds of lazy parsons and lazier church communicants, there were enough filled with religious zeal to support scores of these small groups which met in private, looking and praying "for the consolation of Israel." In any estimate of what was now, under the inspiration of the Wesleys, to happen in England credit must be given the quiet work of preparation which had been done by these societies.

By the time Wesley got back to London from Herrnhut, there were almost no pulpits open to him. His brother had been preaching during his absence in a way that had made the name Wesley a bogey to most of the city's rectors. There was nothing wrong, they admitted, with a Wesley sermon so far as its content went. It was the tone.

For Charles Wesley had been preaching, not only as though he believed what he was saying, but as though he expected those who listened to believe, and to do something about it. And the last—the doing something—was more than the rectors could stand. The last thing in the world they wanted around their comfortable parishes was something doing. They were for peace.

In this situation the Wesley brothers turned to the only opportunity which remained open. They began to speak before the various religious societies. Here they immediately found a place of leadership. Soon John Wesley was recognized as the leader of the society in Fetter Lane. It was his first great responsibility as a religious reformer.

§ 5.   WHITEFIELD

Almost from the first Wesley had a hard time with the Fetter Lane society. Even at this distance it seems that the group contained rather more than its share of cranks. And John Wesley never did have much luck with cranks. He was too well balanced himself. He must have welcomed with joy the return of his old friend, Whitefield, as the year was drawing to its close. "God gave us once more to take sweet counsel together," he says.

Whitefield had been spending the year preaching in Wesley's old mission field, Georgia. He had found it as easy to get along with the colonists as Wesley had found it hard. He had witnessed some remarkable religious triumphs. Now he was back in London to secure money for the work he had started.

When he left for America Whitefield had been something of a pulpit idol. His preaching had crowded church after church. There had been all sorts of guesses as to what his final honors were to be. But when he returned he found himself facing a far different situation. The same parsons who had turned the Wesleys out of their pulpits treated Whitefield to a like discipline. They found that he was even more "enthusiastic" than the Wesley brothers, and they sought as ruthlessly to put a silencer on him.

To all outward view, the parsons had succeeded fairly well in squelching the Wesleys. To be sure, the brothers were speaking to private groups and to the felons in prison. But that was a form of service so inconspicuous that it scarcely entered the calculations of the rectors of London. What must have been their dismay when they found that George Whitefield refused to accept the seclusion they had thrust on the Wesleys!

It is said of George Whitefield that when he preached his voice could be heard a mile, and when he sang his voice carried two miles! Obviously, it had never been intended that such a man should conduct his ministry in a back parlor. What he did do is history. He went back to Bristol, then the second city in England. Before his journey to Georgia, he had been a prime favorite in Bristol. Now, one or two sermons, and the bars were up in all the pulpits.

GEORGE WHITEFIELD

The next Saturday afternoon the evangelist took the step which was to thrust Methodism forever out of the back rooms into the midst of the current of life. Standing on a little knoll he began preaching to two hundred miners from Kingswood, a mining district just outside Bristol. "I thought," he said, "I might be doing the service of my Creator, who had a mountain for his pulpit and the heavens for a sounding-board." Whitefield knew how to use the heavens for a sounding-board.

We cannot tell the story of what happened at Bristol in detail. If Whitefield's first open air congregation numbered two hundred, his second was just ten times as large. It was not long before he was preaching to twenty thousand people. The miners came straight from the pit to listen, and there is no picture in all the annals of that early Methodism easier to imagine than that of the white furrows that appeared on their blackened cheeks as they listened spellbound, and the tears came coursing down.

But Whitefield stayed in Bristol for only six weeks. By that time he had the city and its surrounding territory so stirred that men thought and spoke little but religion. To some, such a condition would have been a challenge to further preaching. To Whitefield it was only a challenge to move on. If he could do this in Bristol, he could do it elsewhere. And God knew that all England needed a similar shaking. So he sent for the one friend he had whom he could trust to carry the work ahead. And thus it was that John Wesley came into Bristol, and into the most significant portion of his life-work.

§ 6. WESLEY MOVES OUT OF DOORS

It is not certain that John Wesley knew what he was getting into when he answered Whitefield's call to Bristol. He had been such a stickler for churchly form that he had a hard time in bringing himself to the place where he was ready to stand in the open air, letting the wind blow on his bare head, or sometimes while the rain or snow pelted down, and preaching to such folks as he had never faced in a church. But he thought of the career of Jesus, of the Sermon on the Mount, and saw that there was at least "one pretty remarkable precedent of field preaching," as he called it. And the success of Whitefield was so obvious that his scruples were overcome.

On a Monday afternoon in May, not quite a year after his awakening in Aldersgate Street, he took up his stand on a little rise outside the city and began preaching.

Wesley's first text in the open air was prophetic. He chose the same words which Jesus used in announcing his mission in Nazareth: "The Spirit of the Lord is upon me, because he hath anointed me to preach the gospel to the poor; he hath sent me to heal the broken-hearted, to preach deliverance to the captives, the recovery of sight to the blind; to set at liberty them that are bruised; to preach the acceptable year of the Lord." In a few days he was before the miners of Kingswood, crying: "Ho, every one that thirsteth, come ye to the waters; . . . yea, come, buy wine and milk without money and without price."

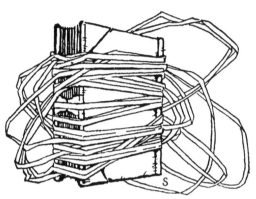

"GARROTER EXTRAORDINARY!"

So, if sometime you are in England, and can make your way to Bristol, you will do well to seek out a little mound near Kingswood, not quite four miles away. Here it was that George Whitefield first preached in the open air in Great Britain. Here it was that John Wesley soon followed him. Here it was that a pulsing tide of religious fervor burst the dikes which had been raised by the conservatism of the Established Church for the salvation of England and the enrichment of the world.

If the history of red tape should ever be written, what a tale it would be! What a garroter extraordinary red tape has been for all the comfortable conformists of history! How much more often it has lent itself to securing spiritual defeat than any other weapon! How largely has the fate of men hung on such heroisms as that first seen outside Bristol when Whitefield and Wesley wrestled with the red tape of a reactionary ecclesiasticism; wrestled and came off more than conquerors!

With the first open-air preaching in Bristol the Methodist movement may be said to have been fairly launched. For the rest of that year, 1739, John Wesley divided his time between Bristol and London. Charles stayed in the capital most of the year. Whitefield went storming into Wales, back to Bristol, to London, finally away again to America. One or two other clergymen, intimates of the Wesleys' Oxford days, began definite evangelistic preaching.

The work in the open air was the most distinctive mark. Authorities of the church inveighed against it, but it grew rather than slackened. From the point of view of a strict interpretation of churchly law the Methodist preachers were in the wrong. From the point of view of the needs of England and the English people they were gloriously right, and history has not hesitated to say so.

The distinctive genius of John Wesley for leadership was early shown. He was not, like Whitefield, content to sway great crowds with his preaching. He had a way of picking the individuals who were really moved out of the crowd and forming them into groups for further instruction. Thus, under his ministry, regular societies began to come into existence. The first of these was at Bristol. The most famous was in London.

The London society was known as the Foundry. It took its name from its location, an arsenal which had been blown up by accident in the early years of the century. Wesley leased the abandoned building, refitted it for his purposes, and opened his indoor services there late in November, just as the winter began to close down. There were between five and six thousand people in that first congregation.

It is worth while to note the preacher's comment: "I preached . . . at five in the evening in the place which had been the king's foundry for cannon. Oh, hasten Thou the time when nation shall not rise up against nation, neither shall they learn war any more!" For thirty-nine years the Foundry remained the headquarters of the Methodist movement.

§ 7. DIFFICULTIES

It was at about this time that the parting of the ways came

with the Moravians. The Moravian influence had become more and more strong in the Fetter Lane society in London, where Wesley had been the unofficial leader. A Moravian from

THE FOUNDRY, LONDON

Bohemia brought a majority of the members to a belief that the best means to spiritual blessing was through "stillness"— refraining from all work, all study, all participation in the services of the churches, until a blessing came.

It requires only a small knowledge of John Wesley to know how impossible it was for him to accommodate himself to an idea of that kind. He made several attempts to patch up the trouble, but, before the next year was over, it became clear that this could not be done. Sadly the Wesleys and those who agreed with them withdrew. Fetter Lane was given up entirely to the Moravians. The streams divided, the Moravians to do their work in testifying to the reality of the inner life, the Methodists to do their larger work in proclaiming holiness to the multitudes.

§ 8. A Lord Bishop Is Scandalized

The opposition, especially within the Established Church, mounted as the Methodist work prospered. There is a church in London, one of Sir Christopher Wren's great gifts to the beauty of that city, where to-day one of the most alert of the ministers of the Church of England preaches to great throngs. "I am in a hurry to bring in the kingdom of God," says the present rector of Saint Martin's-in-the-Fields, "and I don't care who knows it." But in 1739 the Rev. Joseph Trapp, D.D., who chanced to be rector of the same Saint Martin's, thought otherwise.

Doctor Trapp preached a sermon on "The Nature, Folly, Sin, and Danger of Being Righteous Overmuch; with a Particular View to the Doctrines and Practices of Certain Modern Enthusiasts." This is the way Doctor Trapp felt about it: "For a clergyman of the Church of England to pray and preach in the fields, in the country, or in the streets of the city, is perfectly new, a fresh honor to the blessed age in which we have the happiness to live. I am ashamed to speak upon a subject which is a reproach not only to our church and country, but to human nature itself. Can it promote the Christian religion to turn it into riot, tumult, and confusion? to make it ridiculous and contemptible, and expose it to the scorn and scoffs of infidels and atheists? To the prevalence of immorality and profaneness, infidelity and atheism, is now added the pest of enthusiasm. Our prospect is very sad and melancholy. Go not after these imposters and seducers; but shun them as you would the plague."

Finally, Wesley was brought to book by the Bishop of Bristol. The conversation closed in this way:

"I hear you administer the sacrament in your societies," said the bishop.

"My lord, I never did yet; and I believe I never shall."

"I hear too," the bishop charged, "that many people fall into fits in your societies, and that you pray over them."

"I do so, my lord, when any show, by strong cries and tears, that their soul is in deep anguish; and our prayer is often heard."

"Very extraordinary indeed," ejaculated the bishop. "Well, sir, since you ask my advice, I will give it freely. You have no business here; you are not commissioned to preach in this diocese. Therefore, I advise you to go hence."

Then the little cutter of ecclesiastical red tape rose to new heights. "My lord," he replied, "my business on earth is, to do what good I can. Wherever, therefore, I think I can do most good, there I must stay, so long as I think so. At present, I think I can do most good here; therefore, here I stay. Being ordained a priest, by the commission I then received, I am a priest of the church universal; and being ordained as Fellow of a college, I am not limited to any particular cure, but have an indeterminate commission to preach the word of God in any part of the Church of England. I conceive not, therefore, that in preaching here by this commission I break any human law. When I am convinced I do, then it will be time to ask, shall I obey God or man? But if I should be convinced in the meanwhile that I could advance the glory of God and the salvation of souls, in any other place more than in Bristol, in that hour, by God's help, I will go hence; which till then I may not do."

CHAPTER VI

"THE VERY SOUL THAT OVER ENGLAND FLAMED"

§ 1. The Poet's Picture

SEVERAL years ago an American poet, Richard Watson Gilder, sat rapt before the portrait of the man about whom we have been talking—John Wesley. As he studied the picture words came struggling for expression. He reached for paper and pen, and the result is one of the great odes in the English language:

> "In those clear, piercing, piteous eyes behold
> The very soul that over England flamed!
> Deep, pure, intense; consuming shame and ill;
> Convicting men of sin; making faith live;
> And—this the mightiest miracle of all—
> Creating God again in human hearts. . . .
>   Let not that image fade
> Ever, O God! from out the minds of men,
> Of him, thy messenger and stainless priest,
> In a brute, sodden and unfaithful time,
> Early and late, o'er land and sea, on-driven;
> In youth, in eager manhood, age extreme—
> Driven on forever, back and forth the world,
> By that divine, omnipotent desire,
> The hunger and the passion for men's souls!" [1]

From the day when, encouraged by Whitefield, John Wesley cast aside all restraints of churchly custom and stood in the open air to preach the gospel to the miners of Kingswood, until the day he died, fifty-two years later, England felt the presence of this flaming soul, this messenger driven on forever,

---

[1] Reprinted by permission of Houghton Mifflin Company, publishers.

back and forth the world. We wish it were possible, in the limits of one brief chapter, to give some idea of what John Wesley's life crusade was like.

If you take up your New Testament at the first of the Gospels to be written, that according to Mark, you find a story of the life of Jesus filled with the rush of action. The characteristic word, recurring again and again, is "straightway." There is a sense of immediacy, of on-pushing, that fills every chapter. If, now, you will take up the journals in which John Wesley kept the day by day record of his life, during the more than half century of active ministry, you will find that same sense. There are the same crowds in the cities and along the roadways; the same sense of appalling human need; the same eager response; and the same pressure impelling the preacher on and on. The servant here is as his Lord.

§ 2.   WHAT WESLEY ATTEMPTED

It is, in one way, a strange picture. Outwardly, this is no man for the rough-and-tumble of such a life. This is an Oxford scholar and a son of scholars. As delicate and frail, to all seeming, as a piece of rare porcelain, he is the last sort of person whom you would expect to brave successfully the bickerings and riots of the soap-box.

Nor would it be thought that such a man could ever reach the minds of the rough populace in a way to produce any profound effects. Yet here he stands, a target for a thousand rocks and vegetables, preaching his way calmly while the mob rages, finally stilling the mob by the contagion of his own self-possession, stirring mightily the hearts of the very men who have come to harm him, and at last mounting his horse and riding away to his next appointment, while the mob follows to the end of the street, shouting, "God bless you, sir!"

The more you think about it, however, the more you come to understand that there was really nothing surprising about

this.   England was desperately sick spiritually.   The whole
nation needed a fundamental changing.   No mere talker, no
superficial player on the emotions—such as the evangelist frequently proves to be—was sufficient for such a need.   Such a
man never profoundly affects even the crude crowd, no matter
how many saw-dust trails he may fill.   When there is anything
really fundamental to be done it takes the scholar, the man
who can probe to the bottom, to do it.   That had been true in
Europe when Luther gave birth to the Reformation.   It was
true now in England when Wesley gave birth to the Evangelical Revival.

Wesley saw at the very beginning that there was nothing
in particular the matter with the *doctrines* of the Church of
England.   When, in his old age, he drew up a set of twenty-
five articles of religion for the new Methodist Church in the
United States, he used the old articles of the Anglican Church,
merely leaving out some of those he felt to be debatable or un-
important.   But the thing that he felt needed to be done in
England was to put energy into Christian living.

Christianity had come to be thought of as the same thing
as respectability, and respectability was largely conceived as
refraining from gross sin, not because it was sin, but because
it was not good form.   Wesley gave his life to making religion
a vital force in life.   In the greatest of his defenses for his
course, he wrote, "The problem of problems is how to get the
principles of Christianity put into practice."   That, in a sentence, was what the Methodist movement under John Wesley
was—an attempt to rouse men to act up to the principles which
they already possessed.

The way in which the flaming evangelist set about accom-
plishing his purpose was said by the Established Church to be
irregular.   Of course it was irregular!   What great movement
ever stirred the religious life of men that, from the standpoint
of settled ecclesiasticism, was not irregular?   God inspires such

movements for the precise reason that the regular order has become sterile and ineffectual.

It was the genius of Methodism that it followed no set forms. John Wesley met each day's problems as they arose; he acted as the need seemed to demand; he soon learned to spend little time worrying about the precedents of the past or the portents of the future. Like the hymn-writer, he could say,

"FORTY-FIVE HUNDRED MILES A YEAR"

"I do not ask to see The distant scene; one step enough for me."

A thousand locked church doors became for him only a thousand reasons why he should go into the open fields and, finally, into the whole wide world.

§ 3. WESLEY THE TRAVELER

The ground covered by John Wesley in trying to awaken his age to a conception of Christianity in earnest has been the marvel of many a writer. When we remember that he lived long before that Scotchman, MacAdam, had made his name immortal by teaching men how to build good roads; when, in fact, there was not a single post road north of York in England, it seems incredible that he could have covered the distances he did.

To ride from sixty to seventy miles, besides preaching at least three times, was a common experience. Nor was it only now and then that he did so. He kept it up, day after day.

He was always up at four; he almost always preached at five; by six he was in the saddle and away.

Until he was seventy he made all his journeys on horseback. Not only did he push his horse along at the clip which his mileage indicates, but he learned to read while in the saddle. Unless it was Dr. Samuel Johnson, it is doubtful whether John Wesley had a contemporary who was as omnivorous a reader.

In his later years Wesley calculated that he had never journeyed less than 4,500 miles in any year! The average must have been even greater than this.

"He crossed Saint George's Channel," says Dr. S. Parkes Cadman, "nearly fifty times, and traveled two hundred and fifty thousand miles on land—this when there were no turnpikes in the north of England, and the London stagecoaches did not run beyond York. In June, 1750, he was nearly twenty hours in the saddle and covered ninety miles in one day; in 1778 he speaks of having made 280 miles in forty-eight hours, and in the winter weather of Scotland he rode an equal distance in six days.

"His northern route in February, 1745, was one of the severest he ever undertook. Gateshead Fell was covered with snow, no roads were visible; wind, hail, and sleet, accompanied by intense cold, made the country one sheet of impassable ice. The horses fell down and had to be led by Wesley and his companions, who were guided by a Newcastle man into the town. The following winter he was crusted from head to foot by a blizzard as he struggled on from

"PETER, FEAR NOT; THOU SHALT NOT SINK"

Birmingham to Stafford. In 1747 the drifts almost swallowed him upon Stanford Heath.

"In his eighty-third year he was as fearlessly energetic as ever. While traveling in the 'Delectable Duchy' he came to Hayle, on his way to preach at Saint Ives. The sands between the towns were covered with a rising tide, and a sea captain begged the old hero to wait until it had receded. But he had to be at Saint Ives by a given time, and he called to his coachman, 'Take the sea! take the sea!'

"At first the horses waded; ere long they were swimming, and the man on the box feared that all would be drowned. Wesley put his head out of the carriage window to encourage him—'What is your name, driver?' he inquired. 'Peter, sir,' was the reply. 'Peter, fear not; thou shalt not sink,' exclaimed the patriarch. When they reached Saint Ives, after attending to Peter's comfort, he went into the pulpit, drenched as he was, and preached.

"The philosophical coolness and brevity with which he recorded these and similar adventures show that he regarded them as merely incidental to that cause he had assigned as the sole purpose of his existence, and to which he had consecrated all his gifts.

"He delivered forty-two thousand sermons in fifty years, an average of over fifteen a week. He was beyond seventy when thirty thousand people gathered to hear him in the natural amphitheater at Gwennap Pit, Cornwall. Ten days later he wrote, 'I have entered the eighty-third year of my age. I am a wonder to myself, I am never tired, either with preaching, writing, or traveling.' "[1]

§ 4. METHODISM AND THE INDUSTRIAL REVOLUTION

It is a mistake, however, to think of this enormous amount

---

[1] From The Three Religious Leaders of Oxford. Reprinted by permission of The Macmillan Company, publishers.

of travel as having carried Wesley into every nook and corner of England. There were whole counties in the kingdom into which the message of Methodism had hardly penetrated by the time of Wesley's death. The fact is that Wesley was as careful in laying out his plan of campaign as any Wellington. He picked the places where he felt the pulse of the nation's life to be beating strong. There he went; there he put in his contribution. Then he left it for natural forces to carry his message from those centers to the rest of the land.

As it happened, Wesley's work came at the very time when England was beginning to change from an agricultural island to the marvelous industrial nation it is to-day. It was at the moment when the manufacturing cities were being born. During Wesley's life London was to see its supremacy challenged; Bristol was to be outstripped by cities which, for years to come, were not even to have representatives in Parliament.

So it happens that if you will take the record and study it carefully you will see that, far from riding around the map indiscriminately, John Wesley spent his half century visiting not much more than half a hundred cities and important towns. London he entered more than two hundred times; Bristol, one hundred and seventy-five; Kingswood, more than a hundred; Leeds, Manchester, Birmingham, Newcastle-on-Tyne, between fifty and seventy times each; Canterbury, Bolton, Chester, Sheffield, forty visits apiece.

In truth, John Wesley and the industrial revolution rode stirrup to stirrup in England. Perhaps that is one reason why Methodism has played so large a part in the life of the industrial masses who have come into being in the last two centuries.

§ 5. Typical Days in Wesley's Work

Let us take a few moments to watch Wesley at typical points during his career. In 1742 he comes for the first time into Newcastle-on-Tyne, most northerly of the great cities of

England, center of the coal industry, and—after Stephenson has made his great invention—fated to be the birthplace of the railways of Great Britain. Wesley entered Newcastle on foot, and never, so he says, had he heard so much swearing, both from children and adults. This, from the veteran of Kingswood, is significant testimony. Newcastle must have appeared about as hard a proposition as could be imagined.

On Sunday morning Wesley goes, with a single friend, to the very center of the worst quarter of the town. Utterly unknown, he begins to preach. His text is, "He was wounded for our transgressions, he was bruised for our iniquities: the chastisement of our peace was upon him; and with his stripes we are healed." It was the sort of text with which he usually approached people who had themselves been bruised of life.

When he finishes preaching the crowd has swelled to more than twelve hundred. It stands open-mouthed, wondering what new thing this is which the little man in the preacher's robes has brought to Newcastle. "My name is John Wesley," says the stranger. "I will be here again this evening, and I will preach again in this place."

That evening an immense crowd gathers, a vaster crowd than Wesley has ever faced at Moorfields or on Kennington Common in London. Again he preaches, and at his words the hearts of some of his hearers are warmed. By the time that second sermon is finished there is a characteristic Methodist revival under way in Newcastle, which is to grow in vigor until it has spread throughout all Northumberland, Durham, and North Yorkshire, transforming the miners and yeomanry of those counties.

Here's another picture, showing the evangelist under quite different circumstances: It is an April morning in 1745, the day after Easter. Wesley, again in Newcastle, is up early and preaches at half past four. Then he mounts his horse and starts for London, almost three hundred miles away. At eight o'clock his horse rests while the rider preaches. Away again, he reaches Northallerton in the early evening, and, as is his custom when he can, preaches to a little company that gathers in the inn.

In the congregation is an unusual hearer, a Roman Catholic priest named Watson Adams, who has listened to Wesley in Newcastle. Father Adams has brought some of his neighbors, including a Quakeress, Elizabeth Tyerman, to hear this strange preacher. One day there is to be a wonderful life of John Wesley written by a Methodist preacher named Tyerman, but that is running ahead of our story.

Father Adams presses Wesley to come and preach in his house in Osmotherley. Wesley accepts; the tired horse is brought out from his stall; the company mounts and, a little before ten that night, Wesley is in Osmotherley.

It is long after dark; the people in the village have been abed for hours; but the priest and his friends go pounding from door to door and, in about an hour, the chapel which has once been the property of the Franciscan friars, is filled with a congregation. Wesley preaches and, after midnight, goes to bed, having traveled sixty miles and preached four times, but feeling, he writes in his journal, "no weariness at all."

At five in the morning he comes back into the little Roman chapel to preach on justification by faith—the very question on which hinged the Protestant Reformation!—and he finds his congregation there ahead of him, for most of them have sat up all night long for fear lest they might oversleep and miss his message.

As the preacher leaves the pulpit and starts toward his horse and the long road again, the Quakeress who has had a part in bringing him there blocks his path.

"Dost thou think water baptism an ordinance of Christ?" she demands.

"What says Peter?" replies Wesley. " 'Who can forbid

water, that these should not be baptized, who have received the Holy Ghost even as we?' "

The woman is in a mood for quick decision. " 'Tis right! 'tis right!" she cries. "I will be baptized."

The preacher takes her into an adjoining house, baptizes her, and, full daylight having come, mounts and resumes his way toward London. There is a Methodiist society in Osmotherly within a short period after.

One more scene, this of a different character: Again we will take Newcastle as our location, but this time the reason for John Wesley's presence is changed. England is in turmoil. Bonny Prince Charlie has landed in Scotland; the clans have risen; after one or two preliminary skirmishes the Stuart prince is marching on London. The troops loyal to the house of Hanover are being concentrated in Newcastle. There, characteristically, Wesley makes his way.

No sooner has he reached the city than the news comes of the defeat of the Hanoverian forces at the battle of Preston Pans. Immediately there is a panic. Most of the well-to-do flee from the city, taking as much of their personal property with them as they can carry. Wesley stays. More, he stays calm. "At eight," he writes on the day of the panic, "I preached at Gateshead, in a broad part of the street, near the popish chapel, on the wisdom of God in governing the world."

In a short time sufficient re-enforcements of German and English soldiers, under Prince Maurice of Nassau, have reached Newcastle to render that town safe from attack. But these bring their own moral problems. Finally Wesley cannot stand it longer. He writes to the mayor that the moral conditions of the camp have become so horrible that something must be done. This something, he suggests, shall be a series of sermons which he shall preach.

The mayor passes the suggestion along to the commanding general. Five days later Wesley is preaching to the troops.

It cannot be said that he sees the kind of results he has become accustomed to in other places. His own explanation is that the soldiers have become so inured to hard language from their officers that they are not reached by his own chaste speech, however simple. A lay preacher, taken from the common ranks, he feels might have done better. Perhaps he is right.

But there is one thing the lay preacher could not have done! Sunday comes. Wesley stands up to preach, and a multitude gathers. Horse and foot, rich and poor, soldier and civilian, there they stretch away by thousands from the man who is proclaiming, "There is no difference; for all have sinned and come short of the glory of God."

Away off on the edge of the crowd he sees a number of homesick German troopers, not understanding a word of what is going on, but attracted by the commotion. And to the astonished ears of these aliens there comes the swift message, carried in the language of their homeland! It took the scholar to do that.

§ 6. PERSECUTIONS

Of course there were experiences of other kinds. There were, it must be admitted, plenty of people, both high and low, who had no desire to hear the preaching of Wesley and his helpers. And these again and again formed mobs which frequently threatened the lives of the dauntless evangelists. The time came when Charles Wesley claimed that, in certain parts of England, he could pick out the houses of the Methodists by the marks of violence on them!

Nor were these persecutions solely the work of irresponsibles. Here, for example, is an official document that is worth reproducing for the idea that it gives of what some of the early Methodists had to face:

To all High Constables, Petty Constables, and other of His Majesty's Peace Officers, within the county of Staffordshire, and particularly to the Constable of Tipton:—

Whereas, we, His Majesty's Justices of the Peace for the said county of Stafford, have received information, that several disorderly persons, styling themselves Methodist preachers, go about raising routs and riots, to the great damage of His Majesty's liege people, and against the peace of our Sovereign Lord the King:

These are in His Majesty's name to command you, and every one of you, within your respective districts, to make diligent search after the said Methodist preachers, and to bring him or them before some of us, His said Majesty's Justices of the Peace, to be examined concerning their unlawful doings.

Given under our hands and seals, this 12th day of October, 1743.

J. LANE.
W. PERSEHOUSE.

All sorts of methods were used to break up the meetings. Rowdies brought bulls from the ring in which they were indulging in the barbarous sport of bull-baiting and tried to drive them through the crowds. Drummers were hired to drown out the preacher. Horsemen rode recklessly into the ranks of listeners. Stones, vegetables, filth were showered down. Bullies were hired to pummel the preachers. The press-gang took some of the lay preachers, forcing them to serve in army and navy.

In more ways than we can here enumerate the very lives of the converts were endangered. Thus, we are told that in the town of Darlston women were knocked down and abused in an unmentionable manner. Their little children meanwhile wandered about the streets, and no neighbor dared give them shelter. Houses were looted, and sometimes destroyed.

§ 7. FACING THE MOB

Through the midst of all this tumult Wesley moved with a serenity that remains a marvel. Not even his enemies were ever able to tell of a time when he had acted as though he were frightened. He himself tells us that he made it his rule "always to look a mob in the face." Of course John Wesley always looked everything in the face. But this proved as effective a method with mobs as with any of the other problems of his ministry.

We have several records of wounds suffered by Wesley. It is significant, however, that most of these came from stones thrown from a distance or from blows delivered from behind. When John Wesley got a man in front of him and close enough to look him in the eye, it was seldom that there was any violence. Wesley never used a weapon, never lifted his hand in self-defense. But his bearing and the flash of his eyes were defense enough.

Perhaps the worst time that he ever had was at Walsal, in Staffordshire, where he had been hustled by a mob before the justice, Persehouse, who had signed the proclamation already quoted. Persehouse refused to act, on the plea that he had gone to bed and did not want to be disturbed. This left Wesley alone, at night, in the hands of a surging mob. One brute struck him several times, from behind, with an oak club. This emboldened another, who rushed up with arm lifted to strike. But, as he reached Wesley, his arm fell and he began to stroke the little preacher's head, exclaiming, "What soft hair he has!"

Missiles thrown from other parts of the crowd brought the blood. The headless mob pushed their victim from one end of the town to another. In a sudden moment of quiet he cried, "Are you willing to hear me speak?" "No, no!" came the answering roar, "knock out his brains; down with him; kill him at once!"

Reduced to utter helplessness, Wesley began to pray. The words could not carry far, but they reached the mob's leader, one of those, undoubtedly, who held his arms pinioned. "Sir," he suddenly said, "I will spend my life for you; follow me, and no one shall harm a hair of your head." And, with three or four of his comrades, this ruffian, who turned out to be a prize-

fighter, carried the preacher safely out of the crowd. The
rescuer was himself rescued, and later became a lay preacher.

Terrible experiences at the time, these early persecutions
did not prove wholly harmful to the young Methodism. For
one thing, they deterred unworthy or weak-willed persons from
joining the movement. For another, they proved the sincerity
of those who underwent such fire as nothing else could have
done. They provided just the sort of public testimony that
would, in the long run, prove irresistible. Long before Wesley's death they had become things of the past, and some of the
very men who were most conspicuous in the early rioting were
most conspicuous in the later honors which were showered on
the leaders of the Methodist Revival.

As an example of the way in which good came directly out
of this evil, it is of interest for Americans to remember that the
center of this most bitter persecuting in Staffordshire was the
village of Wednesbury. But Wednesbury means for us to-day
not riots, but something far different. It means the Methodist
society which weathered the riots; it means the little Methodist
chapel which was built as soon as the attacks had ceased; it
means the sermon that John Wesley preached in that chapel in
1761; it means the young man who heard that sermon and was
converted; it means Francis Asbury! And, later by a few
years, it means another young Wednesbury man who knew by
what a rugged road the Methodists had walked to their place
in the town's confidence. The second young man was named
Richard Whatcoat. And between them, Francis Asbury, the
first, and Richard Whatcoat, the third bishop of the Methodist
Episcopal Church, those two young men made the riots of
Wednesbury contribute to the evangelization of a continent!

§ 8. THE WESLEY MESSAGE

So, through the years, John Wesley rode up and down
England, preaching the gospel of Christianity in earnest. The

places in which he preached were beyond mention—jails, grave-yards, horse-fairs, mining pits, inns, private houses, street corners, the open fields, the hillsides and the valleys. The subjects on which he preached were not many.

There were only forty-four sermons in the collection which he gave to the public as containing his message, and these he used over and over. Twenty-four of this number have to do with the practical concerns of Christian living. Many of these are based on texts taken from the Sermon on the Mount. The other twenty deal with the abstract theological and doctrinal questions concerning which Wesley thought his converts should be instructed.

For the sake of some people who have utterly mistaken the attitude and interests of John Wesley it is a good thing to look quickly at those twenty doctrinal sermons. When it came to such matters, with what was John Wesley concerned? Not with the sort of doctrines that some would now try to declare "fundamental." Wesley has not a single sermon on the virgin birth; not one on inspiration; not one on the second coming. This does not mean that he did not have beliefs on those subjects; he had, but evidently he did not consider them doctrines of importance when it came to instructing people in the way of salvation and right living. The doctrines he preached on were salvation by faith, justification, the witnesses of the Spirit, the new birth, and the way of the Kingdom. These were Wesley's fundamentals.

The manner of Wesley's preaching was in violent contrast to the usual manner of his day. He lived at the time when Lord Chesterfield was telling men how they should talk if they were to be regarded as persons of breeding. No gentleman, said Chesterfield, would congratulate a friend on his approaching marriage with a mere, "I wish you joy." No, the proper form was, "Believe me, dear sir, I have scarce words to express the joy I feel upon your happy alliance with such or such a family." And if it was another kind of a message that was to be given, the proper form would then be, "I hope, sir, you will do me the justice to be persuaded that I am not insensible of your unhappiness, that I take part in your distress, and shall be ever affected when you are so." Most of the parsons preached in just that ornate, artificial style. Not so John Wesley.

Wesley's printed sermons cannot give the atmosphere of intense reality which always accompanied his preaching. But they do show the simplicity of word and the directness of logic by which he approached his goal. It was the logician of Oxford, using words fitted to the understanding of a child, when Wesley preached.

John Nelson, one of the greatest of the early lay preachers of Methodism (of whom more hereafter), gives us, in his account of his own conversion, an indication of the sort of effect this preaching had. "Whitefield," confesses Nelson, "was to me as a man who could play well on an instrument, for his preaching was pleasant to me and I loved the man, . . . but I did not understand him. I was like a wandering bird cast out of its nest till Mr. John Wesley came to preach his first sermon at Moorfields. . . . As soon as he got upon the stand, he stroked back his hair and turned his face toward where I stood, and, I thought, fixed his eyes upon me. His countenance fixed such an awful dread upon me, before I heard him speak, that it made my heart beat like the pendulum of a clock; and when he did speak, I thought his whole discourse was aimed at me. When he had done, I said, 'This man can tell me the secrets of my heart; he hath not left me there; for he hath showed the remedy, even the blood of Jesus,' . . . I durst not look up, for I imagined all the people were looking at me. Before Mr. Wesley concluded his sermon he cried out, 'Let the wicked man forsake his way, and the unrighteous man his thoughts; and let him return unto the Lord, and he will have mercy upon him; and to our God, for he will abundantly pardon.' I said, 'If that be true, I will turn to God to-day.' " And John Nelson did!

Wesley's texts varied marvelously with his congregations. We have already seen the words with which he approached the pitiful bruised folk of Newcastle. But when he faced a different congregation he struck a different note. "Seeing many of the rich at Clifton church," says his journal, "my heart was much pained for them, and I was earnestly desirous that some, even of them, should enter the kingdom of heaven." Well, what text would he use for such a congregation, under such an urge? "I came not to call the righteous, but sinners to repentance"!

At another time, having a similar fashionable congregation, he chose, "Ye serpents, ye generation of vipers, how can ye escape the damnation of hell?" Someone thought that was a little too strong, and remonstrated with Wesley for his choice of text. "Oh," said he, "had I been preaching in Billingsgate I would have taken, 'Behold the Lamb of God, which taketh away the sins of the world.' "

§ 9.   THE DUCHESS OF BUCKINGHAM IS INSULTED

Naturally, such direct preaching provoked all sorts of reactions. One of the best known is the reply of the Duchess of Buckingham, the illegitimate daughter of James II, to the invitation of the Countess of Huntingdon. The countess had become a Methodist, particularly under the influence of Whitefield, and gathered the fashionable of London in her drawing-room to hear the new sort of preaching. But when she invited the duchess, that lady, who had evidently already heard some of it, replied in this wise: "I thank your ladyship for the information concerning the Methodist preaching; their doctrines are most repulsive, and strongly tinctured with impertinence and disrespect toward their superiors, in perpetually endeavoring to level all ranks and to do away with all distinctions, as it is monstrous to be told that you have a heart as sinful as the common wretches that crawl on the earth. This is highly offensive and insulting."

But if it were insulting for a duchess to be told that she had as sinful a heart as a "common wretch," there were others who received the message in a different manner. In the first years of the Methodist movement there took place, while Wesley was preaching, many remarkable outbursts, during which people went through physical contortions, or periods of apparent catalepsy, as evidence of the effect of the preacher's words. A good many attempts have been made to explain these outbursts. They never happened while Charles Wesley was preaching, nor George Whitefield. This is the more remarkable, since both men preached with much more fire than John Wesley. They never happened except in Bristol and the region contiguous. They never happened after the first few years of Methodist preaching.

It seems as though Bristol was in a psychological condition where the portrayal to men and women of their sins was almost more than they could bear, and where the cooler and quieter the preacher, the greater the effect. At any rate, while these things undoubtedly took place, they were never considered as normal or even desirable effects of the Methodist preaching. It was well when they ceased entirely.

§ 10. CONTROVERSIES

It was, of course, impossible for such a movement as the Methodist Revival to get under way without a certain amount of controversy. It is astonishing that there was not more of it than there was.

Mention has already been made of the controversy that early developed between the Wesleys and the Moravians in London on the subject of "stillness." John Wesley was a quiet man, but he was no quietist. Later there was a distressing break between the Wesleys and Whitefield.

Whitefield, while in America, had come under the influence of the Calvinistic doctrine preached by Jonathan Edwards and the preachers of New England who produced the Great Awakening in the colonies. When Edwards preached of "Sinners in the Hands of an Angry God" it was no wonder that strong men trembled and whole congregations cried out for mercy. It was a terrible and dark doctrine, and had little relation to the words spoken in Palestine by Jesus.

Whitefield brought the New England Calvinism back to old England with him. He insisted especially on the doctrine of predestination. Wesley could not accept such a doctrine. In his hands Whitefield, as a logician, was helpless. There came a break, out of which there grew one branch of Methodism known as Calvinistic, which continues until this day in England.

The break between the leaders, however, was soon mended. They were too big for separation. Whitefield was almost as ready to "think and let think" as was Wesley, who had called that his life-motto. When Whitefield finally died it was Wesley who, when the word reached England, preached his funeral sermon.

The third, and the most serious, of the controversies which the Methodists had to undergo was with the Established Church. It was never an official quarrel; officially, the Methodists never separated from the Established Church during the Wesleys' lives. But a good many bishops, and any number of lesser clergy, rushed into their pulpits and into print with accusations.

One of the reasons John Wesley wrote so many books was in an attempt to meet the worst of these attacks. We will not speak of them here at any length. Wesley, it can be said, never showed himself to better advantage than in the magnanimity of spirit and the keenness of intellect with which he conducted the

Methodist side of these disputes. As an indication of the way in which argument undoes good men it is saddening to note that the severest of the attacks on the Methodists was made by that same Augustus Toplady who wrote:

"Rock of Ages, cleft for me,
Let me hide myself in thee."

§ 11. METHODIST CONFERENCES

By 1744 the Methodist movement, under the impetus of this flaming evangelist, had reached such proportion that he felt it wise to ask his principal helpers to meet with him in London for conference. Thus assembled the first Methodist Conference, which was to be the beginning of the annual sessions of Methodists held from that day to this, and now meeting year by year on every continent.

At that first session there were present six clergymen of the Church of England and four lay preachers. The time was taken up in defining what was meant by repentance, saving faith, justification, sanctification, free will, the witness of the Spirit, and other doctrines. John Wesley would have none of his preachers using pious phrases for which they could not give a definition in words that the humblest could understand.

These Annual Conferences grew in size and importance from year to year. They were curious institutions. They consisted largely in the asking and answering of a series of questions. The questions were drawn up and asked by John Wesley. John Wesley supplied most of the answers. He carried on a sort of a monologue with himself. The preachers had the right to engage in the discussion, and they did so. But the answers had a way of coming out where John Wesley wanted them to.

Even in the case of what came to be the most burning question of all—Should the Methodists separate from the state church and form a church of their own?—the answer so long as

John Wesley lived came out as he wanted it to, despite the fact that an overwhelming majority of the preachers were anxious to have it come out somewhere else.

With the twenty-first of these Annual Conferences John Wesley seems to have felt that the Methodist Revival had come of age. In that year, 1765, the minutes of the Conference were for the first time given to the public. They showed that there were 25 regular circuits with 71 recognized Methodist preachers in England; 4 circuits with 4 preachers in Scotland; 2 with 2

1765 A.D.	CIRCUITS	PREACHERS
England	25	71
Scotland	4	4
Wales	2	2
Ireland	8	15

preachers in Wales; and 8 with 15 preachers in Ireland—a total of 39 regular circuits with 92 lay itinerants, besides the local preachers, the Wesleys, and the clergymen of the Church of England who cooperated with them.

It was found·impossible that year to give satisfactory lists of the Methodist membership, but two years later evidence which could pass the searching test of John Wesley was presented showing that there were 22,410 members of the Methodist societies in England, 2,801 in Ireland, 468 in Scotland, and 232 in Wales.

§ 12. "Captains Courageous"

It has been the purpose of this chapter to try to give some sense of the way in which John Wesley, traveling his more than 4,500 miles a year, gave a new conception of Christianity to his land and time. We have tried to tell the sort of preacher he was, the sort of people he preached to, and the way in which they responded to what he said. It may easily be that, with all these words, the picture is not clear. Then listen to this story:

While yet in Georgia young Wesley preached from the text, "Whosoever is born of God overcometh the world." When he had finished, one of his hearers exclaimed, "Why, if this be Christianity, a Christian must have more courage than Alexander the Great!" That was always the sort of Christianity Wesley preached; a religion that demanded more courage than that of Alexander. But, when the days of his great evangel came, Wesley not only called men to a life which demanded more courage than that of Alexander, but he showed them a sure supply of courage on which to draw. It was with the new army that he thus formed of "Captains Courageous" that John Wesley conquered and transformed England.

CHAPTER VII

HOW THEY SANG A NEW DAY INTO BRITAIN

§ 1. A Joyous Religion

CHARLES WESLEY once said that he could tell the houses of the Methodists by the marks of violence on them. But there was a better way to discover the house of an early Methodist. It was to look for a distinguishing mark that Charles Wesley himself had put there. That mark was the sound of singing.

The Methodist Revival was a singing revival. The Methodists were happy folk. They sang at meeting, on the way to meeting, on the way home from meeting, at home, at work, at leisure. In fact, that was one of the charges sometimes brought against them—that they sang too much.

In some way or other the idea has gained root that piety and dolor walk hand in hand. The Puritans helped to make that belief current in England. The first Methodists had no such idea. "Sour godliness is the devil's religion," said John Wesley. The two Wesley brothers and Whitefield were from the beginning eager to hear their congregations sing. When the congregation wasn't singing as though it enjoyed the singing, the Wesleys took it for granted that there was spiritual trouble somewhere about, and they probed for it until they thought they had found it.

It was said of Whitefield, as we have already written, that when he spoke his voice could be heard for a mile, but that when he sang he could be heard for two miles! In a way, that difference in radius characterized the Methodist Revival. It was a revival marked by great preaching. But it was a revival made by great singing. It was the singing voice which carried farthest.

The hymns of the Wesleys and their friends carried the characteristic message of the evangelical revival into scores of communities which never heard any of the outstanding preachers. And they carried that message in such a form that it could be easily remembered. Perhaps it would be nearer to the facts to say in such a form that it could not be easily forgotten.

"A DISTINGUISHING MARK OF A METHODIST"

The Methodist Revival sang a new day into Britain. It sang a new day into the churches of the English-speaking world. Before the coming of the Wesleys there had been no singing of hymns, in our modern sense, in the churches. The ancient chants, with metrical versions of the Psalms, had been the only music thought fit to be heard in the house of God.

Charles Wesley changed all that. The meetings of the Methodists were not at first considered as church services, and the attendants caught the habit of singing the Wesley hymns without any thought of incongruity. From that it was only a short step to a new concept of sacred music.

In an incredibly short period this new fervor for Christian praise had swept through the united kingdoms. It was no mere chance that Handel's great oratorio, "Messiah," made its appearance two years after the publication of the first of the famous Wesley hymnals. It was the Wesleys who had discovered a public who would appreciate and support the oratorio.

§ 2. CHARLES WESLEY

Charles Wesley was a remarkable complement to his older brother. With Whitefield in America—to die there long before the work of John Wesley was done—Charles Wesley remained in England to give fire and warmth to the Methodist movement. His brother was always a bit austere; Charles had his heart on his sleeve for any bystander to see, and it was a big heart.

He was, to be sure, a man of moods. He could drop to some black depths at times. But he always came back into the sunshine, and, once there, he could move vast audiences with the ardor of his evangelism. Someone, calling his brother the commanding general of the Methodist Revival, has called Charles the cavalry leader. It is not a bad figure.

The active career of Charles Wesley was not as varied nor as long continued as that of his brother. He married ten years after his conversion, and soon became so limited by family cares that he could do little preaching beyond the confines of Bristol. Later he moved to London, where he spent the last seventeen years of his life in looking after certain Methodist societies in that city, ministering to the prisoners, acting as host to many distinguished men, and holding musical evenings at which his sons, Samuel and Charles, displayed their remarkable talents before some of the greatest in the kingdom.

Unlike his brother, as he grew older Charles Wesley grew more conservative. But he retained the Methodist note to the end, his last publication being a collection of hymns for those about to be hanged, *Prayers for a Condemned Malefactor,* which he employed with evident effect, since there is preserved a copy with this manuscript note by the aged author: "These prayers were answered, Thursday, April 28, 1785, on nineteen malefactors, who all died penitent."

The Wesley brothers came from a home in which musical and poetic talents were many. Their father wrote better hymns than any other form of poetry he essayed. One, at least, remains in most collections, that beginning, "Behold the Saviour of mankind." The older brother had some talents of the same kind; one sister, Hetty, might have made a name for herself in a more feminist age.

As a student at Oxford, and in his first years in the ministry, Charles Wesley wrote a few hymns. But it was not until the day of his conversion when, as we have seen, he wrote, "Where shall my wondering soul begin?" that the full power of his gift was revealed. From that day on he never ceased writing.

For several years the Wesley brothers published a new hymn book almost annually. Then they began to gather their various collections in larger books. But all the time Charles Wesley kept adding, adding, adding to the flood of sacred lyrics which came pouring from his pen.

Much of his hymn-writing he did on horseback. He wrote shorthand, as did his brother, and would jot down the verses as his mind formed them on any odd scraps of paper he had about him. Returning home, or to the City Road headquarters of the Methodists, he would fling himself off his horse and come rushing in crying, "Pen and ink! Pen and ink!" And the people about knew better than to disturb him until the work of composition was done.

It is said that Charles Wesley actually wrote 6,500 hymns! About two thousand of them have never been printed; by far the larger majority have long since been forgotten. The latest *Methodist Hymnal* to be adopted in the United States—that of 1907—contains only 121 hymns by Charles Wesley, a heavy reduction over the previous compilation. Even more significant is the fact that he now furnishes but sixteen per cent of *The Methodist Hymnal;* he who once was almost the whole! But his mighty stature as a hymn-writer is not to be questioned by that fact. With the single exception of Isaac Watts, he still stands unrivaled among the troubadors of the modern church.

§ 3. WHAT METHODISM SANG ABOUT

It is astonishing what a range of interests Charles Wesley managed to touch in his hymns. Because he almost always wrote to meet a definite human need, and because his evangelist's eyes were so keen to see such needs, the hymns came pouring forth to be sung under almost any conditions which might conceivably occur to mortals.

There were hundreds of funeral hymns, for he never let the death of a Methodist preacher pass without one or two memorials, always of a gloriously triumphant nature. Dr. Abel Stevens, one of the great Methodist historians, says that, besides Charles Wesley's hymns for Sunday public worship, there were collections of his hymns for watch-nights, for the celebration of the Lord's Supper, for Christmas, for Easter, for the ascension, to the Trinity, for public thanksgiving, for a time of earthquakes, for times of trouble and persecution, for times when invasion threatened, for preachers, for New Year's day, for families, for children, for funerals, for times of tumult, and for the nation.

As an indication of the range of subjects dealt with in any one of these volumes we can glance over the *Hymns for the Use of Families.* Here we find "For a woman in travail," "Thanksgiving for her safe delivery," "At the baptism of a child," "At sending a child to boarding school," "Thanksgiving after a recovery from smallpox," "Oblation of a sick friend,"

"Prayers for a sick child," "A father's prayer for his son," "The colliers' hymn," "For a persecuting husband," "For an unconverted wife," "For unconverted relations," "For a family in want," "To be sung at the tea table," "For one retired into the country," "A wedding song." In addition, there are in this volume other hymns for parents and children, masters and servants, for domestic sorrows, for the Sabbath, for sleep, for going to work, for morning and evening.

Is it to be wondered that the early Methodists could find inspiration and, indeed, guidance for almost every moment of their lives in the hymns of Charles Wesley?

John Wesley told his followers that they might find in the hymns of his brother "a body of practical and experimental theology." It was the practical and experimental note which made them the power that they were.

If you will make a simple test, you will find the difference between Charles Wesley and most of the hymn-writers who had gone before him. Take the hymns of half a dozen of them. You can make your own choice, but here are six that will be sung for generations yet to come: "Before Jehovah's awful throne," one of the great hymns of Isaac Watts; "The spacious firmament on high," best known of the hymns of Addison; "While shepherds watched their flocks by night," Tate and Brady's Christmas hymn; "God moves in a mysterious way," one of the best of the hymns of Cowper; "How gentle God's commands!" by Doddridge; or that hymn of Wesley's father, "Behold the Saviour of mankind."

Now take six of Charles Wesley's hymns. Here, for example, are six that you at once recognize: "A charge to keep *I* have"; "Depth of mercy! can there be mercy still reserved for *me?*"; "Arise, *my* soul, arise"; "O come, and dwell in *me*"; "Jesus, Lover of *my* soul"; "And are *we* yet alive?"

Do you notice the difference? Not that the hymns of Wesley are better than the others mentioned; in several cases we do not adjudge them so. But note the pronouns! Wesley started the Methodists singing personal pronouns, and that was what made his hymns a turning point in English history.

§ 4. TYPICAL HYMNS OF CHARLES WESLEY'S

The temptation, of course, when writing about the hymns of Charles Wesley is to fill the chapter by quoting and quoting. What shall we take as the most representative?

The most famous is, of course, "Jesus, Lover of my soul." There is scarcely a Christian communion which has not sung it, and there are tales of its being translated into Japanese and used by Buddhists, with the name of Buddha substituted for that of C h r i s t. Characteristically, this was one of his brother's h y m n s

CHARLES WESLEY

which John Wesley did not particularly like. If he had followed his own inclinations, it would never have appeared in a Methodist hymnal. Its imagery was a little too intimate for the taste of the meticulous Fellow of Lincoln, Oxford. But the hymn won too wide an acceptance to permit its exclusion, and while some will always object to it on the same grounds as did John Wesley, it will go on providing spiritual comfort for thousands for years to come.

Isaac Watts, perhaps the greatest of all hymn-writers, once said that he would have given all the hymns which he had written to have been the author of the group of Charles Wesley's hymns known as "Wrestling Jacob." In the original form there were about thirty verses in this hymn group. This has been gradually reduced until the latest American *Methodist Hymnal* prints only seven.

It is a pity that the modern church does not know these seven verses better than it does. Nowhere else is there to be found a description of a biblical scene given with such power and leading to so lofty a climax of religious truth. The present condensation is well done. It begins with the man alone in the night, wrestling with the angel:

> "Come, O thou Traveler unknown,
>   Whom still I hold, but cannot see;
> My company before is gone,
>   And I am left alone with thee:
> With thee all night I mean to stay,
> And wrestle till the break of day."

All through the night the wrestling continues, the man helpless in the hands of his opponent, but desperately holding on until he can discover the name and nature of this visitor from above. Finally the revelation comes in the climactic verse:

> " 'Tis Love! 'tis Love! thou diedst for me!
>   I hear thy whisper in my heart;
> The morning breaks, the shadows flee;
>   Pure, universal Love thou art:
> To me, to all, thy mercies move;
> Thy nature and thy name is Love."

If any one hymn were to be chosen as expressing Charles Wesley's own religious experience, it would be hard to find a better than the familiar, "O for a thousand tongues to sing!" Written on the first anniversary of his transforming experience, the hymn throbs in every line with the ecstasy which marked its writer's spiritual life when at its best. The hymn has always appeared first in *The Methodist Hymnal,* and will hold that place for a long time yet to come.

It is, perhaps, necessary to remember that not all the hymns Charles Wesley wrote, and his brother made public, were worthy. Both brothers could be tragically mistaken, and were on some subjects. When that happened Charles had a way of bursting into rime, and his brother generally wrote a pamphlet. History tries to be kind by saying little about such productions. But, lest we get the idea that neither brother ever was wrong, it is as well to cast a glance in passing at such mistakes.

A good example is to be found in the hymns they published for British Methodists to sing at the time of the American Revolution. Here, for instance, is a verse in a hymn supposed to describe the Continental Congress:

> "Thou know'st thine own appointed time
>   Th' ungodly homicides to quell,
> Chastise their complicated crime,
>   And break their covenant with hell;
> Thy plagues shall then o'erwhelm them all,
>   From proud Ambition's summits driven;
> And Faith foresees the Usurper's fall
>   As Lucifer cast down from heaven."

There was another published at the same time that began with the tender lines,

> "Father of everlasting love,
>   The only refuge of despair."

Who were the afflicted ones thus commended to the especial care of heaven? They were the American Tories, surrounded by the perfidious patriots of the colonies, as the second verse made abundantly clear:

> "The men who dared their king revere,
>   And faithful to their oaths abide,
> Midst perjured hypocrites sincere,
>   Harassed, oppressed on every side:
> Galled by the tyrant's iron yoke,
> By Britain's faithless sons forsook."

Strangely enough, these hymns were never much sung in the Methodist societies of America! It is satisfying to be able to report that they were never widely accepted in the societies in England either.

But we must not stop long with such wanderings from the main track. It was in singing of God, his love, his mercy, his abundant pardon, and the consequent transformation of the sinner's life, that the genius of Charles Wesley found its true expression.

It is difficult to pick one hymn as a type of this genuine Methodist singing. There are so many which might be used! But perhaps "Arise, my soul, arise" will serve as well as any other. Read that hymn and you have, in essence, the Methodist Revival. It is there more vividly than it is to be found in John Wesley's sermons or pamphlets. It is there more compactly than any history—including this one—has ever been able to tell it, or ever will. It sings triumphant in every verse until it reaches that ecstatic climax:

> "My God is reconciled;
>   His pardoning voice I hear;
> He owns me for his child,
>   I can no longer fear:
> With confidence I now draw nigh,
> And, 'Father, Abba, Father,' cry."

It is the confident voice which marks the true Methodist, in this day as in that.

The best of Charles Wesley's hymns were written within a few years after the beginning of the Methodist Revival, but there was never a year in which he was not producing others. When at last he came to die, lying helpless in his home in London, he called the wife who had been in the truest sense his comrade and dictated to her these words:

> "In age and feebleness extreme,
> Who shall a helpless worm redeem?

> Jesus, my only hope thou art,
> Strength of my failing flesh and heart,
> O could I catch one smile from thee,
> And drop into eternity!"

And so, with a song still on his lips, this minstrel of Methodism, this troubador of God, fell on sleep.

§ 5. JOHN WESLEY'S HYMNS

We cannot overlook the contribution that John Wesley made to the singing mission of Methodism. It is the belief of the writers that this contribution was much larger and more important than has generally been recognized. It was threefold.

In the first place, John Wesley acted as editor for the hymns of his brother and of the other early Methodist writers. He was a remarkable editor. Mention has been made of his objection to a hymn like "Jesus, Lover of my soul." That was a hymn with an appeal too great for him to smother it. But again and again he did save his brother and others from extravagances of expression which would have weakened their productions. In the excitement of the Methodist Revival it was possible for such "enthusiasm" as this to find its way into verse:

> "I rode on the sky,
>   Freely justified I,
> Nor did envy Elijah his seat;
>   My soul mounted higher
>   In a chariot of fire,
> And the moon, it was under my feet."

It was from balderdash of this sort that John Wesley's blue pencil saved Methodism. His changes in the poetry of his brother, and of even such a writer as Doctor Watts, were almost always for the better.

In the second place, John Wesley, as translator, gave to Methodism a group of hymns of the finest spiritual temper. He took from the Moravians and other German pietists twenty-four great hymns. In rendering these into English he achieved translations in almost every case better than the originals. Of the twenty-four, there are still fourteen to be found in the American *Methodist Hymnal.* When compared with the fate of his brother's hymns—now reduced from 6,500 to 121—it will be seen how much better such hymn-writing as John Wesley did do has worn.

Every one of these translated hymns is worth study, and singing. Perhaps the best known is the one beginning, "Jesus, thy boundless love to me," but there are few sacred lyrics to equal:

> "Thou hidden love of God, whose height,
>   Whose depth unfathomed, no man knows,
> I see from far thy beauteous light,
>   Inly I sigh for thy repose;
> My heart is pained, nor can it be
> At rest, till it finds rest in thee."

Finally, John Wesley lifted congregational singing to a new dignity by insisting that it be dignified, and that his followers should consider the meaning of the words they were singing.

It was possible to do this while lining out the hymns, as was then the custom. Wesley went further. He printed his Methodist hymnals with the important words and ideas in italics, so that the most casual reader could not miss the point. Thus, verses in the Methodist hymnals of Wesley's day looked like this:

> "Father, whose *everlasting love*
>   Thy only Son for sinners gave,
> Whose grace to *all* did *freely* move,
>   And sent him down a *world to save.*"

Besides this, John Wesley set his face like flint against cheap music and vulgar verses in Christian worship. And his standards as to what constituted vulgarity were high. Here is a characteristic letter to his brother: "Pray tell R. Sheen I am hugely displeased at his reprinting the nativity hymns and omitting the very best hymn in the collection, 'All glory to God in the sky.' I beg they may never more be printed without it. Omit one or two, and I will thank you. They are namby-pambical."

Namby-pamby hymns stood no chance with John Wesley. One wonders what he would have said of the musical slosh that passes for "gospel songs" to-day! Probably he would reiterate the refusal he placed in his hymnal of 1780 to "longer be accountable either for the nonsense or for the doggerel of other men"!

§ 6.   Other Methodist Hymn Writers

It was one of the glories of the Methodist movement that it not only gave Charles Wesley a field for the use of his matchless talent, but it also called forth great hymns from other and far more unexpected sources. There was, for example, John Cennick, the master of the school that Wesley built for the children of the miners of Kingswood. Cennick, the schoolmaster, is almost forgotten, but Cennick himself will live while Methodists sing, "Jesus, my all, to heaven is gone," or while the whole Christian world joins in, "Children of the heavenly king."

William Williams, of Pantycelyn, Wales, is a name that means nothing to the present generation. Even his enormous labors as a Methodist itinerant in Wales have been forgotten, but it will be a long time before "Guide me, O Thou great Jehovah" is forgotten.

And so with John Bakewell. Who was he? If you look at his tombstone in the City Road churchyard, London, you will find that this Methodist class-leader "adorned the doctrine of God our Saviour 80 years, and preached his glorious gospel about 70 years." But the fact that makes John Bakewell important is that one day he was moved to write, "Hail, thou once despiséd Jesus."

Edward Perronet is not quite so unfamiliar a name. His close comradeship with Charles Wesley has gained him a certain remembrance. But it is to be doubted whether one reader of this page will recognize his name to fifty who can sing from memory, "All hail the power of Jesus' name."

The most striking figure among those early Methodist hymn-writers was Thomas Olivers. Totally unlettered, Olivers was caught from a wild youth into the full tide of the Methodist movement. His attempts to go back over the route which he had traveled in the days of his dissipation in order to undo some of the evil he had done and to make restitution where that was possible is a story in itself.

We cannot tell that story in these restricted pages. It is enough for us to remember and marvel that it was this rough, untutored field preacher who sat down one day in John Bakewell's house in London and wrote one of the most majestic odes in Christian hymnody: "The God of Abraham praise." There is another of Olivers' hymns in the modern hymnal, perhaps even more commonly sung: "O thou God of my salvation."

So it was that they went out, those early Methodists, to sing a new day into Britain. What some of them lacked in head they made up in heart; when their tongues failed they had an inexhaustible supply of song on which to fall back. And this song they used with marvelous power, not because of its poetic merit, but because it expressed a personal experience which the singers truly longed to share with all those who listened.

One can almost hear them, leaving their Annual Conference in some English city and trudging out to the market places and the country lanes to lift that strain of praise and invitation:

"Jesus! the name to sinners dear,
    The name to sinners given;
It scatters all their guilty fear;
    It turns their hell to heaven.

"O that the world might taste and see
    The riches of his grace!
The arms of love that compass me
    Would all mankind embrace.

"His only righteousness I show,
    His saving truth proclaim;
'Tis all my business here below,
    To cry, 'Behold the Lamb!'

"Happy, if with my latest breath
    I may but gasp his name;
Preach him to all, and cry in death,
    'Behold, behold the Lamb!' "

CHAPTER VIII

MEN OF MIGHTY STATURE

§ 1. Rise of the Lay Preachers

ONE day in the year 1741, John Wesley, who was supposed to be in Bristol, stepped into the parsonage room in the Foundry, London, in which his mother was resting. A single glance was enough to tell her that this unexpected visit had been caused by news which had upset her son. She inquired, therefore, what the trouble might be. "Thomas Maxfield," he blurted, "has turned preacher." Poor Thomas Maxfield! The little field marshal's tone of voice and the glitter in his eye boded no good for the presumptuous young layman.

Thomas Maxfield had been one of the first and most promising of Wesley's Bristol converts. When Charles Wesley had found the care of the Methodists in London too great a burden for one man, young Maxfield had been brought in to assist. In the humming Foundry, with its varied activities, he had found plenty to do. The Wesley brothers had told him that he was to give advice to such as needed it, to pray with those who asked for prayers, and to expound the Bible in band-meetings.

But the line between expounding and preaching is a thin one, and almost before Charles Wesley was aware what was happening, Maxfield was across it. If the testimony of the Countess of Huntingdon is to be accepted, the young layman proved a preacher of extraordinary power.

John Wesley had been helped by laymen in Bristol, notably by John Cennick. But he had always been so close at hand that this help had never seemed to take the form of independent preaching. When the word came of Maxfield's course Wesley's loyal Anglican soul—which had already had so much trouble with field preaching and preaching within the parish limits of the established churches—rose in final protest. He rushed off to London to put an end to such a clear irregularity.

Then it was that Susannah Wesley rendered her final service to the shaping of Methodism.

She knew her son too well to cross him outright. But she also knew the kind of argument which would overpower him. Looking at him standing there, all hot and tired after his unwelcome journey, all determined to make an example of poor Maxfield, she quietly said: "John, you know what my sentiments have been. You cannot suspect me of favoring readily anything of this kind. But take care what you do with respect to that young man, for he is as truly called of God to preach as you are. Examine what have been the fruits of his preaching and hear him also yourself."

From an appeal of that kind John Wesley could not turn away. He examined and he heard. And when he had done both he said, "It is of the Lord; let him do what seemeth him good." From that day, the lay preacher was a recognized part of the Methodist movement. Before Wesley died, the lay preacher had become its most distinctive worker. A very large part of the Methodist preaching in England is still done by laymen.

§ 2.   WHAT LAY PREACHERS ACCOMPLISHED

It would be a sad mistake to think of the Methodist Revival as all the work of the Wesleys. The tale of the achievements of the two brothers is so astonishing that we can fill page after page in such a book as this with it. But all the while that the Wesleys were working it must be remembered that there were working with them what came to be hundreds of devoted men, who left behind almost every earthly comfort for the joy of carrying the glad tidings of the Kingdom into every part of the British Isles.

For when Wesley found that the Lord could work through a Thomas Maxfield, he immediately concluded that he could work through others also without ordination. And he set out to find the others. That was the nature of Wesley; he had only to stumble on a hint and he followed it until it became an institution.

Methodism, in employing lay preachers, was following some historic precedents. Saint Francis had used his "brothers minores" to purify the religious life of medieval Europe. John Wyclif had employed "hedge preachers" to carry the first reforming gospel about England. In fact, as Wesley himself observed, it was the comment of his contemporaries that Jesus was a carpenter, and the first Christian apostles and preachers were fishermen.

From the point of view of Anglican church order the lay preachers of Methodism might be totally irregular. From the point of view of England's spiritual needs they were a help sent of God. When punctilious parsons tried to annoy Wesley with the church regulations in the matter the best they drew from him was the somewhat savage comment: "Soul-damning clergymen lay me under more difficulties than soul-saving laymen."

It was a call to "come and suffer" that Wesley gave his itinerants, and, as has been so often the case, such a call proved exactly the one for which brave men had been waiting. There were no salaries promised; in fact, besides such food as the various Methodist societies gave them these preachers were allowed only enough money to cover their traveling expenses—and when they traveled they were supposed to walk! A few of them, being expected to cover long distances, had horses, but for the most part they trudged.

So zealously were those early Methodist preachers guarded against the temptations of money that even at the time of Wesley's death, when Methodism was a strong connection, with many well-to-do members, the salary of a member of Conference was only twelve pounds a year!   But Wesley never seemed to lack for heroes who would face mobs, brave death, work as few men ever worked, live on the scantiest of fare, and have a glorious time doing it.

§ 3.   Wesley's Discipline

He ruled them with a rod of iron.   Once a month, at least, he wrote to every one of his circuit superintendents, and from each one he expected at least a monthly report.   At one of the earliest Conferences it was voted that these preachers "had nothing to do but to save souls."   But when the Wesleyan definition was added it was found that the business of saving souls meant, for a Methodist preacher, preaching at least twice a day; spending from six in the morning until noon, daily, in reading, writing, and prayer; from noon until five in visiting; from five until six in private communion with God.   There seems to have been no time specified for eating, but then, the Methodist preachers of John Wesley's day spent little time at that!

Some of the pastors who sigh because they have so little time for study nowadays, when their parish work is so exacting, would do well to cast an eye over the normal schedule of a Methodist preacher of the vintage of 1745.

Nor did this discipline suffice.   In addition to this daily schedule John Wesley wrote a series of rules for his preachers which have rightly become famous.   The first one was this: "Be diligent.   Never be unemployed a moment.   Never be triflingly employed.   Never wile away time; neither spend any more time at any place than is strictly necessary."   The succeeding eleven were in the same strain.   They are all still printed in the Methodist *Discipline.* Every young minister who enters a Methodist Conference affirms his cheerful acceptance of them. He may accept them; certainly few to-day pretend to obey them. When Wesley lived they were obeyed.

As might have been expected in the fellow of Oxford, Wesley insisted on his preachers studying. "Steadily spend all the morning in this employ," said the Conference minutes of 1766, "or at least five hours in twenty-four."

Suppose a young carpenter, who felt called to preach but had hard work getting interested in books, objected, "I have no taste for reading"? Wesley's reply was uncompromising: "Contract a taste for it by use or return to your trade." And so incessantly and successfully did the Methodist leader keep hammering away on this point that the time finally came when he felt confident that his preachers, recruited from every rank and trade, could pass better examinations in theology than the graduates of Cambridge.

There has long been an utterly mistaken notion that most of those early Methodist preachers were rude men. It is true that many of them had few educational advantages in childhood. They were not, save in rare instances, college trained. But they had the finest stuff in them.

Wesley did not pick men at random. He had an uncanny ability to discover the men who could take a polish. In the most exacting sense of the word, the preachers who came through his mill came out gentlemen. In their blue frock coats, with the high stiff collars, the immaculate linen stock, the knee breeches, the clean stockings, and the three-cornered hats of the professional man, the Methodist preacher could take his place without apology in any company.

Because Methodist preachers thus came to be, under the hand of Wesley, men of culture, Methodist homes did likewise. If you want to know what that early English Methodism was really like, read that story, *The Tramping Methodist,* by Sheila

Kaye-Smith. Follow the boy who leaves the rectory with its brutish parson. Watch him stand spellbound listening to the Methodist preacher: "He had not been speaking for ten minutes before I knew that he could tell the name of every star that trembled on the dun breast of the sky and of every flower that colored the grass; that he knew the roosting places of the birds and the variations of their notes; that he regarded as familiar friends the wild, timid creatures of the forest, the conies of the fallow, and the butterflies of the hedge and clover-field."[1] See him as he finds refuge in the Methodist home, where for the first time he discovers people to whom Shakespeare, Chaucer, and Spenser are dear familiars. That was the Methodism which John Wesley and his lay preachers brought forth!

And what, you ask, did the preachers preach? What need to ask that question? They began with the message that all men needed salvation. Then they promised that all men might be saved. Not only that; they might know themselves saved. If they had this experience, the preachers declared it to be the duty of those thus saved to tell the good news to others. And they never ceased to exhort their hearers to go on toward the "entire sanctification" which consists in the devotion of all one's life to the service of God.

The sermons had to be short. John Wesley himself could preach for three hours and hold an immense crowd motionless, but he would not trust his preachers to such expansiveness. Half an hour he held to be long enough for any service. A hymn to start; the exhortation; a hymn to close—that was the standard Methodist service.

Texts were to be chosen to fit audiences; the exposition of these texts was to be as simple and direct as it could be made; there was to be no shouting. "Scream no more," Wesley wrote one of his preachers, "at the peril of your soul." But it must

---

[1] Copyright by E. P. Dutton & Company. Used by permission.

have taken a fairly stout voice to have been heard at all in many of the places in which those pioneer Methodists preached!

§ 4. JOHN NELSON

And now, having thus looked hurriedly at the itinerant preachers as a body, it will do us good to come to closer acquaintance with a few individuals among them.

JOHN NELSON

There was, of course, John Nelson. It would be as impossible to tell the story of Methodism without John Nelson, the famous stonemason of Birstal, as without John Wesley. Nelson was a grave, introspective man, with huge physical strength, who had come to London to earn the high wages of the capital. An earnest member of the Church of England, he found no inner satisfaction of soul until, caught in the crowd at Moorfields, he was converted, as we have already seen, under the preaching of Wesley. From the day of his conversion he was called on to meet tests of the hardest kind.

These began in his work. When he refused to lay stone on government buildings on Sunday, his employer threatened to dismiss him. But Nelson would not compromise, and the quality of his work kept him his job. Then his landlord would have turned him out, but that ended when Nelson took a member of the family to another Wesley meeting and watched his conversion. Finally, Nelson went back to his own town, where

his zeal soon brought a Methodist society into being. When
Wesley reached Yorkshire, he placed the seal of his approval
on what had been done, and enrolled Nelson as one of his regular "helpers."

Then began a career truly apostolic. He carried the revival into the city of Leeds. He went with Wesley into Cornwall, sleeping generally on floors and living on blackberries.
So successful was he in gaining a hearing and winning converts as he traveled about that finally the Anglican clergy of
that region brought it to pass that Nelson was taken by the
press-gang for army service.

All sorts of offers were made to buy his release, but without avail. The stonemason refused to bear arms, because fighting was against his conscience, but he was marched back and
forth over a large part of England for three months until
finally Lady Huntingdon secured his release. On the night of
his discharge from the army he started preaching again in
Newcastle!

Soon he was pioneering again in wholly new sections of the
country. No Methodist ever underwent more bitter persecutions. At the town of Harborough the whole populace seemingly turned out to drown him. A halter was placed about his
neck, and the local butcher was selected to drag him to his
death. But Nelson started preaching and so awed the crowd
that finally a constable, who had been siding with the rioters,
took matters in hand, released the prisoner, and bade him God-
speed on his way.

But he came immediately into worse trouble at Hepworth
Moor. There, as he was leaving the spot on which he had been
preaching, he was hit in the back of the head with a brick, and
dropped senseless. Finally managing to get up, he staggered
away, with blood streaming down his back, while the mob followed, waiting until he should pass the limits of the village,
where they promised to kill him. But just before he reached

that spot a resident of the town opened his door and invited him in, giving him shelter until a surgeon could dress his wound.

The next day he was in Acomb. There he was set upon by a crowd of young roughs, knocked down, and jumped on until he was senseless. The wound in his head was again opened, and he lost added quantities of blood.

Recovering his senses, Nelson staggered out into the street, where a crowd again set upon him, and knocked him down eight times. When at last he lay unable to rise, he was dragged by the hair along the cobblestones for nearly twenty yards, the bystanders kicking him as he passed. Six of them jumped on him at once, to "tread the Holy Ghost out of him."

At the moment when even Nelson's robust frame could hardly have survived more punishment, the ruffians saw two women pass in a carriage who recognized them. Surprised in their bloody work, one of those sudden panics fell on them which sometimes befall mobs, and they ran away.

The very next day the itinerant had ridden forty miles, and stood in the evening, resting against a gravestone in Osmotherly churchyard, listening to Wesley preach! Such was the life of the man who planted Methodism in Leeds, Sheffield, Manchester, and York.

§ 5. John Haime

For another example, take such a man as John Haime. Here was a preacher with a different sort of circuit from that of Nelson. For Haime was a soldier, converted under fire during the battle of Dettingen. It is surprising how many of the early Methodist preachers had seen army service. Soldiers and cobblers seem to have fitted easily into Wesley's methods. In several great army camps Haime formed Methodist societies. The regular chaplains complained, but the commander, the Duke of Cumberland, approved, and the Methodist preaching among the soldiers went on.

Haime had his justification when Fontenoy was fought. Here the Methodist preachers and their converts established a name for courage. Evans, one of the preachers, had both legs carried away by a cannon-ball. As he lay dying he kept praising God until his strength was utterly gone. Another preacher, Clements, twice dangerously wounded, cried, "I am as happy as I can be out of paradise."

Coming out of the battle, Haime met one of his Methodists wounded, and so covered with blood that he did not at first recognize him. The wounded man said, "Brother Haime, I have got a sore wound." "Have you Christ in your heart?" Haime responded. It was that kind of spirit which made the Methodists marked men. After he left the army Haime spent years in the itinerancy in England.

§ 6. SILAS TOLD

Still another type of ministry was that of Silas Told. Here was a man who had been a sailor, shipwrecked, captured by pirates, brutalized by years in the slave-trade, and had finally settled down in London. There he had been brought to hear Wesley at the Foundry and had been converted. For a time Wesley used him as a school-teacher. But one morning he took his class to hear Wesley preach at five o'clock. The text proved to be, "I was sick and in prison, and ye visited me not." That sermon ruined a schoolmaster, but it made one of the greatest of the Methodist preachers.

Told took the prisons of London as his circuit, and for the rest of his life he devoted himself to the welfare of the wretches with whom they were crowded. Those were the days when it was thought that the way to reduce crime was to hang early and often. Condemned felons would be taken to Tyburn Hill by the dozen and launched into eternity while huge crowds looked on to jeer and cheer.

Silas Told went with most of the condemned to their

deaths. The hardened jailers came to know him and believe in him; they saw to it that he had his chance with the men and women—sometimes they were the boys and girls—who were about to die. Literally hundreds of these poor people met death with courage, upheld by the promises of a religion they had received at the hands of this former slaver.

§ 7. ALEXANDER MATHER

Then there was a man like Alexander Mather, totally different in background and manner from the men already mentioned. Mather grew up in a Scotch home, and was trained as a Presbyterian boy should be. In London, however, he heard Wesley preach, and his life was changed.

Mather was a baker by trade. He became a Methodist band and class-leader, and finally an itinerant preacher. While still working at his trade he found it necessary to spend so much time in preaching and in looking after the Methodist converts for whom he was responsible that he could spend only about eight hours a week in sleep!

In 1757 Mather turned his back on the bakery and walked one hundred and fifty miles to his first circuit. From that day on he was one of the recognized powers among the Methodist preachers. He faced riots as dangerous as those known by John Nelson.

One experience, in the town of Monmouth, must have outraged his orderly Scotch soul. He had been haled before the mayor in the town hall, where he found not only the mayor, but all the chief men of the place. The rector and his curate opened the proceedings with a general list of accusations; one after another jumped into the verbal fray; finally all were shouting at once and at the tops of their voices.

"Gentlemen," suggested the Methodist, "be pleased to speak one at a time." But this proved too much of a demand for the local sanhedrin, which kept up its shouting until Mather walked out.

Mather was one of the men ordained by John Wesley himself; in fact, Wesley ordained him as a "superintendent" for England, just as he ordained Coke as a "superintendent" for America. He came as close to being a British Methodist bishop as any man ever did.

§ 8. THOMAS WALSH

It is a temptation to continue these tales indefinitely, but we will look at only one more of Wesley's lay preachers. But that one is worthy close scrutiny, for he is Thomas Walsh.

Thomas Walsh was one of the first fruits of the successful revival which Wesley launched in Ireland. Brought up in a Roman Catholic home, Walsh remained a good member of that communion until he was eighteen. Then an older brother, who had already broken away, convinced him of the flimsiness of the foundations on which rest many of the pretensions of the Roman Church, and the boy joined the Church of England.

Walsh never manifested, as do so many converts, a bitter spirit toward the church which he had left. "They have a zeal for God," he wrote afterward of Catholics, "but it is not according to knowledge. Many of them love justice, mercy, and truth, and may (notwithstanding many errors in sentiment, and therefore in practice, through invincible ignorance) be dealt with accordingly, since as is God's majesty, so is his mercy."

It was not until the Methodist preachers reached his native town that Walsh found the religious certainty which he craved. Then he threw himself into a life of such tremendous exertion and austerity that by the time he was twenty-eight the last ounce of his strength had been consumed, and he died. Yet in the short eight years of his ministry he accomplished prodigies.

To the Irish, or Gaelic, which was his native tongue, he

added a mastery of English, Latin, Greek, and Hebrew. This was a real mastery, for the time came when Wesley testified that Walsh, being given any Hebrew word, could tell how

"THE REVIVAL WHICH WESLEY LAUNCHED IN IRELAND"

often it was used in the Old Testament, or how often any Greek word was used in the New!

He walked thirty miles to his first appointment, and before long found himself the best known preacher in Ireland. His services were attended by Catholics as well as others, and the number of converts won among the Romanists brought upon him the opposition of numbers of the priests.

Walsh had his share of the rough handling which seemed to be the common lot of Methodist itinerants. One day, while on his way to a place called Roscrea, he was set on by seventy-eight men armed with clubs. They gave him his choice between being thrown into a well or being converted either to Romanism or Anglicanism—apparently without it making any difference which. When Walsh refused to choose either alternative, the crowd hustled him toward the well, but a minority was enough impressed by his bearing to protest. After considerable bickering, during all of which his life was in momentary danger, he was given a chance to mount his horse, from which pulpit he addressed his persecutors and prayed for them, and then rode away, as he himself said, "in peace of conscience and serenity of mind."

There were several other times when Irish crowds threatened him, but he showed such a quickness of wit and such a spirit of devotion flamed through his preaching that he finally won out against all opposition. The time came when certain priests were reported to be trying to frighten their ignorant parishioners from attending Walsh's services by declaring that the preacher was none other than the devil, who had taken possession of the body of the Methodist!

For a time Wesley kept young Walsh at work in London. He had success there equal to his success in Ireland. "I do not remember ever to have known a preacher," said Wesley, "who in so few years as he remained upon earth was an instrument of converting so many sinners." In London, Walsh, armed with his remarkable knowledge of Hebrew, was able to carry the Methodist message to many of the Jews in the synagogues of that city. But his career closed, as we have said, almost before it had started.

Someone remonstrated with the man at the way in which he was burning out the candle of his life. "Will a man rob God?" he retorted, utterly unaware that his prodigal expenditure of vigor was robbing the Kingdom of years of service which it might have expected. But his death left a memory—

almost a legend—of prodigious labor and accomplishment that served to inspire Methodist preachers for years after his passing.

§ 9. Helpers in the Church of England

The Methodist preachers of whom we have been speaking —Nelson, Haime, Told, Mather, and Walsh—were members of the large company of laymen who came into the itinerancy called by John Wesley from the ranks of the toilers. With rare exceptions, they were not school-educated men.

There was another type of Methodist preacher of a far different kind who stood beside the Wesley brothers. This was the clergyman of the Church of England who experienced the religious awakening characteristic of Methodism, who believed in the Methodist message, and who was willing to break over the routine of parish life in order to bear a hand in the conduct of the Methodist Revival. There were not a great many of these men, but, such as there were, they exerted a powerful influence.

§ 10. George Whitefield

At the head of this group stood, of course, George Whitefield. Companion of the Wesleys at Oxford, first preacher of the evangelical gospel in London, successor of the Wesleys in Georgia, pioneer in the open fields, Whitefield deserves to rank as a fellow-father with John and Charles Wesley of the Methodist movement. In fact, in his own day Whitefield was almost universally regarded as the leader and John Wesley as a subordinate figure in the revival.

Whitefield himself had no illusions on that point. He knew that John Wesley had a permanent contribution to make far beyond his own. "My brother Wesley acted wisely," he once said. "The souls that were awakened under his ministry he joined in societies and thus preserved the fruit of his labor. This I neglected, and my people are a rope of sand."

It was as a preacher that Whitefield excelled. Perhaps there has never been a preacher who could attract and hold such congregations, and move them so mightily. Benjamin Franklin, who was anything but a sentimentalist, has left record as to the effect made on him by Whitefield's preaching. He could gather crowds of twenty thousand to listen to him preach in Scotland, where Wesley largely failed. When he passed through the American colonies, as he continually did during the closing period of his life, his coming meant the end of all other business.

His common practice was to preach at least forty hours every week, and this he frequently raised to sixty. And after the strain of preaching thus continually to such crowds as few preachers ever face, he held incessant sessions of private prayer and praise in every house to which he could gain admission. Except John Wesley, no man ever left behind him such a record of work.

§ 11. WILLIAM GRIMSHAW

Whitefield was the type of Anglican clergyman who gave up all parochial work and became a Methodist itinerant pure and simple. William Grimshaw, vicar of Haworth in Yorkshire, followed a different course.

Grimshaw opened his pulpit to the Wesleys, and his rectory became a sort of haven for the Methodist itinerants. Despite the opposition of many clergymen, he accepted an appointment from Wesley as superintendent of a Methodist circuit, which he traveled regularly, and formed several Methodist societies. In his parish church he awoke a spirit of zeal that transformed what had been an "ignorant and brutish" community, until the number of communicants had increased from two to twelve hundred.

Grimshaw had a belief in direct methods that might not have met with John Wesley's entire approval, had he known

of it. When he thought it time to preach on Sabbath-break-
ing in Haworth, he appeared, whip in hand, at the taverns and
marched the tipplers there before him to the church, so that he
could be sure that the folks who needed the message would be
in the pews!

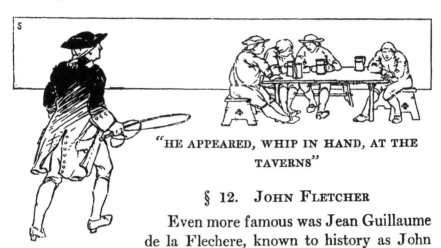

"HE APPEARED, WHIP IN HAND, AT THE
TAVERNS"

§ 12. JOHN FLETCHER

Even more famous was Jean Guillaume
de la Flechere, known to history as John
Fletcher. After a short career in the French army, Fletcher
drifted to England, where he became a tutor in an English
family. Moved by a longing to find friends who could minister
to his spiritual nature, Fletcher came into contact with the
Methodists, and at Wesley's advice was ordained as a minister
of the Established Church. On the very day of his ordination
he went to a Methodist chapel to administer the communion.

For twenty-five years Fletcher acted as vicar of Madeley,
in Shropshire, a country church which he made among the
best known in England. His devotion to his parish knew no
bounds. At the first he was met with the same brutal opposition which Methodism everywhere encountered, but long
before his death he was the acknowledged saint of the whole
region.

Wesley would have designated Fletcher as his successor in
the Methodist leadership, but Fletcher would have none of it.

He knew that his talents were not primarily administrative. And, as it turned out, he died six years before Wesley.

The great service which Fletcher rendered Methodism was in his writing. It is hard for us to-day to get up much interest in the debates on pre-destination and election which so nearly wrecked the Methodist move-ment. We k n o w , vaguely, that the feeling was so keen that the Wesleys and Whitefield divided on these issues, but to us the whole thing seems far, far away and utterly uninteresting.

JOHN FLETCHER

The reason for this is largely that after Fletcher had finished writing his books there was little left to be said on the subject. There are still people who call themselves Calvinists, but in the sense that Whitefield and Jonathan Edwards and others were Calvinists in the eighteenth century, there are almost none extant. Fletcher's writing just swept that old, harsh, implacable Calvinism out of the realm of concern. He gave the Methodist Revival an intellectual and theological foundation which is to-day almost universally accepted as a matter of course.

It is a happy thing to be able to say that he did it without using a bitter word. He showed that argument might be Christian. John Fletcher was a saint if ever one lived. Even Robert

Southey, who wrote on the Methodists in those days with the detachment and sense of superiority which might be expected of a poet laureate, proclaimed the sanctity of Fletcher's life.

§ 13.   THOMAS COKE

John Fletcher was, in a way, responsible for the addition to the Wesleyan movement of another Anglican of whom we will see more in another chapter. Here we will take only time to mention his name. Thomas Coke was a Doctor of Laws of Oxford and curate in the Church of England. Deeply moved by reading Wesley's sermons and journals and the books of Fletcher, Coke sought out Wesley and offered himself to the Methodist movement. He lost his post for doing so, but he found a field of service that was to spread all the way from the young United States of America and the Barbados to that lonely spot in the Indian Ocean to which at last his worn body was consigned.

§ 14.   VINCENT PERRONET

There is, perhaps, one more name that should be mentioned in this list of Methodist clergymen of the Church of England. That is Vincent Perronet, vicar of Shoreham, another Oxford man, who was later to give two sons to the Methodist itinerancy. Perronet assisted so widely in the Methodist movement, and lived so close to its heart, that he was called by Charles Wesley "the archbishop of Methodism." There is something of a question as to whether he or Fletcher—both clergymen in good standing in the Established Church—was the first to use the expression, "the Methodist Church." Neither of the Wesley brothers ever countenanced that title for use in England.

§ 15.   WOMEN OF THE METHODIST MOVEMENT

One of the best books on the early Methodist movement,

and one which most of the readers of this book have probably read, is George Eliot's *Adam Bede*. In that book you will recall that a chief figure among the Methodists is a woman. It would not be right to close a chapter on the men of mighty stature who stood beside Wesley without reminding ourselves that some of the mightiest of these were women.

As class-leaders, prayer-leaders, sick-visitors, teachers, and occasionally as preachers, women took a prominent place from the start in the evangelical revival. In fact, they were allowed a larger part in the Methodism of John Wesley's time than they were for generations after. Recent action by Methodist bodies in allowing women called of God to act as preachers is not the advance it has been made out to be. It is, in fact, only a return to the practice of John Wesley, who, in this matter as in so many others, was not ready to try to thwart a condition with a theory.

The most difficult thing in writing a chapter of this kind is the necessity of excluding the names and achievements of so many. Name after name comes crowding up, each with its claim to special remembrance. Joseph Benson, Peard Dickinson, Howell Harris, Martin Madan, James Rogers and his wife Hester Ann Rogers, Ann Cutler, Robert Brackenbury, John Downes, John Hodges, John Merriton, Henry Venn, Samuel Bradburn, John Evans, Christopher Hopper, Grace Murray, Mary Bosanquet—later the wife of the saint Fletcher; Joseph Bradford, Benjamin Ingham, John Pawson, Sarah Crosby—every name in the list stands for a definite contribution of some kind to the making of the Methodist Revival.

And when these are named the tale is just begun. For no record, however full, will ever tell of all the hundreds of humble folk who felt their hearts strangely warmed, as John Wesley's heart had been strangely warmed, and who went in the glow of that kindling to touch their neighbors into new warmth.

And, finally, England was changed, and all the world

moved, not because two brothers went out, the one to speak and the other to sing a new word of life, but because there came to stand beside them these hundreds and hundreds of others, who "through faith subdued kingdoms, wrought righteousness, obtained promises, stopped the mouths of lions, quenched the violence of fire, escaped the edge of the sword, out of weakness were made strong, waxed valiant in fight, turned to flight the armies of the aliens."

CHAPTER IX

METHODISM CROSSES THE ATLANTIC

§ 1. "Who Will Go?"

THE Methodist Conference of 1769 met in Leeds. The local newspaper reported that "Wesley had held a kind of visitation with several hundreds of his preachers." Since there were only one hundred and eleven Methodist preachers of all kinds at that time, and only a part of these could be present at such gatherings, it would seem that the press exaggerated somewhat the size of the meeting. Such things have been known to happen.

But if the size was exaggerated, the importance of the Conference could not be, for in the course of the proceedings Wesley, by that time sixty-six years of age, arose and said: "We have a pressing call from our brethren at New York, who have built a preaching house, to come over and help them. Who is willing to go?" And two young ministers, Richard Boardman and Joseph Pilmoor, who seem to have known that the call was coming, immediately volunteered, and within two weeks were on their way to the colonies.

The local press, rounding out its report of the Conference, said that "a large sum of money" had been collected to pay the way of the two young missionaries. As a matter of fact, they were given seventy pounds, and fifty of that was to be turned over to the chapel in New York for the payment of its debt.

It has been figured that it cost Spain about three hundred dollars, invested in the expedition of Columbus, to discover a new world. It cost British Methodism only one hundred dollars to establish its spiritual presence in that same world!

141

It was a prophetic moment at which Boardman and Pil-moor sailed. On the little island of Corsica, in the Mediter-ranean, a mother was crooning over the new-born baby who was to attempt to grasp the power of both Old World and New. In the city of Glasgow the instrument-maker to the uni-versity was bringing to perfection the steam-engine. Through the scattered towns of the American colonies the flaming evan-gelist of two worlds was setting out on his last journey.

Napoleon, Watts, Whitefield—all sought power; all found it; all changed the course of human affairs. The influence of the first passed quickly. The influence of the second has yet to reach its consummation, though the new order of industrial-ism which Watts made possible has brought human problems which sometimes appall us. But the influence of the third also abides, and that largely because, when the voice of the great preacher was stilled, there were men like Boardman and Pil-moor and their fellows to carry on the work.

§ 2. Religious Awakenings in the New World

Methodism did not spring to life in America without long years of preparation. There is always a background for spir-itual marvels, even when it is least apparent. Even the work which John Wesley did in Georgia, little as it seemed to amount to, made its contribution to the later triumph of the evangelical revival in this country. "The good John Wesley has done in America is inexpressible," Whitefield wrote. "His name is very precious among the people, and he has laid a foundation that I hope neither men nor devils will ever be able to shake."

At about the same time that Wesley was laboring in Georgia the Great Awakening was sweeping New England and New Jersey. Here was a revival within the ranks of Puri-tanism and nonconformity, rather than within the life of the Church of England. But it was a revival of such power as has seldom been equaled.

There were elements in it that we find it easy to criticize. The message was largely an appeal to fear. The preachers of the Great Awakening—notably Jonathan Edwards in New

"WITHIN TWO MONTHS THEY WERE ON THEIR WAY TO
THE COLONIES"

England and the Tennants in Jersey—painted a God with a dark face, and the refuge of souls which they depicted was a refuge for those seeking to hide from the anger of a punishing Deity.

Reaction from preaching of this kind was bound to come, and it brought much backsliding and excess to the settlements where the revival had blazed most fiercely. Yet it must not be forgotten that for years before the coming of the Methodists the soil of the northern and central colonies had been plowed deeply by the preaching of the Great Awakening.

Added to these elements was the work of Whitefield. Whitefield made separate journeys to the colonies. His general plan seems to have been to land at the south and preach his way northward. He was as much at home with the Puritans of New England as with the churchmen of the Southern colonies.

In a Quaker city like Philadelphia—then with a population small enough so that all could listen to the stentorian preacher at one time—Whitefield had a ministry of such lasting value that his statue stands to-day on the campus of the University of Pennsylvania as a founder of that famous school. He bridged exactly the gap between the departure of Wesley and the coming of Wesley's itinerants, for as he landed in Savannah in 1738 to take up the work Wesley had just left there, so, at the end of his course, he came into Philadelphia to bless Boardman and Pilmoor, and then passed on to Newburyport in Massachusetts and to his coronation there.

§ 3.   BEGINNINGS IN NEW YORK

Behind that "preaching house at New York" to which Wesley referred when he made his call for volunteers at the Leeds Conference there lay a most romantic story.

In one of his first preaching tours in Ireland Wesley found, in the county of Limerick, a colony of Palatines who had been driven out of their homes in Germany by the advance of the armies of Louis XIV of France. During their residence in Ireland these emigrants had fallen into evil ways, but the Methodist message proved able to bring many of them back to an active religious life. These Protestant Germans were never very happy in Limerick, and they early enrolled themselves in that great migration which was to bring so much of the best blood of Ireland to the New World.

It was in 1760, nine years before the Leeds Conference, that a group of these wayfarers landed in New York. Among them was a young carpenter, Philip Embury, who had been a local preacher in the Methodist societies of Ireland. Likewise, the company contained Embury's cousin, a young married woman named Barbara Heck. The newcomers seem to have spent their first years trying to find places for themselves in the new city.

Embury was a diffident sort of a chap. He apparently found it hard to obtain work at his craft, for he advertised for pupils and tried to support himself by teaching. Both he and the Methodists who had come with him from Ireland, while they did nothing to outrage their religious professions, fell back on a sort of quiet inactivity which was far from representing the ardor of the true Methodism of that period.

It took Barbara Heck to wake things up. Some five years after landing in the city she found herself one night where a group of card-players were gambling. It was a form of amusement then almost universally practiced, but it proved the spark needed to kindle once more the flame of her religious zeal.

Sweeping the cards into her apron, the aroused woman threw them into the fire, warned the players of the unhappy fate which awaited them, and exhorted them to repent of their evil ways. Then, while the passion was still on her, she rushed off to the house of her cousin and cried, "Brother Embury, you must preach to us or we shall all go to hell, and God will require our blood at your hands!"

Poor Embury! His conscience had been pricking him for a long time, for it did not seem just right that a Methodist local preacher should be in a city with as apparent moral needs as New York, and nobody be the wiser. But he had worked out an excuse for his inactivity that at least satisfied his own mind, and this he tried now. "Where shall I preach?" he asked. "How can I preach, for I have neither a house nor a congregation."

But Barbara Heck was not the kind to be put off with an answer like that. "Preach in your own house and to your own company first," she retorted. And the story runs that she herself went out and drummed up the first congregation, which proved to number five persons. At that, if the old prints which have come down to us are at all accurate, the congregation must have nearly filled the house in which it met!

It was not long before the congregation outgrew the house of the carpenter-preacher. Then an empty room in the neighborhood of the British barracks was rented. The sound of Methodist singing, so different from that in the churches, attracted to the meetings some of the musicians from the regimental bands, and two were converted and began to preach.

Then one day the congregation was amazed to see a stranger enter in the full regimentals of a captain in his Majesty's army. While the service continued there was an apparent undercurrent of apprehension. The experiences of Methodists with the army in England had not been happy. Had not Nelson and other preachers been impressed? Had not soldiers tried to break up several societies? Perhaps this officer was about to make trouble over the musicians who had turned preachers, or over the other converts won from the barracks.

But as soon as the meeting closed these forebodings disappeared. The officer marched to the front and introduced himself as "Captain Thomas Webb, of the king's service, and also a soldier of the cross and a spiritual son of John Wesley."

Within a week the officer was preaching. Again the quarters proved too small. Embury's voice, once it had taken courage, had proved sufficient to gather a congregation, but the sight of a British captain in uniform, with his sword laid across the pulpit, preaching in the characteristic Methodist fervor proved enough to draw large crowds. Behold, here was a new kind of warrior!

Captain Webb remains one of the most engaging figures in Methodist history. He lost one eye in the siege of Louisburg, and so appears in Methodist histories with his famous green patch. At the storming of the Plains of Abraham, in the battle of Quebec, he watched Wolfe die, and was himself wounded again in the arm. Five years later, on duty once more in England, he heard John Wesley preach in Bristol. Soon he was preaching, and before long Wesley had given him a local preacher's license.

Webb always was a favorite of John Wesley's. He commends him frequently in his *Journal,* and after the captain had passed the years of active service, Wesley exerted his influence with Lord North to secure a suitable pension for the old hero. Charles Wesley seems to have liked him too, but he did not wholly approve of the exuberance of the officer. He felt, for one thing, that Webb was altogether too optimistic in his forecasts as to the future of the colonies and of such places as New York.

When Webb pressed work in New York on some of the leading Methodist preachers of England, painting glowing pictures of the future importance of such a field, Charles Wesley was ready with a bucket of cold water. The idea that New York should ever rival Bristol in importance! "The captain," he said, "is an inexperienced, honest, zealous, loving enthusiast," and let it go at that.

John Adams, who later became President of the United States, heard Webb preach, and described him as "one of the most eloquent men I ever heard; he reaches the imagination and touches the passions very well, and expresses himself with great propriety."

As has been said, the sight of a British captain preaching

drew too large a crowd for the storeroom near the barracks. So the Methodists of New York moved again, this time to a rigging-loft on William Street. It is a coincidence that the Methodist societies in New York, Philadelphia, and Baltimore all spent their early days in rigging-lofts. Was there something about the smell of a ship which attracted the Methodists without their realizing it? Methodism itself was a new-launched ship in those days; did its members instinctively resort to the spot where men were fitting sails to spars and testing ropes and cords against the day of gale and tempest? Whatever the reason, when you think of the first Methodists in America you can almost smell tar.

It was from the rigging-loft that this Methodist society moved to the "preaching house" mentioned by John Wesley. Again, Captain Webb was the central figure in the move. He gave the first subscription—thirty pounds, a third more than any other giver's—and he loaned the society ten times that amount, besides going out and drumming up contributions in all parts of the city.

It is interesting to note, on the original subscription paper which is still preserved, the names of Anglican clergymen, of the artistocratic families like the Livingstons, the Stuyvesants and the Lispenards, the name of the mayor, and even the names of African slaves! The lot on which that first church stood still holds a Methodist church—the John Street Church, which has become something of a shrine for the Methodists of America.

§ 4. In Maryland

While Captain Webb and Embury and Barbara Heck were thus forming the first Methodist society in New York another Irish Methodist, Robert Strawbridge, had emigrated to the colonies, and settled on Sam's Creek, in Frederick County, Maryland. Strawbridge had none of Embury's hesitancy. He had hardly settled before he had built a log chapel, without windows, door, or floor, but which was, from its first service, filled with a spiritual power which mightily moved that whole region.

It was not long before all Maryland, including Baltimore, had felt the impact of this Methodist preacher. Soon he had carried his message into Pennsylvania, Delaware, and Virginia. It was one of the glories of the ministry of Strawbridge that wherever he preached, he raised up other preachers.

§ 5. The First Methodist Preachers Land

Such was the state of affairs when Boardman and Pilmoor, bearing Wesley's commission, landed in Philadelphia. Captain Webb was there waiting for them, and they started their work at once by having Pilmoor preach from the steps of the State house. Then Boardman rode on to New York, preaching to the British troops in Trenton on his way, and Pilmoor settled down to the direction of the society in Philadelphia.

The two men changed appointments every three months, thus certainly making the American Methodist ministry from its start as much of an itinerancy as two preachers could make it!

After the arrival of the first two regular Methodist preachers in the colonies, Methodism grew rapidly. Embury moved away from New York, and soon after died as a result of an accident suffered while mowing.

Barbara Heck, with her family, also left the city, coming to rest finally in Canada, where her remains lie to-day in a churchyard near the Saint Lawrence. It is a tribute to her character to be able to say that at every point where she lived along that journey she established a Methodist society!

Strawbridge kept preaching in his part of the country, and his path almost never crossed that of the other itinerants.

Captain Webb, and one or two other local preachers, preached as opportunity offered.

§ 6. THE COMING OF ASBURY

But Captain Webb was not satisfied. He felt that Wesley was not giving the new field the attention it deserved. He

"BUT THE OTHER WAS FRANCIS ASBURY"

kept goading Wesley on the subject, and others helped, until at last Wesley, in the Conference held at Bristol in 1771, called for more volunteers.

Five preachers responded. Wesley chose two. One of them proved a failure. But the other, a young man not yet twenty-six years of age, was Francis Asbury!

The son of a gardener, Asbury had begun to preach at Wednesbury, scene of some of the worst of the riots against the Methodists, when he was seventeen. After five years as a local preacher he was called to the itinerancy, and he had spent five years in this kind of training when John Wesley sent him to America.

There is no better way of finding out what sort of a young man he was than by looking again at the words he wrote in his journal while on the voyage: "I will set down a few things that lie on my mind. Whither am I going? To the New World. What to do? To gain honor? No, if I know my own heart. To get money? No; I am going to live to God, and to bring others so to do."

With the coming of the two new men American Methodism was ready to swing into its stride. Leaving the recruits in the settled societies, Asbury in Philadelphia and his companion in New York, Pilmoor started out to storm the South and Boardman invaded New England.

In a few months a commission arrived from Wesley making Asbury the superintendent of the American work. But he was soon relieved of this command by the coming of two more preachers from England, Thomas Rankin and George Shadford.

Perhaps there is no one piece of evidence of the sublime assurance with which John Wesley did his work more convincing than speaks out of the letter with which he sent Shadford to his task:

Dear George—The time has arrived for you to embark for America. You must go down to Bristol, where you will meet with T. Rankin, Captain Webb, and his wife. I let you loose, George, on the great continent of America. Publish your message in the open face of the sun, and do all the good you can. I am, dear George, yours affectionately, John Wesley.

Both the new arrivals were older than the men already at work in America. Rankin, on whom now devolved the command, was a Scotchman. He and Asbury did not get along well together from the start. Asbury felt hurt that he should

have been superseded, and Rankin was more than a little critical of affairs as he found them.

Wesley received letters from both men which showed how
close they were to a break. He did his best to try to better
matters. "Let brothers Shadford, Asbury, and you," he wrote
Rankin, "go on hand in hand, and who can stand against you?
Why, you are enough, trusting in Him that loves you, to over-
turn America!" But the preachers in America were a bit too
irked by their personal differences to make it possible for them
to respond with enthusiasm to their leader's vision of a captured continent.

The preachers held their first Conference in America in
1773. While their differences did not come into the open, they
all felt their influence. Perhaps Rankin sat looking at Asbury,
wondering what he could do to bring that extremely opinionated
young man to terms. And Asbury sat looking at Rankin,
wondering how long he could stand it to remain under the
orders of that Scotch martinet.

Rankin finally made an issue of the matter with Wesley,
and Wesley, like any man at the head of a ramified organization, felt it necessary to back up his deputy, and ordered Asbury
back to England. But Rankin had himself prevented the order
from going into effect, for he had, in the meantime, shipped
Asbury to the edges of the Methodist world, stationing him
at Norfolk, Virginia, so that the word of recall did not reach
him until the political lid had blown off in the colonies, and an
entirely changed aspect had been placed on Methodist affairs.

§ 7. The American Revolution

For while the Methodist preachers were going through this
period of personal stress and strain, the colonies were girding
for the struggle which gave them their liberty. It was in the
year that Rankin and Shadford landed that the tea was pitched
into Boston harbor. It was in the year that Asbury was ordered

back to England that the first Continental Congress met. It was in the year that Lexington and Concord were fought that all the preachers except Asbury left the country. Thus, in three short years, did the political upheaval change the entire outlook for the Methodist work.

John Wesley had a good deal to do with this change, although in a way he never anticipated.

At the beginning of the quarrel between the colonies and the mother country Wesley was a strong supporter of the position of the colonies. But when the issue came to the point of rebellion, he took the other side in a pamphlet which, ironically enough, was called *A Calm Address to Our American Colonies*. Ironically, because the pamphlet stirred up more trouble than anything else Wesley ever published.

There were three reasons why Wesley switched to the wrong side of that quarrel. In the first place in his earlier position Wesley was pleading the cause of British citizens. In his calm address he was opposing rebels against constitutional authority; then again, he hated war, and knew too well the devastating effects which war always has on the religious life of the people who engage in it. "In all the other judgments of God," he wrote Rankin, "the inhabitants of the earth learn righteousness. When a land is visited with famine, or plague, or earthquake, the people commonly see and acknowledge the hand of God. But whenever war breaks out, God is forgotten, if he be not set at open defiance."

In the next place, he was convinced by the arguments of his friend, Dr. Samuel Johnson. In fact, his ill-famed pamphlet was nothing but a rehash of another pamphlet written by Doctor Johnson. Wesley was not the kind to fall down at the mere word of a great man, but Doctor Johnson's standing as a source of wisdom was so high that it must have disposed Wesley to regard his words with especial care. At any rate, it seems to have been Johnson who turned Wesley against the colonists. Or perhaps it would be nearer the truth to say that Doctor Johnson gave Wesley an intellectual excuse to let his hundred-per-cent British patriotism come boiling out.

Finally, it must be acknowledged that while Wesley was a liberal in a good many lines, he was a thorough Tory in politics. Three years after George Washington had been inaugurated as President of the United States, and six years after the Methodist Episcopal Church had come into being, Wesley was still unyielding on this point. "We Methodists are no republicans and never intend to be," he wrote.

The whole political movement which came to birth at Lexington, and which led to the Revolutions in France and in Latin America, was utterly repugnant to this Oxford graduate. He was against it as instinctively as many of the churchmen of the present day have been against the revolutionary movements which have followed the World War—and for the same reason, because he did not understand.

This explanation of Wesley's attitude has been given, in this book which intends to spend so little space on details of this kind, because it is well to know why he took such a mistaken position, and because the consequences of his mistake were so far reaching.

For one thing, his mistake had much to do with running all the Methodist ministers, except Asbury, out of America. And why not? Some of them were distributing Wesley's *Calm Address*. Others were preaching much the same political doctrine. Still others were British soldiers, like Webb, or former soldiers, like Shadford.

Asbury seems to have been the only one who could keep from dabbling in the political situation, and always, following the example of their distant leader, it was on the Tory side. Is it any wonder that America became an unhealthy climate? Even Asbury, who had sense enough to keep his sentiments to himself, had to spend much of the period of the war in hiding.

For another thing, the resentment aroused by Wesley's stand spread from his preachers to their society members. All the Methodists came to be regarded with suspicion.

It is easy to rouse suspicion in war time. A few years ago it was a poor community which did not have its eyes on at least one German spy. During the Revolutionary War every Methodist was regarded as a Tory until he proved himself otherwise. This, of course, weeded out the unworthy Methodists.

But it did something better than that. It induced scores and hundreds of them to leave the seaboard, along which the war was raging, and to push back into the pioneer settlements, where the question would not be forever tormenting them. And there, when peace came, Asbury and his handful of native itinerants found them, eager for the coming of the preacher, and offering innumerable new outposts for the Methodist advance.

§ 8. AFTER THE REVOLUTION

It was in 1783 that peace came to America. A new nation entered the family of nations. It was necessary, too, for a new church to enter the congregation of churches. Asbury might well say, "I am truly sorry that the venerable man (Wesley) ever dipped into the politics of America." But, sorry or not, the harm had been done, and a breach created which made it impossible much longer to conduct the work in America merely as a branch of a main movement in England.

The newly liberated Americans may have been a bit too bumptious in their freedom; there are passages in the literature of that time which make that seem possible. But the condition was there. They were no longer ready to take a subservient place, in religion no less than in politics.

Besides this, the religious situation in the new United States required drastic action. In the parts of the country

formerly served by the Church of England there was scarcely
a clergyman left.   All had returned to England, impelled by
the same political reasons which had sent home the British
Methodist preachers.   The resulting religious poverty was appalling.

There were great stretches of country where there were
no ministers to administer the communion, none to baptize the
children into the family of the church, none to place the blessing
of the church on the marriage vow.   Many of the Methodist
preachers, notably men like Strawbridge in the South and John
Dickins, who had been placed in charge in New York, favored
action without further delay.   They would have had the Methodist preachers begin to exercise all the functions of clergymen, and they undoubtedly had the majority of the members
of the societies behind them.

Asbury, however, kept fighting for time.   His soul was
still loyal to Wesley, his spiritual father and the man to whom
he had looked for orders for all the years of his career.   He
could not quite hold all the preachers within bounds; Strawbridge refused to obey him.   But he did manage to have the
issue postponed until finally John Wesley himself came to
understand the situation and took the step which set the American Methodists free, and later placed his benediction on the
course which they adopted for themselves.

Wesley, in England, was between two fires.   From one
side he was beset by the letters and reports from America,
pleading that something be done.   To this there was added his
own good judgment, which told him that something had to be
done.   From the other side there came the warnings of his
Anglican friends, led by his brother Charles, who insisted that
whatever he did must be done within the limits of the Established Church, and that he must under no circumstances ordain
his own Methodist preachers to act as full-fledged clergymen.

Wesley made at least two attempts to escape the dilemma

by suggesting to Anglican bishops that they provide ordination for his American preachers, but without success. Finally he came to see that he must either set his American Methodist preachers aside as ministers, with all the functions of clergymen, or that the work in the new republic must be left to drift into whatever forms might happen. And when that choice became clear, he did not hesitate longer.

§ 9. WESLEY'S FIRST ORDINATIONS

For the last few years Wesley had been relying more and more on the help of Dr. Thomas Coke, the former curate of South Petherton, who had been turned out of his church because of the fervor of his religion. Coke had been placed at the head of the London circuit, and had been Wesley's most trusted adviser in arranging the terms of the "deed of declaration" under which the permanency of British Methodism was assured. When Fletcher refused to be considered as Wesley's successor, Coke had seemed to fit into that place. Naturally, in this time of test, Wesley turned to Coke for help in arranging the affairs of the Methodists of America.

One day he called Coke into his study in London and told him that he thought the situation in America required that the societies there be welded into an independent church. It is likely that Coke was willing to agree without reservation. Then Wesley went on to say that he felt this church should have an episcopal form of government. Coke, like any good Anglican, would agree to that.

But then Wesley went ahead to say that he had been convinced for forty years that there was nothing in the theory of apostolic succession on which the Anglican bishops based their claim to the right of ordination; that, in fact, he thought the practice in the earliest churches showed that any presbyter, or full-fledged minister, had the right to ordain. Acting on this belief, Wesley proposed that he ordain Coke as a superintendent for the work in America, and that Coke, once he reached that country, should ordain the preachers who were at work there.

Doctor Coke seems at first to have shrunk from the proposal made by Wesley, but by the time the Annual Conference met at Leeds he had approved the course proposed.

At Leeds Wesley appointed two others of his preachers, Richard Whatcoat and Thomas Vasey, to go with Coke to the infant republic. Then, gathering them all in his room in the Methodist headquarters in Bristol, early on a September morning in 1784, the father of Methodism laid his hands on the head of Coke, and again on the heads of Whatcoat and Vasey, ordaining the former to act as a superintendent and the latter to act as presbyters, or ministers, in the church which was about to come into being in America.

There has been much argument about this action, and about the validity of the ordination thus granted the three men. To those who require a mechanical basis for religious organization, the material touch of life on life, back through the generations to the time when all Christian organizations were beginning, the scene in the Bristol room seems preposterous.

Let it be granted to all such without argument that Methodism has no ordinations of that sort, and is interested in none. The ordinations of Methodism are entirely outside the mechanical realm. They derive their authority from the fact that their originator, John Wesley, was a man whose ministry was evidently approved of God. And if ever the time comes when the ordaining ministry of Methodism is not thus approved, it will be time to scrap the whole thing, and start again from another life with self-authenticating powers.

§ 10. Coke and Asbury Meet

Coke, Whatcoat and Vasey were in New York early in November. From thence they traveled south, until they reached Delaware, where, one Sunday, Coke preached to a great company at a chapel in the woods. "Scarcely had he finished his sermon," says the oft-told story, "before he perceived a plainly dressed, robust, but venerable looking man moving through the congregation and making his way to the pulpit; on ascending the pulpit he clasped the doctor in his arms, and, without making himself known by words, accosted him with the holy salutation of primitive Christianity." Thus did Coke first meet Asbury.

"HE CLASPED THE DOCTOR"

As soon as the newcomers had familiarized Asbury with the plans for the new church they were bringing from Wesley, Freeborn Garrettson, one of the best of the American preachers who had come to the front during the war days, was sent "like an arrow over North and South" calling the itinerants to a Conference at Baltimore. During the six weeks while Garrettson was gathering the clans Coke covered a thousand miles in a preaching tour, thus gaining some conception of the sort of work that the Methodist preachers were doing and the places where they were doing it.

§ 11. THE CHRISTMAS CONFERENCE OF 1784

The Conference finally met in Lovely Lane chapel, Baltimore, on the day before Christmas, 1784. So unanimous were all present as to what should be done, and so closely were the ideas contained in the letter from Wesley which Coke presented in accord with the desires of the Americans, that actions of epochal importance took place within a few hours.

On motion of John Dickins, it was voted to form the Methodist Episcopal Church. Wesley had already designated Coke and Asbury for the episcopal offices in this church, and had

"GARRETTSON WAS SENT LIKE AN ARROW"

actually ordained Coke for this episcopacy. But Asbury was wise enough to see that an American church should have the privilege of choosing its own leaders, and he refused to accept the high office unless his ministerial brothers elected him to it. This they promptly, and unanimously, did.

On Christmas day Coke, assisted by Whatcoat and Vasey, ordained Asbury, until then only a Methodist itinerant, as a deacon in the new church. On the next day he was ordained an elder. And on the next day, assisted by the minister of a German congregation who was a close friend of Asbury's, the same three made the son of the gardener of Wednesbury a bishop of the Methodist Episcopal Church.

Thus it came to pass that, while there was as yet no Methodist Church in England, and while the Methodist preachers in that country were still regarded as wandering laymen, without the rights of full ministers, there came to birth in America, in a republic still without a constitution and without a President, the first Methodist Episcopal Church in the world. Of what happened after that church had been formed we shall have more to say in other chapters.

CHAPTER X

THE BIRTH OF A CHURCH

§ 1. The First Societies

IF YOU, to-day, reading this book, call yourself a Methodist, the chances are that you are a member of some kind of a Methodist *church*. But if you had lived in England one hundred and fifty years ago, and had been moved by the preaching of John Wesley or one of his followers to declare yourself a Methodist, you could not have joined a Methodist church, for there was no Methodist church to join!

We are apt to think of religious history in terms of churches. Indeed, we generally call the study of this branch of knowledge "church history." Methodism, however, has never been careful to follow the patterns set by others. So it is no surprise to find that, in this respect too, Methodism was a law to itself.

Methodism did not begin as a church. It was not formed, as so many new religious bodies have been, by one man, or a group of men, withdrawing in dissatisfaction from an old church and forming a new one. No, it was, for more than half a century, simply a movement, and it was only by slow stages, and under constant pressure, that Wesley allowed the Methodist movement to crystallize into a separate legal body.

It is not hard to understand why the work that John and Charles Wesley and their friend George Whitefield started in England remained so long an unformed movement. All three of them were, we remember, ministers in a national church. The father of the Wesley brothers had come back into that church after a personal experience which had convinced him that the religious bodies outside its ranks were of doubtful

162

spiritual power.   For this reason he had been strong in his appreciation of the claims of the national church to the obedience of all its members and the observance of all its rules.   It was a subject on which he was even ready to dare a dispute with his formidable wife.

This pronounced churchmanship the old rector of Epworth passed on to his sons.   Charles never lost it.   To the day of his death he never ceased to fight against the evidences which were continually cropping out that the Methodists would one day drop all pretense of allegiance to the national church and set up ecclesiastical housekeeping for themselves.

Adam Clarke, who became one of the greatest students of the meaning of scripture that Methodism has produced, has told how, in 1783, when he was admitted to the Methodist Conference, Charles Wesley—then but five years from his death—preached the sermon to the newly accepted preachers and said: "They which are healed under the ministry of my brother and myself go with us into the church.   Abide in the church.   If you leave the church God will leave you, or you will go halting all the days of your life, should you even get to heaven at last."

The question never became a burning one for Whitefield, because that evangelist never had personal responsibility for such large numbers of converts as looked to the Wesley brothers for guidance.   Probably Whitefield had a vague hope that enough of the clergy of the national church would be inwardly stirred to look after the spiritual needs of most of his converts, while the rest could find refuge in the chapels of the various dissenting congregations—Baptists, Congregationalists, Presbyterians and the like.

For the rest, Whitefield was content to preach wherever a pulpit opened, be it the pulpit of a Congregational church in New England, or an Anglican parish in London, or a desk in the mansion of the Countess of Huntingdon, or a box in the open air. With it all, he remained to the end a clergyman in regular standing of the Church of England, although his bones rest beneath the pulpit of a Congregational church in Newburyport, Massachusetts.

To John Wesley the question presented itself in a different manner than to his brother or his friend.

After the seventeenth year of the Methodist movement Charles ceased to itinerate, held to his home in Bristol and later in London by the mounting cares of a large family. He, therefore, knew what was going on only at second or third hand, and often not at all. Not so with John. That field marshal, always on the move, was so constituted that he knew when the debt on the Newcastle chapel reached a hundred pounds and when one of the sisters attended class-meeting in Bristol wearing a gold necklace. But more than that, he knew all the problems that beset all his preachers, and so he came to know how real and difficult a problem this one of their relation to the national church had come to be.

A condition always had more weight with John Wesley than a theory, and so, although the pleadings of his brother, the example of many clerical friends, and even the advice of one or two eminent legal men drew him back, the force of circumstances pushed him on and on until, before he died, separation between Wesley's followers and his old church—which he, in point of legal fact, never left—had become practically complete. What had started as a movement, what the Wesleys would have liked to have kept as a movement, had become a church. Many to-day will be glad to know how this change came to pass.

§ 2. Life in the Methodist Societies

"In November, 1738," John Wesley told his Annual Conference of Methodist preachers almost thirty years later, "several persons came to me in London, and desired me to advise and pray with them. I said, 'If you will meet on Thursday night, I will help you as well as I can.' More and more then desired to meet with them, till they were increased to many hundreds. The case was afterward the same at Bristol, Kingswood, Newcastle, and many other parts of England, Scotland, and Ireland."

Such were the beginnings of the Methodist societies, as told in the terse language that always characterized their founder. Religious societies were not an innovation in the London of his day. Many such groups formed within the dissenting churches. The Quakers were really attendants upon such gatherings. The Moravians planted their societies in London and many other English centers. It was in the meeting of an Anglican society in Aldersgate street that Wesley himself felt his heart strangely warmed.

When we talk of the wickedness of the England into which the Wesleys and Whitefield brought the transforming power of the evangelical revival, we must not leave out of account these groups of earnest seekers after the benefits of religion who, in quiet rooms unknown to the revelers who made the outer record of those days a scandal, were, with prayer and mutual counsel, laying the foundations of the better order soon to be.

Naturally, no sooner did a religious leader of the stature of John Wesley appear than he was begged to act as the leader of some of these societies, especially of the societies composed of those whose spiritual aspirations had been stirred under his preaching. So rapidly did the formation of these societies spread that the Wesleys felt it necessary to print rules for their guidance, and in these rules they printed their description of a Methodist society that remains a classic to this day.

A Methodist society, they said, consists of "a company of men having the form and seeking the power of godliness, united in order to pray together, to receive the word of exhortation, and to watch over one another in love, that they may help each other to work out their own salvation." There is a lot of worth still left in that old definition. If you wonder at times whether the organization of which you are a part is in the true Methodist succession, you might test it by the standard of the Methodist societies as the Wesleys held it.

In the interest of truth it must be admitted that life in these societies was not always as ideal as their purposes suggested. Frequent house-cleanings seem to have been necessary. What it is about the sort of religious experience that these people were seeking that leads to disorder we do not know, but it is a sad fact that rarely can any large number start in search of a deeper spiritual life without having aberrations appear that cast discredit on the whole movement.

To the extent that this is true the Anglican clergy of Wesley's day who warned against the danger of "enthusiasm" were warranted in their opposition. Wesley himself, as we read his journal, seems to have spent much of his time in the early years of the Methodist movement traveling back and forth between London and Bristol, "purging" the societies at each end of his journey.

There were times when the expulsions and withdrawals outnumbered the faithful allowed to remain within the fold. Wesley was never enamored of statistics. Membership figures were not compiled until Methodism had been a power in England for thirty years, and even then they showed that the society membership was being held down with a firm hand.

It has become the fashion in some quarters to talk about the size of the Methodist movement. Much Methodist time and energy is now spent in making sure that every church member, probationer, baptized child, and even constituent is on the rolls, so that no other communion dare claim a larger company. One wonders what John Wesley would have to say to such a worship of statistics.

There were times when he was warned that the stringent demands he was making of his society members would reduce the societies to extinction, but the warning failed to deter him. He knew that a spiritual revival is not a matter of members but of devotion, and he seems never to have been disturbed, even when some of his closest associates were leaving.

§ 3. THE CLASS MEETINGS

The growth of the societies, however, went steadily on. And the growth brought the most difficult of all Wesley's problems. It was impossible for him or for his brother or for an occasional sympathetic parson who might come to their aid, or even for the handful of lay helpers who were gradually and carefully chosen, to give the thousands soon enrolled the sort of oversight their spiritual needs demanded.

Wesley was the most tireless of itinerants. But he could not be everywhere at once, and where he was absent trouble had a way of cropping out. It was by chance that he hit upon a plan that characterized Methodism for years, and that solved his problem of personal supervision—the plan of dividing the main societies into class meetings.

The society in Bristol was in debt. Methodist societies had been in debt before, and have been since. But John Wesley could never be fully happy with a debt around, and he gathered the society members to see if some plan could not be worked out for getting rid of the bugbear. It was proposed to divide the debt by the number of society members, and then ask each to give his share.

But it was protested that some were too poor. Then, counseled one of the local leaders, divide the society into groups. Let a leader be responsible for each group. Let each group member be asked to give a penny a week, and in a short time the whole will be raised. And, said this counselor, if he was made responsible for a group in which some were too poor to give the penny, he would make up the difference from his own pocket.

Wesley adopted the plan, and then, with his genius for organization, made it contribute to something vastly more important than raising money to pay a chapel debt.

The societies were divided, as had been suggested, into groups of about twelve. Leaders were appointed for these groups. But the groups were called on to meet together each week, and it became the business of the leader to conduct a public examination into the manner of life of each member of the class, to praise those who were living well, to admonish those who were falling before temptation, and to exhort all to go on in the way of holiness.

Raising finances became a very minor—although never neglected—feature of such a gathering. Rightly conducted it was a spiritual clinic, and within it was much of the secret of the persistence and stability of the Methodist movement.

§ 4. Step into a Class Meeting

Too few Americans remember a Methodist class-meeting of the old order. There they sat, twelve persons "having the form and seeking the power of godliness"; in the center, on the plain table, the leader's Bible; around it, the circle of chairs, each with its occupant.

Generally the leader pitched the tune for an opening hymn:

> "All thanks be to God,
> Who scatters abroad,
> Throughout every place,
> By the least of his servants, his savor of grace:
> Who the victory gave,
> The praise let him have,
> For the work he hath done;
> All honor and glory to Jesus alone!"

Followed prayer, fervent, from the heart, that the Spirit of God might be present, to expose the inmost thoughts and imaginings, and to inspire all to new heights of living, and after that the reading of a passage of Scripture, with perhaps a running fire of commentary from the class leader.

"Brother Watson," the leader would demand, the reading done, "how has it been this week with your soul?"

Stammeringly, the lad from the farm just outside the village would rise to his feet. Words would not seem to come. At last, with a mighty wrench, "I thank the Lord, well," he would mumble, and sit down.

But the old leader was not satisfied.

"Praise the Lord," he would encourage, and then the probe would go in. "No wrestlings with temptation?"

"THE LAD FROM THE FARM"

"Yes." The lad's head might hang, but there was never any thought of holding back an answer.

"Did that old temper rise up again?"

"Yes."

"And did you win the victory?"

"Yes, thank God."

"Hallelujah, Brother Watson. Go on as you are and one day the crown incorruptible will certainly be yours.

'I the chief of sinners am,
But Jesus died for me.'"

And the circle would take up and carry to its end the

familiar stanza. The next chair would bring a very different type of problem.

"Sister Lee, has the Lord been your support this week?"

No hesitation now. In a moment Sister Lee is on her feet, pouring out a record of spiritual blessings in rich profusion, the whole interlarded with ejaculations of rapture that stir the little company to increasingly fervent responses.

"The blessing of God is upon me," the rapt woman concludes. "He is my constant portion by day and by night. By him I have been kept all this week from temptation. Life has become a song and a way of glory! Praise his name!"

"Amen!" "Hallelujah!" "Glory to God!" come the cries from the group as Sister Lee finally, and with evident reluctance, takes her seat. But the class leader, a shoemaker with a deep knowledge of human nature, is not quite content to leave the matter there.

"So you feel that this has been a week of nothing but spiritual triumph, sister?" he asks.

A fervent affirmative expresses the class member's assurance.

"No hours when the tempter caught your soul in his toils?"

Equally positive is the response.

"You feel that you have the witness of the Spirit to this blessing which has been yours?"

"Yes, yes; glory to God!"

"Well, Sister Lee, this is glorious. How happy you must be! And how happy your husband must be!"

There is a pause; a sudden drop in the temperature that all feel. Sister Lee's husband is not a Methodist; worse, he is a good deal of a town reprobate. But there have been whispers about the village that the erring husband might not have wandered so far or so frequently if conditions had been different at home.

Sister Lee's eyes flash at the question, but she is slow to

answer. The leader senses the tension. "Doesn't your husband rejoice with you?" he persists.

"Him!" The woman can hold in no longer. "Why, that worthless scamp, he came home the other night and found me singing a hymn-tune. 'Ha!' he says, 'more religion, is it?' At once I saw that he was fixing to make sport of me, so I flung a mop at his head, and he's been quiet since then."

At first Sister Lee is inclined to bridle at the leader's suggestion that there may be certain spiritual deficiencies to make up before she can rightfully lay claim to the sort of experience that Methodism has called sanctification. But the leader has the backing of the other members of the class in his dealing, and presently is able to pass on to the next member, leaving Sister Lee glowing with a sense of such victories as she has truly won, but also with a lively appreciation of the heights yet to be surmounted.

So the conversation passes around the circle. It is doubtful whether in all the record of religious gatherings since the days of the apostles there has been such an instrument for personal upbuilding as this.

The Roman Catholic Church has had its hearing of individual confessions by individual priests—a practice the value of which can never be discounted. Some wit has said that a Roman priest differs from a Protestant pastor in that a priest hears confessions, while a pastor hears excuses. There is a good deal in the idea. Before the priest the faithful Catholic stands stripped of outward disguise, and from the priest there are supposed to come those admonitions which shall enable the penitent to overcome the faults thus disclosed.

The main fault of the Catholic confessional is its secrecy and its individual nature. Moreover, there has attached to it, in the course of the generations, a species of compulsion which has brought in those who were not in the mood where they desired its ministries, and so have obtained little help from it.

The Methodist class meeting showed its strength just where the Roman confessional has shown its weakness. Testimony in the class meeting was voluntary, for, while the class leaders frequently indulged in forms of probing to bring to light problems that they felt were oppressing their class members, no one was required to disclose matters which he wished to keep to himself.

In addition, the system was thoroughly democratic. If Methodism encouraged its followers to seek new levels of life, it provided in the class meeting a jury in whose presence claims to achievement might be judged. If the class leader was not wise enough to speak the word which was needed in each case, the chances were good that some other member of the class could do so. And the whole system of living before the scrutiny of a dozen fellows tended at once to discourage a tendency to yield easily to temptation and to increase the sense of comradeship in the attempt to live a good life.

We have spoken thus at length of the class meeting because it was the most important feature of the early Methodist movement. Societies there were, and these later became the individual churches. But the societies were held together, and made vital, by the class meetings.

How many have been the revivals that have stirred men, but that have evaporated without leaving long-surviving trace! That it was not so with the work of the Wesleys was largely because, after men had been moved, after they had come together in societies, John Wesley was not content to lose them in the anonymity that soon descends upon individual members of a great body, but, by the provision of these little classes, with their weekly review, secured a constant guard against sin and indifference among his followers.

It was the rule that three consecutive absences from the class meeting meant the loss of the "ticket." And without the ticket—a small card given every quarter by the leader to all in good standing—admission into the meetings of members could not be secured.

§ 5. BANDS

To be sure, there were other organizations within the Methodist societies besides class meetings. The most important were called "bands." These were generally confined to persons of one sex, and were designed to make possible an examination of life even more intimate than could be secured in the class meetings. In the early histories of Methodism numerous references to the bands will be found, but the truth is that they were not regarded as essential, that they fell into disuse at an early date, and that we need spend no more time with them than to remember that they once existed.

§ 6. CIRCUITS

The next development in the making of a church was the setting aside of circuits. First the societies, then the classes, then the circuits.

The two Wesleys had not been preaching long before it became clear that they must have helpers to keep the work going. Most of these helpers had to be recruited from the laity, but, in one way or another, they were called to their work and gave it such devotion as has seldom been given any cause. By the year before John Wesley died, there were 541 itinerant Methodist preachers.

The trouble was that this number—and many of them were not active for considerable periods—had to care for almost 150,000 members of Methodist societies. Many of these societies were in such small places that the whole society was hardly larger than the weekly class. The need for spiritual oversight by leaders who gave their whole strength to this work was, however, too clear to admit of argument.

Wesley accordingly began the custom of grouping the

societies into circuits, and appointing his lay preachers to the responsibility of guiding these circuits. When the preacher could not be present—which meant on a majority of the Sundays of the year—some local lay preacher or some class leader was expected to take charge. But it was the preacher at the head of the circuit who was held responsible for the condition of the societies as a whole. He it was who had to take his report to the Conferences which Mr. Wesley called annually.

"WHEN THE POST ARRIVED"

And he it was who never knew, when the morning post arrived, what letter there might be in it, signed by that famous name, calling him to account for deficiencies that had been reported to the founder of the movement.

§ 7. THE QUESTION OF THE SACRAMENTS

It was after the societies had been joined in circuits, and after Wesley had begun the practice of setting men aside for the pastoral care of these circuits, that the pressure grew to separate the Methodists from the Church of England and to take the character of a dissenting church, like the Baptists or the Presbyterians or any of the others.

In one way it was impossible for the Methodists to *separate* from the national church. As Adam Clarke said later, the vast majority of the Methodists had never been in the Church of England, but had been living without any church connections whatever. But the Wesley brothers were regular clergymen of the national church, and desired so to remain. Charles was especially vehement on that point.

When the subject of separation from the church was under discussion it was really the separation of John and Charles

Wesley which was being discussed. So far as the societies were concerned, neither Anglican parish clergy nor bishops ever exercised the slightest authority over them. But it did seem likely that, if certain things were done, it would be impossible for the Wesleys and their handful of Anglican clerical friends to remain Methodists and also clergy in good standing in the state church.

On the other hand, here were these growing societies, with a membership running now into the tens of thousands. They desired to have the church's sacraments administered to them, but this they could not have while their preachers were laymen. Wesley urged them to attend the parish churches to obtain the sacraments, and, in a further effort to maintain the peace, ordered that no services should be held in the Methodist chapels at the hours services were in progress in the churches.

This attempt to keep tied up with the Church of England was only partially successful. In some churches the Methodists, presenting themselves, were repelled from the communion by clergymen who had no sympathy with Wesley's movement. In practically all churches, these converts of the new order, accustomed to the freer ways of the chapels, felt ill at ease. Generally, after one or two visits they stayed away.

The whole issue finally boiled down to about this: Should the sacraments be administered to Methodist societies? If so, it would be necessary to have ordained persons to perform this rite. There were not enough sympathetic clergymen of the Church of England to take care of the needs of the hundreds of chapels. Attempts to induce Anglican bishops to ordain Methodists failed.

It finally became clear that John Wesley would either have to do the ordaining himself, or that the societies would proceed to obtain the sacraments in such ways as seemed best to them, waiting only until his death to act, since that seemed the last barrier in the way of setting up an independent church.

John Wesley was convinced that he had as much right to ordain to the Christian ministry as any Anglican bishop. He held the whole theory of a bishop's miraculous powers, transmitted by touch of hand on head from the first apostles to the present, to be an unproved and unprovable myth. His reading of church history had convinced him that in the early church there was no difference between the standing of a bishop and that of any other church elder or presbyter.

For almost fifty years Wesley felt clear as to his theoretical right to ordain, if he so chose. But for most of that same period he held back from exercising that right on grounds of expediency. He simply could not bear to see the thousands of his spiritual children cutting even the shadowy ties which bound them to the Church of England.

It was, as we have seen, the situation in America which brought things to a head. The societies in America cared little for the Church of England. In fact, after the peace treaty of 1783, which finally established the independence of the United States, there was no Church of England in America, and had there been one the citizens of the young republic would have done everything they could to avoid being identified with it. England was not popular. The final outcome, when Wesley's common sense sized up the situation, was his ordination of Coke, Vasey and Whatcoat, so that the Methodist Episcopal Church could begin its career in the United States.

Charles Wesley was outraged when he heard what his brother had done. His letters sizzled, and, to relieve his feelings, he burst forth, characteristically, in verse:

> "Why should I longer, Lord, contend,
> My last important moments spend
>   In buffeting the air?
> In warning those who will not see,
> But rest in blind security,
>   And rush into the snare?

"Prophet of ills, why should I live,
Or, by my sad forebodings, grieve
When I can serve no more?
I only can their loss bewail,
Till life's exhausted sorrows fail,
And the last pang is o'er."

Such, in truth, remained the mood of Charles Wesley for most of the rest of his life. Too firm in his belief in his brother ever to allow a break to come between them on such an issue, too sunny by nature ever to nurse a disappointment long, Charles Wesley continued to preach occasionally in the Methodist chapels in London, and to write those hymns which were his greatest contribution to the great movement.

Yet in his heart he was never reconciled. He could not countenance the obvious drift of the movement toward a separate ecclesiastical organization of its own. And when death finally overtook him, he would not allow himself to be buried in the burial ground of the Methodist City Road chapel, but insisted on lying in the consecrated ground of Saint Marylebone Church, and on having his body committed to the grave by the Anglican parson of the parish in which he happened to be residing.

§ 8. A CHURCH

We have seen how John Wesley was finally prevailed on to ordain ministers for service in America, and how swiftly there developed from that act a church, where previously there had only been societies. Much the same thing happened in Great Britain. At first it was only for missionary service in Scotland, in Ireland, in Newfoundland, and in similar places, that the aged evangelist was induced to ordain.

Finally Wesley was ordaining a few for the ministry in England. Alexander Mather was even ordained to be a superintendent, or bishop, as Coke had been ordained for the superintendency in America. Nothing seems to have come of this, however, since it was an office that the preachers in England were not ready to adopt or obey.

In the closing years of his life Wesley clearly saw a new, distinct church coming into being. Sometimes he seemed in a mood to close his eyes to what was happening. Once in awhile he would feel afresh the perils that would confront an infant church and would point out how much better it would be if all remained in the fellowship of the Anglican body.

"ANGLICANISM WAS AN ORDER"

He knew, however, in his heart of hearts, that this was not to be. So he made legal arrangements whereby it became easily possible, just as soon as he himself, clad in the garb of a minister of the Church of England, had been placed in his grave, for the societies he had left behind to coalesce in an independent church.

Regarded as the Methodists were by most of the clerics of the Church of England, there could be no other outcome. Methodism was a spirit; it was a movement; it was a life. Anglicanism was an order, a rubric, a theory. The Methodists, in the main, had little commerce of spirit with the Anglicans; the Anglicans had less with the Methodists.

Many who have written on this subject have written as though the Methodists were forced out of Anglicanism, and have tried to point out how much better it would have been if the Anglican bishops had had wisdom enough to hold them. As we have said, this is hardly an accurate statement, for the overwhelming majority of the Methodists never were, in any vital sense, within Anglicanism. But, even taken at its face value, it is far from certain that such a judgment is right. For if the Methodists were forced out, they were forced out to their own good, to the good of all English-speaking lands, and to the good of the world. It was not the only time in which the purposes of God have been secured by means of an exodus.

CHAPTER XI

THE AFTERGLOW

§ 1. AFTER THE TIDE TURNED

IN 1785 John Wesley, now an old man of eighty-two years, sat in his room in Dublin writing to Elizabeth Ritchie, the daughter of one of his old friends, who had become one of his closest intimates. "Many years ago," he wrote, "I was saying, 'I cannot imagine how Mr. Whitefield can keep his soul alive, as he is not now going through honor and dishonor, evil report and good report, having nothing but honor and good report attending him wherever he goes.' It is now my own case; I am become, I know not how, an honorable man. The scandal of the cross is ceased; and all the kingdom, rich and poor, Papists and Protestants, behave with courtesy, nay, and seeming good will! It seems as if I had well-nigh finished my course, and our Lord was giving me an honorable discharge."

It is not hard to understand why the patriarchal evangelist must have been astonished by the change in popular attitude toward him. He was still preaching the same truths that had provoked so much disturbance in earlier years; he was still going into every part of the United Kingdom with his message; until he was eighty-five years of age neither he, nor the onlookers, were able to detect any lessening of the vigor with which he pressed home his message. But, where once his coming had been a signal for riot, now the crowds would gather by the thousands to stand bareheaded, staring at his passing "as if the king were going by."

He had outlived most of those who had figured, either as his supporters or his opponents, in the tumultuous events of earlier years. But, here and there, he still found those who had

180

once haled him before magistrates or warned him to leave the bounds of parishes, now standing in his congregations to do him honor.

Parish churches that had once been closed now sought with eagerness the honor of having him stand in their pulpits. Even in cathedrals he was invited to administer the sacrament of the holy communion. But field preaching remained the main order of his day. Once he had gone to the fields because few other places were open to him. Now he stayed in the fields because no buildings could care for a tenth part of the multitudes that crowded to hear him. There was given to him the satisfaction that comes to but few men who undergo the taunts hurled at a pioneer, namely, that of living long enough to see his work acknowledged as good and himself as a leader of mankind.

From the first century of Christian history there has come down to us a picture something like this. It is the picture of the church that had grown up in the rich city of Ephesus. From humble beginnings that church had multiplied until it held in its membership scores of the families of the proud city. At its head there remained a venerable figure—the sole survivor of the little group that had walked the roads of Galilee and Judæa with the Master. An old man now, worn by the innumerable hardships through which he had passed, the apostle John was carried on the shoulders of young men of his congregation, along the streets of Ephesus and into the sanctuary. Everywhere men and women fell on their knees, beseeching his blessing. And the old man, feebly holding out his hands in sign of benediction, murmured as he was carried along, "Little children, love one another."

In much the same way John Wesley went about England during the closing years of his life, the benediction of his spirit and words falling upon men everywhere as he passed. In one respect he had an advantage over the saint of Ephesus, for he preserved to a remarkable degree his physical energies.

After he had passed his eighty-fifth birthday he began to admit the encroachments of age, but even when he was eighty-seven, and within six months of his death, he could write: "My body seems nearly to have done its work, and to be almost worn out. Last month my strength was nearly gone, and I could have sat almost still from morning to night. But, blessed be God, I crept about a little, and made shift to preach once. On Monday I ventured a little further; and after I had preached three times (once in the open air) I found my strength so restored that I could have preached again without inconvenience."

What a man he was—at eighty-seven "almost worn out" and preaching three times a day!

§ 2.   THE MEASURE OF A LIFE

It is no wonder that, before the end of his long career, the same England that had once reviled him came to honor John Wesley. England has given birth to some wonderful sons, but never to one that surpassed him. Indeed, in the extraordinary range of his accomplishments, he was a man unique. Considered from almost any angle, he appeared like no one who had gone before in that country, and he has certainly not been approached by any who have come after. In certain aspects of interest or effort he was equaled and even surpassed, but the totality of his range and his power gives such an impression as to leave him towering among Englishmen. It is not hard to discover what some of his attributes were that set him apart from most men.

§ 3.   "HE NEVER FOLDS HIS LEGS"

Probably no man who ever lived worked harder or more continuously. Up every morning at four, preaching at five, he was never at rest until after eight in the evening. Deliberately he sacrificed social pleasures that must have appealed mightily to such a nature as his in order that his work might not suffer.

Dr. Samuel Johnson, the grand khan of English letters in that day, growled to Boswell, "I hate to meet John Wesley; the dog enchants you with his conversation, and then breaks away to go and visit some old woman." Seemingly, the great doctor could not get this peculiarity out of his mind. Other men of that day competed for the privilege of hours with him; he had given clear indication of his desire for Wesley's presence. But no, "he is always obliged to go at a certain hour." No wonder the gruff doctor called this "very disagreeable to a man who loves to fold his legs and have his talk out, as I do."

In the letter we have already quoted, Wesley admits, as evidence of the advance of age, his readiness to sit still. It was sufficient evidence.

§ 4.   Typical Days in Wesley's Life

See the way in which he lived his days. Here is a typical portion, as one of his biographers has epitomized it: "His age is seventy-four. On Friday, May 9, he rides from Osmotherly, fifteen miles, to Malton, Yorkshire, suffering at intervals from ague. He preaches. Having heard that E. Ritchie is very ill, he sets out after the service, and reaches Otley, forty-eight miles away, at four o'clock Saturday morning. After seeing the invalid, he rides back to Malton, having, as he says, ridden between ninety and a hundred miles. He rests one hour, then rides twenty-two miles to Scarborough, and preaches in the evening. On Sunday morning he is shaking with fever. He lies between blankets, drinks hot lemonade, perspires, and sleeps for half an hour. Then he rises up and preaches. After this he meets the society. On Monday he is preaching at Bridlington. On Tuesday preaching at Beverley in the morning, and in the evening at Hull, having ridden thirty-six miles that day. On Wednesday he rides twenty-six miles to Pocklington,

preaches, rides twelve miles farther to York, and preaches
again. He admits that he feels his 'breast out of order,' and
would gladly rest. But he is expected at Tadcaster. He starts
at 9 A. M. Thursday in a chaise, which breaks down. He bor-
rows a lively horse, whose movements, he cheerfully says, 'elec-
trifies' him, and he feels better! He preaches, and that same
night returns twelve miles to York. The next day he 'took
the diligence' for London."

Thus John Wesley drove his frail, once tubercular body,
three hundred and sixty-five days a year, for half a century!
Is it any wonder that the total impression given an observer
like W. T. Stead was of a "marvelous body, with muscles of
whipcord, and bones of steel, with lungs of leather, and the
heart of a lion"? Is it any wonder that he accomplished more
than most men?

§ 5. WESLEY THE READER

What an omnivorous reader he was! Master of six languages, he learned to read while in the saddle or in the chaise,
and was thus thrusting his way through ancient classics and
modern productions of all sorts all the while that he was pushing the work of the Kingdom.

"While in Dublin," he remarked, "I read two extraordinary books of different kinds." He was always reading extraordinary books of different kinds. Bolingbroke, Chesterfield, Voltaire, Rousseau were as familiar to him as the writings of Roman Catholic mystics and the fathers of the early
church. After he died one of his preachers was appalled to
find a complete edition of Shakespeare's plays, the margins
covered with notes in Wesley's handwriting, and quickly destroyed the volume lest it betray to the godly their leader's lack
of piety.

Much that Wesley read he felt would be of value to his
followers, and one more evidence of his astonishing ability to

turn out work is the fact that he issued four hundred and forty-one publications, ranging in size from a four-page tract to his three volume commentary on the Old Testament. A majority of these publications were condensations or rearrangements of books that had figured in Wesley's own reading.

Wesley once called himself a man of one book, and in a sense he was that. But in another sense he was a man of multitudes of books. He seemed determined to expose his mind to every wind that might be blowing. He did not care whether he agreed with an author or not. Truth could be trusted to attest itself to the reason. But, until every voice had been allowed to speak, what chance was there for the truth to be discovered?

§ 6. Wesley the Thinker

Out of this eagerness to see the inside of all the minds who had left their records on paper, John Wesley naturally developed into a pioneer thinker on his own account. When we remember the age in which he lived, it is astonishing to find in how many matters he struck out on paths of thought that other men were not ready to walk in until long years after.

He was one of the first to accept the value of the experiments being made by Benjamin Franklin with electricity, and defended that American's discoveries when they were being laughed at by the Royal Society in London. During all his life he insisted on the therapeutic value of electrical treatments.

Even more daring was his anticipation of the modern theory of evolution. Writing under the title of "A General View of the Gradual Progression of Beings," in his "Compendium of Natural Philosophy," he asked, "By what degrees will nature raise herself up to man? How will she rectify this head that is always inclined toward earth? How change these paws into flexible arms? What method will she make use of to transform these crooked feet into supple and skillful hands?

Or how will she widen and extend this contracted stomach? In what manner will she place the breasts and give them a roundness suitable to them? The ape is this rough draft of man, this rude sketch, an imperfect representation which nevertheless bears a resemblance to him, and is the last creature that serves to display the admirable progression of the works of God." And later he adds, "There is a prodigious number of continued links between the most perfect man and the ape"! Remember, this was published exactly twenty-five years before Charles Darwin was born! Such passages, it is true, should be interpreted in the light of Wesley's writings as a whole, and not Wesley's other writings in the light of these brief passages.

More like the attitude of another age than such a particular judgment as that of the paragraph quoted was the spirit in which Wesley approached questions. In his day it was the fashion to work out a theory, generally by introspection, and then to select such facts as fitted it. Wesley turned the process around. In any realm, it was the experience, the fact, that he sought first of all. On the basis of the facts he reached his conclusions. If later facts appeared to discredit his first judgments, he did not hesitate to change his beliefs.

At one time he believed the stars to be inhabited; later he felt obliged to give up the belief in the light of other facts. At one time he believed that men could get into heaven only as the result of one type of spiritual experience; later he acknowledged that proof to the contrary had forced him to change his belief.

Even in his ideas on spooks, he followed the same method. He may not have been critical enough in his examination of his sources of material, but in every case he gave evidence of having no desire other than to discover what had actually taken place when ghostly visitors had been reported in various parts of England. So far as his method of arriving at conclusions was concerned, John Wesley was the contemporary of any modern scientist.

§ 7. WESLEY THE THEOLOGIAN

It was when this method was applied to the realm of religion that the most remarkable results were bound to come. In how many ways did Wesley prove himself a religious pioneer! Not in theology, for he adopted his theological ideas largely from men who had gone before. But in his attitude toward theology, toward the book out of which theology is supposed to spring, toward the basis of Christian fellowship, toward the work of the church Wesley proved himself a thoroughgoing pioneer.

Take his theology as an example. His were the orthodox theological ideas of his time. Had he ever been moved to put down a list of theological fundamentals or essentials, it is certain that he would have included a belief in the deity of Jesus among them. Yet, when he had read the life of Thomas Firmin, a Unitarian, he felt forced to pass it on to his Methodists, with this preface: "I was exceedingly struck at reading the following life, having long settled it in my mind that the entertaining wrong notions concerning the trinity was inconsistent with real piety. But I cannot argue against matter of fact. I dare not deny that Mr. Firmin was a pious man, although his notions of the trinity were quite erroneous." There it is: "I cannot argue against matter of fact"!

He was equally cordial in his recognition of the high spiritual qualities in the saints of the Roman Church. "If most [Catholics] are volunteers in the faith," he observed, "believing more than God has revealed, it cannot be denied that they believe all which God has revealed as necessary to salvation." He commended certain Catholic saints to the study of Methodists.

He went even beyond that. In a day when it was an

almost universal belief among churchmen that the heathen were bound straight for hell, he wrote, after reading the *Meditations* of Marcus Aurelius, "I make no doubt but this is one of those 'many' who 'shall come from the east and the west and sit down with Abraham, Isaac, and Jacob,' while 'the children of the kingdom,' nominal Christians, are 'shut out.' "

More than that, John Wesley was not one of the kind who came to advanced views in his own mind, and then carefully hid them there lest he be called in question by others. If he thought that men like the Roman emperor and Socrates and Plato and many another would find their way into heaven, he let his preachers know it. If you will turn to the minutes of the Conference held in 1770, you will find that the formal proceedings began in this way:

"1. Who of us is now accepted of God? He that now believes in Christ with a loving, obedient heart.

"2. But who among those who never heard of Christ? He that feareth God and worketh righteousness, according to the light he has.

"3. Is this the same that 'He that is sincere'? Nearly, if not quite."

Ponder those questions a minute. You could convict John Wesley, and those Methodist preachers of 1770, of heresy to-day in many a communion on the strength of those three answers! By so much was the founder of Methodism a theological pioneer.

Then, too, he was a good deal of a pioneer in his attitude toward the Bible. Here is a religious question that is making more trouble to-day than it was in Wesley's time. The issue as to the inspiration of the Scriptures had not come up then. If it is asked whether Wesley was a believer in the literal inspiration of the Bible, the answer would have to be in the affirmative. No other answer had then occurred to men who called themselves religious. Even the Unitarians of that day

accepted such an inspiration as an axiom. But, if Wesley believed in a verbally inspired Bible, he did so in what must have
seemed a queer way to many of his contemporaries.

The Calvinists put their proof texts up to him. Did these
not prove their arguments as to predestination and the like?
They certainly did, provided that you accepted a theory of
inspiration which heard the veritable voice of God speaking in
every word. Wesley was supposed to have accepted that
theory. But what did he say to the proof texts? "Let it mean
what it will, it cannot mean that the Judge of all the world is
unjust. No scripture can mean that God is not love, or that his
mercy is not over all his works; that is, whatever it prove beside,
no scripture can prove predestination."

In other words, when a theory of inspiration came in conflict with Wesley's own experience of the nature of God, the
theory was cast overboard.

Other facts might be called up to show how free Wesley
was from the traditional thralldom to the letter of the Bible.
In his commentary on the very first verse of the first chapter of
the New Testament he admitted the possible errancy of the
Scriptures, saying that the evangelists had merely copied
Jewish records that might be wrong. And when he sent a
psalter to America for the use of the infant Methodist Episcopal church, the last paragraph of the preface to his collection read: "Many psalms [are] left out, and many parts of the
others, as being highly improper for the mouths of a Christian
congregation." Again the theory of inspiration had come into
conflict with the experience of Christian revelation, and the
theory had to lose.

Perhaps, however, a still more significant light is thrown
on Wesley's attitude toward the Bible by his reply to another
objector. For something that he was doing it was objected
that there was "no scripture for it." "What of it?" answered
Wesley. "There is none against it."

§ 8. WESLEY THE RELIGIOUS PIONEER

The peak of Wesley's service as a religious pioneer came, however, in his conception of the proper basis of Christian fellowship. On what basis should followers of Jesus form their organized bodies?

There had been just one answer to that question for hundreds of years. The basis had always been a creed; a collection of tenets; a statement of beliefs, or a certain form of worship. The person who would acknowledge adherence to this set of views or would follow these methods of worship would be acknowledged as a member of the true order of Christians; all others were looked upon as of a lesser degree of piety, if not actually on their way to destruction.

Wesley turned the whole Methodist movement squarely against this sort of exclusiveness and externality. "The thing which I resolved to use every possible method of preventing," he later wrote, "was a narrowness of spirit, a party zeal, a being straitened in our own bowels—that miserable bigotry which makes many so unready to believe that there is any work of God but among themselves."

Accordingly, one evening a month he gave to telling his societies of those in other communions, and even in so-called heathen lands, who were carrying forward the cause of righteousness, all, as he said, to hasten the time when the Methodists would know what it means to say, "Whosoever doeth the will of my Father which is in heaven, the same is my brother, and sister, and mother."

The same catholicity of spirit held him back from imposing doctrinal tests on those who came seeking membership in the Methodist societies. "Is thy heart as my heart? Then give me thy hand!" That was always the essence of Wesley's test of those who sought to become members of his movement.

Whatever his modesty may have been on other matters,

here was one of which Wesley always boasted. As an old man, two years before his death, he came into Glasgow to preach to those hard-headed, theologically minded Scots who had always proved such a discouraging field for Methodist effort.

What was his text? "Now abideth faith, hope, love; these three."

What did he say? "I subjoined a short account of Methodism, particularly insisting on the circumstances. There is no other religious society under heaven which requires nothing of men, in order to their admission into it, but a desire to save their souls. Look all around you. You cannot be admitted into the church, or society, of the Presbyterians, Anabaptists, Quakers, or any others, unless you hold the same opinions with them, and adhere to the same mode of worship. The Methodists alone do not insist on your holding this or that opinion; but they think, and let think! Neither do they impose any particular mode of worship on your former manner, be it what it may. Now, I do not know any other religious society, either ancient or modern, wherein such liberty of conscience is now allowed, or has been allowed, since the age of the apostles. Here is our glorying; and a glorying peculiar to us. What society shares it with us?"

There have been times when Methodists, moved by phantom fears, have been ready to cast this glory away. They have set up the very requirement of conformity that Wesley expressly rejected. Gradually, however, they are coming back to his standards. Or perhaps we had better say that slowly, fearfully, they are catching up, on this issue of Christian fellowship, with this pioneer who died more than a century ago.

Of course John Wesley proved himself a pioneer in methods of church work. He started his movement in irregular ways, and he watched and encouraged its development in modes as unusual. For many of his innovations he claimed the authority of ancient church practice, finding parallels in the church of the first and second centuries for his love feasts, his class tickets, his watch nights, even his ordinations. But these were really a sort of defense set up after the innovations themselves had been introduced.

Wesley's principle was always to use whatever methods clearly promised the most success. He really cared little for traditions; he made his own traditions. For example, he prepared catechisms for three different age-groups in his societies. In that he was the forerunner of the psychologist and experts in pedagogy who have brought graded instruction into our church schools, and whom we are apt to consider a distinct product of our own advanced day. That was only one of the scores of changes in religious method that Wesley introduced. His was the restless and resistless energy of the pioneer.

§ 9. WESLEY AND SOCIAL ISSUES

One New Testament note that Wesley sounded again and again warned those who listened against the danger of riches. It is sobering to remember how much of the teaching of the great prophets, including Jesus, has been devoted to this subject. On it Wesley would permit no compromise.

The poet, Robert Southey, who wrote a life of Wesley, thought that he was hopelessly impractical on this matter. A good many Methodists, who were prospering in this world's goods, thought so too. At Manchester once a group of them went so far as to tell him that he did not know the value of money. He was not the only preacher who has heard talk of that sort from laymen. At the moment he said nothing, but later, in the pulpit, he returned to the subject.

"I have heard to-day," he remarked, "that I do not know the value of money. What! don't I know that twelve pence make a shilling, and twenty-one shillings a guinea? Don't I know that if given to God, it's worth heaven, through Christ?

And don't I know that if hoarded and kept, it's worth damnation to the man who hoards it?"

Wesley simply could not believe that a man could accumulate great wealth and have a healthy spiritual life. He made no bones about saying so. Even to Ebenezer Blackwell, the wealthiest supporter he ever had, and a man tried and true, he wrote, "What an amazing thing it will be if you endure to the end!"

In his own life the evangelist exemplified all that he taught about wealth. "Money never stays with me," he told his sister. "It would burn me if it did. I throw it out of my hands as soon as possible, lest it should find its way into my heart." When a student at Oxford he discovered that he could live on £28 a year, and formed the habit of giving away every cent in excess of that.

Because he was, in himself, the Methodist organization so long, large sums of money were continually passing through his hands, and a legend grew up as to this supposed wealth. Thus it happened that, when the kingdom was trying to raise money for its war with America, he was commanded by the tax collectors to "make due entry" of his silver plate, so that he might be properly assessed. His laconic answer is famous: "Sir, I have two silver teaspoons here in London and two at Bristol. This is all which I have at present; and I shall not buy any more while so many round me want bread." It will be noticed that he could not resist the temptation to slip in a bit of a sermon for the tax collector even in that brief note!

During his life Wesley gave away more than $200,000, and he was always so careful to have no more on hand than required by his needs that he said that if, at his death, he was found in possession of more than ten pounds, he would give men the privilege of calling him a robber.

Wesley was constantly calling his followers to a new kind of life in regard to the obtaining and use of money. He

"AS IF THE KING WERE GOING BY"

preached salvation all the time, and salvation from the power of gold was as important a kind to him as any other.

His later-day disciples, with an eye out for six per cent, have been wont to ring the changes on the fact that he counseled Methodists to gain all they can and save all they can. That was true. But for what purpose? Go right on with the same sentence in that sermon—a sermon that he preached again and again—and you find the answer. "Spend not one pound, one shilling, or one penny, to gratify either the desire of the flesh, the desire of the eyes, or the pride of life, or, indeed, for any other end than to please and gratify God. Give all you can, that is, all you have. I defy all the men upon earth, yea, all the angels in heaven, to find any other way of extracting the poison from riches."

Moreover, he was keenly aware of the moral implications that lie in the ways in which money is made in the first place. He was constantly warning his hearers against engaging in the sort of business where success is gained by cheating, or over-charging, or by obtaining usurious rates of interest. "We cannot," he said, "consistent with brotherly love, sell our goods below market price; we cannot study to ruin our neighbor's trade to advance our own; none can gain by swallowing up his neighbor's substance without gaining the damnation of hell."

§ 10. WESLEY THE ORGANIZER

One is tempted to continue to speak without limit of these aspects of Wesley's character and teaching. We must turn, however, to another ability that distinguished him from his con-temporaries. That was his ability as an organizer. Already the story has been told of the way in which what started as un-organized meetings in the fields or fugitive prayer meetings in out-of-the-way places became an intricate and highly organized movement, and later a church as closely tied together in all its parts as any body in Protestantism. It was all a result of the organizing genius of John Wesley. He could not leave things at loose ends.

In this matter, however, it is necessary for us to be just. If Wesley was a great organizer, it was frequently in much the spirit of the man who, as commanding general, can whip great armies into shape, but who cannot brook a moment's insubordi-nation. As he grew older, Wesley's spirit in matters of this sort became as mellow as it always was in matters of doctrine and theological opinion. But during the most active years of his life, his Methodist ministry was an army in which he held absolute power, and where he acted at times in as arbitrary a way as any Oriental despot. That is one of the main reasons why, of the almost seven hundred preachers whom he received into the Methodist ministry, more than half of them left the itinerancy early in life.

As an example of the sort of absolutism of which Wesley was capable, consider his treatment of Alexander McNabb, his preacher at Bath in 1780. McNabb's main fault seems to have been his belief that the formation of a separate Methodist church in England was inevitable, and that the preachers should have the right to perform all the usual duties of preachers, including the giving of the sacraments, to the people called Methodists. With Charles Wesley on the warpath against any such idea, John Wesley was not quite ready in 1780 to admit its possibility. McNabb would not give up his views; Wesley expelled him. The way in which he wrote about the expulsion shows how thoroughly absolute he could be on occasion:

"Whoever, therefore, violates these conditions, particularly that of being directed by me in the work, does *ipso facto* disjoin himself from me. This Brother McNabb has done (but he cannot see that he has done amiss) and he would have it a common cause, that is, he would have all the preachers do likewise. He thinks 'they have a right to do so.' So they have. They have a right to disjoin themselves from me whenever they please. But they cannot in the nature of the thing join with me any longer than they are directed by me. . . . For about six years after my return to England, there was no such thing [as a Methodist Conference]. I then desired some of my preachers to meet me, in order to advise, not control me. And you may observe, they had no power at all, but what I exercised through them. I chose to exercise the power which God had given me in this manner, both to avoid ostentation, and gently to habituate the people to obey them when I should be taken from their head. But as long as I remain with them, the fundamental rule of Methodism remains inviolate. So long as any preacher joins with me, he is to be directed by me in his work. Do you not see, then, that Brother McNabb, whatever his intentions might be, acted as wrong as wrong could be? and that the representing of this as the common cause of the preachers was the way to common destruction? the way to turn all their heads, and set them in arms? It was a blow at the very root of Methodism. I could not therefore do less than I did. It was the very least that could be done for fear the evil should spread."

This is not an attractive Wesley, but it is a Wesley who existed. His Annual Conferences were just what he said they were: a place to which the preachers came to be minutely examined as to all they had done for a year past; to be faced by a series of questions which the little field marshal in the chair believed were important at the moment; and to be required to give assent to a series of answers to those questions which the same field marshal had already formulated. Wesley's Conferences were a good deal of a ventriloquist's performance, with Wesley the ventriloquist.

§ 11. Wesley the Man

With it all we must ask, what kind of a man was he? So very small in his person; quick in his movements; never excited; never unemployed; so simple in his dress as to pass unnoticed in any company; such fire in his eye as to set him apart in any crowd. What sort of a man was he?

Well, he was no man for a bluffer to trifle with. He had no time for simpletons, and the greater their pretensions the greater his scorn. "A weak, washy, everlasting flood" of mere talk was the thing that he dreaded more than anything else, even while he reveled in talk that had some substance.

He seems to have had little sense of humor. His defenders have drawn two or three instances from his *Journal,* which covered half a century, in the attempt to prove that he had a kind of dry humor, but it is a hard case to establish. Once, when his stagecoach was held up, a fat lady was so frightened that she sat in Wesley's lap, completely screening him from the highwayman. He solemnly records this as an instance of divine interposition in his behalf—and it is hard to believe that the man who could do that had much of a sense of humor.

His belief in ghosts shows that he had a credulous streak, which also made him ready to accept the word of others as to spiritual experiences with too great readiness. His notion that God could, and does, work through the casting of lots and the turning up of verses from a Bible opened at random brought him a great deal of misery, for it tore him away from a woman he should have married and left him a prey for another who was to make his days a burden.

As amusing an example as his *Journal* gives us of the way in which this particular kind of credulity marked the career of John Wesley accompanied his decision to join Whitefield in Bristol in March, 1739. That, it will be remembered, was one of the great decisions of Wesley's life, for it took him to the place where he began field preaching, and without field preaching it is doubtful whether the Methodist movement would ever have amounted to much. When Whitefield's invitation came, Wesley began his old habit of opening the Bible at random. His first attempt turned up this verse in Deuteronomy: "Get thee up into this mountain, and die in the mount whither thou goest up, and be gathered unto thy people." Evidently that wasn't precisely the sort of encouragement wanted, so Wesley tried again. The Bible, as is a way with books closed and immediately opened, turned up another verse in Deuteronomy: "And the children of Israel wept for Moses in the plains of Moab thirty days." Again, not much encouragement. So he tried again, and this time he saw to it that the Book opened somewhere else than in Deuteronomy. It proved to be Acts, and at this comforting thought: "And devout men carried Stephen to his burial, and made great lamentation over him"! On the strength of these texts Wesley decided to go! But the Fetter Lane society objected. So *they* began drawing texts. They drew four, in the following order: The first was from Ezekiel, "Son of man, behold, I take from thee the desire of thine eyes with a stroke: yet shalt thou not mourn nor weep, neither shall thy tears run down." Then this from second Samuel: "Now there was long war between the house of Saul and the house of David: but David waxed stronger and stronger, and the house of Saul waxed weaker and weaker." The next try also came from second Samuel: "When wicked men have slain a righteous person in his own house upon his bed; shall I not now require his blood at your hands, and take you away from the earth?" And then, as a clincher, this from second Chronicles: "And Ahaz slept with his fathers, and they buried him in the city, even in Jerusalem." Now it might seem to a casual observer that this collection of texts, if it means anything, is suggestive that the course in view might not be attended with pleasant results. That evidently was the conclusion of the Fetter Lane society, and who can blame them for it? But John Wesley really, in his heart, wanted to go to Bristol. And this funereal collection of verses therefore seemed to him to mean only one thing: Go to Bristol. So he went to Bristol, and had the time of his life!

He had as little use for the lazy man as for the bore. When some of his preachers protested against being hauled out at four in the morning to preach at five, he wrote that he would not employ an apostle if he was not ready to adopt that schedule! He drove his preachers relentlessly, but when their health failed, as too frequently it did, under the rigors of their task, he was as solicitous as a mother regarding their rest and recovery.

As a young man he was much given to argument, and in the first years of his own triumphant spiritual experience he was apt to demand a precisely similar experience in others, and to reflect upon the quality of their religion if they could not testify to its possession. As he grew older, he grew more tolerant. He even came to wonder that the people had not stoned him and his brother for the narrownesses of their early days.

To a young Anglican preacher he wrote, "The longer I live, the larger allowances I make for human infirmities. I exact more from myself, and less from others. Go thou and do likewise!"

He seems to have been about as even-tempered a man as ever lived. He was always trying, after he attained his great age, to discover the reasons why one who had started life so handicapped physically should have lived so long and done so much. It is likely that the serenity of his poise had more to do with it than his getting up at four o'clock, even though he did not suspect it.

He would permit no one to travel with him who could not take the incidental discomforts of the journey as minor matters. He knew as much about bad weather, bad roads, bad beds, and bad food as any man who ever lived, but he summed it all up by saying, "By the grace of God I never fret; I repine at nothing, I am discontented with nothing."

For his own spiritual experience he had a profound reverence and a fitting reticence. He was always dealing with people who were making their spiritual experiences public; he was always preaching that such spiritual certainty could be attained in this life that a man could tell of his inner victories with absolute confidence in the reality of the phenomena of which he spoke. But he never spoke about it himself!

After the experience in the meeting in Aldersgate Street, and the stress of the few months immediately following, he ceased almost entirely to refer to his own soul experiences in his *Journal*. The nearest he ever came to such a testimony in his later years was when, almost shyly, he told his intimate Bradburn that if he wanted to know what his experience was like he would find it most nearly suggested in one of his brother's great hymns:

> "O Thou, who camest from above,
> The pure, celestial fire to impart,
> Kindle a flame of sacred love
> On the mean altar of my heart;
> There let it for thy glory burn,
> With inextinguishable blaze;
> And trembling to its source return
> In humble prayer and fervent praise."

When one of the young girls among his Methodists sought to find out from him what this Christian perfection was about which he preached and to which he called others, he replied, "Read and meditate upon the thirteenth chapter of the First Epistle to the Corinthians. That is the true picture of Christian perfection."

So it was that he came down to the end of life. "If we see God in all things, and do all for him, then all things are easy," he had once remarked. That seemed to be his motto, even more than that other motto he supplied for those who asked him for the rule by which he lived:

> "Do all the good you can,
> By all the means you can,
> In all the ways you can,
> In all the places you can,
> At all the times you can,
> To all the people you can,
> As long as ever you can."

Take the two quotations together, and you have a good measure of the spirit and the aims and the achievements of John Wesley.

CHAPTER XII

THE END OF THE LONG TRAIL

§ 1. CHARLES WESLEY'S PASSING

ONE Sunday morning near the end of March in 1788 John Wesley, now eighty-five years of age, was preaching in Shropshire. Led by his voice, the congregation was singing as only Methodist congregations could sing:

"Come, let us join our friends above,
That have obtained the prize,
And, on the eagle wings of love,
To joys celestial rise:
Let all the saints terrestrial sing,
With those to glory gone;
For all the servants of our King,
In earth and heaven, are one.

"One family we dwell in him,
One church, above, beneath,
Though now divided by the stream,
The narrow stream, of death:
One army of the living God,
To his command we bow;
Part of his host have crossed the flood,
And part are crossing now."

At the very moment the last lines were being sung, the author of the hymn "crossed the flood" from his home in London, more than a hundred miles away. And his brother, who had announced the hymn, walked the rest of life's road a lonely old man.

A fortnight later, preaching at Bolton, he attempted to

announce that greatest of all Charles Wesley's hymns, "Come,
O Thou Traveler Unknown," but when he came to the lines:

"My company before is gone,
And I am left alone with thee,"

it was more than even his disciplined nature could bear, and he
broke down and wept in the pulpit.

The two Wesley brothers did not always see eye to eye.
Charles was subject to fits of despondency or wild outbursts
that may have been a natural result of his poet's temperament.
His extremes of temper must have been annoying to his placid
elder brother. Certainly his extremes of churchmanship were.
Even in the midst of his grief, John Wesley made public a
statement ridiculing the idea of "consecrated ground" that had
moved his brother to refuse burial in the yard at City Road
Chapel and had placed his corpse in a burial ground of the
Established Church, with the service read by the parish parson.
But with all their minor differences, the two brothers were
closer together than two men often come to be. On the essentials of their ministry they saw as one. Each sought his complement in the other. When the younger died, the elder felt
as though a part of himself had gone.

§ 2. WESLEY THE AGED

For two years the flaming evangel was to go on. With
eyes so aged that they could not read the hymns in public serv-
ives, with body so feeble that companions supported him about
the streets and in the pulpit, with memory so overtaxed that
one stood always at hand to suggest the next point in the oft-
used sermons as they were preached, yet the old man continued
to storm up and down England, proclaiming the same message
that he had proclaimed for half a century.

His last birthday found him making his characteristic
entry in his *Journal:* "This day I enter into my eighty-eighth

year. For above eighty-six years I found none of the infirmities of old age; my eyes did not wax dim, neither was my natural strength abated; but, last August, I found almost a sudden change. My eyes were so dim that no glasses would help me. My strength likewise now quite forsook me; and probably will not return in this world. But I feel no pain from head to foot; only it seems nature is exhausted; and, humanly speaking, will sink more and more, till 'the weary springs of life stand still at last.' "

A month later he was putting that famous finish to his account books: "For upwards of eighty-six years [probably he meant to write sixty-eight] I have kept my accounts exactly. I will not attempt it any longer, being satisfied with the continual conviction, that I save all I can, and give all I can, that is, all I have."

On he went to his last Conference, held again at Bristol, where it was shown that there were now 240 Methodist societies, with 541 itinerant preachers, and 134,549 holding tickets as society members in good standing. For three weeks after the Conference he was preaching in Wales. For the rest of the year he was preaching in England.

Vast crowds found themselves able to hear him, feeble though he was. In October he preached for the last time in the open air, standing beneath an ash tree in a churchyard in Winchelsea, and using a text that had been a part of the first outdoor sermon of his Lord: "The kingdom of God is at hand; repent ye, and believe the gospel."

Throughout the winter he was preaching regularly in the churches and chapels of London and near by. January of 1791 came and passed. February came. On the seventeenth of the month he was at Lambeth, and, although forced to pause frequently to gather strength, preached on "The King's business requireth haste." He knew whereof he spoke, for the long trail was almost ended.

Six days later he was at Leatherhead, and stood for the last time in a pulpit. "Seek ye the Lord while he may be found, call ye upon him while he is near"—were ever words more fitting for the closing utterance of such a career? It was a text that, in a way, epitomized the spirit of every one of the 42,400 sermons he had preached since his return from Georgia, more than fifty years before.

He was not yet quite done. He could no longer preach, but he could write. He had one letter at the least that must be written. Three days after the last sermon it was in the post, going to William Wilberforce, to nerve the arm of that young hero as he faced the intrenched slave power of the British empire:

My dear Sir: Unless the Divine Power has raised you up to be as Athanasius, *contra mundum*, I see not how you can go through your glorious enterprise, in opposing that execrable villainy, which is the scandal of religion, of England, and of human nature. Unless God has raised you up for this very thing, you will be worn out by the opposition of men and devils; but, if God be for you, who can be against you? Are all of them together stronger than God? O! be not weary in well doing. Go on, in the name of God, and in the power of his might, till even American slavery, the vilest that ever saw the sun, shall vanish away before it.

Reading this morning a tract, wrote by a poor African, I was particularly struck by that circumstance—that a man who has a black skin, being wronged or outraged by a white man, can have no redress; it being a law, in our colonies, that the oath of a black, against a white, goes for nothing. What villainy is this!

That He who has guided you, from your youth up, may continue to strengthen you in this and all things, is the prayer of, dear sir,

Your affectionate servant,

JOHN WESLEY.

§ 3.   THE CLOSING SCENE

And now but one scene more. It is the following Sunday, in the little room in City Road where the old man of eighty-eight is awaiting his end. He is feeling enough stronger to sit in a chair, and leads those who are about, eager for a chance to serve him, in a verse from another of his brother's hymns:

> "Till glad I lay this body down,
> Thy servant, Lord, attend!
> And, oh! my life of mercy crown
> With a triumphant end!"

That end is at hand. On Monday he dozes through the day. On Tuesday he astonishes the watchers by awakening singing:

> "All glory to God in the sky,
> And peace upon earth be restored!
> O Jesus, exalted on high,
> Appear our omnipotent Lord."

He wishes to write, but cannot, so a bystander offers to act as amanuensis. "Tell me what you wish to say," Miss Ritchie suggests. "Nothing," he answers, "but that God is with us." And a few minutes later he is really sitting up again, and singing:

> "I'll praise my Maker while I've breath;
> And, when my voice is lost in death,
> Praise shall employ my nobler powers."

He follows this with the benediction, tries to sing the doxology, and, when his voice fails, gasps: "Now we have done. Let us all go."

Sleep comes in brief snatches. In the waking intervals he recognizes and bids farewell to the friends that stand by the bed. Frequently he repeats his injunction: "Pray, and praise!" Twice he rouses to repeat, "The best of all is, God is with us!" Tuesday passes into Wednesday.

It is just before ten o'clock in the morning, March 2, 1791. A dozen intimates stand watching the old man go to his crowning. "I'll praise. I'll praise," he keeps muttering, but more

will not come. Joseph Bradford, for long now Wesley's traveling companion, begins to recite: "Lift up your heads, O ye
gates; and be ye lift up, ye everlasting doors; and this
heir of glory shall
come in." And as the
w a t c h e r s bow in
prayer, w i t h o u t a
s i g h , the s p i r i t
passes.

One week later, at
five o'clock in the morn-
ing, lest too great a
crowd assemble, the
father of Methodism
was laid to rest in the
yard of his own City
Road Chapel.   Just
across the street, in
Bunhill Fields, lay
John B u n y a n and
Isaac Watts and Su-
sannah Wesley. Others
w h o h a d wrought
largely for the same
purposes to which he
had dedicated his life
were to be brought, in
later years, to lie beside
him.   But if all the
other shrines should be

"IN THE YARD OF CITY ROAD CHAPEL"

destroyed, if the chapel should disappear, if the surging
life of the city swallowed up every mark, so long as this
single grave remained, the spot would be a goal of world
pilgrimage.

§ 4. What Did Wesley Accomplish?

Dozens of volumes have been written to tell of the contributions that early Methodism, under the command of John Wesley, made to England and the English-speaking world. It would be impossible to review all this material in such a book as this. We can do no more than mention briefly some of the essential differences between the England that John Wesley found and the England that he left.

For one thing, he found a land far gone in moral decay. Of its besottedness we have tried to give some hint. He did not do away utterly with the moral evils, but he introduced a social salvation which has continued to work through all the years.

Frances Willard used to tell of a young nobleman who found himself in an out-of-the-way village in Cornwall, and desperately thirsty. His search for a "pub" proving vain, he hailed a passing rustic.

"How is it that I can't get a glass of liquor anywhere in this wretched village of yours?"

Cap in hand, but with quiet assurance, the old man answered, "My lord, something over a hundred years ago a man named John Wesley came to these parts."

It is doubtful if ever more terrible things have been said about the liquor traffic than John Wesley said. And what courage he showed in attacking that deeply intrenched wrong, he showed in confronting every social iniquity by which some were lining their pockets without thought of the damnation of their brethren.

If you will read Wesley's sermons, you will find that it was the evils of his own time against which he preached. He was not content to talk about "sin" in any large, generic way. He made it immediate, actual, the very evils that the men and women to whom he spoke were committing. And because he made sin so terribly personal, he set on foot in England a moral revolution.

Again, early Methodism gave impetus to the modern movement for popular education. Wesley's first act at Oxford, when he began his spiritual pilgrimage, was to start schools for the children of the poor. His career was dotted with school experiments—most of them failures, for he had queer notions of school discipline that made his schools places of torture for most of the pupils—and he was constantly inspiring others to set educational experiments under way. The quickness with which American Methodists went into the business of conducting schools was an indication of the interest of that early Methodism in the subject.

Even more eventful was the work of Robert Raikes, and the start of the Sunday-school movement. Raikes was not a member of a Methodist society. He was one of the nonconformists who came under the inspiration of the Methodist movement, and his Sunday schools were the result. Those first Sunday schools were not, it must be remembered, planned as places for the teaching of the Bible. They were places in which waifs were gathered from the streets to be given the rudiments of the "three r's." Methodism adopted the idea almost as soon as Raikes proposed it. The discovery of the value of the child that grew out of it remains one of the permanent gifts of the evangelical revival.

Another contribution that Wesley gave to England and the English-speaking world was the sense of the responsibility of religion for all unrighteous conditions. If you are interested, you can read thick books telling of all the plans he worked out at London, Bristol, and elsewhere, for giving employment to men and women out of work, for loaning small amounts of capital to those who wished to start in business for themselves, for providing shelter for the friendless and medical attention for those in need, for enlisting support for John Howard as he struggled to reform the awful prison system of the day, or for William Wilberforce as he began that long fight with the African slave trade.

It may be that he never plumbed the depths of the social and economic issues out of which come such injustices and distresses. Neither economics nor sociology, as such, had been heard of in John Wesley's day. But he saw the evils, and he made Methodism the kind of a religious movement which expressed its sanctification by its devotion to the removal of those evils.

If you sit down to-day and try to analyze that early Methodism you quickly come to the conclusion that it had no intellectual differences from the religious order which had preceded it. Bold as Wesley may have been in some of his thinking, he certainly left no new methods of biblical interpretation, no new creed, no new doctrines. He may not have emphasized some of the doctrines that his old church—the church from which he never formally separated—did emphasize; he may have insisted on other doctrines which that church had almost forgotten it possessed. But in teaching, and even in method, there was little about the Wesley Revival to have made it such a gigantic fact in the history of the church.

What was it, then, that Wesley and his comrades did that has made Methodism such a landmark?

Three things. They made men face the ethical implications of religion. The sort of parson whom you can see depicted in the literature of the hundred years before Wesley became a monstrosity in the face of the Methodist witness. The sort of church member whom you can find revealed in the diaries of the social leaders of that period also became a creature despised. Doubtless there have been, since then, plenty of parsons and plenty of church members who have been contented to observe a few outward forms, and have thought the demands of religion satisfied thereby. But they have not carried the church with them. They have been the exception; not the rule.

Once and for all, the English-speaking world has come to understand that it is the pure in heart who may see God, and that he who would stand in the holy place must come with clean hands. And the universally acknowledged right of religion to demand ethical living from its followers is the first of the great and abiding gifts made by Wesley's crusade to the worship of all the communions.

Again, John Wesley made religion personal. What had been to multitudes merely a formal thing, a creed remote from life, or a convention without a trace of power, became, through the conviction of Wesley's preaching, a real energy in life. Religion was made a personal experience. And in that emphasis on experience was perhaps John Wesley's supreme service to the cause of Christianity and to the world.

The other permanent accomplishment of Wesley was to make clear the social responsibilities of religion. If, in the way we have just mentioned, he left men "going on to perfection," Wesley also left them understanding that they could not pretend to be living the life of God while they saw their fellows hungry, thirsty, lonely, naked, bound, and did nothing to help.

One of the last sermons he wrote attempted to answer the question, "Why has Christianity done so little good in the world?" and was wholly given to the preaching of this sense of responsibility toward others in the use of every talent entrusted to a Christian. Just as the old man could not die content until he had said one last word against human slavery, so he could not lay down his ministry without reminding his followers that they could not win holiness while they spent upon themselves time and money that might have brought help to the needy.

The church in the English-speaking world is not yet what it must one day become. It is not yet wholly devoted to the service of God; wholly lost in the service of men. But if it is not what it once bade fair to become, a body in which casual parsons droned through set ceremonials in the presence of even more casual listeners, the difference, so far as our human eyes can see, is to a large extent due to the fact that, not two hundred years ago, a little man started to preach in the highways of England, who did not cease from speaking until his voice had carried into every nook and corner of that land, and he came at last to the end of his pilgrimage and entered into rest beside the roaring roads of London.

CHAPTER XIII

METHODISM IN THE NEW REPUBLIC

§ 1. George Washington's America

ON THE last day of April, 1789, George Washington was inaugurated as the first President of the United States of America. Less than a month later he was visited by four grave gentlemen, who read him an exceedingly grave address, to which he replied in a manner equally grave. The address and the response appeared in the newspapers within a few days, and something of a furore seems to have been caused by their printing. For the four grave visitors had been the two bishops and two prominent ministers of the Methodist Episcopal Church, and by their act they gave the first churchly recognition and blessing to the officers of the young republic.

As it happened, one of the two bishops was a subject of King George III, and was about to return to that monarch's dominions. There were plenty of American patriots who, in

"FOUR GRAVE GENTLEMEN WHO READ A GRAVE ADDRESS"

view of the late unpleasantness, felt that their President had no business in letting a Britisher address him about anything, even to promise him a share in his prayers. But there is no evidence that the President was disturbed by this teapot tempest. He was so much the father of his country that he knew there was no ecclesiastical organization from which recognition would be more valuable than this church of the circuit-riders. He seems to have been as pleased to receive the address of the Methodists as the Methodists were to give it. With the exchange of greetings, the last charge of disloyalty on the part of the church disappeared.

WASHINGTON'S COUNTRY—
ASBURY'S CONFERENCES

What sort of a country was it over which Washington was taking the reins of government? It was a country alive with premonitions of a tremendous future, yet hesitant in the face of many immediate difficulties. Politically, it was an association of thirteen States, all asserting their separate sovereignty, all jealous of each other, and all suspicious of the political instrument—the Constitution—under which they had been brought together. By the most desperate sort of argument, pleading, and maneuvering enough of the States had been induced to ratify the new Constitution to bring it into effect, but there was still throughout the country an amazing amount of popular skepticism and even resentment.

It was felt that the newfangled government was largely

the creation of a clique of aristocrats like Washington, Hamilton and John Adams, imposed on the true democrats by reason of their inability to cope with the personal prestige and the intellectual finesse of the Federalists.   Men like Jefferson and Sam Adams viewed the new plan of government with suspicion; men like Patrick Henry did not hesitate to call it an abject surrender of the liberties the Revolutionary War had been fought to secure.   There were two attempts at revolt against the government during Washington's administrations, and there would have been more had any lesser man been in the presidency.

If the United States had had nothing to do but consider its political condition it is altogether likely that the form of government adopted by the young republic would have been smashed in a handful of years.   What saved it?   The trails across the Appalachians!   The men who had been most deeply moved by the call to freedom, the men who had echoed Henry's "Give me liberty or give me death!" in every colony along the seaboard, would never have submitted quietly to the fastening of federal authority on States and local communities.   Nor did they.   For they were the men who first heard the call of the wilderness trail, who flung their belongings in an ox-cart, shouldered their rifles, and set off in the train of Daniel Boone and the other pioneers of the early frontier.   The winning of the West, which Theodore Roosevelt was later to recount, was the work of the veterans of the Revolution.

In the new communities of Kentucky and Tennessee, and later Ohio and Indiana, the men of the frontier were not much bothered by questions of authority.   Into Kentucky, to be sure, the Virginians who had crossed the Blue Ridge carried their ideas of local sovereignty; ideas written into the famous Kentucky Resolutions which were to play so large a part in the national debates of a later generation.   The same spirit was to be found in Tennessee.   But there was an academic air about the whole business which tempered the spirit with which men discussed it.

As a matter of fact, there was precious little authority of any kind in those pioneer communities. Elbow-room was a drug on the market. Men ran wild, as we say, because their neighbors placed so little check on them. The time came quickly when the migrants who were trying to form permanent settlements were glad enough to welcome agents of law and order no matter who had commissioned them. And while these frontiersmen were expending their energies in wrestling with the wilderness, the republic of which they had been so suspicious was slowly gaining in power back along the seacoast.

§ 2. FRANCIS ASBURY'S METHODISM

But suppose George Washington had been asking himself, as he stood listening to that address in that dignified New York drawing room that May afternoon, "What sort of a church is this which is thus congratulating me on my inauguration?" What, of necessity, would the answer have been?

It is remarkable to how large an extent the answer would have paralleled the description of the republic. For the Methodist Episcopal Church in 1789 was a church alive with premonitions of a tremendous future, yet hesitant in the face of many immediate difficulties. It had just gone through a period of fierce testing. It had just achieved its independence. It had just adopted its basis of government. Apparently, it was just ready to swing into the full stride of a glorious career. But there were struggles already beginning within the ranks.

If George Washington had his Patrick Henry in Virginia, searching his vocabulary for words to denounce the arbitrary and despotic government set up by the President of the United States, Francis Asbury had his James O'Kelly in the same State doing the same thing regarding the bishop of the Methodist Episcopal Church. Many a man who had proved his readiness to undergo tremendous hardships for the sake of the gospel during the previous ten years was chafing at the firm form of church government which seemed so out of place in a republic.

If the young church had had nothing to do but consider its ecclesiastical condition, it is altogether likely that the form of government adopted in the famous Christmas Conference at

"THE TRAILS ACROSS THE APPALACHIANS!"

Baltimore would have been smashed in a handful of years. What saved it? The trails across the Appalachians! For the men of the Methodist itinerancy had no time to sit down and fuss about the details of church order after the roads opened to the new settlements beyond the mountains. "The Revolutionary War being now closed," writes Jesse Lee, the one historian produced by the church in that period, "the Revolutionary War being now closed, and a general peace established, we could go into all parts of the country without fear; and we soon began to enlarge our borders, and to preach in many places where we had not been before." There were Methodist preachers in almost every wagon-train of pioneers who took the trail to the wilderness.

In the new communities of Kentucky and Tennessee, and later Ohio and Indiana, the Methodist circuit-rider was more familiar than the doctor; ten times more familiar than the judge; a hundred times more familiar than the governor. Astride a horse which could be depended on to plod ahead, day after day, for months on end, even if it seldom cantered; wrapped in a cloak which might be—and generally was— patched and repatched until the confines of the original garment were not to be distinguished; with all his worldly goods that were not on his back in his saddlebags—the Methodist itinerant rode every trail, reached every cabin, and lifted new standards in every community of that magically expanding frontier.

"Neither snow nor rain nor heat nor gloom of night stays these couriers from the swift completion of their appointed rounds," said Herodotus of the messengers of the great Persian king. That boast has now been applied to the agents of the mail service of the United States government; it might have been with equal truth applied to those itinerant preachers of early Methodism.

§ 3.   The Circuit-Riders

So it was that the early Methodist preachers rode to their task. They had no "important" churches to look forward to as rewards for faithful service. In all Methodism there were not more than ten city churches with what might be called a settled pastorate at the time Asbury and Coke presented their address to Washington. Men were appointed to circuits, and some of those circuits were larger than States. They preached wherever opportunity offered—in taverns, in private houses which were frequently nothing more than single-room log cabins, in town halls, in county poorhouses, in courtrooms, in taprooms, in schools, on street corners, in barnyards, in clearings in the woods.

Any family which would receive them was accounted a congregation; any that turned the itinerants away was marked for future attention. While there are records of some large congregations, the work of the preachers was mainly with small groups. They came quickly to grips with the spiritual problems of an individual or of a household. It was, in one way, a day of small beginnings, but so many small beginnings that they mounted rapidly to a great ingathering.

So rapidly, in fact, did the Methodist Church grow in America that even Wesley and the other leaders in England, who had experienced the revival in that country, were amazed. When Asbury landed in Philadelphia in 1771 there were only a half dozen Methodist preachers on the entire continent, and six hundred members of societies in all the colonies. At the time of the organization of the Methodist Episcopal Church in 1784 the number of preachers had grown to eighty-three, and there were almost 15,000 recognized members. Then, in the five years before the inauguration of Washington, the number of preachers more than doubled, and the church membership rose to almost 40,000! By the time of Asbury's death, as we shall see, there were more than 200,000 Methodists named on church rolls which, in those days, were frequently cut down, and the ordained ministry had passed the 700 mark! The church in America quickly passed that in England in size.

When a Methodist minister receives an appointment to a new charge in these days it is a matter of much counsel and labor to transfer him to his task. There are generally hundreds of books to be packed; perhaps heavy files of a Christian Advocate or of the Methodist Review to be brought down out of the attic and boxed once more. There is some furniture to be crated—a piano, a sewing machine, a washing machine. In some parts of the country the preacher will have a complete household outfit to be looked after. The old parsonage must be carefully cleaned. There will be judicious inquiries as to the sort of place the new parsonage is, and expressions of delight or sorrow as the report is favorable or otherwise. In brief snatches, caught between wrapping plates and tying up bedding, the harried minister may try to outline an "opening sermon" for use on his first Sunday in his new pulpit.

Finally the day of departure comes. The motor van backs to the curb, or the local drayman comes to transport the preacher's goods to the freight depot. The committee from the Ladies' Aid Society is on hand to bid the retiring minister and his family farewell, and to estimate the extent of the repairs which will be necessary to put the parsonage in shape for further habitation. The minister, his wife, and their children depart; a few years ago by train, now more frequently by that motor-car which proves such a help in the making of pastoral calls.

Arriving in the new station, there is the scurry of settling. Even to-day a Methodist preacher's belongings seem to have a magical faculty of fitting into parsonages of every kind and condition and wallpaper. The leaders, male and female, of the new congregation are met, always with a momentary initial hesitation which soon passes into warm good fellowship.

Then comes the first Sunday in the new church. The preacher takes his place in the dedicated pulpit. The preacher's wife gathers her brood into the pew almost equally dedicated to the seating of the parsonage family. The sermon strikes fire. There is a warm tone to all the greetings and remarks at the close of the service. And the parsonage family goes off to dinner with the president of the board of trustees, knowing that another pastorate is officially and auspiciously under way.

It was different in the days of Asbury. After the appointments had been read by that "venerable man"—the records persist in describing Asbury as venerable from a time when he was less than forty years of age—the preachers clung together in a few last moments of prayer and praise, then rose from their knees and started out. Most of them were young men, unmarried, hardy, unshackled. Their appointments had been to places which it would be hard to find on any map.

There were no parsonages ahead of them, generally no churches, frequently no towns. There might not even be an organized Methodist society.

There was never any promised, or even expected, salary. In fact, these men refused to allow the word "salary" to be printed in their reports. They talked of "allowances," which gradually, during the years of Asbury's life, worked up to about a hundred dollars a year, and which were never paid in full.

It took the average itinerant about five minutes to pack, and in ten

"IN TEN MINUTES HE WAS ON HIS WAY"

minutes he was on his way to his new appointment. Just where he was going he might not be sure, but there were rumors that one family in the general region of his objective had at one time been members of a Methodist society back in the coast settlements. Sure enough, when the cabin of this family was reached, there were expressions of rejoicing, and the first night was spent in a rousing prayer service, with the reconsecration of the family altar.

On the morrow the preacher starts out, working his way from cabin to cabin, coming to know every family, and almost every individual, in the neighborhood by name, preaching wherever he can gather five or ten hearers, praying in every house which will permit him. In a month he has made his first circuit, which may easily have covered more than fifty miles, established his contacts, and, when he returns to the house from which he started, he has a year's hard work before him. There will be regular classes, with regularly enrolled Methodists, to report from here when next he visits Conference.

§ 4. FREEBORN GARRETTSON

Of what sort were the men who carried on this Methodist evangel in the young republic? We might spend pages in trying to describe them, but that would probably not be as good a way of getting to know them as to look closely at one or two of them.

We have already had one glimpse of Freeborn Garrettson, riding "like an arrow" to summon the preachers to the Christmas Conference of 1784, at which the Methodist Episcopal Church was formed. There was a man worth knowing! The son of a man of property, Garrettson grew up in Maryland, living the trifling life of most other young men of his day, until he fell under the influence of the Methodists.

First Strawbridge, and later Asbury and Shadford, stirred him with their preaching, until he was thoroughly miserable with a sense of his spiritual needs. During a long period of inner struggle he kept trying to put off the day of self-surrender, pleading within himself for a year, for six months, for a week of delay. But at last he could stand it no longer. He went through what was then considered a typical Methodist conversion and on into the Methodist itinerancy.

Garrettson joined the Methodist Conference in the year that the Battle of Lexington was fought. When all the British preachers took ship for England, he was one of the little group of Americans who rallied around Asbury. Throughout the eight years of warfare he kept resolutely at his task. When Asbury was forced to go into hiding in Delaware, Garrettson kept itinerating in the South. The same suspicion which fell on other Methodists fell on him. As a possible British sympathizer he was mobbed, jailed, beaten, and even underwent attempts on his life with poison and firearms.

John Wesley heard of him, and encouraged the young preacher to write of his experiences. "My lot has mostly been cast in new places, to form circuits," he wrote Wesley, "which much exposed me to persecution. Once I was imprisoned; twice beaten; left on the highway speechless and senseless (I must have gone into a world of spirits, had not God in mercy sent a good Samaritan, that bled and took me to a friend's house); once shot at; guns and pistols presented at my breast; once delivered from an armed mob, in the dead time of night, on the highway, by a surprising flash of lightning; surrounded frequently by mobs; stoned frequently; I have had to escape for my life at dead time of night." Such was his record after only nine years in the ministry; he was to serve a total of fifty.

Garrettson's early ministry covered Maryland, Virginia, both Carolinas, and extended into Pennsylvania, Delaware, and New Jersey. Later he became a famous evangelist in Nova Scotia, and was nominated by Wesley for the office of superintendent of the work in what was left of British North America after the Revolution. For some reason, the Methodist Conference refused to elect him to that office, and Asbury sent him back to itinerating in Maryland. After a while he worked his way north again, and finally undertook the task of planting Methodism in the territory north of New York City.

It is hard for the Methodists of to-day to understand that the Methodist Episcopal Church formed in 1784 had more than four fifths of its membership south of where was later to run the Mason and Dixon line. At the time the Methodist bishops made their historic call on President Washington in New York, the church for which they spoke had almost no members north of Westchester! Garrettson was given the job of invading this country. He was given twelve young preachers, and told to start.

"I gave myself to earnest prayer for direction," he writes. "I knew that the Lord was with me. In the night season, in a dream, it seemed as if the whole country up the North river, as far as Lake Champlain, east and west, was open to my view. After the Conference adjourned, I requested the young men to meet me. Light seemed so reflected on my path that I gave them directions where to begin, and which way to form their circuits."

It was "the whole country" which those Methodists were after, and twelve young men, under a flaming evangelist like Garrettson, proved enough to open it all the way from New York to the Canadian border, and westward to Niagara. In two years the territory which now makes up three great Conferences—the New York, the New York East, and the Troy—had been thoroughly aroused, a large accession of members had begun, and Garrettson was ready to have the churches founded in the older settlements set aside in another district, while he and his pioneers pressed on.

There is one other incident in the life of Garrettson which should be mentioned; not that it suggests the extent of the work he did, but that it shows the sort of man he was.

Not long after his entrance into the ministry his father died, and the young preacher inherited his estate. A good part of that inheritance, as was not unusual in Maryland, proved to be slaves. Garrettson had never so much as heard the question of the moral implications of slavery raised, and accepted the heritage without misgiving. But soon he began to feel his preaching grow feeble. He had no inkling as to what the matter could be, but he knew something was wrong, and he began to agonize over it. At last, he called his whole family together for a session of common prayer. As he stood before them, about to announce a hymn, he seemed to hear an inner voice saying, "It is not right for you to keep your fellow creatures in bondage; you must let the oppressed go free." Without a moment's hesitation he told the slaves that they were free men, and then, in his own words, "I was now at liberty to proceed in worship. After singing, I kneeled to pray. Had I the tongue of an angel, I could not fully describe what I felt: all my dejection, and that melancholy gloom which preyed upon me, vanished in a moment, and a divine sweetness ran through my whole frame."

§ 5. JESSE LEE

Jesse Lee was another of the giants of those days. He, too, was converted just before the outbreak of the Revolution, and became one of the little band of native-born preachers who carried on through that struggle.

While preaching in North Carolina in 1780 he was drafted for the army. His conscientious scruples made him refuse to bear arms, and he was accordingly thrown into the guardhouse. There he began to deal with the soul of his guard; soon his exhorting brought a crowd of soldiers. Soon he was out and, while nominally still under arrest, standing on a bench near his colonel's tent, preaching. A revival broke out among the troops. The colonel begged him to reconsider his decision not to bear arms, for he did not want to appear as an oppressor of such a man. Lee replied that he could not bring himself to fight, but that he would drive the regiment's baggage-wagon. And in this way he served for four months, when his discharge came.

Asbury was naturally attracted to a man of this caliber, but Lee seems to have feared to undertake the full vows of a regular itinerant. He felt his own shortcomings so keenly that he could not see how the ministry would gain by his entrance into it. Asbury, at the Conference of 1782, swept these misgivings aside. Between sessions, seeing Lee standing with a number of the preachers in the yard, Asbury cried, "I am going to enlist Brother Lee!" Falling quickly into army metaphor, one of them replied, "What bounty do you give?" "Grace here and glory hereafter will be given him if he is faithful," answered the leader. And on those terms Lee found himself in the itinerancy.

Lee's record can be placed alongside that of Garrettson. He was, if anything, even more of an evangelist than Garrettson. He was always on the go, always pressing ahead. He frequently rode one horse, and led another, so that, by shifting back and forth, he might not be delayed by tired horses.

His best-known work was, probably, that done in New England, where he took the four Methodists in Boston who remained as the sole survivors of the early preaching of Boardman and developed them into a church well established in all the New England States. It was hard going; in many a town, as his *Journal* relates, there were no beds for the Methodist preacher; no tables at which he might eat. The strict Calvinists of Massachusetts regarded the gospel of the Methodists with suspicion. Added to that, the natural reticence of the New Englander made them hold back from this church which was characterized everywhere by its loud "Amens!" its "Hallelujahs!" and its exultant hymns.

Lee covered the Eastern States, as he himself said, from Georgia to the border of Maine as no itinerant, except Asbury, covered them.

Once, at the General Conference of 1800, he was defeated for the bishopric by only four votes. He was the first in a long line of men who have come within sight of that office, only to have it denied them. One of the early historians charges that Lee was defeated by the circulation of private rumors which were wholly without foundation, as Asbury proved, but not, alas! until after the election. If so, he was not the last to be defeated in a Methodist election in that fashion.

But he accepted his defeat in a manner different from that of some others. "I believe we never had so good a General

Conference before," he said of the session in which he had been defeated. "We had the greatest speaking, and the greatest union of affections, that we ever had on a like occasion."

Lee served for a time as chaplain of the House of Representatives of the United States. He was thus probably the first Methodist preacher to come into close official contact with the government. Characteristically, his brethren felt that he was becoming thus entangled with the world, and made their disapproval so manifest that he finally resigned the position.

But Lee always found it easy to get along with folks. He never hesitated to speak his mind; he never let up in his efforts to bring all whom he touched into serious religious conversation; yet there was something human about the man which made him a welcome entry into almost every company. The tales of his repartee are legion. One of the oldest, yet one that may still serve to dispel the notion that the original Methodist preachers were long-faced, lugubrious fellows, tells of the time when, riding between Boston and Lynn, he fell in with two young lawyers, who promptly ranged themselves on each side of the itinerant and prepared for sport.

"I believe you are a preacher, sir?" asked the one who rode on his right.

"Yes; I generally pass for one."

"You preach very often, I suppose?"

"Generally every day; frequently twice, or more."

"How do you find time to study when you preach so often?" the young lawyer on Lee's left asked.

"I study when riding, and read when resting."

"But do you not write your sermons?"

"No; not very often."

"Do you not often make mistakes in preaching extemporaneously?"

"I do, sometimes."

"How do you do them? Do you correct them?"

"That depends upon the character of the mistake," Lee replied. "I was preaching the other day, and I went to quote the text, 'All liars shall have their part in the lake which burneth with fire and brimstone;' and, by mistake, I said, 'All *lawyers* shall have their part—' "

That so venerable a joke as this should not have been known seems strange, but evidently it was not. The young lawyer on Lee's left rushed into the trap. "What did you do then?" he interrupted. "Did you correct it?"

"No, indeed," said Lee calmly. "It was so nearly true, I didn't think it worth while to correct it."

"Humph!" snorted the young fellow on the right, "I don't know whether you are the more knave or fool."

JESSE LEE

"Neither," the preacher quietly replied, looking from one to the other, "I believe I am just *between* the two!"

§ 6. HEROES ALL

The temptation is great to continue with the stories of scores of the men who carried the warm vigor of the Methodist gospel into every cranny of the young republic. Robert Southey, in England, and later James M. Buckley in this country, gave pages to the tale of Benjamin Abbott, and with reason. John Dickins is worth a long section. So is Caleb Pedicord. So is Thomas Ware. There was hardly a man in that first Conference of 1784 who should not, by rights, be treated here at length. But there are limits to the size of such a book as this, and these limits must shut them out. Look at Garrettson and Lee—and, in our next chapter, look at Asbury—and you see these other men as well. Not quite as gifted perhaps; not quite as useful; but men of the same spirit, poured into the same molds, fired with the same ambition, crowned with the same glory.

There is one thing about that early itinerancy which should not be overlooked. It was as merciless a calling as ever challenged brave men. We have spoken of mobs, of jails, of long rides through the rain, of nights in the open, of days in the malaria-soaked swamps of the new frontier. "How did they ever stand it?" someone asks. The answer is that they didn't stand it. They died under it.

They died, most of them, before their careers were much more than begun. Had there been insurance companies in those days, no Methodist itinerant could have secured protection, except by paying the high premiums of an extra hazardous risk. Of the 650 preachers who had joined the Methodist itinerancy by the opening of the nineteenth century, about 500 had to "locate," as the term was used for those too worn out to travel farther, before they died. Many of the rest had to take periods for recuperation before they could go on with their work. Others, however, located not because of health, but by reason of lack of support and desire to marry and establish a home.

Of the first 737 members of Conferences to die—that is, all who died up to 1847—203 were between 25 and 35 years of age and 121 between 35 and 45. Nearly half died before they were thirty years old! Of 672 of those first preachers whose records we have in full, two thirds died before they had been able to render twelve years of service! Just one less than 200 died within the first five years! True, there were a few who seemed to be hardened to live to a vigorous old age by the

sort of life demanded of the early Methodist preachers. But
the majority burned themselves out for God in a few years.
When we read of the way in which these men threw their lives
away, we wonder whether that may have had something to
do with the marvelous results they achieved.

When he had been fifty years in such a ministry as this,
Freeborn Garrettson was called on to preach a special sermon
before the New York Conference. In the course of that sermon he had occasion to try to picture the sort of a task which
had been his. "I traversed the mountains and valleys, frequently on foot, with my knapsack on my back, guided by
Indian paths in the wilderness, when it was not expedient to
take a horse," he said. "I had often to wade through morasses,
half-leg deep in mud and water; frequently satisfying my
hunger with a piece of bread and pork from my knapsack,
quenching my thirst from a brook, and resting my weary limbs
on the leaves of the trees. Thanks be to God! he compensated
me for all my toil; for many precious souls were awakened and
converted to God."

Souls! That was the one fixed thought of the early
Methodist preacher. His interests might be as varied as the
communities which he entered, but, with it all, he had at bottom
only one overpowering interest. That was the passion for
souls. Well might he have exclaimed, in the words which
F. W. H. Myers put into the mouth of that other great
itinerant, Saint Paul:

"Oft when the Word is on me to deliver,
   Lifts the illusion, and the truth lies bare:
Desert or throng, the city or the river,
   Melts in a lucid Paradise of air—

"Only like souls I see the folk thereunder,
   Bound who should conquer, slaves who should be kings,
Hearing their one hope with an empty wonder,
   Sadly contented in a show of things;

"Then with a rush the intolerable craving
    Shivers throughout me like a trumpet call—
Oh, to save these! to perish for their saving,
    Die for their life, be offered for them all!

"Give me a voice, a cry, and a complaining,
    Oh, let my sound be stormy in their ears!
Throat that would shout but cannot stay for straining,
    Eyes that would weep but cannot wait for tears.

"Quick in a moment, infinite forever,
    Send an arousal better than I pray,
Give me a grace upon the faint endeavor,
    Souls for my hire and Pentecost to-day!"[1]

----

[1] From "Saint Paul."   Reprinted by permission of The Macmillan Company.

CHAPTER XIV

METHODISM'S MAN ON HORSEBACK

§ 1. RIDERS

ACROSS the closing years of the eighteenth and the opening years of the nineteenth century there lies the shadow of a single man. Born on the obscure island of Corsica; a stranger in France, without influence, without wealth, without position; called to assume control in an hour of national chaos—this man rode to power until the greater part of western Europe acknowledged his rule and all the world trembled at his name. It is still easy to trace in the affairs of the nations the influence of this single man, Napoleon Bonaparte—Europe's man on horseback. God protect us from such another!

Across the closing years of the eighteenth and the opening years of the nineteenth century of American history there lies the shadow of another man. Born in an obscure village in mid-England; a stranger on another shore, without influence, without wealth, without position; called to assume control in an hour of chaos—this man rode to the service of his fellows until thousands had come to new life at his word and all the nation held his name in honor. It is still easy to trace in the affairs of the United States the influence of this single man, Francis Asbury—Methodism's man on horseback. God send us such another!

There are pictures and statues of Napoleon without number. The memorials of Asbury are few. There are only three portraits which can be surely accepted as authentic. There is just one statue. But that statue tells, in a glance, the story of

232

the man, and what it is which sets him apart from Napoleon and all the other men on horseback whom history has known.

The statue stands in Washington, on a little triangle of ground where three streets cross. It shows a rider in bronze

"A RIDER IN BRONZE"

—but a rider far different from the others to be found so numerously in that city. For this is a weary rider, astride a weary horse. The fatigue of hard trails lies heavily on man and beast. Even the high collar of the riding cape has failed to keep out the chill and the rain and the snow. The legs of the horse are heavy with mud. The boots of the rider are alike

bespattered. There is a feeling of intense exhaustion, even in
the cold bronze. But, from under the wide brim of the low
hat, two burning eyes look out. Those eyes see little of the
wilderness trail, with all its hardships. They see a new nation
at birth. They see that nation devoted to the service of God.
And it is not so much because of the incredible toils which he
endured as because of the boundless visions which he followed
that Francis Asbury rides to-day in the nation's capital.

Already we have had several brief glimpses of Asbury.
We have seen him on shipboard, coming to the colonies, asking himself, "Whither am I going?" and "What to do?" We
have seen him in those colonies, bringing an infant church
under the strict discipline which has characterized the Methodist societies in England. We have seen him during the Revolutionary War, casting his lot with this infant church when all
the other preachers returned to their homeland. We have seen
him at the Christmas Conference, accepting election at the
hands of his brethren rather than at the appointment of Wesley, and going out as the active head of a new church. We
have seen him standing before the new President of the new
republic, and tendering to him the allegiance and blessing of
this new church.

But now the time has come to look at this man more
closely. We need to know him as the men and women came
to know him who served with him and under him for more
than forty years. We need to see him, not as a figure in bronze,
and much less as a legendary giant in some dim past, but as a
living, breathing man. For until we have become acquainted
with Francis Asbury, we cannot understand this Methodism of
ours.

§ 2. Asbury's Episcopal Area

The first thing which will strike most of us about Asbury
is that he was just what we have called him—a man on horse-

back. He was always on the go. Already in this book we have emphasized the amount of ground covered by John Wesley in establishing Methodism in England. Wesley had a decade more of service than had Asbury; he worked in a country which, by comparison with the America of Asbury's time, was settled and easy to travel in; although not robust, he had much better health than the man who traveled the malaria-ridden marshes of the new frontier. But Asbury outrode Wesley! All in all, it has been estimated that he covered 275,000 miles! Most of this, remember, was wilderness trail. He crossed and recrossed the Alleghany Mountains more than sixty times.

We have spoken of the sort of circuits which the early Methodist preachers like Garrettson and Lee were expected to cover. But no circuit in all the history of the Christian Church is to be compared with that of Asbury. "From Maine to Virginia, through the Carolinas, wading through swamps, swimming the rivers that flow from the eastern slopes of the Alleghanies to the Atlantic, on down to Georgia, back to North Carolina, through the mountains to Tennessee, three hundred miles and back through the unbroken wilderness of Kentucky, back again to New York, to New England, then from the Atlantic to the Hudson, over a rough road, mountainous and difficult, on to Ohio"—this is not the record of a single extraordinary expedition, but the round of the circuit which Asbury and his horse plodded over every year!

"Where are you from?" asked a stranger who met him one day on the prairies of Ohio.

"From Boston, New York, Philadelphia, Baltimore, or almost any place you please," the bishop truthfully answered.

One of the few worthy biographies which Methodism possesses is a life of Asbury written by Dr. Ezra Squier Tipple. If only every reader of this book could be counted on to read Doctor Tipple's *The Prophet of the Long Road,* there would be no need to write this chapter. At least, we can give this glimpse of the man on horseback, as Doctor Tipple sees him go riding by:

"Where did Francis Asbury not go? In what place did he not lift up the cross? He literally went everywhere. In his annual or semiannual episcopal journeys he visited practically every State in the Union every year. His *Journal* shows that he went into New York State more than 50 times; New Jersey, over 60; Pennsylvania, 78; Maryland, 80; North Carolina, 63; South Carolina, 46; Virginia, 84; Tennessee and Georgia, each 20; Massachusetts, 23 times after his first visit there in 1791; and in the other States and Territories with corresponding frequency.

"Take an atlas and follow him on the map as he makes a typical journey. Leaving New York in the early part of September, he proceeds by Philadelphia, Wilmington, Baltimore; Alexandria, Petersburg, and Norfolk, Virginia; Raleigh, North Carolina; and Charleston, South Carolina, to Washington, in Georgia. Returning through South Carolina, he enters North Carolina; passes on to the western counties; crosses the mountains to the Holston River, in Tennessee; plunges into the Kentucky wilderness as far as Lexington; returns to the Holston; passes up on the west side of the Alleghanies, over a most mountainous region, through the whole breadth of Virginia, to Uniontown, in Pennsylvania; crosses the Alleghanies by Laurel Hill and Cumberland to Baltimore; goes on to New York; proceeds directly through Connecticut and Massachusetts to Lynn; passes west across the valley of the Connecticut, by Northampton, and over the Berkshire Hills by Pittsfield to Albany, and then down the valley of the Hudson to New York, where he arrives on the 28th of August, 1792. In later years his episcopal circuit was even more extended."[1]

Asbury kept a *Journal*, just as Wesley called on all Meth-

---

[1] *Francis Asbury: The Prophet of the Long Road*, pp. 162, 163. The Methodist Book Concern. Used by permission.

odist preachers to do. Compared with Wesley's, the book has little of the polish, and almost none of the keen observation on multitudinous affairs which makes the diary of the founder of Methodism an unequalled source of information concerning the social life of eighteenth-century England. But there is one fact about Asbury's *Journal* which no reader can miss, and which will never be

FRANCIS ASBURY

forgotten. That is the sense of movement. Pick it up almost anywhere, and it reads like this:

"We have ridden little less than four hundred miles in twenty days, and rested one. Under the divine protection I came safe to Philadelphia, having ridden about three thousand miles since I left it last."

Or again:

"Since the 16th of April, 1805, I have, according to my reckoning, traveled five thousand miles." (Asbury was sixty years old when, in 1806, he wrote that.)

Or again:

"We have traveled one hundred miles. My feet are much swelled, and I am on crutches."

Or again:

"I have frequently skimmed along the frontiers, for four

and five hundred miles, from Kentucky to Greenbrier, on the very edge of the wilderness; and thence along Tigers valley to Clarksburgh on the Ohio. These places, if not the haunts of savage men, yet abound with wild beasts. I am only known by name to many of our people, and some of our local preachers; and unless the people were all together, they could not tell what I have had to cope with. I make no doubt that the Methodists are, and will be, a numerous and wealthy people, and their preachers who follow us will not know our struggles but by comparing the present improved state of the country with what it was in our days."

§ 3. WHAT ASBURY'S ROAD WAS LIKE

So the man on horseback plodded ahead. But the mere addition of the number of miles he traveled gives only a faint idea of the sort of a road the rider came to know. Hear him as he writes from Tennessee, after one of those trips when he has found himself in the midst of that early American migration over the mountains:

"We have made one thousand and eighty miles from Philadelphia; and now, what a detail of suffering I might give, fatiguing me to write, and perhaps to my friends to read. A man who is well mounted will scorn to complain of the roads when he sees men, women, and children, almost naked, paddling barefoot and barelegged along, or laboring up the rocky hills, while those who are best off have only a horse for two or three children to ride at once. If these adventurers have little or nothing to eat, it is no extraordinary circumstance; and not uncommon, to encamp in the wet woods after night—in the mountains it does not rain, but pours.

"I too have my sufferings, perhaps peculiar to myself— no room to retire to; that in which you sit common to all, crowded with women and children, the fire occupied by cooking, much and long-loved solitude not to be found, unless you choose to run out into the rain, in the woods. Six months in the year I have had, for thirty-two years, occasionally, to submit to what will never be agreeable to me; but the people, it must be confessed, are among the kindest souls in the world.

"But kindness will not make a crowded log cabin, twelve feet by ten, agreeable; without are cold and rain, and within six adults, and as many children, one of which is all motion; the dogs, too, must sometimes be admitted.

"HE WAS CONSTANTLY IN PERSONAL DANGER"

"On Saturday I found that among my other trials I had taken an uncomfortable skin disease; and, considering the filthy houses and filthy beds I have met with, in coming from Kentucky Conference, it is perhaps strange that I have not caught it twenty times. I do not see that there is any securing against it, but my sleeping in a brimstone shirt."

"Asbury was constantly in personal danger," writes Doctor Tipple. "Wolves follow him; his horse falls; he crosses the Potomac in an open boat; he is lost in the swamps of South Carolina—'O how terrible to be here in the dark!'; in the blackness of the night he is bruised by the trees; his saddle turns and he falls from his horse; he fords the Catawba and finds himself

'among the rocks and in the whirlpools,' escaping with difficulty; through another's carelessness he is 'nearly burnt up'; he
falls downstairs; his horse, startled, throws him into a millrace,
and his shoulder is hurt; a whirlwind, accompanied by hail-
stones 'of such a size that three stones filled a pint measure,'
nearly overcomes him; his horse falls on the ice, and Asbury's
leg is caught under him; night overtakes him in the mountains,
'among rocks and woods and dangers on all sides'; he has to
'swim a long creek'; ruffians seek his life, a bullet grazing his
head as he rides through the forest."

But it was not alone such perils of a new road which made
the onward march of this man a marvel. The ills which often
accompany frontier life, with its poor food, its exposures, its
epidemics, early fastened on him.

"He needed someone with him, for he journeyed when he
'had a kind of chill and headache'; he 'went' more than six hundred miles 'with an inflammatory fever and fixed pain' in his
breast; he traveled for a period of four months during which he
was continuously ill, and covered 'not less than three thousand miles'; he 'went' when he had a boil on his face and another on his eye; when his leg was inflamed; when his 'breast
was inflamed'; when he had influenza; when he had 'a putrid
sore throat'; when he was so ill that he had no appetite for anything except 'a watermelon that Mrs. Tillottson was kind
enough to give us as we came by her house'; when he had a
toothache; when he had a high fever; when he was so weak that
he was ready to faint; when he was in pain from head to foot;
when he had a running blister on his side; when he was so ill
that his friends expected his speedy death, so ill that to him
death would have been welcome; when he had only strength to
write in his *Journal*, 'Pain, Pain, Pain'; through rain and snow,
through heat, drought, and dust, without food, without drink,
over mountains, through deep rivers and muddy creeks, on, on,
on, day after day, month after month, year after year, one

decade, two, three, four decades, until he reaches the end of the Road and is at rest."[1]

§ 4. ASBURY'S RELIGIOUS CONTRIBUTION

There are no words wherewith to describe the passion of soul which must have possessed a man who could live like that. With much the same reticence about his own inner experience that characterized his "father in Christ," John Wesley, Asbury makes few references to his own spiritual condition. We have to gauge that for ourselves, as we watch him at his task, knowing that no material rewards could be offered which would tempt such a man to such a career.

It can hardly be claimed that he was a great preacher. One of his contemporaries tells of a time when Jesse Lee and Asbury preached to the same congregation. Lee was generally mistaken for the bishop, and there was general praise of his sermon. But many were heard to say that they didn't think much of the sermon of "the old man" who had followed Lee.

Asbury's sermons were logical, cogent, imperative, and he knew well how to make the appeal which would move men to instant decision. He had a knowledge of the Bible so large that he was able to adapt his texts to his circumstances with remarkable facility. He did not preach "topical" sermons; he kept to the path marked out by the Methodists of England, proclaiming salvation to sinners, and letting other matters very largely look after themselves.

Here is an outline of one of his sermons, preached on one of his favorite texts: "Men and brethren, children of the stock of Abraham, and whosoever among you feareth God, to you is the word of this salvation sent." Asbury's own account of the way he handled that passage from Acts is: "This salvation; the gospel, to be sure; who the author, what the nature, means, conditions, spirituality, and degrees of this salvation; from whom

---

[1] *Francis Asbury: The Prophet of the Long Road*, p. 172.

it is sent, by whom, and to whom it is sent. It was sent to Jews first, afterward to the Gentiles, and continued to be sent, and is still sent to the children of men by the written Word, by the ministers of that Word, and by the influence of the Holy Spirit. The consequences of its reception—eternal life; of its rejection —everlasting damnation."[1]

"WOLVES FOLLOW HIM!"

There is nothing about the outline of such a sermon as that to set it off from thousands of sermons which were being preached in Asbury's day.

It is likely that Asbury enjoyed preaching. Most preachers do. He certainly did enough of it. It is possible to enumerate from his *Journal* something like sixteen thousand five hundred sermons preached by him. But most of these were preached in out-of-the-way places, and to very small congregations. It was only occasionally, at the time of the Annual Conference, and while he was in the cities along the seaboard, that he had the exaltation of preaching to a great multitude. It is hard to believe that just the chance to preach drove him on.

Asbury had an extraordinary sense of the solemnity of life. In fact, he had a little too much of it. "My conscience smote me severely for speaking an idle word in company," he

---

[1] *Francis Asbury: The Prophet of the Long Road*, p. 231. The Methodist Book Concern. Used by permission.

wrote. Or again, "I was condemned for telling humorous anecdotes." What a horrible time he would have had in the company of most modern Methodist preachers! Or, more likely, what a horrible time they would have in Asbury's company!

"May the Lord make me more serious," he prayed in his *Journal.* Poor man, he was serious enough. The sense of the brevity of life, of the awful issues for eternity which hung over every mortal, never left him. That, too, played its part in making him what he was. But it is doubtful whether that alone would have carried him to the end.

He was a man with the flair of an administrator. Like his great preceptor, Wesley, he found unlimited joy in seeing a chaotic movement taking form and substance under his hand. He was a statesman of the first order, never more happy than when he was laying out his plans of campaign, saying to one "Come," and seeing him come, to another "Go," and seeing him go. He liked power, and he used it with zest. In his lifetime he laid out an ecclesiastical empire which has remained to this day the largest in the republic. But even the chance to exercise authority was not enough, alone, to hold him to his long road.

Every record which we have of him agrees that, in a degree seldom witnessed, he was a man of prayer. To the very end, when the Methodist ministry had grown until it numbered its members by the hundreds, he made it his invariable practice to pray for every Methodist preacher every day by name! Freeborn Garrettson said of him that "he prayed the best, and prayed the most of all men I knew."

In addition to the prayer which came welling up spontaneously in every moment of difficulty, he had regular habits of prayer which sustained him during the normal round of his life. At one period he made it a point to pray at least three hours every day. Again, he set aside seven stated periods every day for prayer. Later, he spent ten minutes in every waking hour praying. "My desire is that prayer should mix with every thought, with every wish, with every word, and with every action, that all might ascend as a holy, acceptable sacrifice to God," he wrote.

All these things must be taken into account when we try to decide what made him the man he was. Not the desire to preach, alone; not the sense of life's solemnity, alone; not the joy of administration, alone; not the moving power of prayer, alone. But each of these in their measure, and all taken together, were at work in the man. And while they worked, he could not rest. The road held him. He could neither turn back nor halt.

§ 5.   ASBURY THE DICTATOR

At that, it must be confessed that there were things about Asbury which must have made him a difficult person for some people to get along with. To those who would subject themselves to the same iron discipline which he imposed on himself, who would never question his authority, who would grant him the same complete obedience which Wesley required of his preachers in England, life with Francis Asbury must have been a glorious experience. But to the man who showed reluctance to treat his word as law, Asbury could be as cold as ice and as hard as iron.

When he first landed in America, a young graduate of Mr. Wesley's school of absolute obedience, he was outraged by what he conceived to be the laxness in discipline of the Methodists he found here. When Thomas Rankin came over, Asbury found it hard to get along with him, but he greeted him just the same, because he thought Rankin had the look of a disciplinarian and would make the lawless colonial Methodists toe the mark.

Under Asbury's rule, the Methodist societies—and later

the churches—were always places of rigid discipline. Expulsion was the lot, for example, of any person who married a non-Methodist who was not thought to be living up to the standards the Methodists set for themselves.

Along with his demand for absolute obedience, Asbury placed a refusal to take advice from others. In his later years the one thing he disliked most in the policy of Bishop Mc-Kendree, his greatest successor, was the asking of presiding elders for advice as to the proper appointments for the ministers. Asbury had presiding elders, but they never served him as the "Cabinet" has come to serve most Methodist bishops. He felt that he knew all there was to know about the places which were to be filled and the men who were available to fill them. If others gave him counsel, he said that he feared they would merely pass on their own prejudices. So the bishop steered his own course, and few men ventured, after the first attempt, to suggest to him the way which he should go.

One young fellow who was ordained at the last session of the Western Conference held by Asbury tells this characteristic story of what happened to a Methodist preacher who tried to infringe on what the bishop felt to be the prerogatives of his office: "Bishop Asbury said to the preachers: 'Brethren, if any of you shall have anything peculiar in your circumstances that should be known to the superintendent in making your appointment, if you will drop me a note, I will, as far as will be compatible with the great interests of the church, endeavor to accommodate you.' I had a great desire to go west, because I had relatives, which called me in that direction, and it would be more pleasant to be with them; so I sat down and addressed a polite note to the bishop, requesting him to send me west. My request was not granted. I was sent a hundred miles east. I said to him, 'If that's the way you answer prayers, you will get no more prayers from me.' 'Well,' he said, 'be a good son, James, and all things will work together for good.' "

In one way, it is amazing that Asbury accomplished what he did in the young republic. He came at a time when men's minds and mouths were filled with the watchwords of democracy, and he hadn't the slightest idea of the meaning of the word. He was a born conservative and born autocrat. Had it not been for the completeness of his devotion to his task, and the transparent righteousness of his life, he could not have carried the men of revolutionary America with him as he did.

O'Kelley, whom he drove out of the church, made his fight on the issue that there should be some appeal from the appointments of this self-sufficient bishop. Surely that was the kind of an issue which might have been expected to appeal to men who had fought a war on the principle that "resistance to tyrants is obedience to God"! Among the men who stood with O'Kelley was McKendree, a veteran of the Revolution, and afterward a bishop. And many who stayed in the church agreed with O'Kelley.

The way in which Asbury handled the situation during the plastic years while the war was in progress, holding what amounted to rump Conferences which voted him supreme and unquestionable authority, shows a man of iron will, the kind of a man who could provide wonderful leadership for the campaign which lay just ahead of Methodism, but it does not show a democrat.

§ 6. THE BETTER SIDE OF ASBURY

But with it all, he remains one of the great men of American history, and one of the mighty figures in the growth of the kingdom of God. If he held others under a rigid discipline, it was no more than he demanded of himself. Body, mind, spirit—all were required to give a day-by-day return to an owner who judged them with a severity even beyond that he visited on others. He drove his body to incredible accomplishments, almost, as it seemed, with whips. He took a mind which had never been trained in the schools, and made it an instrument of the first rank.

Never a scholar to rank with Wesley, he yet became at home in the Greek and Hebrew Testaments, and year by year absorbed a quantity of reading of amazing range. He had almost no place to study except in the saddle, yet when he died he was the intellectual peer of any man he met, and the superior of most. He had the self-trained man's suspicion of schools—"The Lord called neither Mr. Whitefield nor the Methodists to build colleges," he wrote when he heard that Cokesbury College had burned—and such academies as he founded could not flourish under the sort of discipline he demanded. But he knew the value of a mind well stored and able to function. He fashioned such a mind for himself, and he sought it in his preachers.

While he was never easily jarred out of his path, he did know when he was beaten. One of his defeats came when he formed what was to be known as a general council—a little group of presiding elders who, with the bishop, were really to run the church. Since the other members would be dominated by the bishop, the church saw quickly that all vestige of popular government would vanish if this council once became established. It met twice; then the protest reached such proportions that Asbury saw there was no chance for the project. Accordingly, the council died.

Another matter on which he acknowledged defeat was small in itself, but significant. After he had been ordained deacon, elder, and bishop, all in the space of three days, he began to go about his appointments wearing vestments like those of a bishop of the Anglican Church. His failure to understand the spirit of the newly liberated republic is clearly indicated by this. Of course, he could not keep it up for long.

Jesse Lee was the man who dared to tell him so. Again, Asbury knew when he was defeated, and the vestments disappeared.

Later, he tried to make his preachers keep to knee-breeches when the majority of men had adopted trousers. He could not do so. He never ceased to express his disapproval, but he at least knew better than to make the length of the preacher's trousers an issue of church discipline—something which in his early days he would have been likely to have done.

On the other hand, if he could acknowledge defeat when he was clearly defeated, and could compromise when he thought he had no chance of winning—as he compromised with the Methodists in the South on the matter of slavery—he could fight to the last on an issue where he was sure he was right.

The delegated General Conference was one such issue. The first Conferences were annual affairs to which all the preachers came who wanted to do so. Since all the preachers then worked in a very small territory, it was comparatively easy for most of them to reach Baltimore, where custom placed the sessions. But as the church spread west of the mountains and into New York and New England it became impossible for a majority of the preachers to attend. And the preachers who, because of their service on the farthest fighting line, could not attend Conference became extremely dissatisfied.

Asbury agreed that they had cause for their dissatisfaction. He held, with them, that a Conference, meeting only at widely separated intervals, and attended by delegates elected on a proportional basis, with their expenses paid, was the only fair arrangement. When this proposal was first offered, the Baltimore and Philadelphia and Virginia Conferences—the ones who were holding the balance of power in the church because of their geographical location—turned it down. But Asbury stuck by his guns, and pushed the issue. Methodism is ruled to-day by a delegated General Conference because that was an issue on which, being sure he was right, Asbury refused to acknowledge defeat.

§ 7. THE END OF THE LONG ROAD

It was in 1771 that Mr. Wesley appointed Francis Asbury, a young English preacher of twenty-six, "general assistant" for the work of Methodism in America. It was in 1784 that he was ordained to the office of a "general superintendent" in the new Methodist Episcopal Church. It was in 1788 that he himself changed the title in the *Discipline* to "bishop." It was in 1816 that he died, leaving a church with more than seven hundred ordained ministers and more than two hundred thousand members.

To the very end, although wasted by consumption and enfeebled with age, he kept up the journeyings by which he is best remembered. He was no longer a man on horseback; death, as Wesley phrased it, had taken him by the hand, and he had to ride in a carriage, constantly cared for by a young preacher detailed for this single service. But he could not be stopped.

Leaving Boston in the early summer of 1815, after having held the New England Conference for the last time, the indomitable old man dared lay a course of sixteen hundred miles, along his familiar circuit of the nation. The flesh, however, proved too weak, and he had to turn away from the west, and back to New York, and from there to Delaware. A brief rest there somewhat recruited his strength; immediately he was off for Ohio, where, although ill, he held the Ohio Conference. McKendree met him there, and traveled with him to Cincinnati, where the two made their last farewell. Slowly the old man made his way into Tennessee, where once more he essayed to preside over a Conference.

It proved his last Conference session. He placed his hands for the last time on the heads of men to set them apart for the ministry; he read for the last time the marching orders of a brigade of his devoted army. Then he wrote, with faltering pen: "My eyes fail. I will resign the stations to Bishop McKendree. I will take away my feet. It is the fifty-fifth year of ministry, and forty-fifth of labor in America. My mind enjoys great peace and divine consolation."

"HE PREACHED HIS LAST SERMON"

"I will take away my feet." It was, indeed, the end. How better could this man have recognized its coming?

From the Conference, he went back to the familiar road. He seemed to have no definite objective. He had no home to which to go. So he just kept going. As night came on he stopped with friends who eagerly vied with one another for the honor of keeping him. Once and again he stayed over a few days with those who would not permit him to proceed immediately. Back to the southern end of his familiar circuit, in South Carolina, he made his way; then northward. On the seventh of December, 1815, he made his final entry in his *Journal*: "We met a storm and stopped at William Baker's, Granby." But though his record stopped, the journey did not.

The idea seems to have taken hold of him that he should reach Baltimore in order to resign his office in person at the session of the General Conference soon to meet there. Although he was now so sick a man that a few miles of travel utterly exhausted him, he kept pushing on. Finally, late in March, he reached Richmond, in Virginia, where he was placed in a chair on a table beside the pulpit of the Methodist church, and preached his last sermon.

The next Sunday, after he had reached the home of an old friend about twenty miles from Fredericksburg, still on his way to Baltimore, he died. The end came as he sat in a chair, resting his head against the hand of the young preacher who had been his traveling companion.

"The brave pilgrim's journey," says Doctor Tipple, "is over. The greatest itinerant of the ages has come at last to the end of the Long Road, and behold there is a House at the end of the Road, and a light in the window and a welcome. At last the man without a home has found his Home."

CHAPTER XV

CAMP-MEETING DAYS

§ 1. As an Englishman Saw Us

NOT long after the War of 1812 had settled the relations of the United States and Great Britain, there began to visit this country that long line of English literary celebrities which stretches down to the present day. Now these famous folk come to "lecture," which, being interpreted, means that they come to obtain the most money by the easiest means they know. A good many of them quickly show that they have little to lecture about, but there are thousands of Americans still ready to pay good prices in order to hear these British lions roar.

Nowadays, it is the fashion for these visitors to express their admiration at much they see in America; their amazement at much more; and almost all of them apparently feel it politic to cover what small doses of criticism they may feel like giving with a thick coating of sugar. It was not ever thus. When the feet of English celebrities first turned toward the new republic, there was little desire manifest to compliment the Americans.

This young country, which had dared to declare its independence, and even to support that daring with a second war, seemed a most upstart, bumptious and brash member of the family of nations to many of those early visitors. Our manners were bad, and our morals were not to be envied. When we were not hypocritical, we were "slick"; and when we were not slick, we were crude.

Mrs. Trollope went home to give all good Englishmen

a shuddering realization that it had been only the direct favor of Providence which had rid the mother country of responsibility for this land of dirt, boorishness, and bad grammar. And if there were any of Mrs. Trollope's readers who had lingering doubts, these must have been dissipated when Charles Dickens came home to tell of a land flowing with tobacco juice and dotted with cuspidors, with the manners of the sty and the morals of the wooden nutmeg manufacturer.

Yet these were not, heaven be praised, the only reports of America which reached the rest of the world. Even before Mrs. Trollope and Charles Dickens and others with much the same opinions wrote their accounts—for which it must be admitted that there was a considerable measure of justification— a more informing and more just picture of American life had been given Great Britain by Captain Frederick Marryat.

Captain Marryat was a fine type of naval officer who had served in American waters before and during the War of 1812, had traveled extensively in the "backwoods" sections where the real America was being born, and had the ability to tell what he saw in a fair and graphic manner. Later he was to prove one of the greatest writers of sea stories the English-speaking world has known.

There is nothing, however, in any of his sea tales more vivid than this bit, which is to be found in his *Diary in America.* It describes a Methodist camp meeting of those early days, just as it looked to a total outsider:

"The camp was raised upon . . . a piece of table-land comprising many acres. About one acre and a half was surrounded on the four sides by cabins built up of rough boards; the whole area in the center was fitted up with planks, laid about a foot from the ground, as seats. At one end, but not close to the cabins, was a raised stand, which served as a pulpit for the preachers, one of them praying, while five or six others sat down behind him on benches. There was ingress to the area by the four corners; the whole of it was shaded by vast forest trees, which ran up to the height of fifty or sixty feet without throwing out a branch; and to the trunks of these trees were fixed lamps in every direction, for the continuance of service at night.

"Outside of the area, which may be designated as the

"THEY HAD COME MANY MILES TO ATTEND"

church, were hundreds of tents pitched in every quarter, their snowy whiteness contrasting beautifully with the deep verdure and gloom of the forest. These were the temporary habitations of those who had come many miles to attend the meeting, and who remained there from the commencement until it concluded —usually a period of from five to ten days, but often much longer. The tents were furnished with every article necessary for cooking; mattresses to sleep upon; some of them even had bedsteads and chests of drawers, which had been brought in the wagons in which the people in this country usually travel. At a farther distance were all the wagons and other vehicles which had conveyed the people to the meeting, whilst hundreds of horses were tethered under the trees, and plentifully provided with forage. Such were the general outlines of a most interesting and beautiful scene.

"The major portion of those not in the area were cooking the dinners. Fires were burning in every direction; pots boiling; chickens roasting, hams seething; indeed, there appeared to be no want of creature comforts.

"But the trumpet sounded as in the days of yore, as a signal that the service was about to recommence, and I went into the area and took my seat. One of the preachers rose and gave out a hymn, which was sung by the congregation, numbering seven or eight hundred. After the singing of the hymn was concluded he commenced an extensive sermon; it was good, sound doctrine and, although Methodism, it was Methodism of the mildest tone and divested of the bitterness of denunciation, as, indeed, is generally the case with Methodism in America. . . .

"In front of the pulpit was a space railed off, and strewn with straw, which I was told was the anxious seat, and on which sat those who were touched by their conscience or the discourse of the preacher. On . . . one side . . . about twenty females, mostly young, squatted down on the straw; on the other a few men; in the center was a long form, against which some men were kneeling, with their faces covered with their hands as if occupied in prayer. Gradually the number increased, girl after girl dropped down upon the straw on one side, and men on the other.

"At last an elderly man gave out a hymn, which was sung with peculiar energy; then another knelt down in the center and commenced a prayer, shutting his eyes and raising his hands above his head; then another burst into prayer and another followed him; then their voices all became confused together; and then were heard the more silvery tones of women's supplication. As the din increased so did their enthusiasm; handkerchiefs were raised to bright eyes, and sobs were intermingled with prayers and ejaculations. It became a scene of Babel; more than twenty men and women were crying out at the highest pitch of their voices, and trying apparently to be heard above the others.

"Every minute the excitement increased; some wrung their hands and called for mercy; some tore their hair; boys lay down crying bitterly, with their heads buried in the straw; there was sobbing almost to suffocation, and hysterics and deep agony. One young man clung to the form, crying: 'Satan tears at me, but I will hold fast. Help! Help! Help! He drags me down.'

"It was a scene of horrible agony and despair; and, when it was at its height, one of the preachers came in and raising his voice above the tumult entreated the Lord to receive into his fold those who now repented and would fain return. Another of the ministers knelt down by some young men, whose faces were covered up and who appeared to be almost in a state of frenzy, and putting his hands upon them, poured forth an energetic prayer, well calculated to work upon their over-excited feelings. Groans, ejaculations, broken sobs, frantic motions and convulsions succeeded; some fell on their backs with their eyes closed, waving their heads in a slow motion, and crying out—'Glory, glory, glory!' "

What do you suppose Charles Dickens would have made of that?

§ 2. A Child of the Frontier

Most Englishmen must have found it hard to understand, let alone sympathize with, such an event as Captain Marryat was describing. An attempt was made to introduce similar meetings into British Methodism, but the staid ministers of that careful church would not countenance the plan. To them it seemed a wanton insult to all the decencies of religion, and proof that the parsons of the old Church of England had justification when they charged that the Methodists were a parcel of "enthusiasts" without balance or proportion. It is not hard to understand why they took that view. Yet Captain Marryat was right in judging the gathering under the forest trees as of sufficient importance to be described at length to his British readers. For in the camp meeting he had stumbled on the most distinctive feature of American religious life in the first half of the nineteenth century.

The camp meeting was a child of accident. Nobody planned it in advance. It grew spontaneously out of the conditions of that early American border. The frontier lured then, as it always has, a large number of those who wanted, more than all else, to be freed from restraint. There was little moderation, in any direction. Men lived lustily. Whisky was the common drink of most of the populace. There was a distillery for almost every 600 inhabitants in Indiana in 1810, and each distillery averaged almost 1,300 gallons of whisky as its annual output!

Duelling was common. Men shot each other on the flimsiest pretexts. The struggle with the Indians made human life seem of little value; it also worked to close the minds of most of the settlers to any feelings of responsibility toward the red men. Few felt compunction over any chicanery that might be practiced on a savage, with the result that the whole standard of ethics in the border territories was lowered.

Of such restraints as have accompanied a carefully observed Puritan Sabbath, the border knew nothing. "Sunday was a day set apart for hunting, fishing, horse racing, card-playing, balls, dances, and all kinds of jollity and mirth," said Peter Cartwright. Take it almost any way you will, and you will come to the conclusion that the Middle West, during those years of the great migration, was a tough territory. The more remarkable, then, is the way in which the camp meeting gripped it and transformed it. For the camp meeting came with an evangel as clear-cut as was the sinning of the border.

The camp meeting brought the scattered units of those early communities together and made them face their sin as a body. It shook them with conviction of sin as only a crowd can be shaken. It inspired them with hope of better things as only a crowd can be inspired. In the warmth of the large group, in the touch of elbow against elbow, men and women by the thousand found courage to face the temptations of the raw, new life which they had not found before.

It is doubtful whether, with all their faithful cabin-to-cabin preaching, the circuit-riders could have held the advance of religion in those pioneer communities equal with the advance of sin. Indeed, during the last decade of the old century, the membership in the Methodist societies of Kentucky and Tennessee—scene of the first migrations—actually showed a falling off. And later, the War of 1812, with its aftermath, brought another great outburst of riotous living, in the face of which thousands who lived in the new communities gave up all pretense of decency.

Individual dealing, however faithful, was not powerful enough for such a situation. Neither was that of the small, secluded class meeting. What was needed was something dramatic, as violent toward righteousness as the rest of the border was toward license, something explosive and arresting. That need the camp meeting supplied.

§ 3.   THE SOCIAL IMPORTANCE OF THE CAMP MEETING

But the camp meeting not only supplied a great religious need of the frontier. It was of equal importance as a social factor. In fact, it was as powerful as it was because of this social factor. The reason that the day of the camp meeting has passed is because this social need no longer exists.

The great lack of the frontier is always contact. In a community where any person within a day's horseback ride is reckoned a neighbor, any excuse for coming together is eagerly seized on by almost everybody. Thus, the raising of a house or a barn was a holiday for the greater part of a county, but even less important events were also considered legitimate excuses for coming together. Huskings, quiltings, harvestings, log-rollings, and, of course, weddings and funerals, were the signal for a general turnout.

In such a community, the camp meeting was a social godsend. As Captain Marryat reported, families came from miles around, carrying enough provisions and bedding to make possible a stay of a week or longer. It was not, primarily, a religious urge which brought many of them. In the records of that period we have again and again word of the presence of roughs, bullies, intoxicated individuals and groups, scoffers—persons who looked forward to the meeting as a chance for some excitement, but hardly for edification.

To be sure, once these people were actually in the meeting, the sweep of emotion over the crowd often proved too much for them, and they were among the first to respond to the call for penitents. But this did not always happen. Sometimes the preachers had to whip the worst of their tormentors before enough order could be secured to make preaching possible.

In our last chapter we saw a young Methodist preacher praying Bishop Asbury for a certain appointment, and not getting it. How did that young man become a Methodist preacher? As a young frontiersman he had been among the most reckless along the Kentucky border. How did he find his way into a Methodist Conference? The camp meeting supplies the answer, and because the experience was so typical we will let him tell it. He had come to a camp meeting at Cane Ridge, Kentucky—this was in 1801, just as these meetings were starting—partly out of curiosity, and partly to rub against folks.

"THE SCENE WAS INDESCRIBABLE"

"A scene presented itself to my mind," he says, "not only novel and unaccountable, but awful beyond description. A vast crowd, supposed by some to have amounted to twenty-five thousand, was collected together. The noise was like the roar of Niagara. The sea of human beings seemed to be agitated as if by a storm. I counted seven ministers all preaching at the same time, some on stumps, some on wagons, and one, William Burke, standing on a tree which in falling had lodged against another. Some of the people were singing, others praying, some crying for mercy in the most piteous accents. While witnessing these scenes, a peculiarly strange sensation, such as I had never felt before, came over me. My heart beat tremendously, my lips quivered, and I felt as though I must fall to the ground."

So the young backwoodsman did a natural thing. He fled into the woods to regain his poise. As soon as he felt sure of himself he came back to the seven preachers and the noise like Niagara, but he was not as safe as he thought.

"The scene that presented itself to my eye was indescribable," he writes. "At one time I saw at least five hundred swept down in a moment, as if a battery of a thousand guns had opened upon them. My hair rose up on my head, my whole frame trembled, the blood ran cold in my veins, and I fled to the woods a second time, and wished that I had stayed at home."

The next day he tried to turn the wish into thought. With a friend he actually started away. But the sense of sin was on him, and before he was well started he was praying for forgiveness, and, with the help of an old man, he found peace.

"Suddenly my load was gone," he says, "my guilt removed, and presently the direct witness from heaven shone fully upon my heart. Then there flowed such copious streams of love into the hitherto waste and desolate places of my soul that I thought I should die with excess of joy."

That is what the Methodist camp meeting did to one young fellow who came to it, as did thousands of his fellows, just to enjoy the novelty of finding himself in a crowd!

§ 4. Why Methodism Used the Camp Meeting

The camp meeting is always spoken of as a Methodist institution, but it did not originate with the Methodists. The first preachers to hold camp meetings were Presbyterians. For years the Presbyterians bore almost as large a part in the conduct of the meetings as did the Methodists. In fact, one of the causes of a split in Presbyterianism that brought about the formation of the Cumberland Presbyterian Church was the refusal of the staid, established Presbyterianism of the seaboard to approve the meetings in the woods. The Baptists, too, had a hand in the beginnings. But there was something about the Methodist spirit, the Methodist machinery, the Methodist message, and, more than all else, the character of the Methodist preachers, which tended to make the camp meetings more and more a Methodist institution.

That early Methodism, as we have seen, was a mobile affair. Its preachers were not tied down to single churches and congregations. Almost the only church buildings which the frontier afforded were Presbyterian or Congregational. The Methodist preacher rode a circuit, and frequently that circuit was four hundred miles or more in length. Even the bishop was mobile. It is indicative of the closeness with which Asbury kept in touch with every development of the religious life of the America of his time that, although the camp meeting first came into existence in an out-of-the-way part of the mountains during the spring of the year 1800, the Methodist bishop had taken part in such a meeting by October of the same year.

There were certain preachers who proved particularly adept at the sort of preaching the camp meeting demanded. These the Methodism system made it easy to move from meeting to meeting, bringing their peculiar talents to bear at the strategic points. In their absence from their own circuits the junior preachers—for whenever possible a young preacher was linked with an experienced one on each circuit—could carry on their regular work.

Then, when the camp meeting was over, and the crowds went back to the isolated homesteads, they were not left to their own spiritual resources. For the Methodist system then made it possible for the preachers on the local circuit, who had, of course, been helping in the meeting, to follow those who had given evidence of spiritual awakening, confirm them in their new resolves, and tie them up permanently with Methodist classes. It was this ability to follow-up which, as much as anything else, made the Methodists more successful than any others in using and conserving the new method of evangelism.

Again, the camp meeting became peculiarly a Methodist institution because Methodist doctrine fitted it better than any other. There were always some Presbyterians and some Baptists who made good use of the camp-meeting method, and here and there a Congregationalist, and some of the followers of Alexander Campbell. But these did so to a large extent in spite of the doctrinal emphasis of their denominations, while the Methodists were tremendously helped by the doctrines on which their church insisted. As a matter of fact, the Cumberland Presbyterians, who split off from the main body at this period, largely gave up the proclamation of a stiff Calvinism in the face of the demands of the camp-meeting crowd.

It is one of the queer twists of history that the churches which came into the frontier with a democratic organization— the Presbyterians, the Baptists, the Congregationalists—came there also with a monarchical doctrine, while the church which came with an organization often accused of being autocratic brought the most democratic of gospels.

The first three churches, which left matters of church government almost entirely in the hands of the local congregations, proclaimed a God absolutely sovereign over the individual, who predestined whom he would to eternal damnation and foreordained whom he would to glory. Some of these frontier Calvinists did not hesitate to go the whole length, preaching the damnation of infants, and that there were infants in hell a span long. With every life foreknown, foreordained, and predestined, it is easy to see that the appeals of the evangelist would lack something of promise.

The Methodists, on the other hand, preached that every man was the master of his own spiritual fate. "So then every one of us must give an account of himself to God," was one of their favorite texts, used over and over again in the camp meetings. Their preachers might seem to be helpless in the hands of an autocrat-bishop, and their congregations might have nothing to say as to who should minister to them or what rules of discipline should be enforced, but their gospel was a gospel of individual responsibility, with an immediate and conscious salvation freely offered to anyone who would exert the will to accept it.

On the frontier, where every man was supposed to be the equal of every other—and ready to fight at any whisper which impugned otherwise—this doctrine, which denied that there were any elect in the eyes of God, naturally won a response. And it made the Methodist camp meeting a place in which men and women, conscious that they were sinners, were brought squarely up to the warning that they must either be converted and live a new life, or they would go to a hell of endless torment.

§ 5. Camp-Meeting Preachers

More than all else, the Methodist spirit and the character of the Methodist preachers seemed made to the order of the camp meeting. From its birth, Methodism had been a child of irregularity. Every significant advance which John Wesley had made in England had been irregular, in the eyes of the Established Church. The very formation of the Methodist Episcopal Church in this country was not only an ecclesiastical irregularity but, in the opinion of some, almost an ecclesiastical outrage. The moment Methodism becomes regular, it becomes just another Protestant group, not much more significant than any one of a half dozen other groups. But in its days of irregularity, it has found glory and strength.

The camp meeting was as irregular a churchly proceeding in America as field preaching had been in England. But it met the same sort of demand. And Methodism, which had made a continent-transforming bishop out of an unlettered gardener's son, and preachers out of the rough products of the frontier class meeting, was now able to make cathedrals and

tabernacles out of these tent and hut begirt clearings in the open forest.

The Methodist preachers of the frontier were men who fitted perfectly into this rough-and-ready order of things. They were not college bred. There was not a single college graduate in the Methodist ministry in the whole State of Indiana until the forties, and the total number of college-bred ministers in the whole West could at that time be numbered on the fingers of both hands. They did a good deal of reading, mostly while in the saddle, and more thinking. But they never desired to copy the niceties of pulpit practice that some of the Presbyterian and more of the Congregational preachers brought with them from beyond the mountains.

Their scorn was reserved for the preacher who tried to use a manuscript, and in this they reflected the views of the whole frontier community. Peter Cartwright tells of one such missionary from New England whom he tried to instruct in the ways of the new States: "I told him to quit reading his old manuscript sermons and learn to preach extemporaneously; that the Western people were born and reared in hard times, and were an outspoken and off-hand people; that if he did not adopt this manner of preaching, the Methodists would set the whole Western world afire before he could light his match." The poor chap thus admonished "tried it for a while," says Cartwright, "but became discouraged and left for parts unknown."

Such is human nature that, if the Methodist preachers

looked down on those who could not enter a pulpit without a manuscript, the objects of their scorn retaliated by scorning men who had never trod a college campus. But the circuit-riders of the frontier refused to apologize for their lack of formal education. In fact, they rather flaunted the sort of training which they had obtained, believing that it had peculiarly fitted them for their peculiar task.

"My Alma Mater," wrote John Strange, one of the best known of the camp-meeting preachers of a hundred years ago, "my Alma Mater was Brush College, more ancient, though less pretentious, than Yale, or Harvard, or Princeton. Here I graduated, and I love her memory still. Her academic groves are the boundless forests and the prairies of these Western wilds; her Pierian springs are the gushing fountains from the rocks and the mountain fastnesses; her Arcadian groves and Orphic songs are the wildwoods, and the birds of every color and song, relieved now and then with the bass hootings of the night owl and the weird treble of the whippoorwill; her curriculum is the philosophy of nature and the mysteries of redemption; her library is the Word of God, the *Discipline* and the *Hymn Book,* supplemented with trees and brooks and stones, all of which are full of wisdom and sermons and speeches; and her parchments of literary honors are the horse and the saddlebags."

Reading which we may conclude that, meager as his schooling may have been, the saddlebag parson did not need to take a back seat in any company when it came to the employment of highfalutin' language.

One inclines to believe, after reading of scores of the preachers of those days, that they rather tended to magnify their roughness. They were the religious leaders of the part of the country which elected Andrew Jackson and William Henry Harrison Presidents of the United States—the one idolized as "Old Hickory" and the other as "Tippecanoe," the hero of the log-cabin and hard-cider campaign. It was more than a coincidence that Harrison held the candle by which the Methodist parson read his text and lined out the hymns for the first Methodist service in the Indiana capital.

Religiously as well as politically it was an asset in those days to be known as a rough-and-ready sort of fellow, and the Methodist parsons emphasized their rough-and-readiness to the limit. When Henry B. Bascom tried to enter a Methodist Conference he was turned down twice and later taken in with reservations, largely because he dressed well and used careful speech. Yet he was later to become one of the most, if not the most, powerful preacher in the denomination, and to die a bishop!

One of the immediate effects of this rough period on Methodism was a change in the singing at Methodist services. This does not mean that camp-meeting congregations sang less than did the congregations of the Wesleys. Probably they sang more. Certainly they sang more lustily. But they sang in a manner that would have appalled the Wesley brothers. Their efforts had been devoted to dignifying the hymn as an element in Christian worship; the camp-meeting preachers, and their congregations, reduced the hymn at times to doggerel. Dr. William Warren Sweet, who has done more than any other man to make this period known to us, tells how the camp meetings, after starting out with the hymns of Charles Wesley and Isaac Watts, would "warm up," and, as the temperature increased, the cruder and the more vociferous would be the singing.

Some of the hymns were no more than a description of the scene in which the singers were participating:

"Sinners through the camp are falling,
Deep distress their souls pervades,
Wondering why they are not rolling
In the dark infernal shades.

Grace and mercy, long neglected,
  Now they ardently implore;
In an hour when least expected
  Jesus bids them weep no more.

"Hear them, then, their God extolling,
  Tell the wonders he has done;
While they rise, see others falling!
  Light into their hearts hath shone.
Prayer and praise, and exhortation,
  Blend in one perpetual sound;
Music sweet beyond expression,
  To rejoicing saints around."

There were other hymns, theological in content, which did not scruple to use figures at which John Wesley would have brought his editorial blue pencil into furious action. The same direct appeal was used which Charles Wesley had employed so effectively, but it was in a way that Oxford scholar might have hesitated to approve:

"Stop, poor sinner, stop and think,
  Before you further go:
Can you sport upon the brink
  Of everlasting woe?
Hell beneath is gaping wide,
  Vengeance waits the dread command,
Soon will stop your sport and pride,
  And sink you with the damn'd."

That hymn, as it is to be found in *The Camp-Meeting Hymn Book: Containing the Most Approved Hymns and Spiritual Songs, Used by the Methodist Connexion in the United States,* contains another innovation characteristic of that period in the form of a chorus:

"Then be entreated now to stop,
  For unless you warning take,
Ere you are aware you'll drop
  Into a burning lake."

There is another hymn in this same collection which appeals to us. There are nineteen verses in it, the whole giving an account of the adventures of Daniel with the lions. What the tune was is not known, although it is impossible to read the

"AND PUNISHED THEIR OFFENDERS WITH AGONIES EXTREME"

words without realizing that they fit naturally into a popular rhythm. The first verse of this hymn sets the stage in this manner:

> "Among the Jewish nation one Daniel there was found,
> Whose unexampled piety astonish'd all around;
> They saw him very pious and faithful to the Lord,
> Three times a day he bowed to supplicate his God."

The hymn then describes the trial of Daniel, his triumph, the remorse of Darius, and the fate of the accusers of Daniel:

> "The lions rushed with vengeance upon those wicked men,
> And tore them all to pieces ere they to the bottom came.
> Thus God will save his children who put their trust in him,
> And punish their offenders with agonies extreme."

But do not think that this was all the moralizing which the incident occasioned for the camp-meeting singers. No, there were six more verses, culminating in this:

> "Glory to God, O glory, for his redeeming love,
> Religion makes us happy here, and will in worlds above;
> We'll sing bright hallelujahs, and join the holy song,
> With Moses, Job, and Daniel, and all the heav'nly throng."

A great many of the preachers of the days of camp-meeting glory were famous weepers. Asbury did a lot of weeping, as any reader of his *Journal* will discover. McKendree also wept often. Most of the preachers who have left us records of their ministry seem to have let their emotions run away with them almost as often as they preached. The more they wept the better they seem to have felt, and the more they seem to have accomplished. At times their weeping would start tears in the congregation; again, while the preacher wept the congregation would take to shouting hallelujahs. When there was neither weeping nor shouting the preachers—and the congregations as well—were sure that there was something wrong.

So it was that Methodism, with a system more mobile than that of any other church, with a message more democratic and inclusive, and with a ministry which was part and parcel of the life of the frontier, came over the mountains with the great rush of emigration, and took over the spiritual command of the commonwealths which men were hewing from the wilderness—a command which it maintains to this day. For Ohio, Indiana, Illinois, Michigan, Kentucky, and Tennessee still remain the strongholds of Methodism on the American continent. And if there are times when we are inclined, in looking back to those days, to think the preachers a bit too emotional, too rough, too informal in their ways, we need to remember the sort of days that those were, the sort of people with whom they worked, and the sort of results they achieved. Even to-day, with all the niceties of our settled communities, it might not be a total loss if a few preachers here and there would take whatever irregular course was necessary to make their hearers believe that they were as desperately in earnest as were those frontier preachers.

§ 6. THE FRONTIER CHURCH

There is one point at which we need to be careful lest we

misunderstand the effects of the camp meetings. It is true that the people of the Middle West came to these meetings by the thousands. It is true that they were moved at the preaching by the thousands. But it is not true that they were then received into the church in any such numbers. The church grew marvelously in all the new States, to be sure. The Western Annual Conference, which included everything west of the mountains until it was divided up in 1812, had a total membership of only two thousand eight hundred at the beginning of the century; by 1811 it had grown to more than thirty thousand! Yet this did not include a quarter of all those who had professed conversion in the camp meetings.

Membership in the Methodist Church was still a prize to be sought; it was still offered only to those who gave lasting evidence of a change of life, who entered a class and continued in attendance there, and who, after the most searching examination by local leaders and the traveling preacher, were formally recommended for the great honor. The Methodist *Discipline* in those days was not a little black book filled with curious admonitions of interest mainly as remnants of a past history; it was a way of conduct in which Methodists walked with meticulous care. And if they departed from it, they were acknowledged to be backsliders, and as such they were cast out. Even the great McKendree—of whom more presently—was twice a member of a Methodist class, and twice allowed to go his own way, before he was finally admitted to the membership of the Methodist Church.

As was true of the rounds of John Wesley in England, so in America one of the chief duties of the Methodist itinerants as they went from class to class on their circuits was to purge the church of those who were not living up to the standards set in the *Discipline*. The Methodism of that day expected that conversion and admission into the church would have a recognizable effect; that it would lead to a different kind of living than had been the case previously. Otherwise, what good was it? That would seem like a grotesque notion to the people who join the church to-day just because it seems the proper thing to do, but it was not so considered in the days of our great-grandfathers. And the result was a church of high religious voltage.

For this church, the Methodist system provided a type of care very different from that of the camp meeting. The core of every Methodist church was the class meeting. In fact, there were hundreds of class meetings on the frontier where there were no churches. In the class meetings were discovered the young men of especial aptitude for testimony, prayer, and exhortation, who were induced to become local preachers, and, as they developed in that service, were led on and on until they found themselves in the full-time, itinerant ministry. As the circuit-rider made his rounds he made it a point to meet all the classes, and, so far as he could, to visit and hold some sort of service in every home.

But the great meeting for the members of the church was not the camp meeting nor the class meeting, but the quarterly meeting. Then it was that the sacraments were administered and the love feasts held. To these meetings came both the senior and junior preachers of the circuit, and church members from all points of that circuit. Preaching began on Friday evening or Saturday morning and lasted until Monday morning. On Sunday the presiding elder did the preaching. There was no call for converts until Sunday night. Sometimes the converts were gathered here by the hundreds, and always these meetings were regarded as an evangelistic opportunity. But fundamentally they were the meetings at which church membership, as such, was most magnified.

If the discipline held over Methodist church members was severe, that held over the preachers was even more so. It hardly needs to be said that they were disciplined by poverty.

From 1800 to 1816 the salary for all preachers—bishops, presiding elders and all—was $80 a year and traveling expenses; in 1816 this was raised to $100. This seems small enough, but hardly anybody ever expected to receive this in full, and few ever did. Each Annual Conference session found it necessary to have a "committee on deficiencies" which spent its time figuring out means by which enough might be raised to make it possible for the brethren who had not received enough to live on to pay their debts and go to their next appointment. Naturally, under such conditions, bachelor preachers were in favor. Asbury remarks at one place in his *Journal* that "the high taste of these Southern folks will not permit their families to be degraded by an alliance with a Methodist preacher, and thus involuntary celibacy is imposed upon us." But this was no loss in the eyes of the bishop. "All the better!" he writes.

THE FRONTIER

Beyond all that, the Methodist preachers were disciplined by the watchfulness of a Conference—bishops, presiding elders, and fellow ministers—who took the rules of their church seriously. A reader of the minutes of the Western and Ohio Annual Conferences, beginning with the opening of the century and covering its full first quarter, will be struck by the fact that there was hardly a session in which somebody—and frequently more than one—was not expelled. Often the offenses complained of seem to have been trivial. Sometimes men who had rendered magnificent service were cast out where a bit more brotherliness, a bit more of the will to understand, might have made such drastic action unnecessary. But the preachers were almost fanatical in their determination to make and keep the Methodist ministry a peculiar calling, against which no scoffer could raise a finger of scorn.

Some curious things happened as a result of this determination to enforce discipline among the preachers. Among others, Methodism was introduced into Illinois! For it is a matter of Conference record that in 1803 Benjamin Young, a preacher on trial in the Western Conference, was hauled before the bar and charged "of haveing said, that he composed a certain song, when in truth he did not; that he had the misfortain to get his horse's thye broke, when it was not so; and that he has baptized contrary to the order of the M. E. Church." Apparently, Young was able to make the case against himself seem less serious than the charges portended, for "after a plain talke, and hopeful promises" he was admitted. But he was sent as a missionary to Illinois, and the record more than hints that this was a measure adopted to chasten him. Thus did a sovereign commonwealth first come to receive the message of Methodism!

§ 7. William McKendree

It is obvious that a movement of the fluid type of the camp meeting and the saddlebag ministry required leadership of the highest order. Religious emotion is not especially difficult to stir; hundreds of "evangelists" have demonstrated this in every generation of American life. But the emotion thus stirred is not easily harnessed to the rigors and perseverances of a settled church order, as the results of hundreds of revivals have proved. It took a master hand at the point of control to insure that Methodism not only awoke the frontier from spiritual lethargy with the camp meeting and the itinerant, but that it gathered the stark individualists thus awakened into a compact church. In the providence of God, Methodism found this leader. As the great bishop of the days of the church's founding, Asbury, drew near the time of his departure, this new leader was ready to take up the task. Let us look for a bit at this remarkable man, William McKendree, first American-born bishop of the Methodist Episcopal Church.

In the fall of the year 1800 three men made their way along the well-worn trail over the Cumberland Gap and down into the new State of Kentucky. By their dress, all three were preachers. Two of them were old; one young, tall, hardy, commanding. The two elders had ridden as far as they could through Virginia in a light carriage; it was only after the roads had turned into trails that they had taken to the saddle. The younger man would have scorned an easier seat than on the back of a horse. The two old men were Francis Asbury and Richard Whatcoat, at that time the bishops of the Methodist Church. The younger man was William McKendree, who, at forty-three, was being transferred from the presiding eldership of a district in Virginia, his native State, to the same position in the Western Conference which was now about to be formed. The minutes of the first session show that there was only one district—named the Kentucky district, although one circuit was in Tennessee and one in Ohio—and only one presiding elder.

McKendree had made a record for himself as a presiding elder in Virginia, but so thorough an itinerant was he, so little wedded to the settled life of the older colony, that he had started on his way to Kentucky within three hours after word of his new appointment reached him! He tackled a hard job on the western side of the mountains. The growth of the church there had, for various reasons, come to a pause; indeed, it was losing in membership. But soon after his arrival what has been known as the "great revival" broke out, during which the camp meeting came to being and to power, and from that point on McKendree was the leader of a valiant, conquering host.

For eight years McKendree labored as a presiding elder. By 1807, when he received his last appointment, there were five districts, in Kentucky, Tennessee, Ohio, and Mississippi, and forty-four full members of the Conference. Then, early in the next year, McKendree rode back over the Cumberland Gap and into Baltimore, as one of the seven delegates of his Conference to the General Conference of 1808. That Conference was to do two things of superlative importance. It was to adopt the permanent constitution of the church, and it was to elect a new bishop to take the place of Whatcoat, recently deceased, in standing beside Asbury, and later to succeed that great pioneer.

WILLIAM MC KENDREE

On the Sunday before the Conference opened McKendree was prevailed on to preach in one of the churches of Baltimore. Several descriptions of that sermon have come down to us. The frontier presiding elder was wearing frontier clothes. He seemed ill at ease in the city pulpit. As he started preaching it was apparent that his vest and his trousers would never keep company, and soon the congregation was confronted with a growing expanse of red undershirt. For a while everybody seems to have seen nothing but red undershirt; then, suddenly, nobody saw it. The mysterious thing had happened which almost always did happen when McKendree was preaching. The congregation had been lifted out of itself. Its attention had been riveted on other than material things. When the sermon was over, a great sigh passed over the listeners. The impression which they had received was testified to a few days later when William McKendree, red undershirt and all, was elected bishop.

"THE MYSTERIOUS THING HAPPENED"

The Conference over, McKendree turned back toward the land from which he had come, and which was now to be the center of his episcopal activity.

The approach of a Methodist bishop to his area in those days varied somewhat from to-day. McKendree made the journey on horseback, accompanied by five other men, not all ministers. They carried provisions for four days, that being approximately the time they would be between habitations at some parts of the journey.

"Lying out," writes the new bishop, "was no hardship, but the water was extremely bad and the flies intolerable. Some persons had attempted to go through the prairies and had turned back and advised us not to try it; but we resolved to go, trusting in the Lord. On the third day the flies afflicted us sorely, when a kind Providence sent us a strong breeze and blew them all away. After twelve hours a shower of rain succeeded and blessed man and beast with water to drink. On Friday a little after dark we got to Brother Scott's, in the settlement. The old people were gone to the camp meeting, about fifteen miles off, but the children received and treated us kindly. On Saturday morning one of the most affecting scenes I ever witnessed occurred. As we drew near to the encampment about thirty of the neighbors fell in with us. We rode two deep, and a number of excellent singers went in front. We were all glad, and as we moved they sang delightfully with the spirit and the understanding. As we approached, the congregation met us with open arms and welcomed us in the name of the Lord."

Some episcopal reception, that!

From then on, McKendree entered on labors as monumental as those of Asbury or Wesley. Eventually, he presided over Conferences in all parts of the church, but the West was always his stronghold. Tennessee became his headquarters; from it he moved on a round of administration which would quickly have killed a less rugged man. It came near to killing him. In 1812 the General Conference, out of deference for the feelings of the aged Asbury, left him in the active ranks, and did not elect another bishop. The practical effect was that for four years McKendree had to bear the full brunt of leadership in a church which had grown by that time to tremendous proportions. The effort of that quadrennium to be everywhere and do everything made a partial invalid out of him for the rest of his life.

He did not give up. He kept plodding on as faithfully as Asbury had, but from that time it was in constant weakness and pain. We even have the record of his holding one of the new Conferences, with a small membership, in his bedroom, with the ministers sitting around his sickbed. But he managed to keep going until 1834, by which time the camp meeting and the circuit-rider had established Methodism in power to the line of the Mississippi and beyond. Then at last, honored and loved as few Methodists have been, he came back to his beloved Nashville, and on a farm near that city, in the home of his brother, he died.

McKendree was one of the greatest preachers Methodism has ever produced, yet it was not as a preacher that he made his abiding contribution. He was an administrator of the first order, but it was not merely his wise stationing of preachers which made his influence of lasting importance. The thing for which McKendree deserves lasting remembrance was his deliverance of the church to the control of a constitutional and legal order. The constitution was adopted in the year he was elected a bishop. It became his task to turn Methodism away from the personal absolutism of Asbury to a settled, legal order, in which bishops, presiding elders, General, Annual, Quarterly and local Conferences alike felt themselves bound to a line of action definitely laid out by rules in the making of which all had had a part. McKendree, in other words, knew how to blow the great revival of the camp meeting period to white-hot flame, and at the same time how to weld a new church, in the heat of this flame, into a firm and lasting order. Few other men have ever accomplished two such gigantic tasks, calling for such dissimilar powers.

§ 8. PETER CARTWRIGHT

If William McKendree was the great administrative leader produced by the camp-meeting period, Peter Cartwright was its typical preacher. Here was another Virginian, born two years after the close of the Revolution, but reared on the rough Kentucky border, and as rough as any other young blood of that frontier. Converted at sixteen, Cartwright was a junior preacher at eighteen, and was appointed to a circuit on McKendree's Kentucky district. In his first twenty years in the ministry he preached eight thousand sermons!

Cartwright was built for the rough life of the border.

On a superb body there was set a rugged head, topped with a mass of iron-gray hair which was always in disorder. Shaggy eyebrows could not hide eyes which instantly attracted attention, and which, in moments of excitement, seemed to snap fire. The camp meeting was made to his order. When bullies sought to make trouble, he did not hesitate to tackle them single-handed, if need be, clap them in jail, or force them to promise to keep order. When, after such disturbances, other ministers confessed themselves too upset to preach, Cartwright, after a moment of prayer, was ready to go to the improvised pulpit and preach until "the people fell in every direction, right and left, front and rear. It was supposed that not less than three hundred fell like dead men in a mighty battle; and there was no need for calling mourners, for they were strewed all over the camp ground."

Naturally, a man of that kind feared no mortal. Once, in Nashville, Cartwright was called on to preach in a Presbyterian church. As was always the case when he preached, the church was crowded. Soon after the sermon started the idol of Tennessee, General Andrew Jackson, stalked in and, finding no pew vacant, leaned against a pillar in the rear. The pastor of the church was in a flutter lest the visiting preacher fail to comprehend the honor done him and the church by the presence of the great man. He need not have worried, for Cartwright had served as a chaplain in Jackson's army at the battle of New Orleans, and knew the general probably better than the Nashville preacher did. But the pastor leaned forward and tugged at the preacher's coat-tails, whispering, "General Jackson has come in."

Cartwright seemed not to hear.

Again the pastor whispered: "General Jackson has come in."

That was too much for Cartwright. "Who is General Jackson?" he blurted out. "If he doesn't get his soul converted, God will damn his soul to hell as quick as he will a Guinea Negro."

The poor pastor almost had apoplexy; the next day he went around to apologize to the general for the manners of his backwoods visitor; but Jackson sought Cartwright out on the street and said: "You are a man after my own heart. A minister of Christ ought to love everybody and fear no mortal man."

There were times when Cartwright did not hesitate to face a situation even more formidable than that presented by "Old Hickory." Once when visiting one of his preachers, he found the poor man at his wits end under the goading

PETER CARTWRIGHT

of a wife who had no interest in religion, and would not allow the practice of its simplest forms inside the house. She started to heap abuse on Cartwright, and we will let him tell what happened:

"I caught her by the arm and, swinging her round in a circle, brought her right up to the door and shoved her out. She jumped up, tore her hair, foamed; and such swearing as she uttered was seldom equaled and never surpassed. The door was very strongly made to keep out Indians. I shut it tight, barred it and went to prayer, and I prayed as best I could, but I have no language at my command to describe my feelings; to conquer or die in the attempt. While she was raging and foaming in the yard and around the cabin, I started a spiritual song and sang loud, to drown her voice as much as possible. . . . I sang on and she roared and thundered outside till she became perfectly exhausted and panted for breath. At length when she had spent her force, she became calm and still, and then knocked at the door, saying: 'Mr. Cartwright, please let me in.'

" 'Will you behave yourself if I let you in?' said I.

" 'Oh, yes,' said she, 'I will.'

"She had roared and foamed until she was in a high perspiration and looked pale as death. After she took her seat, 'Oh,' she said, 'what a fool I am.' " The woman later experienced a genuine conversion.

As Cartwright grew toward the fullness of his powers an element entered the camp meetings and the other religious services of the Middle West which was not there in the days of McKendree. That was doctrinal disputation. As the frontier became settled, as preachers became more and more fixed figures in the local community, they seem to have had more time to discover their differences and to try to find a logical basis for those differences. The result was a species of bickering which lasted almost down to the present century. In this sort of thing Cartwright excelled, for his natural wit gave point to the arguments which he knew how to cast in the sort of language his audiences would best understand.

It was with the denominations which required the immersion of their members—the Baptists and the Christians—that Cartwright did most of his debating. Slinging texts back and forth at each other in those days when one Bible verse was thought just as authoritative as another, the doughty champions stirred many a community to its depths, but it is doubtful whether or not they accomplished much for the cause of vital religion. "Water! water! water!" Cartwright once snorted after one of his encounters with a Baptist. "You might think that heaven was an island, and the only way to reach it by swimming there!"

Cartwright followed the frontier from Kentucky to Indiana, and finally into Illinois, where he did the most notable work of his life. After he had been in that State a while he got into politics, and was twice elected to the State Legislature. Strange as it will seem in the Methodist churches of the north nowadays, the Methodists of the period of which we are now speaking were almost all Jeffersonian Democrats, and it was as a Democrat that Cartwright's name went on the ticket.

After two successful terms in the Illinois Legislature, the Democrats nominated him for Congress. His opponent was another Kentuckian who had also moved from that State to Indiana, and finally had settled in Illinois. He was as unusual a character in his way as Cartwright was in his. He had successfully resisted the efforts of Cartwright and all the other preachers of the period to induce him to join a church, and, in fact, the common report of the neighborhood was that he was a skeptic. His following seemed to Cartwright to consist principally of the unregenerate. So Cartwright felt it well to combine a good deal of preaching with his campaigning.

One night Cartwright's opponent wandered into the meeting he was holding, and took a back seat. The preacher was hot after souls that night, and, after he had put all the fervor he could summon into his appeal, he called sinners to the mourner's bench. He even dared to do a thing which he had done time and again in camp meetings. He singled his opponent out and called on him by name. "If you are not going to repent and go to heaven," he asked, "where are you going?"

The gangling politician thus addressed took his time in getting to his feet, but once there he answered, with apparent confidence, "I am going to Congress, Brother Cartwright."

The event proved him to be right. For Cartwright's opponent was Abraham Lincoln.

. . . .

So the new country took on a new form as new life flowed over the mountains, and into the new communities of the new States beyond the mountains. And, as the country grew, so the Methodist Church grew with it. As the country changed, so the church changed. When McKendree first passed through the Cumberland Gap both State and church were little more than a promise. But when forty years had passed, and the day of the circuit-rider was done—except in the regions in the far West still to be opened—there stood not only a group of populous States, able to dominate the life of the whole republic, but a Methodist Church recognized as the most powerful moral and religious force in those commonwealths. The camp meeting and the circuit-rider had brought victory.

CHAPTER XVI

THE WINNING OF THE WEST

§ 1. WESTWARD HO!

THE story of the expansion of Christianity could be told with fascinating interest in terms of the ships and other means of transportation by which it has been carried. In that fleet of ships would be enrolled the little sailboat on which Paul crossed with the good news from Asia to Europe, the Mediterranean galley in which he sailed to Rome a prisoner, the daring vessels which rounded the Pillars of Hercules and put out into the Atlantic, the channel boats which carried the gospel to savage Britain, and the Mayflower, which ferried across the Atlantic the seeds of a Christian civilization.

A minister with a fine gift for exaggeration once said that the three greatest transports in history were Noah's ark, the Mayflower and the Prairie Schooner. They were ships of very different style of architecture but they were all alike in this, that each one carried the best of an old world over into a new one. No chapter in the age-long westward march of Christianity is a more gripping and stupendous one than that of which our story of the expansion of Methodism now becomes a part. The story of Methodism for sixty years, from approximately 1800 until 1860, becomes a vital part of the occupation of the continent of America from the Alleghany Mountains to the Pacific Coast. That long parade was one of the greatest migrations of all time. It was one of the epic adventures of the human race. In rapidity of movement, in extent of territory covered, in the permanence of results, that pushing westward of the American frontier from the Great Lakes, the

Ohio and Southern Appalachian Mountains to the Pacific has never been matched. It shaped the destinies of a continent and profoundly affected the history of the world.

If we are to catch the true significance and feel the thrill of the history of Methodism for this half century, we must

"ON FLATBOATS DOWN THE OHIO"

always have in mind this moving column of humanity of which it was a part and into which it poured its stream of influence. Nor must we ever allow ourselves to think of Methodism as an isolated or separate force. It was in the midst of and a part of the whole Christian advance made up of many other denominations in which were the spirit and daring of the pioneer and the passion of the missionary.

There seemed to be no end to the migrants, as, indeed, there was none for half a century. They poured along through every natural route. The emigrants from the Carolinas crossed the mountains and came up through Tennessee and Kentucky. Those from the Middle States came through Pennsylvania and then on flatboats down the Ohio. Pittsburgh continued for many years the main gateway to the West, a key position which forty years later was held by Westport, Missouri, the point of departure of the covered wagons on their journey across the prairies and the Rockies. The banks of the Ohio at Pittsburgh were occupied by hundreds of families with their household goods awaiting the completion of their flatboats. Sometimes as much as $3,000,000 worth of goods was piled up at Pittsburgh awaiting high water. In 1810 more than 200 flatboats passed the little settlement of Louisville, while a few years later an upstream traveler on the Mississippi met 2,000 flatboats in twenty-five days. In one year more than 97,000 persons passed through Buffalo for the West, and in another year 90 vessels reached Detroit filled with settlers. A popular song of the time will reflect the spirit of the day:

> "Come, all ye Yankee farmers who wish to change your lot,
> Who've spunk enough to travel beyond your native spot,
> And leave behind the village where your pa and ma do stay,
> Come follow me and settle in Michigania."

§ 2. THE FIRST MELTING POT

In the new settlements throughout all of what is now the Middle West, the various elements of the American people for the first time really mixed. Thus the frontier was the first "melting pot." Next to the New Englander, with his clean and neat family and orderly ways, would squat down a family of Irish from the uplands of Pennsylvania or Virginia, with rough manners, half-clothed children and as one prominent bit of furniture a jug of home distilled whisky. (Whisky was such an easily portable form of wealth that it frequently served as money on the frontier.) On the other side might be the tall, gaunt "poor white" of Virginia or the Carolinas, with good blood in his veins but the victim of generations of competing with slave labor. He too settled down on the "gov'ment lands." Sprinkle in the Yankee peddler, with his tinware Dutch oven, the land speculator, and last but not least the

itinerant preacher, and you have the materials for a new stirring of the nation's cast of characters.

Yet the picture of thousands of settlements and thousands
of wagon trains stretching all the way from Ohio to Colorado
and Oregon is not complete without a glance at and reverent
salute to the mother of the new nation—the woman in the
pioneer drama. Mute testimony of how hard the early life
was on the woman of the family is still to be found in hundreds
of graveyards. The patriarch buried beside two, three or four
wives who preceded him is much more common than the hardy
woman who outlived her husband. The housewife came to her
new home young and raw. She bore the children and buried
a staggering number of them, for doctors and medicine were
out of reach of the cabin. She fed her men and raised her
children and stocked up food for the winter. She was butcher
and baker and candlestick-maker all in one, and weaved the
clothes of the family. It was she who kept religion alive and
became the nucleus of the circuit-rider's church.

While the settling of the West was steadily going on,
there were at least four great waves. The first reached its peak
about the year 1800 in the overflow of people into the central
plain east of the Mississippi. The second, the so-called "great
migration," began in 1815, at the close of the War of 1812, and
continued until about 1820. The third was the so-called
Jacksonian migration of 1837, stimulated by the panic of that
year and pushing across the Mississippi and up into the Northwest and down to the Southwest. In this wave of migration
two great highways beyond the Mississippi and Missouri were
mapped out, two of the most famous and historic trails in the
world, the Oregon Trail, running up from Kansas City across
what is now Nebraska, Wyoming, Idaho, and Oregon, and the
Santa Fe trail, the great trader's route to the Southwest. This
movement of population completed the organization of six new
States between 1816 and 1821. The fourth great wave—a

gigantic tidal wave which broke over the whole continent, was the transcontinental gold rush which followed the discovery of gold in California in 1848.

The communities which these successive migrations formed were, to a remarkable extent, communities of youth. They were thrown on their own resources to make success or failure, and that necessity created a spirit of self-confidence, of impatience and independence. There was a background of equality which was something utterly new, not only on the American continent but in the world.

Into the very midst of this moving civilization there came the Methodist preacher, a circuit-rider on circuits of incredible distances, except in the most thickly settled regions. We have already seen him in action and caught the flavor of the frontier life in the chapter on "Camp-Meeting Days." Here we can try only to get an impression of the astounding swiftness of his movement in carrying the Gospel and expanding the church into every quarter of this newly opening world. The Methodist preacher crossed the mountains into Kentucky only ten years behind Daniel Boone, and he gained on Boone's successors. He reached Oregon and California ahead of the first division of the on-coming migration and was there to welcome it!

§ 3.   THE MAN ON HORSEBACK

Mary Carolyn Davies has drawn a composite portrait of a thousand circuit-riders and of a whole era in the history of American Christianity in her poem:

THE CIRCUIT-RIDER[1]

"God tramps on through the scourging rains,
   God vaults into the saddle,
Rides alone past the dusty plains,
   God's back bends to the paddle—

---

[1] From the Epworth Herald. Used by permission.

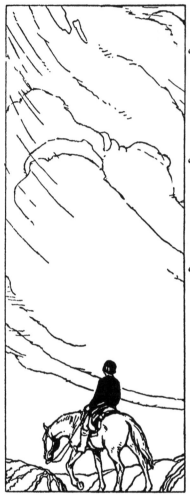

Cedar branches and sunlight through!
And on, still on, speeds the lone canoe!

"God rides out on his ancient quest,
    Healing, saving, commanding;
Here in the savage, unknown West;
    Settlement, cabin, landing—
Well they know the steady beat,
In the stillness, of God's horses' feet.

"God leads to grace the pioneers,
    Who walk each hour with danger;
Knows these grim men for his peers,
    Gives his bread to the stranger;
Doing all that a neighbor can,
God rides still, a weary man.

"God rides out! And found three states;
    Their scourger, their defender;
Guides their loves and tones their
        hates,
    Leads them into splendor!
God—in the Circuit-Rider's breast—
Once more, God built a world—our
        West."

The genius of the Methodist system, as well as the intrepid spirit of the itinerant, is seen in the amazing swiftness in which the preacher "got on the ground" either with the first settlers or at their very heels. This record of the expansion of Methodist circuits is in itself an epic. Look at it a moment.

As early as 1788 Ohio appears as an appointment, fifteen years before Ohio was admitted to Statehood. Methodist preachers had entered Kentucky four years earlier, in 1784. Illinois was first penetrated by Americans in 1780 and was only very sparsely settled in a few spots when the first Methodist preacher appeared on its soil in 1804. For twelve years, from 1803 until 1815, "Illinois" was one appointment. The preacher appointed might well have preached on the text, "Thou hast

"THIS MOVING CIVILIZATION"

set my feet in a large room." Fifteen years later there were thirty circuits. Indiana was entered by Methodist preachers in 1800, sixteen years before the State was admitted to the Union. The first Methodist sermon in Michigan was preached in 1808; the same year was preached the first Protestant sermon in Alabama. In 1800 Methodist preachers went into what is now Mississippi at Natchez, eighteen years before it was admitted into the Union. In 1805 Asbury sent a preacher into Louisiana, just two years after that great empire known as the "Louisiana purchase" had been secured from Napoleon, and two years later, in 1807, another itinerant swung out into the remote Southwest.

Jesse Walker, a veteran of the trail in many States, introduced Methodism into Saint Louis in 1818, the very year in which the first steamboat reached that city. The story of his descent upon Saint Louis might well epitomize the entrance of the preacher into thousands of frontier settlements in the Middle and far West. "I have come in the name of Christ to take Saint Louis, and by the grace of God I will do it." By the grace of God he did! Before a year was over he had a church membership of sixty, a church building and a free school for poor children.

In 1830 we find the same irrepressible and heroic Walker introducing Methodism into a tiny settlement of some eight or ten houses on the south shore of Lake Michigan. The little cluster of houses was less than a year old. It bore a queer sounding Indian name, destined to become somewhat better known—Chicago.

By 1830 the frontier of the United States was west of the Mississippi. By that time the circuit-rider was west of the frontier—its advance agent! Kansas, when still populated by Indians and only a few whites of heroic mold, was entered by Methodism in 1830. John Clark, traveling a thousand miles in a wagon, entered Texas in 1841, and three years later Joseph Hurlburt was sent into Minnesota by the Rock River Conference, these two men thus demonstrating the northern and southern reach of the expanding church. Gold was discovered in Colorado in 1859, but on the heels of the first miner came the first Methodist preacher. Dakota was entered by Methodist preachers in 1860.

§ 4. Getting on the Ground

One classic remark of a characteristic preacher named Nolley gives a vivid view of the expansion. In a remote section of Mississippi one day he saw fresh wagon tracks and overtook a settler just unloading his goods and placing his family on a new homestead.

After learning who Nolley was, the settler exclaimed in disgust: "Another Methodist preacher! I left Virginia for Georgia to get clear of them. There they got my wife and daughter, and I came here, and here is one before I get my wagon unloaded!"

"ANOTHER METHODIST PREACHER!"

"My friend," said Nolley, "if you go to heaven, you'll find Methodist preachers there; if you go to hell, I'm afraid you'll find some there; and you see how it is on earth, so you had better make terms with us and be at peace."

"Here is one before I get my wagon unloaded" might have been spoken in hundreds and thousands of localities from the Ohio to the Pacific. Methodism was neither omnipotent nor omniscient. But it came rather close to being omnipresent!

Two chapters in this Methodist expansion over the continent should be here glimpsed, for they are both notable in themselves and are characteristic samples of this heroic period in the history of the church and the nation. The first is the planting of Methodism in the far northwest country of Oregon. The second is the introduction of Methodism into California in the spacious days of '49. Each must be pictured with just a few strokes.

§ 5. THE OREGON MISSION

The story of the Oregon Mission is one of the most stirring chapters of American Christianity and records one of the outstanding services of the home missionary in the development of the nation.

One afternoon in the winter of 1831-32 three Nez Perces and one Flathead Indian appeared on the streets of Saint Louis with a request which probably no white man had ever heard before. They explained that they had come from the land of the setting sun. They said they had heard of the white man's God and they wished to learn about him and get a copy of the Bible. General William Clark, who had been with Captain Meriwether Lewis on the famous Lewis and Clark exploration trip to the Northwest Pacific in 1804-06, was then Indian agent at Saint Louis. He gave religious instruction to the Indians but did not give them a Bible. The Indians left to go back to Oregon with a feeling of disappointment, not knowing that they had set forces in motion which would work results beyond anyone's dream. It happened that a Methodist half-breed of the Wyandott tribe had been sent by the United States government to Saint Louis and he met these Indians. He sent letters which awakened the Methodist Church and led to the first transcontinental mission in America, that to the Oregon Indians. This same journey of these Indians also led the American Board, then representing the Congregational, Dutch Reformed, and Presbyterian Churches, to send out three missionaries.

President Wilbur Fisk of Wesleyan University, Middletown, Connecticut, was one of the first to be stirred by the challenge and was instrumental in securing and helping to prepare Jason Lee to set out to Oregon. Lee was a young teacher who accepted the call to go as a missionary. Lee set out from Saint Louis in April, 1834, on the long journey over what was for the most part unbroken wilderness, a journey destined to rank as one of the notable missionary pilgrimages of all history.

He crossed the plains with a company of some seventy men, largely hunters and fur traders, two hundred and fifty horses, and some cattle taken by the missionaries. By the middle of June he had reached the summit of the Rocky Mountains. Pushing on to Fort Vancouver, Lee preached the first Protestant sermon on the Pacific Coast September 28, 1834. There he opened his missionary work among the Indians.

It was literally a leap in the dark. The War Department of the government was consulted before the mission started, but it reported that it knew nothing of "a tribe of Flathead Indians." So the missionary society projected the Mission under the general title of "an aboriginal mission west of the Rocky Mountains." The charter reads like that of some of the companies formed in England for "the discovery and settlement of parts unknown, somewhere."

With the mission once located in the Willamette valley log cabins were begun with magical swiftness, ground was broken, and a school for Indian children established. Here and elsewhere the circuit-rider's saddlebag proved a true conjurer's bag out of which the magician drew, not live rabbits, but things far more miraculous—church, school, college, Christian civilization.

§ 6. SAVING THE GREAT NORTHWEST

Here the story becomes a national epic, with the theme of saving to the United States the whole territory of what is now Oregon, Washington and Idaho, a fabulous empire. This whole territory was occupied (to the small extent that it was occupied at all) jointly by Great Britain and the United States, under an agreement which had been extended in 1828 to run indefinitely, until one or the other nation should ask for a settlement. Jason Lee, with other missionaries, did much to awaken the nation to the opportunity and need for swift action if the United States was to possess the territory. They first saw that here was a new world destined to become a field for civilized settlements. Statesmen at Washington and the nation in general were sound asleep on the matter. The first task was to persuade the government and people that the country was valuable. Daniel Webster was proclaiming oratorically that the country was too far away to be governed by the United States. Meanwhile the Hudson's Bay Company was extending its operations to all this vast territory and so bringing it into the actual possession of Great Britain, but the United States had hardly acknowledged, much less encouraged, any occupancy by its citizens. The danger was that the entire coast would eventually become British soil. It was a dramatic struggle of the preacher and school-teacher, of the farmer and home-maker against the trapper and hunter; and the Methodists were the leaders on the American side in that struggle.

The Methodist missionaries sent three petitions to Congress to extend the jurisdiction to the Pacific Coast. These petitions were quietly pigeonholed. Then Jason Lee started east to secure funds and reenforcements to awaken the nation. He brought five Indians with him who proved a great aid in this campaign. His tour of the country was like Peter the Hermit preaching a crusade, and his description of Oregon and the danger of losing it helped greatly to create the immigration which later saved Oregon to the United States. As a result of Lee's trip and the work of other missionaries, the movement of population began to flow freely. In 1843 over a thousand settlers went on the long trail up the Missouri, across the mountains and down the Columbia, the largest band of immigrants which had ever crossed the Rockies up to that time.

The long boundary dispute with Great Britain was finally settled in 1846. The American migration had decided the issue. The boundary between the United States and Canada was fixed at the 49th parallel, dividing the territory as it is to-day.

§ 7. In the Gold Rush to California

The other stirring chapter of the Pacific is that of California. One of the indirect but far-reaching results of the

SUTTER'S MILL

Oregon Mission was the beginning of Methodism in California. In 1847 two ministers on their way to Oregon stopped in San Francisco and preached there and formed a class and started a school. In the same year was formed the first Methodist Society at San Francisco. This was the first Protestant organization in California.

Whenever William Taylor comes upon the scene of Methodist history, whether it be in Baltimore, in California, in India, South America, Africa, or Australia, it is like the advent of Hercules. Then the plot thickens. Then the mountains move. He was the Giant with the Seven League Boots. The world-wide strides of this world apostle are marked out in the chapter on "A Spiritual Forty Niner." Here can be given only a suggestion of his rôle in the high and hectic days of early California.

The lure of gold has always been a chief *motif* in human history. Never has it precipitated such a sudden, such a swift and gigantic avalanche of humanity as that which went toward California between 1848 and 1851. Hold in your mind a moment two facts and dates. In 1848, when the United States acquired California at the close of the Mexican War, there were only a few hundred Americans in the territory. But on January 19 of that year a few small bits of gold were discovered at Sutter's mill in El Dorado County. By 1850 a hundred thousand "gold diggers" had swarmed into California and had already taken out over thirty million dollars' worth of gold. In the few intervening months there was a "gold rush," principally from the eastern and central parts of the United States but also from all the world as well that was like the crusades of the Middle Ages. The mania for migrating to California spread with lightning rapidity and affected all classes. The fever that raged all over the country is well expressed in a verse of one of the popular songs of the day:

> "I soon shall be in Frisco,
>   And then I'll look around,
> And when I see the gold lumps there,
>   I'll pick 'em off the ground.
> I'll scrape the mountains clear, my boys,
>   I'll drain the rivers dry,
> A pocket full of rocks bring home—
>   So brothers, don't you cry."

So wild were the expectations that several companies brought steam dredges with which to "scoop up" the gold!

This great procession of "argonauts" went by two routes, the overland route across the plains, and that by sea to Panama,

then across the Isthmus and then by sea again to San Francisco.
By land there was also the northern route, the famous Oregon
Trail. Along this way the line of "prairie schooners" stretched
for miles. So steady was the onrush that frequently two hundred wagons would be waiting at a ferry. One traveler counted
four hundred and fifty-nine wagons in ten miles along the
Platte River. The men were picturesque in their woolen shirts,
canvas packets, and enormous boots. Usually each man carried
a gun and two revolvers. Many of the women trudged on foot,
some carrying children. Here and there was left a little mound,
with a board at the head, upon which a child's name had been
burned with a hot iron. The trail was strewn with household
goods cast off to lighten the load.

The sea route had as its worst obstacle the dread trip across
the Isthmus of Panama. By the end of 1849 over thirty-five
thousand had arrived by sea and forty-two thousand by land.
In the San Francisco harbor at one time there lay four hundred
ships deserted by their sailors, who had gone to the gold
diggings.

Methodist pioneers flung themselves into this procession.
Taylor went by sea clear around Cape Horn, a journey of one
hundred and fifty-five days. Owen went overland from Indiana, traveling two thousand miles in farm wagons drawn by
oxen. From the moment of Taylor's landing the gospel was
fairly let loose amid the wild and lawless conditions of gold-
crazed California. The very churches which were first created
were "emigrants" also. The frame for the first church was
prepared in Oregon and shipped in sections to San Francisco.
Another church had been shipped all the way from Baltimore.
Standing at Sacramento amid the heap of lumber lying on the
ground, Owen preached his first sermon October 22 and declared, "We will occupy our new church next Sunday." A
society of thirty members was organized on the spot that day
and by the next week the church was raised. The church

shipped from Oregon was erected in San Francisco and dedicated.

From these beginnings there came a speedy success and development such as has seldom crowned the lot of Christian workers.

The old frontier has now passed into history. But the importance of the conquest of the Western mind and heart for Christian ideals is not surpassed by anything in the history of European Christianity.

CHAPTER XVII

THE MISSIONARY SPIRIT

§ 1. Thomas Coke

SHORTLY before sunset on the afternoon of the fourth of May, 1814, a little fleet of five vessels, which had sailed from England for India, came to stop in the Indian Ocean. A heavy sea was beating all around them. The tolling of a bell on one of the ships sounded out above the wind and waves. On the deck of the ship could be seen a coffin covered with signal flags being solemnly borne up to the leeward gangway. Soldiers were drawn up in rank on the deck. The crew and passengers, deeply moved, crowded around the coffin. A missionary among the passengers read the burial service, and just at the moment of sunset the coffin was lifted over the side of the vessel and dropped into the deep.

THOMAS COKE

That sunset scene marked the end of a life. But it marked also the beginning of a movement. It was a sunrise hour as well as sunset. For the man who was buried at sea, almost in the sight of the India to which he was making his way,

301

at the age of sixty-seven, was Thomas Coke, well called "the Foreign Minister of Methodism," the man who more than any other may justly be regarded as the beginning and source of the foreign missionary enterprise of Methodism. The voyage to India, at that advanced age, was the last flaming of a missionary passion which had burned in his breast all his life. His body was buried at sea, but no seas could quench the flame of missionary ardor which was the soul of Thomas Coke. Any story of Methodism in its world outreach must set in a central place the portrait of "the little Oxford Doctor." For we can look at that portrait and say truly, "That was the face that launched a thousand ships," missionary argosies that in his train and in his spirit have sailed all the seven seas of the earth with the evangel of Christ.

There were many streams of influence which contributed to Methodist missions. The Wesley Revival was an essentially missionary movement and cannot be understood in any other light. At the General Conference of 1820, at which the Missionary Society, organized the year before, was adopted and indorsed, the Conference declared: "Methodism itself is a missionary system. Yield the missionary spirit and you yield the very life-blood of the cause." Wesley himself had eyes focused to world horizons, sent out missionaries to America, and in his word, "I look upon the whole world as my parish," uttered one of the undying watchwords of Christian history. Francis Asbury's little memorandum book in which he recorded the sums he collected for the support of itinerant preachers who could not find their support in the districts to which they were sent, was a real "source-book" of Methodist missionary history. The work of John Stewart among the Indians of Ohio, which led directly to the organization of the Missionary Society in 1819, is usually held to be the beginning of Methodist missions and was so celebrated in the Centenary of 1919. The first corresponding secretary of the Missionary Society, Nathan

Bangs, has often been regarded as the father of the missionary work of the Methodist Episcopal Church. These men played a great part, an indispensable part. But Stewart's connection with the origin of missionary work was largely accidental; Bangs' was largely official. Before the form or organization of foreign missions comes the spirit. And the spirit was Coke's.

Coke's appearance in the Methodist movement was one of its outstanding providences. Like Wesley he was an Oxford man. In learning and culture he was the peer of any clergyman of his time, a Doctor of Laws of Oxford. Evicted from his Established Church parish at Petherton, on account of his "Methodist" teaching, he found refuge in the Methodist Conference and became the coadjutor of Wesley, a providentially equipped "Prime Minister" for the hour of world expansion which had arrived in the Methodist movement. He was the first world traveler of Methodism and brought into its consciousness its first vivid sense of world mission and responsibility. In a manner unique in the annals of Christianity he strode the Atlantic like a Colossus of Rhodes, a large feat for a little man with legs as short as his! For all the time during which he acted as one of the two bishops of the Methodist Episcopal Church in the United States he had virtual charge of the Irish Conference, presiding over it more often than Wesley himself, and also traveled incessantly throughout England and the West Indies. He crossed the Atlantic eighteen times, defraying his own expenses, for he was a man of large fortune and lavished on Methodist missions during his lifetime practically all of it. A strong claim could be made for Coke as the first of that modern company of large givers to Christian enterprises, for he gave more money to religion than any other Methodist and perhaps more than any Protestant of his time.

Coke was ordained by Wesley as a Superintendent of the Methodist work in America. Coke, however, was never a bishop of the Methodist Episcopal Church in the sense in which all the other bishops, from Asbury down, have been. He was never elected to that office. He occupied it largely by sufferance as Wesley's representative. He exercised his powers very intermittently. While he made nine visits to the United States, he spent only three years in all there. Yet his personality and work were pivotal in the organization of the church. He has been overshadowed by Asbury, but deserves a place as one of the great triumverate of founders of the church in America, with Wesley and Asbury.

It should not be forgotten that, even though he spent only three years in all in America, those years had packed into them an amazing sum of itinerant preaching. If Asbury had left a few more traces of having possessed a sense of humor we would suspect a sly twinkle in his eye as he calmly arranged itineraries for Coke of a thousand-mile horseback trip through rough and, at times, impassable territory. But any backwoods preachers disposed to discount the "dapper little doctor" as a tenderfoot soon revised their estimate. He could ride with any of them, being frequently sixteen hours a day in the saddle.

It is a mark of Coke's courage and his thoroughgoing missionary spirit that his was the most impassioned and earnest voice raised in early Methodism in America against slavery. He was mobbed many times for his outspoken protests against it. He made a determined but ineffectual effort to have slaveholding made a bar to partaking the communion. Through his influence the Virginia Conference petitioned the General Assembly of Virginia to pass a law for the immediate or gradual emancipation of all the slaves. Coke and Asbury visited George Washington at Mount Vernon to plead with him to sign the petition. Washington agreed to signify his indorsement if the Assembly took the matter under consideration.

In his own person, to the date of his death, Coke represented what might be called the whole foreign-missionary operations of Methodism. He founded the Wesleyan Missions in the West Indies, in many parts of England, Wales and Ireland, and, though he himself never reached either continent, in Africa and Asia. On his first voyage to America he read the lives of Francis Xavier and David Brainerd. Of Xavier's life he wrote in his *Journal:* "O for a soul like his! I seem to want the wings of an eagle and the voice of a trumpet that I may proclaim the gospel through the East and the West and the North and the South." Of Brainerd he exclaims, "O that I may follow him as he followed Christ!" It

"I MADE A COLLECTION"

is one of those picturesque coincidences in the romance of Providence that on the very day on which David Brainerd, that missionary to the American Indians, whose journal played so great a part in launching the missionary movement of the nineteenth century, died, Thomas Coke was born.

Everywhere Coke was intent on the sending of missionaries to new territory, usually becoming himself responsible for their support. The real beginning of Methodist foreign missions in America was at the very birth hour of the Methodist Church, at the "Christmas Conference" of 1784. In Coke's *Journal* he records, "One of the week days at noon I made a collection toward assisting our brethren who were going to Nova Scotia; and our friends generously contributed fifty pounds of currency." This puts foreign missions in the Methodist Episcopal Church at the same hour as the church itself and Coke deserves all the credit. Yet inadequate recognition has been paid to Coke in this connection.

Before the days of William Carey, Coke was possessed with a consuming zeal for foreign missions. He proposed a mission to India before Carey and Thomas went out in 1793. As early as January, 1784, he had framed "A plan for the establishment of Missions among the Heathen," and his name led the subscribers for its support. It was a poetic culmination of his life that its last enterprise should be the organization of a mission of the Wesleyan Church of England to go to India and that just at the threshold of that work he should die at sea.

This heritage of the missionary spirit was never lost. An organized Missionary Society was not formed in the Methodist Church until 1819, but a large amount of early pioneering work was missionary and supported by collections in the more settled portions of the country. It would not be entirely fantastic to describe the service of foreign missions from the United States as the gift made to the world by the American Indian. For it was the missionary experience gained in efforts to evangelize the Indians and the passion generated by that experience which was turned to the wider fields of non-Christian lands.

The development of the missionary interest in England, in the days of William Carey, coincided with a revival of interest in the evangelization of the Indians in the churches of the United States. There had been very early missions to the Indians, largely personal on the part of a few apostolic souls such as John Eliot and David Brainerd. But that interest sadly lagged until about the close of the century. Then, as the settlers pushed out to the frontier across the Alleghany Mountains, contact with the retreating Indians was reestablished. This contact often took the form of battle, capture, and massacre of the whites. No doubt there was an aspect of selfish prudence which made many thoughtful people perceive that the surest way of dealing with the Indian menace was not through military attack but by his conversion to Christian ideals of conduct.

That does not explain, however, the new missionary movement. It was part of the birth of interest in world evangelization and the birth of conscience on the world's spiritual destitution. A great many in the churches in America, which sent out missionaries, first to the Indians and later to the white settlers on the frontier, looked on their program as part of one common enterprise in Europe and America to Christianize the whole world.

It was in such a time that the famous "Haystack Prayer Meeting" at Williams College in 1806 occurred, and Samuel J. Mills and others definitely offered themselves as "missionaries to the heathen." Then followed, as a result, the organization of the American Board of Commissioners for Foreign Missions in 1810. In 1814 the Baptist Missionary Union was founded and in 1819 the Methodist Missionary Society. Such development was inevitable. For years the religious needs of the frontier on the west had been breaking down a provincial idea of the gospel. It had been training the churches to send out both men and money. The missionary movement beginning with the haystack group of missionary volunteers simply enlarged the missionary horizon of the churches from the frontier to the far non-Christian lands.

This general process can be distinctly traced in the Methodist Church. The missionary work among the whites of the frontier preceded that among the Indians. Both led to the enlargement of the undertaking to include "foreign" missions.

§ 2. John Stewart

No romancer ever imagined a tale surpassing in interest and surprise that of John Stewart, a Negro, the first Methodist missionary to the Indians.

Methodism was much later than some other denominations in the evangelizing of the Indian, except as here and there some of the Indians came under its influence. And its first missionary to the Indians was a Negro.

In the little town of Marietta, Ohio, on a Sunday in 1815, an itinerant preacher was addressing a congregation in a voice so loud and penetrating that it sounded far beyond the building in which he spoke. Had the voice been sweet and low, restrained and cultured, history would doubtless have been different. But the preacher was in the true

"HE RESOLVED TO GO TO THE INDIANS"

apostolic succession of Whitefield, as far as voice was concerned. And his tones reached a Negro, John Stewart, addicted to drink. Some traditions say that he was drunk at the time, some that he was on his way to throw himself in the Ohio River. Those may be bits of embroidery in the story to add to the thrill. But the story is thrilling enough in its irreducible facts. Stewart followed the voice, listened to the sermon, which reached his conscience, and as a result he was converted. The next Sunday he joined the church and it was not long before he had resolved to go as a missionary to the Indians. He could read and had a fine voice for singing. He first went to the Delaware tribe on the Muskingum, then to upper Sandusky. It was no jaunty camping trip he had undertaken and he was frequently in danger of his life. He often saved his life by giving a vivid demonstration of the claim that "music hath power to sooth the savage breast." Among the wigwams of the Wyandotts he found a captive Negro, stolen as a child in Virginia, who became his interpreter. Stewart's work spread until he had the whole Wyandott clan under his influence. He was made a local preacher and continued his work until his death eight years later, in 1823.

§ 3. THE MISSIONARY SOCIETY LAUNCHED

This enterprise awakened wide interest in the church. The Ohio Conference adopted the mission in 1819 and other missionaries were sent out. The Indian mission spread so rapidly that three years after Stewart went out into the wilds the Missionary Society came into being.

Under the urgent need, and due to awakened interest, local missionary societies had sprung up in Philadelphia, Boston, and other localities. The New York Preachers' Meeting drafted a constitution for a general missionary society and in the Bowery Church, April 5, 1819, the Missionary and Bible Society of the Methodist Episcopal Church in America was organized. In 1820 this society was indorsed and adopted by the General Conference.

Strange as it may seem, this infant Society had to perform the prodigious labors of the child Hercules and strangle boa constrictors that would have crushed a less lusty infant. If there are any arguments against foreign missions which were not hurled at the Society, it was surely an oversight, soon remedied. Worse than all opposition was the apathy and indifference from the great majority of the church at first. That terrible word, "unmethodistic," was hurled at the innovation.

Though the Society proposed to work in the home field, many suspicious souls feared that it would soon branch out into foreign lands. Well founded fears! "Bitter-enders" railed against such "foreign entanglements" of the church. Several of the managers tendered their resignations. All this made all the more creditable and heroic the determination of those who stuck by the ship while it was running against such heavy seas.

The movement, however, was too inevitable an expression of the genius of Methodism and of the growing missionary temper of the times to be long retarded, and after the General Conference of 1820 the Society began its work and gained strength with every passing year. The Bible part of the work was soon turned over to the American Bible Society.

It is worth remembrance that the birth of the modern missionary movement in Protestantism, one of the great epochs in Christian history, was in itself to a very large degree the result of the Evangelical Revival of the eighteenth century, which was set in motion by the Wesleys and Whitefield. So that when the Methodism of America felt the impulse of that movement, which resulted in the great missionary societies of Great Britain, and had now crossed the Atlantic, it was receiving the spiritual impulse which had originally started in the Methodist movement.

The first twelve years of the work of the Society was occupied with work in the United States. The line between home and foreign missions was not and could not be clearly defined. California and Oregon were then much farther in point of time, effort in reaching them, and expense than are India and China to-day.

The first missionary sent out by the Society went to the French in Louisiana, an effort which met with practically no success.

Missions among the Indians were spread among the Creeks and Cherokees in Georgia and Tennessee and the

Choctaws in Mississippi, the Oneidas and the Onandagas in New York, the Mohawks in Canada, and, as we have already seen, the Flatheads in Oregon. Among the white settlers of the frontier missionaries carried the work of the church into Oregon, Texas, California, Montana, Idaho, Nevada, Colorado, New Mexico, and Arizona. Distinctive work among the Negroes was among the earliest efforts of the Society and was continued till the division of the church in 1844.

§ 4. THE FIRST FOREIGN MISSION

The first foreign missionary was sent to Liberia in 1832.

The sailing of the first missionary to a foreign land ever sent out by the Methodist Episcopal Church is so significant a date that it deserves a pause to grasp its large meaning. For it marks the advent of a new epoch in the story of Methodism. It marks the time and place at which the Methodist Church became a part of the greatest spiritual movement of the nineteenth century. In the second chapter, "A Tale of Two Villages," we have already linked the great spiritual movement of the seventeenth century, the Puritan Reformation and the consequent founding of New England, with that of the eighteenth century, the Evangelical Period, led by the Wesleys and Whitefield. The modern foreign missionary enterprise is likewise the distinctive spiritual movement of the nineteenth century. It was a Christian Renaissance, a new flowering, a fresh springtime that swept over the church in Europe and America and in the course of a century profoundly affected the whole status and future of the Christian religion in the world. Only as we see the growth of Methodist missions as one current in this great stream do we get the setting and background necessary to its understanding.

It is natural to ask, "Why, if the missionary awakening can be fairly described as nothing less than a renaissance, a rebirth of the churches, did foreign missions move so slowly in the Methodist Church?" For the idea was at least forty years in taking a really effective form. One explanation is undoubtedly that foreign missions was such a thoroughgoing innovation, such a radical expansion of the thought and life of the whole Christian Church at large, that it could only win its way slowly, just as the Reformation itself moved slowly. It was a springtime, but spring does not come in a day. The first great souls in Great Britain and America who felt the missionary call as a personal obligation had to convince an incredible and reluctant church. The springtime of missionary awakening took approximately fifty years to reach the full summer of wide and sustained interest.

In addition to this, the actual undertaking of foreign missions in the Methodist Church was held back for years by the lack of suitable candidates. There was no "haystack" group of young men, such as that headed by Samuel J. Mills, whose insistent demand to go to India led to the organization of the American Board of Commissioners for Foreign Missions in 1810 and the sailing of the first missionaries only two years later, in 1812. One reason for this was undoubtedly the lack of Methodist colleges at this time, for colleges have been the most fruitful centers of missionary contagion.

In 1825 the Missionary Society asked the bishops to appoint missionaries to Africa and South America. Yet it was seven years before one was found for Africa and ten before the first missionary was sent to South America. Africa was evidently chosen as the first field because of the familiarity gained through religious work among Negroes in the United States. There was the additional appeal of Liberia, in that it was the project of an American Colonization Society, then in its first stages, an undertaking which was itself partly missionary in its conception. By act of Congress Africans recaptured from slavers were authorized to be restored to the coast of Africa under the care of agents of the United States.

The honor of being the first foreign missionary of the Methodist Episcopal Church belongs to Melville Cox. One indication of the changed conceptions of foreign missions at the end of a century since Cox went out is to be found in the fact that a man in Cox's broken-down health would not to-day have a chance of being sent to the field of any mission board in the world. He had repeatedly failed to stand the strain of pastoral work in the United States. He had just buried his wife and child and was badly depleted in spirit as well as in health. He had reached the point of despair over ever being able to achieve anything important. Yet, on expressing willingness to go to Liberia, the first of the following May he was appointed. There seems to have been no question raised about the wisdom of sending this young man with a pronounced case of tuberculosis to one of the worst climates in the world!

"LET A THOUSAND FALL!"

Yet his going out, his courageous and intrepid spirit, his heroic death, gave an impetus to the missionary spirit of Methodism which it has never lost. It may be said with truth that Cox's missionary career of only four months (a shorter time than he spent on the voyage out) stirred Methodist missions into life. His legacy to the church in the watchword, "Let a thousand fall before Africa be given up," coupled with the inspiration of his own courageous, devoted spirit, has undoubtedly done more for the cause than fifty years of successful missionary work would have done. The immediate effect was felt in the going out of five new missionaries the next year, notwithstanding Cox's death.

Cox lived long enough in Africa to demonstrate that he had some genuine missionary ability as well as spirit. In particular, he soon grasped the idea that has been central in real missionary success in the last century, that the evangelization of a land must be done by its own natives. After a month on the field he reported (April, 1833), "I have thought too that *through them* [the natives] the gospel might be more readily communicated to the natives around them." It is worth recording that the first foreign missionary of the church, in his first month on the field, should have forseen this major line of strategy. Three months later Cox died.

The mission to Liberia was continued despite enormous difficulties. Eleven missionaries were appointed in the first three years—just one third of the whole number of thirty-three who went to Liberia in the first fifty years. The mortality was high. Three others beside Cox died on the field in the first three years. This first foreign mission of Methodism has never been either relatively important or successful, compared with other missions of the church. After fifty years the membership in Liberia was less than twenty-three hundred. Not until fifty years passed did Methodism spread to other sections of Africa. But numbers are never a fair or full measure of spiritual endeavor. The first missionary venture deepened the interest of the church in foreign missions and has done service in holding the great continent of Africa in the imagination and close to the heart of Methodism.

§ 5. SOUTH AMERICA

The field for which Melville Cox had first volunteered, South America, was the second foreign mission undertaken by Methodism. Nearness, of course, had directed the interest to the continent on the south and this appeal of proximity was increased by a decided patriotic appeal. South American republics had been set up after successful revolutions against Spain and Portugal. These revolutions could not help but awaken enthusiastic sympathy in a nation only two generations away from its own Independence Day. The Monroe Doctrine, so recently promulgated, was a stimulant both to the feelings of interest, and to a certain extent, of obligations and responsibility.

Yet it was thirty-five years from the time that the missionary society first decided to undertake a mission in South America, until a permanent work among the native Spanish-speaking people of South America was established. This thirty-five years extended from 1832 to 1867 and was a long time in which to test the endurance and patience of the missionary interest of the church. It was also a long lesson in the difficulty and complexity of the missionary enterprise, a lesson which the church has been rather thoroughly taught during a century of endeavor and experiment.

In 1836 the two first missionaries went out, one going to Rio de Janeiro, Brazil, and the other to Buenos Aires. The mission to Brazil had only a short life, being abandoned in 1841. The mission at Buenos Aires had a longer and somewhat more successful history, but it too was abandoned for a time in 1841. It was renewed, however, after a few years, and in 1867 work among the Spanish speaking peoples was opened, which has proved permanent and has expanded into ten countries in South America.

Evidently during these years the church was not only learning its first lessons in missionary technique but also in missionary faith. Later ventures were not so readily abandoned from lack of immediate results, or in the face of difficulties either on the field or financial difficulties at the home base. The church had learned patience.

§ 6. CHINA

The next field to be entered by Methodism was China in 1847, eleven years after South America. Some Protestant missionary work had been already carried on in China for forty-three years. Robert Morrison was the first Protestant missionary to China, being sent out in 1807 by the London Missionary Society. He had done monumental work in translating, including his translation of the New Testament and the Chinese Dictionary.

China was the most distant missionary field yet entered by American missionaries, yet there had been forged a link of strong interest in China and the Far East by the New England shipping trade in the early part of the nineteenth century. Yankee clipper ships had spread swift wings for the South Seas and China, lured by the profitable trade. The towns of Salem, Boston, New Bedford, Providence, and others had a distinctly Oriental aspect, a fantastic and gay color against the Puritan background. Even to-day the porcelain, brocade, and lacquer brought from China still shine against the plain white walls of many New England homesteads. This interest and touch with China and the East helped to stimulate and direct missionary activity in that direction.

Perhaps partly due to the lesson learned in the South American mission, the China mission was established by the Missionary Society with a clear understanding that "immediate results" of a large nature could not be expected. A number of yearly pledges to run through ten years were made for the support of missionaries before they were sent out. The first two missionaries arrived in Foochow, in September, 1847. Foochow had been selected because it was unoccupied by other missionary forces, had a population of over half a million, and was the center of an important province.

The enormity of the task of these first missionaries to

China is almost beyond the power of the imagination to conceive. The ponderous mass of the population and its effect on the missionary is very well summed up in the remark of a new missionary on arriving at Canton a century later: "I had always heard there were four hundred million Chinese. I never quite believed it, but they were all down at the dock with me." The whole procedure was then an experiment with no paths or traditions to follow. The language difficulty was impressively stated by Milne, Morrison's advocate in the translation of the Bible, "To learn Chinese is a work for men with bodies of brass, lungs of steel, heads of oak, hands of spring steel, eyes of eagles, hearts of apostles, memories of angels, and lives of Methuselah."

One aspect of the entrance of Methodism into China attracted very little attention at the time but has loomed larger and larger in the seventy-five years which have followed, until to-day it is the pivotal aspect of the whole missionary enterprise in China. That is that the missionary was ushered into the country by the gunboat. The very city in which the Methodist work began, Foochow, had been forced open to Western trade and occupation at the end of a victorious war, "the Opium War," conducted by Great Britain against China. "The Opium War," by which the curse of opium was forced on China by British armies, is one of the blackest pages in the whole history of Christendom. The vicious traffic in opium had been introduced from India and the British opposed the prohibition placed upon it by the Chinese. The efforts of China to rid itself of this monstrous plague were desperate and sincere. In 1838 the Chinese government made the use of opium a capital offense. But opium was forced on China by the military power of a Christian nation, and unequal treaties were wrung from her by force. What a fine prelude for the missionary of Christ! To-day this past record is giving basis for China's anti-foreign feeling.

Nothing can better show the difference between the missionary motive and feeling at that time and to-day than the fact that of the incongruity of the means by which the way was cleared for the missionaries was not then keenly realized. In-

deed, the forcing open of port cities by unequal treaties forced at the cannon's mouth were heralded as "a marvelous opportunity prepared by the providence of God!" The ethical aspect of the situation did not clearly appear as it appears to-day.

Five months after the missionaries arrived in Foochow a school was opened. Preaching was begun, some recruits soon arrived and eight years later, in 1855, the first church was erected. These years were crowded with massed discouragements, including sickness and death of missionaries. Not until ten years had passed was the first convert baptized in 1857. But Morrison had endured the same test of patience and faith, for he labored seven years before baptizing his first convert. When he died in 1834, after thirty years' work, he had seen only ten converts baptized. It is doubtful if by 1850, after almost a half-century of terrific labor, there were a hundred Christian converts in all China.

CHAPTER XVIII

METHODIST BREAKS AND FRACTURES

§ 1. Gains and Losses

SO FAR the story of Methodism as we have been telling it has been a tale of uninterrupted growth. Beginning with the first preaching in London and Bristol, we have seen a new church come into being and, in a century, become almost the largest Protestant body in the English-speaking world. We have tried not to burden our story with statistics, for we have not been writing a cold and formal record of this movement. But perhaps it may give something of a standard by which to gauge the power which the Methodist movement developed when we say that when 1839 came and the Methodists in all parts of the world turned to celebrating the one hundredth anniversary of John Wesley's transforming experience in Aldersgate Street, they found that there were more than 6,000 regularly appointed Methodist preachers in Great Britain and the United States; more than 1,400,000 communicant members of the churches; and missionaries at work in Sweden, Germany, France, Cadiz, Gibraltar, Malta, western and southern Africa, Ceylon, India, New South Wales, Van Dieman's Land, New Zealand, Tonga, the Habai islands, the Vavou islands, the Fiji islands, and throughout the West Indies! The number of missionaries alone was larger than the whole number of Methodist preachers at the time of Wesley's death, and the number of communicants on these mission fields was about equal to the whole number of Methodists in Europe when the founder died! No wonder that the centenary of 1839 was a signal for rejoicing throughout the Methodist world.

But if Methodism, both in America and in England, had

been growing at a marvelous rate, it had also known its losses. It seems to be true of every religious movement that, as it gains in age and power, it also gains in conservatism and rigidity. The result is generally that there arise within it some persons who chafe under the restrictions imposed by this conservatism, and who finally feel impelled to launch out on new spiritual adventures.

John Wesley recognized this tendency, and well he might, for the Methodism he knew was essentially just such a launching out from an old and settled church order. He quoted a remark of Luther's that a religious revival seldom continues more than thirty years, and held it to be a sign of divine blessing that the Methodist movement had kept its evangelistic fire for a period at least longer than that. But he knew that the danger would be that, with the passing of time, the new church would become almost as timorous as the old Anglicanism had been, and in this prevision he was later proved to be justified.

In this chapter it is our purpose to tell the story of some of the breaks that came within Methodism. We do this with some hesitation, for it is not pleasant to have to admit that a church which started on the broad basis of fellowship laid down by John Wesley could ever prove too small for any of its members. But these secessions did come, and there may be more than passing value in seeing why they came. Perhaps if we can see the sort of blunders made in the past, we can guard against a repetition of such mistakes in the future.

Against one thing we need to be on guard in reading about such unhappy events of the long ago. We who are reading are, in most cases, members of the church or churches from which the men and women of whom we shall read went out. We love our church. We can see little fault in it. We find it hard to understand why any person should ever have withdrawn from it. One easy explanation that springs to our minds is that there must have been something the matter with the person who withdrew, or he would never have taken such a step.

Several times the story of the incidents we are about to relate has been told as though the men most immediately concerned were not only mistaken—which they may or may not have been—but as though they were morally at fault. Some have talked of these men, and written of them, as though they were bad men. And that they certainly were not. Some of them were extraordinarily good men; saints. All of them were men moved by high motives. Therefore it is the more important that we should understand why they felt that they must leave our ranks. For we do not want that sort of bitter choice to be forced on good men and women again.

§ 2. The O'Kelley Movement

The first great break in the Methodist ranks, after Methodism had become a church, came in Virginia, and resulted in the withdrawal of one of the best known of the preachers and presiding elders of that day, together with a considerable following of preachers and church members. The man who withdrew was named James O'Kelley, and the cause of his withdrawal was his belief that the young Methodist Episcopal Church—for this happened only eight years after the church had officially been formed—was becoming an ecclesiastical despotism which had no proper place in a republic.

The new church which O'Kelley tried to found he called the Republican Methodist Church, to indicate the essential difference between him and the communion from which he had withdrawn. The new church was not a permanency; its founder lacked the qualities necessary to make it such; but the division which brought it into being was much more a result of the spirit of those times than, as some have tried to say, of any defect in O'Kelley's character.

To understand the O'Kelley secession we must remember that it all took place in the years immediately following the Revolutionary War. Freedom and equality were the catchwords on every lip. Those words were probably held more strongly in Virginia—the Virginia of Patrick Henry and Thomas Jefferson—than anywhere else. There was everywhere a fear of aristocracy, and a determination never to submit to another despotism. The ostensible issue on which the war had been fought was the right of representation in government. But here was this Methodist Episcopal Church, growing within the young republic, with a Britisher as its bishop —for Asbury never took the oath of allegiance to the United States—and a form of government which made the bishop the absolute arbiter of the fate of the preachers. Asbury, be it remembered, would never consult with even his presiding elders as to what the appointments were to be. And O'Kelley became convinced that the system was wrong.

The issue on which O'Kelley finally took his cause to the Methodist General Conference was that, after the bishop had announced the appointments of the preachers, if anyone felt himself to have been wronged, he should have the right of appeal to the Conference, and if the Conference felt that he had just cause for his appeal, the bishop should then give him another appointment. The debate continued for three days. Some of the best men in the church—among them Freeborn Garrettson—supported O'Kelley. But at last the vote was taken, and O'Kelley lost. The argument which prevailed seems to have been that if the bishop was thus forced to change one appointment it would derange the whole list of appointments, which shows the readiness of Methodism to be guided by considerations of practicability rather than of theory.

Then O'Kelley withdrew. We feel that he made a mistake in so doing, but we are judging with the advantage of more than a hundred years. He felt that the church had been delivered into the hands of a one-man autocracy, and that he would not abide.

As we have said, the O'Kelley withdrawal did not bring about the creation of any permanent church. Some of the best of the men who went out with O'Kelley came back again. William McKendree was one of them. Asbury went out of his way to convince McKendree, for whom a great career was already opening, that, whatever the theory, the bishop would not abuse his powers, and McKendree, the veteran of Yorktown, was soon back in the ranks.

But O'Kelley never came back. He lived a long and honorable life as a Christian preacher, and died respected, even beloved, throughout the region in which he had centered his ministry. The church lost heavily in Virginia and North Carolina by his secession. It was really but the start of a process which has been under way ever since, by which the powers of the episcopacy have gradually been curtailed.

§ 3. THE FIRST BREAKS IN ENGLAND

Another important Methodist separation came in England, and led to the formation of what is known as the Primitive Methodist Church. After the death of John Wesley, as we have seen, British Methodism swiftly moved from its rather ambiguous position as an organization of religious societies, partly within and much more without the state church, into a position as a recognized free church.

At the same time there came the transformation which changed England into the world's greatest manufacturing country, and the men who had been the small shopkeepers and the small factory operators of Wesley's day became the merchant princes of what we call the industrial revolution. By the thousands these people were in the Wesleyan Church, and when they grew wealthy and settled and conservative in their outlook on life, they insensibly made their churches much the same. So that the Wesleyan Church soon became the most formal, most stately, and most rigid of all the non-Anglican churches in England, and that position it holds to this day.

Of course, there were many English Methodists who did not take easily to a rigid church order. John Wesley had hardly been dead five years before independent societies, with their own chapels and leaders, began to spring up here and there, and to carry on religious services in a way they felt to be according to the original Methodist pattern. These adventures were generally discredited by the main church body as the work of "revivalists"—which seems a strange enough taunt to be thrown at any part of the Wesleyan movement! Then, just a little more than ten years after Wesley's death there appeared in England a strange figure, a wandering American evangelist, Lorenzo Dow.

Dow started his career as a regularly appointed Methodist preacher in Maine, but he had the same impulsion in him that Whitefield and the Wesleys knew, and before he died, in middle life, he had conducted a notable ministry in many lands. He was undoubtedly an eccentric, and it would have taken a superelastic church order of any kind to have held him. But he did great good in the world. In England he told of the development of the camp meetings in America, and recommended them as a means of reviving the evangelistic fires which were burning lower and lower in the Wesleyan Church.

The dignified leaders of the British church could see nothing but danger in such a strange form of Christian worship as a camp meeting. They forbade their preachers or their members having anything to do with the meetings. And when two local preachers, one named Hugh Bourne and the other William Clowes, persisted in conducting such meetings, they were expelled.

Neither man seems to have wanted to start a new church, but the situation thus created made that inevitable. There was a whole range of Wesleyanism which could not rest content within a church that had no room for irregular and unusual forms of service. Out of the multitude who felt in this way there came those who gathered around Bourne and Clowes to form the Primitive Methodist Church—a body which has had a great part in the life of modern England.

Not long after the expulsion of Bourne and Clowes had led to the formation of the Primitive Methodists, another body, known as the Bible Christians, came into being. The man who is generally regarded as the founder of this communion, William O'Bryan, was also a local preacher expelled from the older body. His fault seems to have been a determination to preach anywhere he felt there were needy people, whether he had been regularly appointed to such places or not. He was accused of not being regular in his attendance at class meeting, which was probably true, since he spent so much time away from home preaching in otherwise unevangelized communities. He, too, formed the nucleus of a work which displayed extensive spiritual power, and which finally became one of the principal parts of what is now known as the United Methodist Free Church, the third of the principal Methodist bodies in England.

§ 4. The Methodist Protestant Church

The separation of O'Kelley and his followers from the Methodist Episcopal Church did not, as we have seen, lead to the establishment of any large or permanent church. The next important break in American Methodism, however, did so.

In a way, this trouble arose out of the same cause as did the earlier one. The departure of O'Kelley had not lessened the feeling of many Methodists that there must be more democ-

ARRIVING AT GENERAL CONFERENCE, 1820

racy in the government of the churches. One result was an effort to have the presiding elders elected—a provision actually voted by the General Conference of 1820, with several of the leaders of the church, such as Bishop George, Beverly Waugh, and John Emory, favoring it. Another was in increasing agitation for the admission of laymen into the Conferences.

Looked at from this distance, and in the light of history, it is hard to understand why the good men who proposed that laymen should enter the Annual and General Conferences should have been treated as they were. They called themselves reformers. Their opponents called them radicals. The upshot of a long and heated controversy was that the reformers withdrew and formed the Methodist Protestant Church.

The center of their agitation was in Baltimore, and that has always been the center of the church which they founded. It has held a steady course through the years, bearing a worthy part in the religious life of the nation. And as the years have passed its leaders have had the satisfaction of seeing some of the proposals out of which the separation came adopted by the body which had no room for the "radicals" of 1830.

§ 5. THE BREAK OVER SLAVERY

Of course, the great break in American Methodism came in 1844, when the slavery issue led to the formation of the Methodist Episcopal Church, South. It is not our purpose to tell the story of that rupture in great detail, for we do not wish to uncover old wounds. But the way by which the break came to pass has some suggestions of value for the church's future.

The position of John Wesley on slavery was clear-cut. He called it "the sum of all villainies." Doctor Coke, who brought Wesley's plan for the formation of the new church to America, brought also an equally unequivocal conviction as to the evil of the slave trade, and never hesitated to proclaim his views when he was preaching in this country. In certain places in the South, the courageous little Doctor came near being mobbed for his plain speech on the subject. Coke and Asbury, going together to Mount Vernon, obtained from George Washington that hero's private condemnation of the traffic, and it will be remembered that at his death Washington freed his slaves.

The early Methodist preachers all seem to have felt about alike on the subject. They not only liberated their own slaves, as in the case of Garrettson, but they wrote into the conclusions of that first Conference of 1784 the necessity of taking immediately "some effectual method to extirpate this abomination from among us." Rules were adopted requiring members who owned slaves and lived in States where emancipation was possible to free them or to withdraw from the church. If they refused to withdraw, they were to be expelled.

What the outcome might have been, proceeding from such a start, no man can now say. But in the year 1793 a Yankee schoolmaster, temporarily living in the Carolinas, invented a machine that made it possible to separate the seeds from cotton at a rate to make large-scale cotton-growing one of the world's most profitable industries. And immediately, the African slave became not a luxury, but the backbone of the commercial life of the South. Slavery acquired an economic importance which made its continuation seem to spell the difference between wealth and poverty to the cotton planters. The result was that, overnight, the institution grew to be almost sacred in the eyes of the ruling families who lived on the plantations, and so the issue came to be formed out of which came misery and bloodshed to millions.

The Methodists found it impossible to maintain their absolute rejection of slavery as morally indefensible in the face of this changed condition. From the clean-cut stand of 1784 they kept retreating by little and by little, until finally they reached the place where they left it largely to each Annual Conference as to what the attitude of the Methodists in the region should be. By 1808 the church had reached the point where it had nothing to say about slaveholding by its individual members, and only refused to admit slaveholders to official positions in cases where they failed to emancipate their slaves when the laws made that possible.

Then began the growth of the abolition movement in the North. Soon, abolitionists began to crop out in the Methodist Church. But, so anxious were the authorities to keep the peace, that these abolitionist preachers—most of them young men— had a hard time. Young men were refused admission into the Methodist ministry because they favored abolition. Bishops refused so much as to let Conference committees consider resolutions bearing on the slavery issue. Men were suspended from the ministry for having attended anti-slavery meetings, or having written anti-slavery tracts. This, remember, was not in the South; it was in New England and in New York. Finally, after the General Conference of 1840 had turned its face against the abolitionists, not even allowing a minority report to be presented, some of the most uncompromising withdrew and formed the Wesleyan Methodist Church, which continues to this day.

The great break came with startling suddenness only four years later. During the quadrennium there had been a great increase of anti-slavery sentiment in the North, and an equal stiffening of sentiment in the South. The tense situation resulting was thrown into the General Conference in unexpected fashion. Up to that time the church had managed to escape any dramatic tussle with the slavery question by electing to its high offices only men who were not themselves slaveholders. But during the quadrennium of 1840-1844 Bishop James O. Andrew had married a second time and, through his wife, had come to be legally an owner of slaves. Bishop Andrew held the respect of every member of the church who knew him. No doubt has ever been cast on his nobility of character or purity of purpose. But he held the Southern point of view on the institution of slavery and here he was, a slave-owner!

Of the twists and turns of the great debate which grew out of the presence of a slaveholder in the bishopric, we will not tell here. If you care to read about it, you can go back to the books which tell the whole story, giving almost every word that excited debaters uttered during nearly a month of argument. But at the end, the Northern delegates pushed through a resolution which held that Bishop Andrew should "desist from the exercise of this office so long as this impediment remains." Nothing was said about other Methodists in the same situation. Reports at that time declared that there were 200 traveling preachers holding 1,600 slaves; about 1,000 local preachers holding 10,000; and about 25,000 church members holding 207,900 more. The Southerners felt that, if Bishop Andrew was to be punished, the others should be punished with him. But the Northerners were content to hold to the dramatic issue presented by the slaveholder in the episcopacy.

The most influential single figure in the church at that time was Bishop Joshua Soule. Bishop Soule was a Maine product who had been in the Methodist ministry from the beginning of the century. He was a granite-like figure; probably the most influential interpreter of Methodist law the church has ever known. In 1820, when the General Conference voted to make the presiding eldership an elective office, Soule refused to be consecrated to the bishopric to which he had already been elected, and was thus largely instrumental in forcing a reversal of that decision.

Now, in 1844, Soule summoned all the prestige of his reputation as a legalist to withstand this action leveled against Bishop Andrew. He showed that the rule of the church against slave-owning officeholders applied only in States where emancipation was legally possible. As Bishop Andrew lived in Georgia, which did not permit the freeing of slaves, he was clearly within the letter of church law. Moreover, the resolution seemed to Bishop Soule another attempt to question the rights of a bishop, as well as an attempt to punish a bishop without due process of law.

For this reason it came to pass that, when the Southerners

declared they could no longer remain in a church which had deprived a bishop of the rights of his office on the slavery issue, Joshua Soule, son of Maine, but much more son of some legalistic forebear whose name we do not know, marched forth at their head to lead them in the establishing of the Methodist Episcopal Church, South.

§ 6. WILLIAM BOOTH

Of one more rupture within the ranks of Methodism we must tell, and this time we again go back to England. When we do, we see a great man forced to break away from one of the Methodist c h u r c h e s which had itself felt forced to break away a handful of years before. The Methodist N e w Connection was the first of the important seceding Methodist bodies to be formed in Great Britain, being organized in 1797 largely on the issue of lay representation in church government. It had been marked from the beginning by evangelistic passion, and was less rigid in its regulations than the older Wesleyan body. Yet it could not find a place in its ministerial ranks for a man whose fault was that he wished to preach beyond the bounds of an ordinary circuit.

WILLIAM BOOTH

William Booth was born within the Wesleyan Church, but as he grew to manhood and felt the tug of the gospel ministry he passed into the membership of the New Connection. Even before his ordination he had given evidence of remarkable powers as an evangelist, and when he came into the regular ministry it was with the assumption that he would be free to do a widespread evangelistic work. He was fortunate in marrying one of the great women of modern times, a woman whose resolution carried him through many of the hours of discouragement which were to be his lot. She, more than any other person, held him to the conviction that his primary obligation was to the remarkable gifts which he had shown in evangelistic preaching.

The story has been told many times of the way in which William Booth and his wife went to the Annual Conference of 1861, held that year in Liverpool. Objection had already been made by many of the brethren to allowing the young preacher to go gallivanting all over England, holding meetings. And the sort of people to whom he persisted in preaching! Why, they were the dregs of society! It was clear to the veterans in the Conference what the outcome of such practices would be. On the one hand, they would lead other young preachers to undertake irregular missions, with a consequent end to all ministerial discipline, and, on the other, they would introduce a most undesirable element into the churches. So they insisted that something should be done to curb the young preacher. Yet Booth and his wife went to Conference praying that some measure of accommodation could be worked out.

The Conference, however, was not in a conciliatory mood. It did offer Booth what was regarded as a compromise, but it was really a means by which the young preacher would have been hopelessly shackled. At that, he might have accepted it, so much did he wish to avoid controversy, so deeply did he reverence all authority, and so great was his love for his church. But, when the moment of choice came, and the Conference watched to see whether he would come to heel or not, his wife settled the issue for him by springing to her feet from where

she sat in the gallery, exclaiming, "Never!" At that, Booth
rose, bowed to the chair, passed to the door, where his wife
met him, and together they walked out.

The rest of the Conference, we are told, accompanied
their departure with cries of "Order, order," which exactly
epitomized the issue at stake. For it was because of insistence
on the regular order, because, as William Booth's biographer
puts it, the other members of the Conference "wanted the
machine to run smoothly," that the apostle to the outcast had
to go outside Methodism to found the Salvation Army.

§ 7. WHY THESE LOSSES?

There have been other breaks during Methodism's less
than two centuries of history. No attempt has been made to
list them all here, just as no attempt has been made to tell all
the ins and outs of the ruptures which have been mentioned.
But there are a few reflections which come almost inevitably
to our minds as we review, even thus hurriedly, these sad
experiences.

In the first place, it seems almost ironical to find so many
of these secessions coming as protests against legalistic interpretations of church custom and order. For that was precisely
what Methodism itself was in the beginning! John Wesley
sought the fields and Charles Wesley went to the class meetings
and George Whitefield preached in the most unheard of places,
not because they particularly craved that sort of experience—
the Wesleys, at least, would much rather have stayed inside
the churches—but because they were determined that no deference to the details of ecclesiastical routine should keep the word
of salvation from masses of people who were in utter spiritual
destitution. The Wesleys were utterly irregular; John Wesley was an ecclesiastical rebel of the first order. Methodism
is the child of irregularity.

But, with Methodism once established, it soon solidified
into a regularity, an institutionalism of its own. That process

was well matured before John Wesley had been dead ten years. As long as Methodism remained a sort of a personal weapon wielded by one man, the atoms in that weapon had little responsibility for their relation to one another, and so little interest in the question. But that figure of speech could not be applied to the Methodism cut loose from Wesley, in America by the Revolutionary War, and in England by his death. After that, Methodism became, of necessity, a machine. It was, and is, a wonderful machine, which God has used in many marvelous ways during these years. But with the coming of the machine there came also the feeling which machines in running always arouse. "Don't monkey with the machinery," we warn. "If you tinker you are likely to do more harm than good."

The third point is this, that, while it is important to keep the machine running, it is important also that neglected truths should have their chance. Perhaps they will improve the machine. If they hurt the machine, it means that the machine needs changing.

The striking thing about the Methodist breaks we have been talking about in this chapter is, that, with the single exception of the great division of 1844, time has tended to bring support and a goodly measure of approval to the position taken. Methodism is getting further and further away from an autocratic bishopric every year, yet that is the issue on which O'Kelley went out. Both American Methodist Episcopal churches have laymen in their General Conferences now, and the Southern church has them in its Annual Conferences, yet that is the issue on which the founders of the Methodist Protestant Church went out. Nobody upholds the morality of slavery now, yet that is the issue on which the men who formed the American Wesleyan Methodist Church went out. In England, time has amply justified the formation of the Methodist New Connection, the Primitive Methodists, the Bible Christians, and the Salvation Army.

CHAPTER XIX

SOUTHERN METHODISM

§ 1. How the Break Came to the South

IN THE previous chapter the story has been told of the famous General Conference of 1844, which witnessed the break between the Northern and Southern Conferences of the Methodist Church. That story, however, is given much as any member of the Northern part of the church would tell it. It will be worth our while to look back for a few minutes at the same events as they appeared to the Methodists who lived in the South, for they were just as ardent Methodists as those in the North; just as sincere, just as devoted. And the church which, under the compulsion of those bitter days, they founded has been abundantly blessed of God.

Long ago in this record we noticed that early Methodism in the United States was largely a Southern affair. True, it is claimed that the first Methodist class was formed in New York—although Maryland vigorously contests that claim—but the Methodists first ran their roots down deep in the soil of the South. The membership of the church as long as Francis Asbury lived lay, in the main, south of the Mason and Dixon line. The leadership of the church was largely drawn from the South. Even such men as Freeborn Garrettson and Jesse Lee, Methodism's apostles extraordinary to New York and New England, were themselves Southerners. Bishop after bishop was chosen from the South.

This condition, it may be said in passing, formed only another of the remarkable parallels between the life of the Methodist Church and the life of the nation, for when the United States of America was born its center of influence was in the South. Four Virginians followed one another—broken only by the short administration of John Adams—in the Presidency, holding that office for thirty-two years. The various removals of the seat of government, from New York to Philadelphia, and finally from Philadelphia to the banks of the

THE FIRST CHURCH IN KENTUCKY

Potomac, were symbolic of the direction in which the signposts of power pointed in those days. Indeed, in the nation as in the church, it was only when the young and assertive Middle West found its future identified with the outcome of the free-soil struggle that the rule of the South was broken. The election of Abraham Lincoln, our first true prairie President, led to the formation of the Confederate States of America. The election of the General Conference of 1844, with the balance of power for the first time in the hands of Middle Western delegates, led to the formation of the Methodist Episcopal Church, South.

The seriousness of the slavery issue seems to have burst on the Southern delegates to that General Conference of 1844 as a stunning surprise. Communications in those days were meager. The country had already grown to such a size that its parts were separated by hundreds and even thousands of miles, and this physical separation was not bridged by the swift trains, the cheap and fast mail service, the ubiquitous periodical circulation we know to-day. At the General Conference of 1840, as we have seen, there had been no sign of any desire on the part of the Northern delegates to make the slavery issue an embarrassment to their Southern brethren. Indeed, the small anti-slavery minority from the North had felt the chance of stirring action on this subject so slight that it had withdrawn to form the Wesleyan Methodist Church.

A lot of change in thinking can take place in four years. There had been a decided shift in attitude on the part of the Northern churches during the interval between the General Conferences of 1840 and 1844, for this was the period when the United States agreed to annex Texas, that great slavery empire, and when the war with Mexico, which came in 1845, was looming on the horizon, with its promise of further additions to slave territory. In 1840 the abolition cause in the North had gained enough strength for William Lloyd Garrison to dare denounce the constitution of the United States as "a covenant with death and an agreement with hell" and by 1844 the formation of the Free Soil party was just around the corner. But apparently the Southern delegates came to the New York General Conference without ever realizing that these changes in Northern thinking were taking place.

We have already told of the way in which the technical possession of slaves by Bishop Andrew, of Georgia, became the rock on which the church split. We have admitted that the law of the church was on the side of the Southerners, and that Bishop Andrew was a good man, one of those unfortunates of history whose fate it is to symbolize a cause lost long ago. We will not go over all that ground again. It is enough to say that, whatever the law, the Northerners were clearly right in the attitude which they took on the immediate question. If a bishop was a person who traveled at large through the connection, as the *Discipline* said he was, exercising religious authority wherever he went, then the time had come when, law or no law, the Northern churches must be protected against the travels of a slave-owning bishop. For the coming of such a bishop to the churches of the North and Middle West, with public opinion on the slavery issue what it was after the war with Mexico, would have laid those churches open to such general contumely as would have utterly wiped out their spiritual influence.

JOSHUA SOULE

When, however, the Southern delegates saw that t h e Northerners were determined to push through the resolution which should call on Bishop Andrew to cease to travel as a bishop, they felt that there was only one course to take. They had not dreamed of facing any such contingency when they left their homes. Bishop Andrew was, of all men at the Conference, most surprised and most nonplussed at what developed there. But the Southerners did not hesitate. They did not try to work out a compromise which might have held things together a little longer. They recognized the situation for what it was—one of those famous meetings between an accepted' theory and an implacable fact. So, quietly, perhaps somewhat grimly, but with every evidence of deep sorrow, the Southern delegates, led by stern old Bishop Soule, went home to form their new church.

§ 2. The Birth of the Southern Church

However much the delegates at the General Conference of 1844 may have felt obliged to disagree on the issues there at stake, they came to have a high regard for one another. When it was clear that the Northerners were going to stand by their action on Bishop Andrew, and when it was clear that this meant that the Southerners would leave the church, it became the first interest of men on both sides to see that the break was handled in a spirit of scrupulous fairness and gave rise to as little hard feeling as possible. Accordingly, a plan of separation was adopted which, under seven provisions, did everything that was possible to secure all their rights for the men who were to form a new church. It was a document both just and generous, and, had it been approved by the Northern church, it would have lessened materially the difficulties between the two churches which the years have seen.

The Southern delegates reported this plan of separation to the Conferences from which they had come, and suggested that a convention be called to bring the new church, acting under its provisions, into existence. This convention met in Louisville, Kentucky, a year after the New York General Conference. Bishop Soule and Bishop Andrew were on hand to preside. It provided that a General Conference should be held the next year at Petersburg, Virginia—later to become a fated name in American history—and that the Methodist Episcopal Church, South, composed of thirteen Annual Conferences which would not approve the New York decision concerning Bishop Andrew, should come into being. That General Conference met in 1846 as voted; it began to function at once as though there never had been a break; it elected two new bishops; founded a mission in China; provided for all the general church offices which had been known under the old order, and, in short, started the new church off at high speed.

One other thing that Petersburg General Conference did. It chose Dr. Lovick Pierce, one of the most eloquent preachers in Methodism, to go as its fraternal delegate to the General Conference of the other branch of the church, which was to meet in Pittsburgh in 1848. Doctor Pierce sought, by this mission, to confirm the attitude of mutual brotherly regard in which the Conference had adjourned in 1844. But it was not to be. For the men in control of the Northern General Conference of 1848 were not in the mood of the men of 1844. The plan of separation had been voted down by the Annual Conferences of the North. Editors of church papers, and others whose words carried far, had spent four years berating the Southerners as seceders, defiers of church discipline, champions of slavery. The Pittsburgh Conference refused to receive the Southern delegate. So Doctor Pierce sent word that this would be the last time Southern Methodists would come offering fraternity; that any future advance in that direction must be made by the North. And, sorrowfully, he turned homeward.

The rejection of the plan of separation by the Northern church made the Southerners look to the courts to establish their rights. The plan had provided that they should have their full share of the church's property, both in buildings, real estate, and in the values created by the extraordinarily successful Book Concern. Now, with the North refusing to give them these things voluntarily, the South sought to have the courts compel such action. Of course the Southerners were not primarily concerned with the money involved, although that was an item worth taking into account. What they wanted was a legal decision which would show that they were not seceders but one party to a "plan of separation" mutually agreed upon. And this the Supreme Court of the United States gave them. For when the case finally reached that highest of all tribunals, the Southern contention was sustained on every point. Dr. John Alfred Faulkner, one of the eminent historians of the Methodist Episcopal Church, has said, "Few impartial minds will doubt that the decision of the Supreme Court rendered substantial justice."

§ 3. THE SOUTHERN CHURCH AND THE WAR

After the organization of the Methodist Episcopal Church, South, and the upholding of its legal position by the courts, there was little in its history of an unusual nature until 1861. The General Conferences came every four years, just as they had before the break. The Annual Conferences met every year. The machinery of church government was just what it had been; the methods of working and the content of the preaching had not altered. The Southern church was perhaps a trifle more evangelistic in tone than its Northern neighbor. As the slavery issue grew more acute, this was natural. Northern preachers found it impossible to keep slavery out of their pulpits, nor did they want to do so. Southerners, on the other hand, wanted no attention paid to such a disputed social issue; they preferred "the old gospel." Revival fires burned brightly almost every year in most of the territory of the Southern church.

As a result, the church grew rapidly in membership. At the close of its first official quadrennium of life, in 1850, the membership was just above half a million. Then it went up by more than 80,000 during the next quadrennium, and by almost 100,000 during the four years following that. By 1860 the membership of the Methodist Episcopal Church, South, stood at the remarkable figure of 757,245. (This was approximately one sixteenth of the population of the Southern States.) One interesting feature of these statistics was that almost a third of this membership—207,706 persons, to be exact—was made up of Negroes. It was one of the standing taunts of the Southerners at this period that the Northern Methodists talked about the human rights of the Negro and left the Negro himself severely alone, while the Southern Methodists accepted slavery as an institution of questionable standing but in existence and then claimed that they spent money and men without stint to bring the Negro spiritual help.

Then, in 1861, came the Civil War. That the Southern church lived through the war at all seems a miracle, for the conflict, especially in its later stages, became largely a series of invasions of Southern territory. The Union strategy became that of wiping out the resources of the South, and thus making

it impossible to support armies in the field. Henry J. Grady's famous tribute to General Sherman is a quizzical, but none the less genuine, picture of that period. "We Georgians," said the Atlanta editor years after the close of the war, "think a lot of Sherman, although we do feel he was inclined to be a le-e-et-tle bit careless with fire." Nor was it only on the march to the sea that destruction fell upon the South.

While the war was on, the Southern church could not, of course, do "business as usual." There could be no General Conference held when 1862 came; there was no way of getting money to the mission field; Annual Conferences could not meet except in a fugitive and informal manner. Yet the preachers stuck to their jobs. Some of them stayed on their circuits and at their stations; others acted as chaplains with the Confederate army. A few, as in the North, joined the fighting forces. To a marvelous degree, they held the church together. The end of the war saw a thirty-per-cent decrease in membership, but when one thinks of what had been happening, and what was ahead in the reconstruction years, this decrease seems small.

In fact, it can be almost entirely accounted for by the loss in Negro membership which came with emancipation, reconstruction days, and the beginning of work among the Negroes by the Methodist Episcopal Church and the two African Methodist bodies.

For, with the Civil War, there was injected into the problem of the relation of the two churches an element which still makes its influence felt in the South. North of the battle lines the Methodist Episcopal Church was just as whole-hearted in its support of the Union cause as was the Southern church in its support of the Confederacy; in fact, the Methodists of the North were conspicuously loyal to the government. Lincoln's letter of praise, sent to the General Conference of 1864, is still a matter of denominational pride. There was almost no "copperhead" element in the body. As a result, Methodist preachers made acceptable chaplains, and came to serve in large numbers with the troops.

In the fevered tensity of those days, as the troops moved South, they came to feel that they were redeeming "rebel" territory, occupied by people who must of necessity have something the matter with their morals and religion, as well as their politics, or else they would never have championed the institution which they had championed, nor challenged the government. The needs of the newly freed Negroes added, likewise, to the belief that the Unionists had a religious, as well as a political, responsibility in the reconquered States. And so it came to pass that the Northern Methodists practically set aside one of their bishops to set up the standards of their "patriotic" branch of the church wherever the Union success made that possible. In this they were encouraged by the government, both during the war and the reconstruction period. The Northerners were, of course, acting in good conscience. But who can blame the Southerners for resenting such a penetration?

§ 4.   SINCE THE CIVIL WAR

The close of the Civil War saw the machinery of the Methodist Episcopal Church, South, in chaos. But there was a spirit remaining which quickly brought order. The bishops who had survived the war called for the meeting of the Southern General Conference at the regular time, in 1866, at New Orleans. And the quality of daring and determination which was shown when the delegates gathered there gave the church a new lease on life. When one regards the wonderful career which has been made possible for the Southern church because of the boldness of the New Orleans decisions, one wishes that other churches might more frequently be backed against a wall and made to feel that they were fighting for their lives, as the Southern church then felt. In a crisis such as those delegates faced the only possible course was to take a great venture of faith into untried, untrodden ways. But that leap of faith proved to be the way of salvation.

For four weeks the delegates remained in session at New Orleans. In that time they introduced lay delegations into the Conferences and courts of the church; abolished the six-months probationary period and the requirement of attendance on class meetings; extended the pastoral term to four years, so that a minister could stay with a church until he had given it something like a rounded ministry; and put the mission board, the book concern, and the Board of Bishops—usually called a "college" in the South—back into full running order. Four men were elected to that office. The critical situation among the Negro members who remained—less than a fourth of the number counted before the war—was given careful consideration, and plans were put under way which resulted, four years later, in the setting aside of the Colored Methodist Episcopal Church, having close fraternal bonds with the older body, but its own separate corporate life.

From the day of the New Orleans General Conference to

the present, the Methodist Episcopal Church, South, has grown. It has been for some time the fourth Protestant denomination in America in point of size, with a membership already surpassing two and a half millions. Of late its rate of growth has been more rapid than that of its Northern sister. It is

"AT SOOCHOW, THE ANCIENT CAPITAL"

still characterized by evangelistic zeal, and its missionary endeavors have led to the establishment of missions on three other continents.

The first of these missions to be established, as we have seen, was that in China. There, using Shanghai as a base, the lower Yangtse valley has been the territory occupied. At Soochow, the ancient city captured from the Taiping rebels by "Chinese" Gordon, a university of the first rank has been developed. In Shanghai, two or three of the strongest congregations in all China has been gathered. A remarkable feature of the work has been the emphasis placed on literature. Dr. Young J. Allen, one of the pioneer missionaries of the Southern church, is generally accredited with having given the first impulse to China's national interest in the new learning by the works which he translated and had published in the years immediately after China's defeat by Japan in 1895. During the last five years, this mission has opened work at Harbin, in Manchuria. Here, in the rapidly developing province north of the Great Wall, one of the strongest Christian missions in China may easily arise.

From Asia, the eyes of the Southern church turned nearer home. Mexico was the next field to be entered, with the pioneering being done by a young Mexican, an officer in the army which defeated the Emperor Maximilian. This young man had originally been designed for the Roman Catholic priesthood, but was converted from infidelity during a service in a Methodist church in Brownsville, Texas. The work in Mexico is now a part of the coordinated Protestant program, which allots to each denomination included in it a definite field for activity.

From Mexico, the church moved deeper into the Latin world, establishing a mission in Brazil. This has proved to be one of the most successful evangelical efforts in that great republic. The work in Cuba, the next to be undertaken, went along at about the usual pace until after the American occupation, when it quickly developed into a flourishing community. Brazil and Cuba were for some time unique among the fields of the Southern church in that there were no missions of the Methodist Episcopal Church also at work in the country.

In Japan, the presence of competing Methodist bodies led, in 1907, to the formation of the Japan Methodist Church. This includes the congregations formerly a part of the two American Methodist Episcopal Churches, and of the Canadian Methodist Church. The experiment, if such it can be called, of setting up an independent national church has proved remarkably successful. In Korea the problem of overlapping has been met, as in Mexico, by careful delimitation of the fields in which each denomination is to work. The Korean mission is one of the strongest under the auspices of the Southern church.

In 1918 the Methodist Episcopal Church, South, joined with the Methodist Episcopal Church in the celebration of the centenary of the missions of the two bodies. It was one hundred years since John Stewart, the illiterate Negro local preacher, had begun his work among the Wyandott Indians. Both churches pledged great sums for the enlargement of their work overseas. The most important continuing effect of that great movement on the Southern church has been the opening of work in Europe. In Belgium, in Poland, and in Czecho-Slovakia the new missions are now seeking to establish themselves. These are hard, forbidding fields. But if determination and liberality can bring the desired ends to pass, the work will be carried on until it makes its influence widely felt.

§ 5. Efforts at Reunion

Through all the years, as the Methodist Episcopal Church, South, has pursued her steady way, there have been those who have dreamed of a day when the break of 1844 should be mended. In both churches voices have been raised saying that the causes which brought about the separation are no longer operating, and urging that there is no sufficient reason for keeping the two great bodies apart. Because of this feeling, which has grown from year to year, various approaches have been made toward reunion. But none of these, so far, has succeeded.

We have seen Dr. Lovick Pierce going with his fraternal letter to the General Conference at Pittsburgh in 1848, and we have seen him going away again when the door was shut in his face. We have heard him say, if ever fraternal relations were to be renewed, the Methodist Episcopal Church would have to make the first proffer. In 1872, with the Civil War seven years over, that proffer came. Two years later the fraternal messengers knocked at the doors of the Southern General Conference. In the South, this offering of the olive branch was greeted with joy. Fraternal messengers were appointed to carry back the word of affection and trust to the Northern General Conference of 1876. And at the head of the delegation was named Dr. Lovick Pierce, the same man turned away at Pittsburgh, now ninety-four years of age. What reversals time does bring to pass!

Almost from that day plans looking toward reunion have been under consideration. It would be a waste of time to describe them in detail here, for, as has been said, they have all, so far, failed. Some advances have been won. There have been agreements made—and generally kept—to prevent competition in "border" communities. The eagerness of some denominational officials has produced what would look like a queer "border" to most outsiders, with the Northern church in Florida and Louisiana, and the Southern church in Oregon and Montana! But such incidentals merely testify to the human qualities of even Methodist leaders, and do not seriously affect the success of the comity agreements now in force. There is also a common Hymnal, a common Catechism, a common order of worship, and—most important of all—a large amount of common Sunday-school material. Many ministers, moreover, have transferred north and south.

The latest great effort to bring the two churches together failed in 1925. After long consultation and debate, commissioners appointed by the two churches framed a proposal for union which was reported to the two General Conferences. Since carefully detailed programs had, in the past, failed, the commission this time said, in effect: "Let us just announce that the two churches have united under one General Conference with two jurisdictions, and then go on living and working practically as we are at present. Then, in the course of the years, as we get accustomed to each other, as our preachers transfer from one Conference to another, we will gradually and naturally shake together. The union which we now announce in name will become one in fact, and nobody will be able to tell quite how or when or where it has come to pass."

The Methodist Episcopal Church greeted this proposal with enthusiasm. Neither in its General nor in its Annual Conferences did enough opposition develop to make it worth counting. But not so in the South. There the General Conference approved, but when it came time for the Annual Conferences to take the final step, the votes could not be mustered for the three-fourths majority which was required. A simple majority was on hand, but more than a quarter of the church held back from the union. The presence of the Negro in the Northern church (and perhaps even more of Negro bishops); the danger of being "swallowed" in the larger body; the wounds not yet quite healed from Civil War times—all these and other factors worked to postpone reunion awhile longer.

§ 6. FACING THE FUTURE

Keen disappointment has been expressed in many quarters over the failure of the latest plan to reunite the two branches of Episcopal Methodism. With that disappointment has gone some natural pessimism. "If this plan wasn't acceptable," say some of the Northerners, "nothing will be acceptable." To which the Southerners who hoped for union reply, "You will have to give us time for at least another generation of funerals, and then we can try again."

But after the time has passed, when the question comes up again—as it certainly will—what are the prospects? That union will finally come a majority of the members of the two churches devoutly hope. Yet there is no use in denying the presence of difficulties which will stand in the path for a long time. The thought of the two churches on many questions is not the same. Some of these are ecclesiastical questions, such as the proper amount of power to leave in the hands of a bishop. In the Southern church, for example, the bishops can now question the legality of an act of a General Conference and send it down to the Annual Conferences for decision—a power that would never be admitted in the North. In theological thinking the Northern church is more liberal than is the Southern. In that great realm composed of the application of religion to industrial problems—what is often called "the social gospel"—the very pressure of the times has placed the North in a far more advanced position.

But, more than all these, there is the Negro. It is needless to try to dodge that question. The Negro is in the Methodist Episcopal Church. He has the same standing there which any man has. Two Negroes are bishops of that church, and, legally, they are bishops in the exact degree and with the same power that characterizes all their brethren on the Episcopal Board. The Negro can be put out of the church only by the same process of bringing charges against his personal character which applies in the case of the white man. On the other hand, the Southerner knows what he is talking about when he says that the Negro could be brought into the Southern church only at the risk of social revolution. There are issues, both social and religious, bound up here which it will do no good to discuss. But it does need to be borne in mind that, as between a divergence of opinion as to the method of biblical inspiration and a divergence of opinion as to the social worth of a black-pigmented mortal, the former becomes a question of incidental and academic interest.

It is not at all certain that the mere union of two big denominations in order to form one super-big denomination would, of itself, add greatly to the spiritual resources of America. It might do no more than create another awe-inspiring piece of denominational machinery. If it eliminated overlapping and competition in border communities, it would be of value. But it would not seem necessary to have union in order to secure Christian treatment of one another in such communities. If it blotted out confusing and meaningless sectarian lines on mission fields, it would help. But much of the overlapping is more apparent than real—in China, for example, the names of the two churches are totally different, so that no Chinese, except for foreign influence, would ever think of identifying them—and present sectarian lines are more likely to be blotted out by the passing of congregations into unions much more inclusive than merely Methodist groupings. And if union meant the slowing down of the thinking and action of any part of the church in order to allow the rest to catch up— if it set the army's pace by the step of the slowest marcher— then union might easily be purchased at too high a price.

And yet, having said all this, it is impossible to close this chapter without expressing the hope that union between the Methodist Episcopal Church and the Methodist Episcopal Church, South, may yet be brought to pass. The exceptions already noted will suggest the requirements which we feel must be satisfied if this union is to be worth having. Nor are they easy requirements. Some will think them impossibilities. "With God all things are possible." May he make the way of reunion clear!

CHAPTER XX

THROUGH THE CIVIL WAR AND BEYOND

§ 1. The Civil War

THE intensity of energy and conviction with which the churches in the North flung themselves into the support of the federal government during the Civil War was not alone due to natural emotions of patriotic fervor. It was also due to an ardent sense that a tremendous moral issue was at stake, the issue of slavery, which for a generation had been agitating the churches, to the point of disrupting Methodist, Presbyterian, and Baptist communions. To the churches the issue was not merely that of the integrity of the Union. It took on the aspects of a moral crusade against slavery. It is for that reason that the war became, to so large and unusual extent, the great preoccupation of the churches. The activities of the Methodist Church throughout the war years are typical of the other churches.

The split in the Methodist Church in 1844, seventeen years before the Civil War broke out, was generally regarded as a sinister prophecy of the "irrepressible conflict," as it was called by William H. Seward, in the life of the nation. Statesmen both North and South, such as Henry Clay, Daniel Webster, and John C. Calhoun, had deplored the break, had endeavored to minimize its significance, as a possible shadow of coming events in the life of the nation. Webster had declared the split to have been unnecessary and due to "a lack of candor and charity."

But it was increasingly made plain, as the years intervening between 1844 and 1861 went on, that the break in the Methodist Church, followed by similar splits into Northern and

Southern bodies in the other churches, could not be regarded a mere ecclesiastical division, but was a forerunner of an issue which the nation itself must meet. For over half a century a long and tortuous history of compromise on the question of slavery had been going on. But that chapter, in 1860, had drawn definitely to a close.

By the outbreak of the war the Methodist Episcopal Church had become practically unanimous in its opposition to slavery, although there had been, strangely as it seems, no change in the *Discipline* on the subject of slavery between 1824 and 1860. But the anti-slavery feeling had so gained ground in the church that "the great contest over the question of slavery was practically settled in the Methodist Episcopal Church before the final struggle in the nation began."

"LET MY PEOPLE GO"

In every way possible the ministry and membership of the Methodist Episcopal Church threw themselves into the struggle to preserve the Union. It is estimated that more than 100,000 members of the church enlisted in the federal armies. The records of the membership during the war years show to some extent the loss the church suffered. When the war began, the total membership of the Methodist Episcopal Church was 990,-447, and when the war closed there was a membership of 929,-259, a net loss of 61,188 for the period of the war. Some of this loss was due, no doubt, to the interruption to regular activities which war always brings. Most of it unquestionably was due to army enlistments.

But no statistics can give even a faint glimpse of the loyal devotion and patriotic services which the church rendered the nation during the testing years of the war. In sustaining the spirit of the nation, in ministering to the soldiers in camp and hospital, in keeping before the nation what the church regarded as the moral and spiritual interpretation of the war, a great service was given. This was done in the pulpit and on the platform; by the six bishops of the church at that time, who traveled incessantly throughout the country and made a large contribution to strengthening the morale of the North; by chaplains and other ministers with the armies; by representatives of the church in England; by the church papers continually.

The total number of Methodist ministers who were chaplains in the Union armies during the Civil War was over five hundred. Professor William Warren Sweet gives in his valuable book, *The Methodist Episcopal Church and the Civil War,* some glimpses of the work of these chaplains in the field: "In many instances a regimental church was formed, which held regular services; and where a regiment remained long in camp the chaplain usually improved the time by holding a revival meeting. At the close of such a meeting in an Indiana regiment forty-eight soldiers were received into the regimental church. In a New York regiment a revival meeting was kept up thirty nights in succession in a tent furnished for that purpose by General Hunter, and one hundred and twenty-five soldiers professed conversion. In an Ohio regiment, whose colonel was a well-known Methodist preacher, Colonel Granville Moody, a regimental church was formed called the 'Church of the Living God,' and at one of the evening services of this soldiers' church the colonel himself baptized nine soldiers."[1]

In addition to furnishing over five hundred chaplains, the church participated in a large way in the work of the United States Christian Commission, in which the work of many agencies for the benefit of the soldiers was united. The Chris-

---

[1] Used by permission of the author.

tian Commission did an extensive work for the soldiers, in furnishing supplies and comforts and other forms of welfare aid. Of the four thousand workers of the Commission in the army, four hundred and fifty-eight were Methodist ministers. In the United States the outstanding personal service was doubtless that of Bishop Matthew Simpson, the friend and trusted intimate counselor of President Lincoln. Bishop Simpson was one of the most notable orators of the country, and in public lectures and sermons wielded a large influence for the Union cause.

One of the treasured documents of the Methodist Episcopal Church is the reply of President Lincoln to the address of loyalty and sympathy made to him by the General Conference of 1864. It might almost be said that this reply of Abraham Lincoln has been committed to memory by the whole church. Mr. Lincoln's letter is reproduced on the next page.

The Methodist Episcopal Church, South, was just as loyal and active in the support of the Confederacy as the church in the North was in support of the Union. It was the largest Protestant body in the South, numbering over 700,000 members in 1859. In the same ways and with the same ardor the church in the South contributed men to the armies, and support and sympathy to the leaders. The number of ministers of the Methodist Episcopal Church, South, who served as chaplains in the Confederate armies totaled over 200. Many others went as missionaries to the armies. Especially in the army of Northern Virginia, and, in particular, among the corps of "Stonewall" Jackson, were religious interest and activity pronounced. Prayer meetings and revivals were frequent. During the war the Church South lost over 250,000 members.

The churches suffered much from the war. The deflecting of attention from active religious work to the engrossing anxieties and tasks of the national struggle inevitably slowed up and crippled religious progress. Hundreds of churches in

Gentlemen.

　　　In response to your address, allow me to attest the accuracy of its historical statements, indorse the sentiments it expresses; and thank you, in the nation's name for the sure promise it gives.

　　　Nobly sustained as the government has been by all the churches, I would utter nothing which might, in the least, appear invidious against any. Yet, without this, it may fairly be said that the Methodist Episcopal Church, not less devoted than the best, is, by its greater numbers, the most important of all. It is no fault in others that the Methodist Church sends more soldiers to the field, more nurses to the hospitals, and more prayers to Heaven than any. God bless the Methodist Church—bless all the churches— and blessed be God, Who, in this our great trial, giveth us the churches.

　　　　　　　　　　　　　A. Lincoln

May 18, 1864

LETTER WRITTEN BY PRESIDENT LINCOLN TO THE GENERAL CON-
FERENCE OF 1864.

the South were broken up and destroyed. Hundreds of thousands of members were lost through death in battle or disease, or by the evil influences of army life. After the close of the war the usual period of demoralization followed, with crime, extravagance, reckless speculation, and intemperance. These influences made their effect felt in public life in the decade following the war. Scandals and corruption were frequent blots on the political landscape.

That the churches recovered as quickly as they did from the war was undoubtedly due to the fact that the years immediately preceding 1860 were years of an unusual religious awakening and revival which affected practically the entire country. The years 1857-58 marked one of the high peaks in revivalism in the United States. Following a period of placid and conventional life in the churches from 1843 to 1857, the revival movement which began in New York developed in strength and the religious contagion was rapid. As far as a definite starting place can be assigned, it can be said to have begun at the Fulton Street prayer meeting, New York, in September, 1857. It was not a revival centered around any evangelist or group of them. No extraordinary agencies were employed. It is estimated that in one week 50,000 persons professed conversion and that during the revival more than 300,000 members were added to the churches. The Methodist Episcopal Church in the year from November, 1857, to November, 1858, received 136,000 new members. Unquestionably this religious awakening left a permanent vitality in the church which helped it to a rapid recovery from the war. The rapidity with which the church was enabled to turn to new tasks with new resources is shown by the fact that, while the last war year, 1865, showed a decrease of 65,000 in membership, the year following, 1866, showed an increase of more than 70,000.

§ 2. THE CENTENARY CELEBRATION

The first great advance was planned as a celebration of the one hundredth anniversary of the introduction of Methodism into the United States—1766.

As one goes about the United States and looks at the churches he will note a great many which bear the name "Centenary." Almost every city either has or had its Centenary Methodist Episcopal Church. "How did all these churches come to be called Centenary?" is a natural question which has been asked repeatedly. It would appear that "Centenary" must have been some kind of a Methodist saint. Perhaps the answer would not be entirely wrong! The word "centenary" has, of course, become familiar to the present generation of Methodists from the Centenary Movement and program of 1919-1924. But this flock of "Centenary" churches we have now in mind were standing before the Centenary of the present time was ever dreamed of.

These churches were the products of the Centennial of 1866, which inspired the building of hundreds of Methodist churches, as one phase of a new aggressive program marking the close of the first century of American Methodism. The announced purpose of the Centennial was the strengthening of the spiritual life of the church and, in particular, the strengthening and increasing of the educational institutions of the church.

This Centennial celebration is interesting for many reasons. It was the first general propaganda movement resembling the modern "financial drive," with which the present generation has become so thoroughly and continuously (and, some would add, "painfully") familiar. Meetings were held in all cities and towns, Centenary speeches were given, special books and publications used. The concluding date of the campaign was the last Sunday of October, when throughout the church the financial pledges were made.

The objects for giving were designated at the beginning of the Centennial as being both local and general. Among the general objects for which funds were asked were, first, a Centenary Education Fund, of which great results were hoped, five theological institutions, a Centenary mission building in New York, and for Irish Methodism, and a Biblical School at Bremen, Germany, and a Sunday School Children's Fund to be used for student loans. No apportionments for these objects were made. The outcome, apparently, could easily have been foreseen, but, owing to lack of experience in collections, was not. The stress of the bishops and General Committee was laid on the connectional objects, but the results of the general collections showed a pathetically small amount for the general objects and a surprisingly great sum for local expenditure. Thus the total amount subscribed in this effort from all sources reached approximately $9,000,000. But the general Education Fund received only $9,115!

Undoubtedly, the giving of the churches to their own local projects, mainly new church buildings, in such an overwhelming proportion was a disappointment to those who projected the Centennial celebration. Yet it left results of large and lasting benefit to the church. Hundreds of churches developed an initiative in meeting their ministry to their own communities which they had never shown before. Thus the need of the times for new and better-equipped buildings was met in multitudes of places. Despite the very small amount contributed to the general Education Fund, the Centennial resulted in the formation of a Board of Education, which during over fifty years has greatly stimulated and increased the strength of the colleges and schools of the church. Large gifts were made to particular institutions, including Drew Theological Seminary at Madison, New Jersey; and Garrett Biblical Institute, at Evanston, Illinois; and the Boston School of Theology. One far-reaching result of the Centennial was the institution of Children's Day as an annual observance throughout the church, and the dedication of the collections on that day to a Loan Fund to assist needy students in obtaining an education. The Sunday School Children's Fund of the Centenary amounted to $65,000 and it was this fund which was the starting point for the General Conference legislation of 1868 which provided for the annual observance of Children's Day. This day has become part of the indelible memory of every child who has come up through the Sunday school and church. During fifty-eight years more than 34,908 students have been aided. What this aid has meant in terms of human life and in terms of service rendered to the world is beyond the power of any historian to set down. The story of the Children's Day Loan Fund is a romance in compound interest, of money being loaned, making its contribution to educated personality; repaid, loaned again, endlessly going on in its service.

§ 3. THE FOUNDING OF COLLEGES

The twenty years following the Civil War were years of great educational achievement and expansion in the Methodist Episcopal Church. The Centennial of 1866 gave a great impetus to the founding and development of colleges and schools. This was due in Methodism to the fact that an era of pioneering and all the immediate necessities of a first occupation of new territory was definitely over, in a large section of the United States. The churches were more free to turn their attention to activities that were necessarily curtailed or prevented in an earlier period.

This educational expansion brings into the picture one of the most fascinating and significant achievements of Methodism in the United States, which has not yet been described in this volume except incidentally. That is, the establishment and sustaining of colleges and schools. The era of educational activity which began then has continued with increased energy and devotion until the present hour.

The story of Methodist colleges would take a large volume, crowded with truly great names, for the mere outline. Here only a suggestive glimpse can be attempted.

One of the major reasons for the continuance and

success of Methodism has been, of course, that it united evangelistic Passion to an equally genuine passion for education.

This was a characteristic of its very birthday when a Holy Club came into being in the very center of a university. Those two elements have blended all through its history —the Holy Club—and the university. It is as though the leaders of the church have said continually of these two things, "What God hath joined together let not man put asunder."

This has been a remarkable heritage. For it has often happened that movements which were essentially and earnestly evangelistic in origin and character have shown a tendency, if not to disparage, at least to undervalue education. The Wesleyan Movement was saved from becoming a spent force by both organization and provision for education; and the organization itself was in large part for purposes of education in the class meetings, the books and periodicals, the training of preachers and the schools. Two years after his historic experience in Aldersgate Street—from which the real beginning of Methodism is dated—Wesley took over the school at Kingswood which Whitefield had started in 1739. Beginning as a general boarding school, it was later limited to ministers' children. It had a long and honored history and has sent out a stream of undying influence into the world. Wesley was in many ways a unique and remarkable educator and gave to the whole Methodist Movement throughout the world a permanent passion for education. Yet a study of his rules for the Kingswood school touches the sense of humor at the present time. For coupled with educational genius was a vast practical ignorance of children and their nature. It should be said, however, in Wesley's defense, that his ignorance of children was one he shared with practically all the schoolmasters of his time. No one in the eighteenth century can rightly be blamed for not anticipating all the discoveries of the twentieth in pedagogy and psychology.

Asbury had a genuine zeal for education, but this, after his disastrous first experiences with a college, became centered on primary and secondary schools, with an accompanying distrust of the higher institutions. After founding an academy bearing the name of Ebenezer, in Virginia about 1784, Cokesbury College was founded in Abingdon, Maryland, in 1785. (It was named from a combination of the names of the two bishops, Coke and Asbury. When the name was severely criticized each disclaimed the doubtful honor of originating the idea of the name.) The two bishops collected the money, $40,000 in all, most of it secured in small bits from widely scattered people, most of whom were in real poverty. The achievement represented unprecedented generosity.

The financial load of supporting the college was heavy. Asbury solicited for it on his wide travels. He records in a frank exclamation after the school had been burned down, "Would any man give me ten thousand pounds a year to do and suffer what I had done for that school, I would not do it."

By 1793 the school was almost hopelessly involved financially, and in 1795 it was destroyed by fire. A new building was purchased in Baltimore and a new start made.

The second building of Cokesbury College in Baltimore was destroyed by fire in 1796 and the college was definitely given up. It was too great a strain financially, and Asbury's original idea, that the need for schools was greater than that for a college, was undoubtedly correct. The abandoning of Cokesbury after so much labor did not dull Asbury's interest in the establishment of schools. He returned with unquenched enthusiasm to establish district schools in various parts of the country which were without them.

The first chartered Methodist college in the world was Asbury College in Baltimore, founded in 1816. It lasted only three or four years. The first college to have any extensive existence was opened in 1822 at Augusta, Kentucky. Academies or secondary schools were founded in increasing numbers in this period, the first being that started by the New England Conference at New Market, New Hampshire. It was transferred to Wilbraham, Massachusetts, in 1824, where it still continues as Wilbraham Academy, after more than a century of fruitful service.

Wesleyan University at Middletown, Connecticut, is the oldest Methodist college in continuous existence in the United States.

"THE MOTHER OF COLLEGES"

It is in a very real sense the mother of Methodist colleges as well as the Alma Mater of many of the notable leaders of the church. It was founded by the New York and New England Conferences and incorporated in

1831, with Wilbur Fisk as President. Great names such as Fisk and Olin have adorned its history. Great personalities have continuously been among its teachers and students.

In the thirties two colleges already in existence were taken over by the Methodist Episcopal Church, Allegheny at Meadville, Pennsylvania, in 1833, and Dickinson at Carlisle, Pennsylvania, in 1834. The rapidity with which the educational expansion went on can be seen from the fact that by 1840 there were sixteen colleges and twenty-six secondary schools under the control of the Methodist Episcopal Church. McKendree College, in Illinois, 1834; Indiana Asbury (the name was changed to DePauw in 1885) at Greencastle, Indiana, in 1837; Ohio Wesleyan at Delaware, Ohio, in 1842; and Northwestern University, at Evanston, Illinois, in 1850, were some of the more important institutions which now came into existence. The story of each of these colleges is rich in interest, in sacrificial devotion and in achievement. The equipment of these colleges, on the physical side, measured by the standards of to-day, was painfully meager. Their equipment, on the side of great personalities on the teaching forces, was rich, measured by the standards of any day.

Syracuse University, at Syracuse, New York; Boston University, at Boston; Hamline, at Saint Paul, Minnesota; the University of Southern California, at Los Angeles; Vanderbilt University, founded as an institution of the Methodist Episcopal Church, South, at Nashville; the University of Denver; the Woman's College of Baltimore (now Goucher College), were some of the colleges founded in the seventies and eighties.

This development, of course, was paralleled by the planting of schools and colleges of other denominations. The era between 1830 and 1870 was marked by the establishment of denominational colleges as an outstanding feature of American church life. Two tendencies natural at that time have been to a great extent corrected in the last fifty years. The first was an overmultiplication of colleges. In the States of Iowa, Kansas, and Missouri, more than fifty colleges arose in approximately thirty years. This was while these regions were in the process of settlement. The result was the founding of some institutions with not much better reasons than local pride or in some cases, denominational rivalry. A number of these later languished and died. The multiplication of small colleges has greatly diminished, and the present tendency is to strengthen and develop institutions already established. Thus in Ohio, which has more small educational institutions than any other State in the Union, only five have been established in the last fifty years. Only six have been founded in Illinois during the same period. The other tendency, now almost entirely outgrown, was to call most any sort of a school a university, even when it was little more than a high school or academy.

By 1926 the Methodist Episcopal Church had forty-six colleges and universities, forty-one professional schools, including law, medicine, and theology, and thirty secondary schools. The combined student enrollment at all these is over seventy thousand.

After the college, the next step in education was the theological seminary for the specialized training of preachers. The wise leaders who pioneered this movement deserve a debt of gratitude from the church of later years, the extent of which is not easily realized, for the project of theological education was met with a large degree of suspicion, prejudice, and not a little actual hostility on the part of a large number of both ministers and laymen. This has so largely disappeared, that it is rather hard to put oneself back in imagination and realize the obstacles which had to be overcome. Yet to one familiar with the historical traditions and development of Methodism it is possible to see the naturalness of many of the suspicions. For one thing, as we have seen, the ministers of Methodism during its first half century in America had been untrained. The large majority were not college graduates; they were self-educated men, products, in large part, of frontier life. Their preaching was extemporaneous a n d emotional r a t h e r than predominantly intellectual or theological. There was quite a widespread fear that the qualities which had made for effectiveness, resourceful, arousing, powerful extemporaneous preaching, would be lost and that heavy, d r y written s e r m o n s would take their place. There was also a fear in some quarters that seminary training would rob ministers of spiritual warmth and that a critical spirit would replace evangelistic zeal. Others had fears regarding doctrine. They prophesied that the seminary would become a breeding place of heresies of various sorts. This fear and prejudice continued in regard to the seminaries for many years. For these reasons the very name "theological seminary" was consciously avoided at the founding of at least two of the theo-

"OVER SEVENTY THOUSAND"

logical schools of Methodism. The Methodist General Biblical Institute, opened at Concord, New Hampshire, in 1847 was not called a theological seminary until it moved to Boston in 1867. The school at Evanston retains to-day the name given at its establishment in 1855, Garrett Biblical Institute. The change of attitude from suspicion, on the part of a section of the church, to appreciation of the fruitful service to all the life and work of the church which the seminaries have rendered, has come with the years. Drew Theological Seminary at Madison, New Jersey, was opened in 1867. These three seminaries have sent out to all parts of the world, as well as the United States, a continual succession of influential leaders.

§ 4. The Methodist Book Concern

Not even the briefest glimpse of the educational activity of Methodism could be closed without some recognition of the measureless influence of the publishing business of the church. The part played by The Methodist Book Concern in the life and achievement of the church, in the one hundred and thirty-seven years since the establishment of the Concern, may be truly said to deserve that badly overworked adjective, "unique." It is not merely the largest religious publishing house in Protestantism; it has also contributed in an unparalleled way to the ministry of the church which has controlled it.

The interest in religious literature is one of the major legacies left to the world by John Wesley. It is a mark borne by the Methodist movement from the very beginning. From John Wesley's earliest days he had a passion for printer's ink, and the passion for souls was joined with his passion for ink all through his life. To the church which owes its origin to him ink has always been a redemptive chemical. It was an omen of large meaning that in the old Foundry meetinghouse there was a Book Room. The communion table and the book room have gone on down the centuries together. "Take care that every society be duly supplied with books," exclaimed Wesley to his preachers. "Oh, why is not this regarded?" Wesley's own contribution to the cause of production of inexpensive literature was that of an indefatigable pioneer. A catalogue of his publications, printed as early as 1756, when he was barely launched in his career, contains one hundred and eighty-one different items in prose, verse, English and Latin, on grammar, philosophy, medicine, theology, music, poetry. Two thirds of these were sold for less than one shilling each and one fourth of them at a penny. Perhaps it would not look like a high tribute to say that Wesley was the Henry Ford of literature, yet that comparison has a real meaning. He applied the idea of quantity production at a cheap price, just as Ford did to the automobile. In both cases the idea was cheap prices sustained by large sales.

This life passion of Wesley's was not lost in crossing the Atlantic. The first circulation of religious literature by Methodism in America, was done by Robert Williams, one of the earliest lay evangelists. He, on his own responsibility, printed and circulated Wesley's sermons throughout the country, especially in the South. The Conference in 1773 decided that this work of publishing should be taken over by the Conference itself. This was done, and the profits accruing were at this very early date voted to be used in making up the deficiencies of the preachers and for the relief of worn-out ministers. In 1789 The Methodist Book Concern was organized by the Conference, which met in John Street Church, New York City. The church had been organized only four and a half years and had a membership of fifty-eight thousand. There was no money with which to embark on the printing and publishing business, but John Dickins, the secretary of the Conference, loaned $600, his savings of a lifetime, as capital with which to begin the enterprise. So with this borrowed capital and John

Dickins in charge, as book steward, The Methodist Book Concern was launched. It was located first in Philadelphia and moved to New York in 1804. The first book published was John Wesley's translation of Thomas à Kempis' *The Imitation of Christ.*

To chronicle the work of The Book Concern would require a large volume. The most romantic aspect of its circulation of Christian literature is unquestionably that in which the itinerant circuit-rider played such a heroic part. He carried into all quarters of the country books and periodicals as well as the gospel. He was a sort of intellectual

THE ORIGINAL METHODIST BOOK-ROOM

and spiritual Johnny Appleseed. Jonathan Chapman, better known as "Johnny Appleseed," was an eccentric character with a high nobility in his make up who traveled over most of the territory now comprised in Ohio, Indiana, Illinois, and Michigan, planting apple seed which grew up into orchards. The circuit-rider in like manner planted ideas and purposes through the books and papers he carried with him.

Periodicals as well as books were published. The first publication, issued in 1818, was called *The Methodist Magazine.* Its successor is the *Methodist Review.* This publication has had a continued existence with the exception of one year, 1829. The first official weekly of the church was *The Christian Advocate,* the first number of which was published September 9, 1826. This was the first of a family of Advocates, established as the church spread westward. These journals have had enormous influence in promoting the general interests of the church and contributing to its solidarity.

The Sunday-school publications of the church have a circulation running into many millions. The profits of the publishing business of the church have been applied for the benefit of the retired ministers, their widows and children.

§ 5. LAYMEN IN THE GENERAL CONFERENCE

The most notable single step of progress in the organization of the Methodist Episcopal Church during the decade following the Civil War was unquestionably the admission of laymen as members of the General Conference in 1872. At the General Conference which met in Brooklyn, New York, the law was changed to admit two lay delegates for each Annual Conference. That seems now a rather small concession, when compared with the ministerial representation of one delegate for every forty-five ministers of an Annual Conference. Yet the admission of lay delegates was the victorious culmination of a long and frequently bitter battle for lay representation which stretched over fifty years.

When we consider the important part which laymen have played in Methodism from the very beginning, it seems strange and almost incomprehensible that it should have taken fifty years of struggle by laymen to be admitted to the highest governing body of the church. The earliest Methodism was, in the words of Bishop Matthew Simpson, one of the ablest and most active supporters of lay representation, "from its beginning an uprising and development of lay influence." Its preachers were for the most part lay preachers in the early days. In the pioneering period in America it was lay preachers most frequently who blazed the way. In a church preeminently employing laymen, why did the recognition of lay rights in government require a fifty years' war?

The answer is made up of many elements. One which must be recorded frankly is that American Methodism inherited both from Wesley and Asbury a certain autocratic spirit. At one period Asbury was committed to a scheme for substituting a Council for a General Conference as the chief authority in the church. It should be remembered as one of the causes of gratitude which Methodism should have to Thomas Coke that he effectively opposed that autocratic scheme and helped to preserve the more democratic General Conference. This tendency, exhibited in Asbury and expressed in some ministers, was out of harmony with American democracy, had more in common with the aristocratic temper of the Federalist party in the early days of the country, and was, of necessity, doomed to be overcome by the growing democracy just as the Federalist party went to extinction.

Another reason lay in the essentially military regime which was at the heart of the Methodist itineracy. That centering of authority in the hands of bishop and presiding elders was productive of great results in the expansion of the church, in both settled and unsettled regions. But with the passage of time it bore more and more hardly on a growing number of ministers and church members. It will be remembered that both the O'Kelley secession in 1792 and the break which resulted in the Methodist Protestant Church in 1830, were concerned in part, at least, with lay representation. A system which could be tolerated under earlier conditions became intolerable as the temper of the times and conditions changed.

Another reason was the more or less natural reluctance of a group to relinquish any special privilege which they had. In this connection it is interesting to note how most of the arguments used against the admission of laymen to the General Conference are now being used against their admission to any part in the Annual Conferences fifty years later. These arguments are now quite venerable, but are still employed!

It is not necessary here to follow the long and intricate course of discussion and legislation on the matter. One of the great scenes in the history of the Methodist Episcopal Church occurred in the General Conference in Brooklyn in 1872, when one hundred and twenty-nine lay delegates who had been elected appeared at the door of the General Conference and made their way down the aisle amid a tumult such as that body had rarely, if ever, witnessed. They were seated as delegates and with that act there began a new era in the church. It was, as it were, the completion of the Americanization of Methodism. It was, also, in a sense, the completion of the Protestant principle in Methodism. For there was always a lingering trace of Romanism and papacy in a church government entirely in the hands of the clergy. The idea of the ministry having a divine right to control (an argument frequently made) was never quite in harmony with that cornerstone of Protestantism, the priesthood of the believer. The large results of this change in polity was that the church was enabled to go forward without the handicap of an undemocratic form of government which had become archaic. Among the results was an increase in the interest and energy displayed by the laymen in the church. Years were to go by before the laymen were to be represented in the General Conference on an equal basis. Years were to go by before the logical and necessary completion of the admission of laymen by the admission of women was fulfilled.

§ 6. WOMEN IN THE GENERAL CONFERENCE

While the long struggle for the representation of laymen in the General Conference was going on, it did not take long for keen minds to see that the only logical end of the contention was the admission of women as well as men into the General Conference as lay delegates. But it took the church long years to bring its law into harmony with this unanswerable logic. As early as 1852, a woman, who is known to Methodist records only as "Sister Jenkins," raised the question clearly. In a letter to The Christian Advocate and Journal, she raised the question whether the proposed representation was to include the women. She pleaded that as women had to bear a full proportion of the church's burdens and were as much concerned with its law and life as the men, it was only an outworn form of male tyranny to exclude the women from a share in making the laws.

Sister Jenkins must have been an irritating embarrassment to many of the grave ecclesiastics of that day, for her logic was unanswerable. The editor of the Advocate at that time wrote this comment on her letter, "We cannot say but pure democracy carried out in the church would give Sister Jenkins a place in the General and Annual Conferences." This comment was certainly a flash of light. It took "Sister Jenkins" and all other sisters more than fifty years to win their place in the General Conference and the place in the Annual Conference is not yet won, though many feel that it is a matter of a few years when that place also will be awarded.

The reluctance to grant women a place in the General Conference was due to many causes. It was due to inertia, to conservatism, to the unwillingness on the part of those who had privileges and prerogatives to share them with newcomers. It must not be thought, however, that all this inertia and conservatism was peculiar to the church. It is to the credit of the church that it granted women the right to vote in the General Conference at least fifteen years before they were granted the right to vote as citizens of the nation. The whole story is part of the slow process of the recognition of women as responsible human beings, entitled to equal rights with men. From the time when the laymen were admitted to the General Conference in 1872 until women were finally admitted in 1904, the intervening thirty-two years might almost be called a "Thirty Years' War." On several occasions women were elected from the

Annual Conferences only to have their seats denied them, or else to have the men make such frantic appeals to their good nature that they resigned rather than become the center of a legislative bombardment.

One of the dramatic pictures, very striking although it is not particularly pleasant to recall, is that of the General Conference of 1888, when one who perhaps it would not be over-exaggeration to call the most distinguished layman in the United States was elected to the General Conference, and was refused admission. That layman was Frances E. Willard. And she stood before the Conference as a woman in whose extraordinary achievements the entire church took pride, about whom the ministers never seemed to tire boasting. Yet the only message of the church to her when she came to take her place as part of its chief legislative body was "Not yet!" Of course the General Conference did not use harsh language. All the rhetorical resources of the language were laid under severe strain to pay compliments to Frances Willard and the four other women delegates who were refused admission in 1888. The Conference chivalrously agreed to pay their expenses, but the strong cords of ecclesiastical red tape could not be cut at that time to admit Frances Willard. By the time that women were legally admitted, Frances Willard had passed on to a higher assembly. It is worthy of note, however, that she has been admitted to a place in a slightly more select company than a General Conference in Statuary Hall in the Capitol at Washington. The action in 1888 was a legal victory by the exclusion of women, but it was a moral defeat for the forces trying to exclude them.

It should be remembered, however, to the credit of the General Conference of 1872, that it put itself on record by declaring that in all matters connected with the election of lay delegates, the word "laymen" must be understood to include all the members of the church who were not members of the

Annual Conference. If the church had been able to accept this common sense, fifty years of bickering over the matter would have been avoided.

What were the reasons why Methodism was so slow to recognize the rights of women? No ecclesiastical body has ever owed more to women. Some of the brightest pages of the history of the church are those which tell the story of women, beginning with Susannah Wesley.

One reason is the general one already suggested and is not confined to ecclesiastical bodies. It is the fact that women have had a long struggle from the days of the cave men to secure equal justice with men. Men have been ready to burst into sentimental tributes. Someone has keenly said that "men have blocked the way of women by erecting pedestals in front of them." Another reason is the reluctance of all bodies, religious bodies in some respects more so than others, to do anything new. The reaction to any new proposition for half a century is frequently that of Peter when he saw the housetop vision at Joppa; he replied in a scandalized tone, "Lord, we have never done this before." The third reason for the necessity of the long wait for admitting women to the General Conference was the opposition of a few distinguished leaders who fought it every inch of the way. Among these were many people who were chiefly legalists. Human values did not weigh with them nearly as much as the niceties of ecclesiastical etiquette. But these defenses could not hold out indefinitely, and after many discussions in General Conferences, the Annual Conferences following the General Conference of 1900 ratified the proposal that all lay members twenty-five years of age should be eligible to membership in the General Conference. Accordingly, at the General Conference of 1904 at Los Angeles, the Methodist Episcopal Church finally opened its doors and said with a belated but nevertheless gracious and hopitable gesture, "Enter, Madam!"

CHAPTER XXI

A SPIRITUAL FORTY-NINER

§ 1. GOLD!

ONE day late in January, in the year 1848, a laborer was casually digging away at the bed of a small stream running through Sutter's Mill, near Coloma, in the recently organized territory of California. Captain Sutter, owner of the mill, was also the owner of thousands of acres of ranch land in southern California. He was the wealthiest and most powerful of the Americans who had found their way into this land which Fremont and his followers had wrested from the authority of Mexico. He knew nothing of plans to deepen the mill-race on his property; the chances are that it was not until weeks later that he knew of the bits of yellow metal which the laborer had picked from the bed of the little stream. By that time word of the accidental discovery had been bruited about the whole territory, and companies of men had begun to camp on Captain Sutter's property and to wash out the gravel in the brooks and creeks. Captain Sutter found himself unable to drive off these intruders. Not only were they brought and held by the lure which has always made men ready to risk death itself, but they proved only the vanguard of a tide of humanity which, when the word of discovery had spread to the East, came like a flood across plains, over the mountains, and by the seaways, until at last poor Captain Sutter's last vestige of property right had been erased, and the man who had once been the proud lord of the ranches went to a pauper's death, ruined by the stampede of '49. Gold!

It was a motley crew which made up the Argonauts of 1849. Every great gold strike in history has drawn a wild and irresponsible following, but it is doubtful if there has ever been a strike which brought together as colorful a collection of human beings as reached California in the early days of its gold rush, and scattered from San Francisco through the mining camps, which sprang up wherever the precious metal was found. Bret Harte and Mark Twain, together with many a lesser writer, have given us revealing pictures of the men and manners of those days. They were rough days, full of hardness and of sorrow. But they were days which had their glory too; days when the gold was found in character-seams as unpromising as any worked by the prospectors.

Along with the first of the California Argonauts there went a Methodist preacher. His Conference—the famous old Baltimore Conference—had released him for missionary service in California soon after the word of the annexation of the territory had come back across the Rockies, and before the news of the gold strike at Sutter's Mill had precipitated the great stampede. He made the journey, accompanied by his wife and an infant son, by the long sea route around Cape Horn, and landed in the city by the Golden Gate with one of the earliest of the companies of forty-niners. The little knock-down timber chapel which he had brought with him proved an impressive cathedral in the San Francisco of those days—in most part a city of tents. Day in and day out, in the face of discouragements such as would have paralyzed a lesser man, this Methodist preacher kept at his mission, until he had planted his church firmly in the new State and had seen a lawless frontier community transformed into an orderly and settled commonwealth. Then he passed on to new fields.

It is the purpose of this chapter to tell something about the life of this spiritual forty-niner. We cannot pretend to make the story a complete one. There are several volumes larger than this one you are now reading given to nothing more than the exploits of this single man, and even these do not tell all that might be told. But we can, perhaps, give a few glimpses of him that will prove easy to remember. And we think him worth remembering, not alone for the wonderful life which he lived and the wonderful deeds which he accomplished,

WILLIAM TAYLOR

but also because his life suggested one or two facts about this Methodism of ours which should not be forgotten. For this man was always doing things in unexpected ways; ways in which men had never done these things before. Some people found it hard to justify his use of these untried methods. But long before his death it was clear that he had done as much to make Methodism an agency for the growth of the King-dom by using these ir-regular processes as had the host of those who clung carefully to the time-worn ways. For that reason, in any story of Meth-odism the career of this man is worth pondering.

§ 2. OUT OF VIRGINIA'S HILLS

His name was William Taylor. He was born in Vir-ginia, of that fine Scotch-Irish stock which formed the sturdy character of the hill counties of the old dominion. His father was a tanner by trade, but spent his life farming. Until he reached middle age he was a member of the Presbyterian Church—as any good Scotch-Irishman might be expected to be!—but then he experienced a profound religious awakening at a Methodist camp meeting, out of which there came a change of church relationship. The father developed into a famous local preacher, who spent more of his time inviting seekers to the mourner's bench at the camp meetings and schoolhouse revivals of that part of Virginia than he did in farming. The home life of his boy, who was later to become a world figure, was thus of an exemplary sort. He was formed more by heritage and religious training than he himself ever dreamed.

William Taylor himself was a child of the camp meeting. He was among the penitents almost as soon as he entered his teens; for six years, he tells us, he vainly sought the sort of religious experience which the camp meeting held to be the common one for every person truly converted and "saved." To the end of his life William Taylor was the child of the camp meeting. He knew the moment when he was saved—"about 10 P. M. of the 28th day of August, 1841"—and he could tell the moment when any one of the motley multitude who, in the course of his long career, came to bow before him at the penitent's form, was likewise saved. He carried the spirit, the message, and the judgments of the camp meeting with him from that open-air gathering at Panther Gap to every continent and civilization on the globe.

William Taylor came into the Methodist ministry as did scores of other young men of his time. After his conversion at the Panther Gap camp meeting he became a rural schoolteacher, spending as much time as he could in local Methodist classes and as class leader and exhorter. Finally, at a camp meeting in which he was doing what he could to help the regular ministers, the presiding elder of that district drew him into the tent set aside for the preachers. "He stroked my hair softly," said Taylor years after in relating the incident, "and drew me near his loving heart and said, 'Brother William, I want to send you as junior preacher with Francis A. Harding, on Monroe Circuit.'

" 'Why, Brother Morgan, I never preached in my life. I can't preach.'

"He caressed me kindly and said, 'God has called you to preach, and I know you can do it, and God will bless you and give you success.'

"I was awed and amazed, moved and melted, and hardly knew what to say. After a pause I ventured to ask, 'What books should I take with me from which I may learn to preach?'

" 'Take the Bible and the Methodist Hymn Book.' "

As a young preacher, Taylor was appointed to work on the mountain circuits of the part of Virginia in which he had been reared. He knew the sort of people with whom he had to deal; he allowed no physical difficulties to daunt him; with these advantages and qualities he combined a flaming evangelistic zeal which made revivals and conversions the normal accompaniment of all his labors. When he came up for admission into the Annual Conference, his presiding elder said, "He is a young man whom the sun never finds in bed." But it was probably the record of things other than this early rising which moved Bishop Soule, who was presiding, to rise and say, "Mark my words, brethren, you will hear from that young man again."

§ 3. In California

It was in September, 1848, that William Taylor, by that time the marked junior preacher of the North Baltimore Circuit, striding down the street to the Monday morning preacher's meeting, heard his name called in the crowd, and followed a messenger into the office behind a bookstore. There he found Bishop Beverly Waugh, who, after telling him that the General Conference had authorized the sending of two missionaries to California, asked him if he would be one of the two. It was six months before passage could be secured, but by September of 1849, after a voyage of one hundred and forty-five days, the young missionary, with his wife and two infant children—one of them born off Cape Horn—was in San Francisco, and ready to begin work.

The story of the next few years, while the work of Methodism was being planted along the Pacific Coast, has been told in the chapter on "The Winning of the West." Here it is enough to say that the tall, raw-boned, long-bearded, utterly fearless mountaineer, who had persisted in remaining a mountaineer even when he had been appointed to the "leading" circuit of the "leading" Conference of his church, proved a providential man for the work of God which needed to be done along the docks and on the plaza of the blatant boom city by the Golden Gate.

He had to deal with a rough-and-ready sort of wickedness, and he knew how to face that sort of opposition. The empty whisky barrels which formed a conspicuous element in the civic decorations of that period he turned into an outdoor pulpit. The sounds of revelry from within dance-halls and gambling hells he countered with a thunderous singing voice which carried as far as did ever the voice of George Whitefield. It was on the San Francisco streets that Taylor first raised the song which he was to make the clarion call of his later revivals around the world:

> "Hear the royal proclamation,
> The glad tidings of salvation,
> Publishing to every creature,
> To the ruined sons of nature—

> *Chorus*
> "Jesus reigns, he reigns victorious,
> Over heaven and earth most glorious,
> Jesus reigns!

> "Hear, ye sons of wrath and ruin,
> Who have wrought your own undoing;
> Here is life, and free salvation,
> Offered to the whole creation.

" 'Twas for you that Jesus died,
For you he was crucified,
Conquered death, and rose to heaven;
Life eternal's through him given.

"For this love of rocks and mountains,
Purling streams and crystal fountains,
Roaring thunders, lightning blazes,
Shout the great Messiah's praises.

"Turn unto the Lord most holy,
Shun the path of sin and folly:
Turn, or you are lost forever,
Oh, now turn to God, your Saviour.

Chorus
"Jesus reigns, he reigns victorious,
Over heaven and earth most glorious,
Jesus reigns!"

California offered more than a little preparation for the sort of ministry which was to fill William Taylor's later life.

"WHAT'S THE NEWS?"

Not only did he find men in that mad rush for gold stripped to their elemental passions, but he found men of all nations. He himself says that Peter's congregation on the day of Pentecost could not begin to equal, for variety, the kind of crowds to which he habitually preached on San Francisco's streets.

"Good morning, gentlemen; I am glad to see you this bright Sabbath of the Lord," he cried when he had sung one of his great open-air congregations together one morning. "What's the news? Thank the

Lord, I have good news for you this morning,—'Behold, I bring you good tidings of great joy which shall be to all people.' " And then he tells how he applied that text to all the nationalities which were plainly present in his audience.

" 'My French brother,' " he shouted, " 'look here!' He looked with earnest eye and ear while I told him what Jesus had done for him and his people. 'Brother Spaniard, I have tidings for you, señor,' and told him the news. 'My Hawaiian brother, don't you want to hear the news this morning? I have glad tidings of great joy for you.' I then told him the news, and that his island should wait for the law of Jesus. 'John Chinaman, you, John, there by that post—look here, my good fellow; I've got something to tell you.' " And so he went ahead, naming one nationality after another. But when he got through one voice shouted out of the crowd, "And may it plase your riverence, and have ye nothing for a poor Irishman?" It was demands of that kind which made the street preacher what he was. Quick as a flash he replied, "I ask your pardon, my dear Irish brother, I did not mean to pass you by. I have good news for you. Jesus Christ, by the grace of God, tasted death for every Irishman on the Emerald Isle; and let me tell you, my brother, that if you will this morning renounce all your sins and submit to the will of God, he will grant you a free pardon and clean all the sins and devils out of your heart as effectually as your people say Saint Patrick cleaned the toads and snakes out of Ireland."

§ 4.   OFF TO AUSTRALIA

Taylor was one of the commanding figures of California for seven years. He received no support as a missionary, raising what he needed to live by on the ground—a practice which was later to exert a powerful influence on the work he undertook in other lands. Finally, the institution for which he was directly responsible, a seamen's mission, became involved in the real estate crash which is the usual experience of every boom city. To pay the staggering debts, and to rescue some part of the endangered property, the evangelist was allowed to return to the East on a money-raising trip. As it turned out, he was never again to have an active career in California.

On his arrival in New York, the young minister—for he was still only thirty-five years of age—found himself nationally famous as "California Taylor." For six years he was kept busy in the eastern States and Canada, hastening from one camp meeting to another, telling the story of his work on the Pacific Coast before congregations, committees, and conventions. He would not accept gifts for his own support, nor would he ask for gifts for the debt-burdened work which he was representing. He wrote a book on his adventures in San Francisco street preaching, and he depended on the profits from the sale of that book to pay his own way and to raise the money which he sought. It was a plan which he used throughout his life. California, however, soon became an incidental; his first work, and almost his only work, was preaching for immediate, individual conversions. He became one of the best-known and most effective evangelists in the country.

Just what it was that brought him to the next phase of his career it is hard to tell. It may have been the interruptions which the Civil War brought to all religious work in the United States. It may have been some of the appeals which were constantly reaching him from other lands. Or it may have been the old itch of the pioneer, the heritage of a California Argonaut, that impulse which makes it impossible for the man who has once crossed the ranges to be content with the settled order of long-established communities.

At any rate, early in 1862 William Taylor was on the Atlantic again, and from then until his death his story was one of oceans crossed and continents traversed. His destination he had fixed as Australia, but he was in no hurry to reach there. He spent almost a year in the British Isles, conducting evangelistic services, and incidentally contributing by voice and pen to the defense of the Union cause in a country where the Confederacy had powerful friends. Then he made a short side trip through Palestine, whose many shrines seem to have impressed him, for all his piety, little more than they did Mark Twain. Finally he landed in Melbourne to begin the first of his great preaching tours through the island continent.

There are still to be found evidences of the influence which William Taylor had on Australia during his two visits there. All in all, he was in the continent about four years. He adhered rigidly to the same forms of evangelistic meetings which he had known from his boyhood in the Virginia hills. He used the methods which he had used in the rough pioneer town of San Francisco. By every outward indication the observers who predicted failure for a mission so conducted were right. But with William Taylor doing the preaching they were proved wrong. Men of all classes, leaders of the Australian bar as well as the broken wastrels of the city slums, proved as ready to come at the call of the evangelist's "Royal Proclamation" as had the adventurers of California.

§ 5. "DRIVEN BACK AND FORTH THE WORLD"

From Australia Taylor went to South Africa, and there he had his first contact with an acknowledged mission field. In the cities he preached to large congregations of Englishmen and Dutchmen—and incidentally made little impression on the Dutchmen—but he was not satisfied until he had penetrated into the native portions of the continent. He seems to have preached precisely the same kind of sermons, through his interpreters, to the Kaffirs and Zulus that he had been preaching to the Nordics, and with equal results. Also, he caught a glimpse of the possibilities of supporting a mission by the industry of its missionaries and converts which was later to bear much fruit.

From South Africa, Taylor's route, which if traced on a map would look like a maze of crossings and recrossings, led him back to England, thence to the West Indies, thence to the continent of Europe, thence back to the West Indies again, thence to London, thence to Australia, thence to Ceylon, and finally to India. In every place along the way he preached; in every place he supported himself by the sale of his books— a practice which he claimed paralleled that of Saint Paul in tent-making—and in every place he produced revivals which not only stirred the community, but which left a lasting impression.

But it was in India that William Taylor was to have what was to prove probably the most influential ministry of his life. When he landed in Bombay, in 1870, he found the Christian forces in the country just beginning to recover from the effects of the mutiny of 1857. The Methodist mission, in particular, was weak. It had been founded only a year when the mutiny broke out; settled policy and its slow access of strength had held its labors to a comparatively small territory in what are now the United Provinces. There were already some great men on the roster of missionaries—it was James M. Thoburn who invited Taylor to come from Australia to India!—but there was little evidence of the coming power which the Methodist Church was to wield in that empire.

Much of the importance of the work of William Taylor in India grew out of his discovery of a class of people who had been, before that, largely neglected. These were the Eurasians, or Anglo-Indians, as they are frequently called. It is one of the sad commentaries on the white man's manner of life in the Orient that every great Asiatic port which has a foreign colony of any size has also a large community of persons of mixed blood. And social lines are frequently so drawn as to exclude these from intercourse with their European father's people on the one hand or with their native mother's folk on the other.

Nominally, they are members of the Established Church, if in a British colony, or of the Roman Catholic. Because of their inheritance of language they frequently rise to positions of importance, both in business and, in India, in the government. But they remain, none the less, a people apart.

William Taylor became, in India, the great apostle to the Anglo-Indians. He never ceased to preach to and work with

"SELF-SUPPORTING CHURCHES"

the purely native population, and many remarkable conversions were reported as a result of that preaching, even among Brahmans and Moslems. But it was for the Anglo-Indian that his coming seemed especially providential. During the four years during which he ranged up and down India, he made his greatest appeals to this group, won from them his largest response, and established among them many self-supporting churches which remain powerful institutions to this day.

It was in India that Taylor's belief in the possibility of self-supporting missions first took practical form. He found the established Methodist missions opposed to expansion of territory because of fears of collision with other missions, and because of the extra expense involved. The missionaries agreed, however, that there could be no serious exception taken to advance steps which made no drain on the general treasury, and sought no support from other Christian groups. This was all the permission Taylor needed. Look at the way in which Methodism is established to-day in Bombay, Hyderabad, Madras, Calcutta, Poona, Bangalore, Jubbulpore, Allahabad, Asansol, Cawnpore, Agra, Ajmere, Karachi, Quetta, and other centers, and you have the continuing proof of the way in which his adventurous soul spread the work of his church over an empire.

It must be admitted that the authorities of the church at first looked on much of this activity with a suspicious eye. The mission board in New York, and the bishops who, in those days, made the round of the mission fields once in four years, were sure that this was all irregular, and feared it might be the first portent of a coming secession. But so long as Taylor raised all the money there was little they could do about it, and finally they were persuaded that, in view of the evident success of the work, the best thing to do would be to bless it and regularize it. So the missions which had been established were recognized as regular missions, a new Mission Conference was organized, and William Taylor was regularly appointed as its superintendent. The work of Taylor had to be made regular in order to survive. His method of self-supporting missions has never proved permanent.

§ 6. Bishop for Africa

But William Taylor was so full of an inner dynamite that they no sooner had him regularized in one place than he was over the bounds in another. With the work well established in India, he answered a call from Moody to assist in evangelistic services in England, and then came on to America. While in this country he felt moved to open work in South America. He designed this as self-supporting work of the same kind he had planted in India, and issued a call for volunteer workers. As devoted a band as ever answered an appeal for pioneer Christian service came in response to his summons.

It cannot be said that the missions Taylor established in

South America were notably successful. No Protestant missions ever have been notably successful in that continent. Nor did the church make success any more likely by the attitude which it took. About all that the bishops and mission board secretaries could see in the enterprise was the fact that the workers were not responsible to the board of foreign missions, and hence were in an irregular connection. So the word went out that any minister who continued in the work would have to "locate" in his Annual Conference membership. This means, in effect, retire from the active ministry. All but one of the young preachers who had gone out "located." William Taylor did the same thing. At the end of forty years of continent-shaking service, he was right back where he had started—insofar as his own church was concerned—a layman!

Then an amazing thing happened. The South India Conference, the child of Taylor's work in India, was as unwilling to let this be the final outcome of the veteran's service as he was. When it came to the election of delegates to the General Conference of 1884, some member suggested that Taylor, since he was located, even though he was then working on another continent, be sent as a lay delegate! And so it came that he was given his chance to make his plea for self-supporting missions in person before the General Conference.

He made that plea; the General Conference upheld him in it; by its action the way was opened for Methodist missionaries and missions to support themselves in any continent if they so desired. But before the General Conference of 1884 had taken this action on the question of general policy, it took another action, far more personal, and bound to have a far greater effect on the career of the great evangelist. It elected him, nominally a lay delegate, bishop for Africa!

The Methodist field in Africa, at that time, was no larger than the little republic of Liberia. William Taylor accepted his election with the definite understanding that while he was "to administer the work of the Methodist Episcopal Church in Liberia according to the rules of the denomination in its relation to the missionary society, he was to found missions on his self-supporting plan anywhere within the radius of the African continent." He made sure in advance that there was to be no more of the kind of red-tape trouble he had known in South America. If the church would turn him loose and let him go, well and good.

For twelve years he served as bishop of the Methodist Episcopal Church in Africa. It will h a r d l y b e claimed that he accomplished wonders while in that position. Sticking to his principle of self-support—which in Africa he interpreted to mean that his missionaries should develop industries sufficient to give a livelihood to all those whom their work Christianized and civilized—the missions under his administration were naturally few in number.

"HE WAS A PIONEER ADVENTURER"

But the general strategy of the campaign which he projected was undoubtedly the correct one. The line of battle which he laid out is still a fighting line worth holding and reenforcing. Bishop Taylor divided his time between Liberia and the southern half of the continent. To the Liberian mission he gave one type of leadership; to the missions elsewhere another. In Liberia he was the administrator of a settled missionary order, working under a society with rules and long-established precedents. In the rest of his field he was a pioneer adventurer, plunging along the forest paths and floating on the streams until he reached the stockade of some other king who desired to "make palaver" in regard to a possible extension of the bishop's area.

The menacing feature of the religious life of Africa during the past fifty years has been the slow advance of Islam from the north, making its way through the jungles and winning converts in scores of tribes. Compared with the numerical growth of Christianity, Islam has been advancing by leaps and bounds. While this advance has been under way from the north, Christianity has been establishing itself in the south, in what is now the Union of South Africa.

When William Taylor undertook his work as a bishop, the first decision that he made was to run a line of mission stations, like the trenches of Flanders and France, across the continent, to hold back the Islamic tide. And while this line has never been strong enough to do the work expected of it, its outline is still plainly to be seen, extending from Loanda on the west coast, past Quessa and Malanje, Kapanga, Kambove, and Elisabethville, to Mutambara, Umtali, and Inhambane.

§ 7. AFTERGLOW

It was 1896 when William Taylor, after fifty-four years of such labors as even Methodist history can scarcely parallel, came to the end of his active career. He was not ready to retire. He had come to the General Conference of that year after covering more than four hundred miles afoot through the jungles of Angola. He did not feel that he had reached the end of his period of effective service. But when the Conference voted otherwise, he accepted the decision like a good soldier. Only—he wanted one more trip to Africa.

He made that trip, and no emperor ever had a triumph to compare with it. Part of the time he still walked, but mostly he rode in one of those covered wagons drawn by four pairs of oxen which is the African equivalent for a prairie schooner. On the back end of the wagon a sort of shaded pulpit had been contrived, and when the journey halted, the aged bishop would step out there to speak. As the news spread that the famous white-bearded bishop was making his last journey, the people of jungle and kraal came by the thousands to see and hear him, and, in the case of converts, to have his hands placed in blessing on their heads. Then, when he had done preaching, and the oxen took up their slow pace toward the next stopping place, they would follow the wagon for miles.

To the end, he was the same man, preaching in the same way, to secure the same results, as in the beginning. He had begun his ministry in the mountains of Virginia. He ended it in a wild, primitive spot among the mountains of Africa. He had begun by preaching for conversions. He ended with a service in which there were seventy-eight black-skinned seekers after salvation, and forty who professed to find spiritual satisfaction. Then he went down to the coast, and aboard ship, and over the long sea lanes again, until he had reached the country of his birth. And here he lingered, growing feebler and feebler by almost imperceptible stages, until at last, six years after his retirement, he entered in triumph the Continent toward which his face had always been turned.

CHAPTER XXII

THE TALE OF THE YEARS IN MANY LANDS

§ 1. 'Round the World in Thirty Minutes

IT IS one of the inevitable handicaps of such a book as this that it cannot give to every part of the Methodist movement, and to every period of its life, the attention rightfully deserved. It cannot, because there is too much of it. Methodists have gone to too many places, and done too many things, to make it possible to squeeze the whole story inside a single volume. For much of the story there can only be hints—words and phrases of pitiable inadequacy thrown out more to pique interest than to do the subjects justice—hoping that those who have their attention thus aroused will go to other and more complete volumes for the full account.

This chapter, then, must be no more than a hasty summary of what has gone on in other parts of the Methodist world since the death of John Wesley. It will have to be a sort of Methodist Cook's tour, covering both space and time, and hurrying us along from country to country, from decade to decade, without giving us time to settle down anywhere and become really acquainted with the places we are visiting. But it may at least serve to show us that our American Methodism is not the only Methodism there is, and that in other parts of the earth the followers of Wesley have achieved spiritual victories that may be ranked with any we have known in our own country. Take a good grip, then, on your imagination, and we will start— around the Methodist world in thirty minutes!

§ 2. British Wesleyanism

We start with the mother Methodism of us all, that in

England. We are back, nine years before the close of the eighteenth century, looking at the Methodist societies which have sprung up so marvelously in all parts of that "green and pleasant land." John Wesley has just died, and the English Methodists seem to be holding their breath, wondering what is going to happen. For under John Wesley this English Methodism has been distinctly a one-man affair; and now the one man is gone. Is there anyone to take his place?

Only two men can be seriously considered for such a position. One of them is the Scotchman, Alexander Mather, whom Wesley himself once set aside for the work of a "general superintendent" in England. But Mather does not press any claims which he may have; in fact, he appears to want no more one-man rule. The other possible aspirant is Dr. Thomas Coke, but, as we have seen in the chapter on "The Missionary Spirit," the little doctor is much too busy speeding from the West Indies to America, and from America back to Ireland, and perhaps from Ireland to the Continent, to make it possible for him to settle down to the work of administration in England. So, in the nature of things, British Methodism has to seek other than a personal rule.

We hear these British Methodists everywhere talking about a Deed of Declaration which Wesley, before his death, executed. In that, we are told, is the plan which the founder had for the government of his movement after he should be gone. It seems that the core of his idea is that there shall be a body of one hundred ministers—men speak of them as the Legal Hundred—who shall meet in conference once a year and settle all questions of church administration. When Wesley drew up his plan, a body of one hundred men was large enough to contain practically all the tried members of the English itinerancy. But by this time the limit is too small. As the years go on we shall see the inadequacy and injustice of the situation become more and more apparent.

What is to be done about it? The only way these British Methodists can obtain legal relief is by going into Parliament and asking for a special act setting aside Wesley's plan and setting up some new one. And when you start tinkering with affairs like that in a political body, the result may be to make matters worse rather than better. So these British brethren of ours stay away from Parliament. But what they do do is much what we might have done under the same circumstances. As we watch them we see that, in the course of the years, they make it easier for men to be elected to the Legal Hundred before they are gray-bearded and over-cautious. And, finally, they make the Legal Hundred itself not much more than an empty form —a rubber stamp.

They leave the Legal Hundred still there, of course. The law requires that. But the members of the Hundred ask all the preachers of the church—and, for some questions chosen laymen as well—to sit with them and pass recommendations as to what the church should do. Then the Hundred goes through the necessary legal motions of adopting the recommendations. But they would never think of disregarding the recommendations! It is a left-handed way of doing business, and nobody would ever adopt it out of choice. But it is made necessary because of the fact that even John Wesley wasn't wise enough to lay down cast-iron rules for doing the business of the church which would not, in the course of the years, require change.

But now let us go back and look at those early years again. If we do so, we see that the questions which are making the most trouble are not questions having to do with administration at all. If we listen, we hear men asking again and again: "What is to be our relation to the Church of England?" Or, "Why don't we become a church by ourselves?" Men began to ask those questions long before the Wesley brothers died. But while the Wesleys, devoted sons of the Anglican Church, lived, they were kept in the background. Now they are out in the open, being asked everywhere, and men are demanding an answer.

Somebody once called the Church of England "the church of lost opportunities." Now we are to have the melancholy experience of watching her lose perhaps the greatest opportunity she ever had. Here are the leaderless Methodists, with hosts of them looking for even the promise of half a welcome if they seek a place within the Anglican fold. And here, in place after place, are parsons turning away from the communion altar the Methodists who come there seeking the sacraments. As late as 1842 we may see the Bishop of London professing himself unable to do anything when one of his clergymen refuses Christian burial to a child who has been baptized by a Wesleyan minister, and hear those devoted men called "beings who pretend to be ministers of the gospel, and really are ministers of hell"! Do you wonder that these Methodists are turning away from a church which greets them like them?

"THE CHURCH OF LOST OPPORTUNITY"

The process of separation is very gradual. It is hard for us to put our finger down at any spot as the story unrolls before us and say, "Just here, or here, or here, the Methodist societies ceased to be mere religious societies and became a church." It is 1818, with John Wesley dead more than a quarter of a century, before the Methodist preachers allow themselves to be called "Reverend." It is 1836 before they allow the placing of hands on the heads of the young men being received into the ministry. It is even as late as 1870 before, in some places, the Wesleyans cease going to the parish church to receive the sacraments.

And while all these changes, so gradual but so far-reaching, are taking place we see some great men developing. Here is Adam Clarke, beginning his ministry while Wesley is still alive, but coming to his full powers after the founder's death. Has Methodism ever produced a mind to surpass his? He is a good deal of a "liberal" when it comes to theology— some of his views are so startling that the church feels compelled to repudiate them publicly—but his mental grasp is so astonishing, and his personal piety is so warm and attractive, that we see him go ahead unchallenged in his place of leadership.

Here are Jabez Bunting and Robert Newton. Perhaps you have never chanced on them before. They are worth knowing. Newton is the great preacher. Watch him chasing back and forth across the country, preaching almost every night, covering six thousand miles a year, and by his eloquence stirring the Methodists as they have not been stirred since Wesley died. He is secretary of the missionary society; his golden tongue fills its coffers and makes possible the sending of missionaries to many parts of the earth.

Bunting is a different sort. He, too, is a missionary secretary, but his greatest work is done in Conferences and committees. For years he really rules the Wesleyan Church. He has all the power in the Annual Conferences that Dr. James M. Buckley used to have in American General Conferences, and then between Conferences he has almost as much power as all the American Methodist bishops together would have!

And now as we watch we see that insensibly, almost, during these years when Bunting and Newton and other men like them are in control, the British Wesleyan Church is becoming less and less of a crusading adventure and more and more of a "regular" church. As the countryside gives way to the manufacturing city, the rural circuits lose their importance. And as the manufacturing city begins to spawn its problems of tenements, and child labor, and poverty, the city churches draw more and more away from those hideous things, until they finally are spending most of their time preaching to the people in comfortable circumstances. The people whose stomachs are crying for food seem to have little interest in "the gospel" which the carefully correct preachers are talking about.

Then, suddenly, a flaming preacher named Hugh Price Hughes appears and, in the closing years of the nineteenth century, brings British Wesleyanism to face its responsibility in the cities. Here is a fighting Welshman who goes into the West End of London and founds a "mission" which soon has the eyes of the nation fixed on it. What he calls a "central mission hall" we Americans should call an "institutional church," but we have no institutional churches until Hugh Price Hughes has shown us what a seven-day-in-the-week plant may be. So successfully does this type of religious enterprise deal with the problems it is facing that the central halls spread until there are now about fifty of them, located in all the great cities of England. They are the most attention-commanding feature of modern British Wesleyanism.

This does not mean, of course, that there is not a lot of faithful work being done in other parts of the church. Looking now in our own time, we see the ministers still covering their circuits; the local preachers still meeting their regular appointments. Class meetings persist, as they have not with us. But, outside of the central halls there is very little to differentiate this church from any other British church, except the Anglican. The Wesleyan ministers do not look on themselves as "dissenting" as the Congregational and Baptist and Presbyterian ministers of England do. They regard themselves as rather near in spirit and thought to the Church of England,

and many of them would like to see reunion take place with that church. They sometimes seem a little stiff to their American visitors; a little more concerned with the ecclesiastical proprieties than Methodists might be expected to be. But they are good men and true, and they are deserving well of their day and generation.

§ 3.   OTHER METHODIST BODIES IN ENGLAND

We have but a few moments in which to look at the other Methodist bodies in England. In the chapter on "Methodist Breaks and Fractures" we have seen that there are such bodies, in addition to the British Wesleyan Church, and we have discovered how one or two of them came into existence. We will not go over that ground again. It is sufficient now to know that, as we look at England to-day, we find not only Wesleyans, but Primitive Methodists and United Methodists, and we see that these other bodies, too, are having a pronounced influence on the life of the nation.

These non-Wesleyan bodies seem, as we look at them, to be much more free in their forms of religious expression; to be less anxious about their social and ecclesiastical regularity; to place more insistence on the older type of evangelistic effort. They owed their start, some of them, to the old-style camp meeting, and the influence of that origin remains. Their preaching is apt to be "noisier" than Wesleyan preaching. Indeed, if you listen closely, you may still hear some street urchin point after a member of the Primitive Methodist Church and say, "He's a Ranter." But among these people we do not find it hard to feel at home.

It is not to be taken from this that these non-Wesleyan Methodists in England are without their scholars. At the present moment, for instance, one of the keenest thinkers in all Britain is admittedly Dr. A. S. Peake, of Manchester, one of the few students of the New Testament to whom that abused word, "an authority," can rightfully be applied. And Doctor Peake is a member of the Primitive Methodist Church. It must be said to the honor of these communions that they have kept in view Wesley's ideal of the union of sound thinking with evangelical fervor.

In our rapid trip across England we see bodies other than the Primitive Methodists break out of the Wesleyan fold. First of all there is what in the beginning is called the Methodist New Connection. Then come the Bible Christian Methodists. Then the Protestant Methodists and the Wesleyan Methodist Association, both of which soon unite to form the United Methodist Free Church. There is very little to differentiate these bodies, either in government, message, or aim. As the years pass, this likeness becomes more and more apparent, until it is clear that there is no further reason for their staying apart. About twenty years ago, therefore, the British Parliament passes the required enabling act, and since then these streams have flowed together to form one United Methodist Church.

Now, if you look at England, you see the way being prepared for another union. Having brought so many different kinds of Methodists together, there are many leaders who are saying, "Why do we stop here? Why not go ahead and bring *all* the Methodists together?" Much enthusiasm has been shown for this final union, but, as in the United States, there are some who hold back. Whether it will go through or not cannot yet be foretold; if the writers of this book had to make a prophecy they would say that they fear it will not. That it *should* go through seems clear.

Shall we have a few figures? Not many, just enough to give us some idea of the size of these various Methodist Churches we have been talking about. The Wesleyan Methodists are the most numerous, with more than 500,000 members in England, 30,000 in Ireland, more than 150,000 in South Africa, and more than 250,000 in other foreign missions. That

---

Methodism in England 1926

Wesleyan Methodists   *500000*

Primitive Methodists   *200000 +*

United Methodist Church   *200000 -*

Also a Few Independent Congregations

---

speaks well for them, doesn't it—to have almost as many members outside as within England? It shows how regular has been the advance and how missionary the spirit of the church during all these years.

Next, in membership, to the Wesleyans come the Primitive Methodists with a little more than 200,000 members. Then there is the present United Methodist Church, with not quite 200,000 names on its membership rolls, and a sprinkling of "reform" and "independent" congregations scattered about the country. The inclusion of all these different kinds of Methodists shows a church much larger than any of the other non-Anglican bodies in England.

§ 4. IN IRELAND

We have an unusual interest in the Methodist Church in Ireland. It was from Ireland that Philip Embury and Barbara Heck, and those other Methodist pioneers of America, sailed to New York. From Ireland Robert Strawbridge sailed for Maryland. Ireland was the particular child of Thomas Coke, who was also one of the founders of the Methodist Episcopal Church. And during all the years there have been hundreds of Methodist leaders who have traced their spiritual ancestry straight back to the class meetings and congregations of Ireland.

When we cross the Irish channel to look at Irish Methodism we see some strange, some unwelcome, facts. We see that the success of a church, at least from a numerical standpoint, does not rest on the character of its leaders, the response of the public generally, but to a large extent on economic circumstances which may be entirely beyond control. John Wesley never found a field where people listened more eagerly to his preaching than in Ireland. No church ever had more spiritual or wise leadership than did the Methodists of Ireland under Thomas Walsh, Adam Clarke, and Thomas Coke. And if persecution bravely borne is, as has been claimed, a source of strength, then the church in Ireland had advantages beyond any of its sister churches.

Yet the Irish church to-day is, as we see, small in size, and making little progress in membership. In the last seventeen years, its net growth has been less than fifty members! There was a time, in 1844, when there were 50,000 Methodists in Ireland; to-day there are not much more than half that number. What happened? Nothing to the Methodists in particular, but something to Ireland as a whole. And that something, in two words, was the "potato blight" of the '40s and '50s.

In 1841 there were more than eight million people in Ireland; to-day there are only four million and a half! Even the Roman Catholic Church in that country has more than a million fewer communicants than it had a century ago! The best blood of Ireland was poured into the life of the New World, and no devotion or planning on the part of the churches has been able to hold for the home land the membership or power which it once had. Irish Methodism deserves the highest credit both for giving so much of its strength for the enrichment of America and also for carrying on so heroically with diminished resources. At the present day, Methodism in Ireland, amid great perplexities and handicaps, is showing the same type of heroism and perseverance.

§ 5. In Canada

Captain Webb, the one-eyed hero who had so much to do with the founding of Methodism in America, entered Canada with Wolfe's army. But it remained for other warriors, spiritual adventurers wearing another uniform, to carry Methodism into that great dominion. If we go back to the years when England was first putting the stamp of her authority where previously the lilies of France had been blazoned, we see the first pioneers of the church entering the country. Some of them came by direct appointment of Wesley to Newfoundland and Nova Scotia. Others were Methodists who had settled first in the colonies, and then sought a new frontier to the north rather than to the west.

Barbara Heck, with her family, was one of these. In the year before Lexington was fought, the Heck family emigrated to what was then called upper Canada—now the province of Quebec—and tried one settlement after another. Finally they came to rest in lower Canada—now Ontario—and there their bodies lie to-day. Militant Methodists that they were, it was not long after they had reached a place before there was a Methodist society in process of formation. To Barbara Heck goes the honor of having been a pioneer of Methodism in the two great countries which hold in their keeping the destiny of the west.

As we look back now at the formative period in the history of Canadian Methodism, we can see the streams of influence flowing into the dominion from many different directions. Here is stout Nathan Bangs, a typical knight of the saddlebags, crossing from western New York and penetrating what is to be the most populous portion of the country. Here is William Black, with his commission from Wesley as superintendent when he is still less than thirty, and his mighty labors in that position taking him from Nova Scotia through practically all British America. Here is Freeborn Garrettson, sent in by Coke at the behest of the Baltimore Conference which founded the Methodist Episcopal Church. And so the names might be multiplied.

We see some queer mix-ups in churchly organization during those early years. In the main, these grow out of the differing origins of various parts of the Methodism of Canada.

BARBARA HECK

One part holds its allegiance with the Conference on the American side of the line, even though war between the two countries is in the air. Another part holds its allegiance with the Methodist Conference in England. Still another part seems to be self-contained and independent of all outside alliances. As we watch we see these various elements come closer and closer together; actually meet at certain points; then draw away again; finally come together for all time.

For the last thirty-five years Methodism in Canada has been a united body. It has prospered amazingly. Canadian Methodists have pushed their way westward with the frontier. The roots have gone in deep, and every preparation has been made for that destiny which Canada confidently awaits, when the rich lands of Alberta and Manitoba and British Columbia, as well as the provinces of the East, shall support one of the great populations of the earth.

As we have been watching this Canadian Methodism we

have seen an amazing thing happen during the last few years. We have seen its members drawing nearer and nearer the members of other Protestant bodies, particularly the Presbyterians and the Congregationalists. We have seen them come to look on each other as brothers in a common cause, rather than as rivals for a common prize. So we have seen the movement for union. Now there is no longer a Methodist Church of Canada. Neither is there a Congregational Church. There is a Presbyterian Church still, but it is composed only of a minority who have held back from a great adventure. For Canada, on the tenth of June, 1925, saw the birth of a United Church, and in this United Church what used to be the Methodist and the Presbyterian and the Congregational Churches will find their destiny. How John Wesley would have gloried in such a consummation!

§ 6.   IN AUSTRALIA AND SOUTH AFRICA

The year that saw the organization of the Methodist Episcopal Church saw the streams of British emigration turn away from the New World to other parts of the earth. Up to the time of the American Revolution it had been the habit of the British government to send hundreds of convicts every year to replenish the population of the colonies; with the establishment of American independence these forced colonists had to go elsewhere. Thus it happened that the great penal colonies were founded in Australia, over which Captain James Cook had raised the British flag only five years before the Americans began their struggle for freedom.

If we make the long jump from Canada to Australia, and seek to review rapidly the progress of Methodism in that great commonwealth, we will probably be struck, first of all, by the absence of unusual events in the record. Outside of the visits of William Taylor, of which we have already told in the chapter on "A Spiritual Forty-niner," there have been almost no exciting moments in the life of Australian Methodism. The first Methodists seem to have come to the colony with almost the first convict ships. As has happened in other British colonies, some of the first and best are soldiers in the British army.

And some of them are convicts! Yet we are not to think of them harshly because of that. No Australian feels compunction to-day in admitting that his ancestors came to the country in a convict ship. That was the day when stealing cherries was a hanging offense, and men and women, even boys and girls, were often sentenced to deportation from England for acts which would not be recognized as criminal to-day. Six Methodists were deported to Australia as criminals for meeting at the home of one of them to discuss laboring conditions in the factory where they were employed!

As Australia grows Methodism grows. When pioneers go out from Sydney, the first settlement, to plant other colonies, there are generally Methodists among them, and class meetings come naturally into the life of every new community. As the first settlements grow into great cities, the societies grow into congregations, and the first small chapels grow into large churches. William Taylor brings the breath of revival, putting new energy into these churches. His influence is still to be felt. But for the most part the church has been content to grow normally, until to-day it has not quite 5,000 churches, with about 160,000 names on the rolls of membership.

The various breaks that have occurred among the Methodists of England are, for a time, mirrored in this great commonwealth. Now, happily, they have disappeared, and it is a united Methodist Church of Australia which is considering the same union with Congregationalists and Presbyterians which has taken place in Canada. There are even rumors that when the union comes in Australia it will have the Anglicans also within it. But this seems too much to hope.

The growth of Methodism in South Africa has been some-what different from that in Australia. When we turn our eyes toward Capetown we see a soldier of an English regiment, part of the force which has seized the territory for Great Britain, preaching to his comrades in arms. When he goes back to England the work is continued by a sergeant of dragoons, and in the meetings which are held for years in the open air at the foot of Table Mountain we see hundreds of other soldiers converted. Then we hear an appeal made to England for a regular Wesleyan minister. He comes out, but a red-tape-loving governor refuses him a chance to preach, and he goes on to the Ceylon mission. Another preacher follows. He is a type not to be suppressed by fussbudget governors. He starts the work.

Then we see the governor still fussing about, still doing all that he can to stop the preaching. Finally the preacher grows tired of the argument. But, instead of sailing on to some other mission field, he turns to the mission field just at hand. He starts north. Traveling by oxcart he covers two hundred miles into the interior. The result is a flourishing mission among one of the native tribes.

Those two elements have controlled the life of Methodism in South Africa through all the years that have passed. On the one hand, we see a white civilization coming into being, part English and part Dutch. Where the Englishman has gone, the Wesleyan minister has gone with him. When the great conflicts between the two came, the Methodist churches —especially those in the Transvaal and in the Orange Free State—naturally suffered heavily. But as the years have passed, as the white man has more and more established himself, as a peaceful order has been worked out for the Union of South Africa, the Wesleyan Church has come to the same sort of a place of settled influence and dignity as it has in other parts of the English-speaking world.

On the other hand, that first expedition to the north was

but the first in a long series of similar expeditions. And while great churches have been growing up in the white man's cities, the missionaries have been constantly on the move toward the villages of the blacks. This work has been remarkably successful. The record of the years shows us the name of one tribe after another who have welcomed the missionaries. To-day there are flourishing congregations in many portions of black South Africa. The church membership, in both black and white churches, is about what it is in Australia.

§ 7. IN THE SOUTH SEAS

And now, in the closing few minutes of our thirty-minute trip, we have time for a glance at only one more part of the Methodist world. Let us pause for a look at the islands of the south seas. Perhaps in no other spot on earth have the Methodists seen such marvelous transformations take place. For here whole islands, once shudderingly known as the home of cannibals and the scene of unmentionable voodoo rites, now stand completely evangelized.

Looking toward the south seas we see Wesleyan missionaries from New South Wales reach the Tonga, or Friendly, Islands about a hundred years ago. After a little preaching, first one chief and then another shows the deepest interest in the new message. One of these chiefs becomes converted. In the course of a few years he becomes, as King George, monarch of the whole group of islands. With him as king the islands become for the missionaries as friendly as their name implies.

From the islands of King George the next step of the missionaries is to the Fijis. Here it is that cannibalism is encountered in its most brutal forms. There is a baptismal font in the great church of Bau to-day which was once the sacred stone on which were beaten out the brains of the consecrated victims. Men were roasted and eaten in front of the mission windows. If ever there was a spot where the comic paper's idea of missionary life was fulfilled, and the kettle actually boiled to receive its missionary stew, Fiji was the place.

But the work goes ahead. About twenty years after the arrival of the first missionaries the last of the great warrior chiefs makes public confession of his new faith. "What a congregation he had!" wrote one man who was present. "Husbands whose wives he had dishonored; widows whose husbands he had slain; sisters whose relatives he had strangled; relatives whose friends he had eaten; and the children, the descendants of those he had murdered, and who had vowed to avenge the wrongs inflicted on their fathers."

So it happens that, as we watch, we see that within fifty years the people of the Fijis are all at least nominal Christians, every village with its church and school, and the sons of converted cannibals are starting out as missionaries to other islands!

CHAPTER XXIII

FORMING A WORLD PARISH

§ 1. An Outstretched Hand

"I see Africa and Asiatic towns,
I see Algiers, Tripoli, Derne, Mogadore, Timbuctoo, Monrovia,
I see the swarms of Pekin, Canton, Benares, Delhi, Calcutta, Tokyo,
I see the Kruman in his hut, the Dahoman and Ashantee-man in their
    huts,
I see the Turk smoking opium in Aleppo,
I see the picturesque crowds at the fairs of Khiva and those of Herat,
I see Teheran, I see Muscat and Medina and the intervening sands,
        I see the caravans toiling onward,

. . . .

I see ranks, colors, barbarisms, civilizations, I go among them, I mix
    indiscriminately,
And I salute all the inhabitants of the earth."

THESE words of Walt Whitman's express in picturesque form the outstanding movements of Christianity in the nineteenth century. The foreign missionary development of Europe and America, which began at the time when William Carey from England went out to Bengal in 1793, and which has been increasing in range and momentum for one hundred and twenty-five years, has been a salute and an outstretched hand to all the world in the name of Christ. During that period there have been not only miracles of achievement but also a widening and enlargement of the motive and basis, the goal and method of the whole business of missions. This chapter wishes to suggest some of the part of American Methodism in that world-wide movement.

When John Wesley uttered the watchword "The world is my parish," it was the expression of a spirit, an ideal, a prophecy. During the seventy-five years from 1850 to 1925 that spirit, that prophecy became a reality. The change from prophecy to actuality meant not only three quarters of a century of a great drama of daring, sacrificial, and romantic achievement, but also the emergence of scores of intricate and enormous problems of a world church in the complex fields of international and race relationships, problems which the church of the twentieth century must face and solve.

This story, of course, cannot be told here; it could not be told anywhere in detail. It could be suggested in many ways. It could be hinted at in *figures,* though the story of the human spirit and romance of Providence can never be footed up on an adding machine as though it were a bank balance. Yet even an adding machine can throw out poetic hints of achievement. In 1850 there were not twenty Methodist foreign missionaries in the world and not more than a few score of communicants. In 1925 there were 1,187 missionaries of the Board of Foreign Missions and 738 missionaries of the Woman's Foreign Missionary Society, a total of 1,925, with more than 661,-000 members of the church on foreign missionary fields.

The story could be told in terms of *maps.* Christianity seems to have been born with a map in its hand. The book of Acts is a geography of the Roman world as well as the first history of the Christian Church. Paul's first geographical goal, "I must see Rome," was not large enough for a lifetime. Chained in a Roman jail, he is fired with a new ambition and writes of "whensoever I go to Spain," planning new outbursts of missionary extension at what was then the farthest westward limit of the known world. The passion for maps has never been entirely lost from the church, and in the second half of the nineteenth century it began to burn with a higher, stronger flame in Methodism than ever before.

The foreign outposts of the church were only four in 1850, but they could not have been more widely scattered—Liberia, Buenos Aires, Foochow, and Germany. Then new continents begin to appear in the heart and imagination of the church. The geography lesson of the church goes on somewhat in this fashion: India in 1856 with the advent of William Butler, the first American Methodist missionary; Norway and Sweden, 1853-4; Bulgaria, 1857; Italy, 1872; Mexico, 1873; Burma, 1879; Malaysia and Korea, 1885; the Philippines, 1899; Borneo, 1902; Java and Sumatra and Panama, 1905. And this is only a part of the forty or more countries in which the church finally finds itself at work.

The real inwardness of the story could be told in terms of human *lives*. These would make a roll call like an extension of the eleventh chapter of Hebrews. What an apostolic gallery it would be!—far exceeding the limits of this book, were there to be told even the merest outline of life investment of those who "through faith subdued kingdoms, wrought righteousness, obtained promises."

The story could be told in *pictures,* in gripping historical scenes, such as the Mutiny in India in 1857-58 and the days of martyrdom, sacred with heroic sacrifice, through which Chinese Christians passed during the Boxer outbreak in 1900; the Korean revival of twenty-five years ago; the mass movement in India.

§ 2. Thoburn and India

The story of Methodist missions in India can be glimpsed

as picturesquely as any way through the lens of one life—that of James M. Thoburn, who was one of the first Methodist missionaries to go to that field and who put in fifty tumultuous and fruitful years there. It has been given to few missionaries to leave as large a life record of achievement.

We have already seen that the first Methodist approach to India was made by Thomas Coke, who died on the Indian Ocean while on the way to Ceylon. With Coke were six missionaries, who proceeded to Ceylon and began work there. One of these missionaries was James Lynch, through whom there was a personal link with the founding of Methodist missions in India from the United States. Lynch worked for thirty years following Coke's

JAMES M. THOBURN

death both in Ceylon and on the mainland around Madras. Returning then to Ireland, he had as an assistant a young man named William Butler, who was destined to be the pioneer Methodist missionary to India. Butler came to the United States in 1852, and while pastor at Lynn, Massachusetts, was appointed missionary to India, sailing in April, 1856. The location of his field was left to himself to choose. He chose the province of Oudh, in which there had never been a missionary. The field was about as large as Pennsylvania but was densely populated with eighteen million people. Butler had just begun his work at Bareilly when the India Mutiny broke out, giving a veritable baptism of blood to the new mission. Long smoldering discontent on the part of certain groups of natives led to the revolt of the Sepoys, part of the Indian army maintained by the East India Company, in which the government of India was then lodged. There were some horrible butcherings, and the mutiny was wiped out in blood.

The mutiny had a large effect both on the political future of India and on missionary work. The immediate political result was the revocation of the charter of the East India Company and the taking over of the empire by the British government, with the British queen proclaimed as empress. Christian missions suffered severely during the mutiny. Many missionaries were killed and hundreds of their converts suffered martyrdom. Yet, as often happens, this suffering called forth greater efforts than in the past and deepened the interest in the mission societies in Great Britain and America.

"THOBURN USED

It was in answer to Butler's call for additional missionaries that James M. Thoburn, a young preacher in Ohio, just out of college, offered himself as a missionary. When he sailed from Salem, Massachusetts, in 1859, there were thirteen members of the Methodist Church in India. Fifty years later, when the semicentennial of his sailing was appropriately held at Allegheny College, in 1909, with himself as the central figure, there were about two hundred thousand members. In his last year on the field he baptized in one day over a thousand converts!

When Thoburn landed in India the Methodist Church had

for its field only one province in the North. He was assigned to Naini Tal, a mountain village. The zeal with which he undertook the work is shown by the fact that within one year after leaving Ohio he was preaching with considerable freedom in the native language in the bazaars.

THE MASS MOVEMENT"

But this task called for more than zeal. It called for inexhaustible patience. India is known as "the mother of religions," and she is hardly to be blamed if she thought long before giving herself in any large measure to this new faith that came from the West. As the apparent fruit of the first year's labor, he had only one baptism to show. At the close of the second year there were only six members. Such discouraging slowness was highly typical of missionary work then. It was a small blade to grow into such a marvelous "full corn in the ear" as the present day exhibits. But in entire consecration he had "chosen Christ for a career" and was undeterred by difficulties.

One of the great contributions of Thoburn to Christian evangelization has been in relation to what are known as "mass movements." This is the embracing of Christianity by whole communities as a body, sometimes by villages, sometimes by larger districts, sometimes by whole castes. These mass movements have taken place largely among the lower castes. Protestantism has always held back from such movements *en masse,* waiting until the individual has given evidence of a certain amount of Christian knowledge and experience on his part. Social motives, the desire to better their condition, have entered largely into these movements. Yet they have presented a challenge and an opportunity from which the missionary cannot turn lightly away. Thoburn was one of the first to use the mass-movement method in the extension of Christianity. He deliberately set himself to reach out for the masses of outcaste population, the "untouchables" as they are called. It was a policy which aroused much criticism and has been fraught with dangers but which has produced large results.

The mass movement is not the only vision which Bishop Thoburn realized. Three others must be barely mentioned in any glance at his life. One is the work for the women of India initiated by Bishop Thoburn and carried through by his sister, Isabella Thoburn.

Three years before the Woman's Foreign Missionary Society was organized, in 1866, "sitting down in front of his tent one day, making a pen from the wing of a vulture which soared above him, he used it to write to his sister Isabella of the futility of evangelizing foreign lands unless the women of those lands were reached by the ministry of Christian women, asking her how she would like to leave her schoolroom in America and come to India to begin to train girls for this great service."

After the organization in 1869 of the Woman's Foreign Missionary Society, Miss Thoburn was its first missionary. The school she opened in Lucknow is now one of the first institutions of higher education in India, the Isabella Thoburn College, which has sent out thousands of well-trained Christian Indian women.

Bishop Thoburn was one of the first to see what the missionary movement might mean to the Europeans in India. Work along this line was largely realized during his ministry at Calcutta.

On his invitation, in the early '70's William Taylor came to India and worked in the large cities—Madras, Bombay and Calcutta—with an evangelistic method and zeal which had large results in widening the field of the church. It is only fair to say that but for the organizing and stabilizing ability and influence of Thoburn and his associates in the regular missionary work of the church, the permanence of Taylor's evangelistic efforts would have been seriously jeopardized.

Thoburn was sent to Calcutta in 1876 to conserve and enlarge Taylor's newly established work among English-speaking people there. His idea was to develop the English base and from this base to engage in the evangelization of the great city. In this new venture he was beyond all expectation successful. He had the courage to start building a great church seating sixteen hundred people with an initial capital of twenty-one dollars which a widow put into his hands, and he dedicated it free of debt! This was an apostolic type of "frenzied finance"! More than that, he filled the church with people.

While in Calcutta he was pastor of the greatest Protestant church of Asia, with a revival on his hands at every service; presiding elder of a district covering at first nearly one half of India; editor of the leading weekly journal, striking body blows at intemperance, child-marriage, and other living questions; and had upon him the administrative and financial burdens of all the institutions which had been begun in Calcutta.

From Calcutta he reached out to plant a mission in Burma, at Rangoon. From Rangoon, accompanied by Dr. W. F. Oldham (later Missionary Bishop, Missionary Secretary and Bishop), he set out for Singapore with barely enough money to cover the passage of the party, but in three weeks a church was organized which has since grown into the whole Malaysia Conference. Doctor Oldham was left in charge of the work in Singapore. Years later, the guns with which Admiral Dewey opened up the way into Manila were hardly cool before Bishop Thoburn was on the spot to begin missionary work.

§ 3. Progress in India

Bishop Thoburn, of course, was only one of the hundreds of Methodist missionaries who have given their lives to India.

HIGH SCHOOL BUILDING, LUCKNOW CHRISTIAN COLLEGE

But during his lifetime he was a part of most of the developments and met most of the problems, and his career is a sort of history in miniature. When the first field in the province of Oudh was chosen the purpose was to confine missionary activities to intensive work in that field. But that policy was abandoned by the development of events and pressure of opportunities. During the years the work has expanded into other provinces and other languages, into nearly all the provinces from the Punjab on the North to Mysore on the South, and from Bombay on the west to Bengal on the east, and across the

Bay of Bengal in Burma and southeast into Malaysia, and thence into the islands of Borneo, Java, and the Philippines—a vast tract of territory with more than three hundred million population. To-day throughout southern Asia work is carried on in more than forty languages.

The slowness and difficulty of the work in the early years are indicated by the rate of growth. In 1864, after eight years, there were one hundred and sixty-one converts—not much of a dent in over three hundred millions. But foundations had been laid and thirteen hundred youths were under regular instruction. A school was founded in Lucknow in 1877 which developed into an influential college. Schools were planted continuously. The missionary force multiplied and medical work was added to the activities of the mission. The names of two women physicians, Clara Swain and Julia Lore, deserve a high place in the record of service.

The mass movement has already been referred to. A glimpse of the way it has worked will give an understanding of one of the characteristic evangelistic movements of India. Bishop Fred B. Fisher has given a very clear picture of the process. He describes how once and again he has been called into villages and towns with the request that he should baptize every man, woman, and child. In one instance he began with the head man and baptized the town council and then all the citizens. It might be assumed that this extraordinary harvest was the result of a protracted evangelistic campaign, with the Bishop preaching every night and holding personal interviews during the day. Not so. The method employed was to call the *chaudries,* or mayors of villages, to summer schools where Christian principles were taught to them, the life of Christ, and certain Christian hymns. They were then sent back to their villages to use what they had learned. As he describes the process, the mayors first call the town council together and report the "good news" to them. Then the members of the council scatter themselves among the families of their neighbors and inform all their people. At the end of a number of months of this preparation a native Christian worker and perhaps a missionary will visit them and bring their spirit to bear upon the awakening life of the village. Result: One day the entire population is received into the church.

Between 1896 and 1920 more than 184,000 members have been received in the Indian Methodist Episcopal Church. In 1915, 40,000 were baptized, a large proportion of whom came through the mass movements. There are seven or eight distinct areas in which mass movements are now under way in India.

A development characteristic of practically all mission fields to-day has been going on, particularly during the last quarter century, with great strength. That is the growth of a native indigenous church. In the beginning, and to a large extent still, the work of the missionaries has been among the poor. These proved willing to order their lives in strict accord with the denominational distinctions and details of practice enjoined by the missionaries. Now this is changing. Men of a high type are accepting the fearful social penalty that it frequently entails to become a Christian openly, but at the same time are providing leaders for the Indian Christians who are increasingly taking over the control of the Christian movement. This is a tendency that is bound to increase until the day comes when foreign missionaries are superfluous, and Indian Christianity orders and maintains its own life.

The largest influence of Christianity in India cannot be appreciated without glancing at its far-reaching by-products outside the acknowledged Christian community. These are not the effect of any single society or denomination but are the result of the common and united impact of all. India's most stagnating social custom has been her caste system, whereby men are born into certain places in the social order from which it is impossible for them to move. The attack that Christian teaching, with its doctrine of human equality before God, is bound to make on such a conception is clear. It must not be thought that Christianity has been alone in working to overcome caste. Many agencies, notably the promiscuous travel on the railroads, have worked to the same end. But Christianity has borne its part, and the bands of caste are at least loosening, if they are not breaking, in India to-day.

Equally significant is the restlessness within Hinduism itself. Several centuries before Christ, Buddhism arose in India to reform the religious life of the country. But Buddhism was itself absorbed back into Hinduism, which went on its way without self-examination until the challenge of Christianity's monotheism and ethical requirements began to make itself felt. Popular Hinduism, with its debasing and idolatrous customs, could not well undergo that challenge. As a result, any number of reform movements have appeared within Hinduism in the last few decades. Many of these seek a sort of a combination of the good elements of all religions, and represent a high level of thought. The trouble is that they are mostly just that —systems of thought—without that fervor of spirit which is needed to move the multitudes.

India is in the full tide of an awakened self-consciousness. She has demanded, and obtained, from the British Empire the first measure of self-government, but she presses on toward a status as a self-governing commonwealth, if not complete independence. The sacrifices she made in the World War, when she sent seven hundred thousand men to the front, have earned for her claims the deepest consideration on the part of the British. Many Indian leaders would deny that Christianity has contributed to this movement for Indian freedom. But the nature of the Christian gospel is such that it is impossible to introduce it in any society without the birth of a spirit of self-respect, which leads inevitably to just such a movement as now possesses India.

One Indian in every eighty-six is to-day a Christian. That proportion will constantly be changing as the hundreds of thousands waiting outside the doors of the churches are instructed and baptized. It is not too much to hope that, a century hence, when India has taken her place in the ranks of the world's great self-governing nations, she will acknowledge as a dominating influence in her life the presence of an Indian Christian Church, Indian in thought, Indian in control, yet Christian in all its effects.

§ 4. DEVELOPMENT IN CHINA

The story of Methodist missions in China has been brought up to approximately 1850. But that was merely the beginning of the first trying years.

The record of the early years makes heart-breaking reading. Death, disease, fierce opposition, internal uprisings that scattered the missionaries, all conspired to make the work seem fruitless. In ten years the devoted efforts of some of the best missionaries who ever labored for the Methodist Episcopal Church gained not a single convert!

Then, at the end of the first decade, the tide turned. The first convert was baptized! A few weeks later the name of his wife was inscribed as that of the first woman to be baptized by the Methodist Episcopal Church in China. By the end of that year thirty-eight adults and three children had been gathered in the group. With a church, schools, a press, medical work, members, probationers, class meetings, quarterly meetings, the

UNIVERSITY OF NANKING, NANKING, CHINA

mission was finally established and started upon its memorable career. That was seventy-five years ago.

Ten years sees a permanent foothold won at Foochow. Two years more and the work has spread fifteen miles up the Min River from that city. At the same time the pioneers of the Woman's Foreign Missionary Society arrive, and special work for women and girls starts. Six Chinese local preachers are licensed, the first in that magnificent line of men who have, when called upon, proved faithful unto death.

We cannot follow the spread of the work in detail. Take a map of China, and check off by twenty-year intervals:

1860—and the work is huddled in and about the city of Foochow, just a dot on the map of Fukien Province.

1880—and the work is begun in four provinces, spreading out from Foochow to much of Fukien; at two of the recently opened ports on the Yangtse River; around the capital, Peking; at the foot of China's sacred mountain in Shantung.

1900—the Boxer year!

Chinese Christians thrilled the heart and soul of the entire church with their unflinching endurance of martyrdom. Again and again, bands of Christian Chinese, many of them Methodists, on being offered the alternative of renouncing their faith or losing their lives, fearlessly chose death. Again, the blood of the martyrs proved to be, as in Tertullian's day, "the seed of the church." And the year of that scourge finds the church spreading through the provinces where it has previously been found, athwart the Yangtse in the provinces of Anhwei and Kiangsi, and leaping a thousand miles westward to the heart of the largest and wealthiest of the provinces, Szechuen.

1920—no new provinces, but great new stretches of territory in all the provinces entered. Isolated stations linked. Centers of occupation carefully planned with reference to the new routes of travel that the railroad and the modern steamship are opening.

Wonderful is the record of these seventy-five years! Not only is the church established in seven provinces, and in such cities as Peking, Tientsin, Nanking, Chungking, Chengtu, Nanchang, and Foochow, but there are nine Annual Conferences and one Mission Conference, with more than 2,500 full-time Chinese workers, more than 90,000 members and baptized adherents, and more than 60,000 Sunday-school pupils.

BUDDHA AT KAMAKURA

§ 5. JAPAN

Twenty-six years after the first missionaries of the Methodist Episcopal Church reached China, work was opened up in Japan. Japan opened her ports to foreign commerce in 1854 after the historic visit of the naval squadron commanded by Commodore Perry. Protestant missionaries pressed in, and several daring young Japanese going to America for education returned to take an outstanding part in the Christian advance in their native land. The Methodist Episcopal Church began its work in 1873, with Robert S. Maclay as the first missionary, and was soon established in half a dozen widely separated centers. The country was so eager for the influences from the West that were to reform its life that it welcomed the religion of the West as an expected part of those influences.

For more than two decades the Protestant advance was limited only by the resources of the missions. Had the churches adopted anything like an adequate program in Japan from, say, 1875 to 1885, Japan might have been a Christian country to-day, and the whole outlook of the Orient changed. Timidity at that time marks one of Christianity's great failures to take advantage of a God-given opportunity.

A natural reaction followed the initial rush of the Japanese to embrace Western ways. Finally the present Japan began to emerge, saying: "We will not reject the West. We will take the best of the West and adapt it to our needs."

The same spirit, working within the Japanese churches, brought a powerful movement toward self-control. It was felt that, in order to make a true adaptation to Japanese life, the churches must be under Japanese leadership.

The Methodists were the last of the large Protestant groups to carry this into effect. Finally, in 1907, the three leading Methodist bodies (the Canadian Methodists, the Methodist Episcopal Church, South, and the Methodist Episcopal Church) united to form the Japan Methodist Church. By this union, one Methodist body appeared instead of three, thus eliminating all dangers of overlapping work. Each of the missions was left to carry on its work, particularly in the realm of higher education, but the life of the churches was put under the guidance of this purely Japanese body.

The formation of the Japan Methodist Church was an innovation of the largest significance for the future history of missions. It was a clear recognition of the fact that the ultimate success of Christianity in a non-Christian land is bound up with its becoming indigenous and being led by the nationals of that country. The experiment has justified itself and in all probability will become a model to be followed by other missions.

§ 6. ENTERING SINGAPORE

Page after page in this historic picture gallery could be turned and each would provide a new fascination. One of the most romantic, from the spectacular standpoint, would unquestionably be that of the wharf at Singapore in 1885, when, as noted elsewhere, Dr. W. F. Oldham, accompanied by Bishop James M. Thoburn, landed from India to begin missionary work in Malaysia. Never was there what seemed to the human eye a more preposterous leap in the dark. Oldham had been appointed to "mid-air" apparently. But he soon put solid ground under the "air." He not only met the difficulties incident to work in a totally new field but also had to provide for its support from the very start. He set himself to gain access to the Chinese, and a brilliant lecture on astronomy before a Chinese debating society known by the resounding name of "Celestial Reasoning Association" proved to be the opening door into tutoring work, founding a school and the development of a remarkable chain of schools, including the Anglo-Chinese School for boys, which has been one of the outstanding educational institutions in the Far East, having approximately eighteen hundred students in all departments. From this beginning mission work has been extended into many points in Malaysia and the Netherlands Indies, including the Federated Malay States, Sarawak, Java, Dutch Borneo, Banka, Sumatra.

Korea was entered by Methodist missionaries in 1884, and the church has played its part in one of the most remarkable Christian movements in modern history. Probably no mission field has furnished quite such a parallel to the apostolic church pictured in the book of Acts as has Korea. All the elements of the apostolic days have been and are there—passion, fervor, self-denial, and persecution. With Protestant missions started as recently as 1885, it is claimed that there has been a new convert every hour, day and night, since the work began. To-day approximately three hundred thousand Koreans—one in every sixty—are reported as Christians.

§ 7. In the Philippines

The Philippine Islands were entered in 1899 just a few months after they passed into the possession of the United

States. In March of that year Bishop James M. Thoburn preached the first sermon heard from a missionary in the Philippines. The Philippines, under the control of the United States, offered to the evangelical churches a unique opportunity—that of projecting missionary work in a non-Christian land for the first time under favorable political and social conditions. A quarter of a century's activity has seen amazing results. Of all Protestant bodies the Methodist Episcopal Church has gathered by far the largest membership. There are more than sixty-three thousand members on its rolls. In addition the church in the Philippines is more nearly self-supporting than in any other part of Asia. One reason for the extent of evangelistic success has been in the fact that with the United States government opening schools everywhere and bringing teachers, in the early years, by the shipload, it was unnecessary for the missionary to open schools, thus making possible concentration on the work of evangelism.

So far our glimpse of Methodism's world parish has been confined to the Far East. All the time that these efforts in the Orient were being carried forward similar plantings and growth were going on in other far-distant continents of the globe, in Europe, in Africa, and in South America.

§ 8. EUROPEAN METHODISM

The Methodist Episcopal Church is now working in more than a dozen different countries in Europe. It would be utterly impossible in a few paragraphs to suggest the rich variety of experience and achievement, the patience, the intricate problems, the obstacles and the results which have formed a part of the work of American Methodism in Europe.

The beginnings of Methodist work in many of the countries of Europe were due to converts among the immigrants from those countries to the United States. This was true of the first work in Europe, which was in Germany and Scandinavia.

The beginnings of Methodism among the Germans of this country form one of the remarkable chapters in the history of the church. William Nast, a young German scholar, had been brought into a deep religious experience in 1835, and became a Methodist preacher in Cincinnati, Ohio. Among the German people he became an active missionary, and the German work of Methodism extended rapidly over the country, developing into many Conferences. It was inevitable that this vigorous development of Methodism should reach back into Germany, and in 1849 a missionary was sent by the Missionary Board to Germany. The work spread and additional missionaries were sent and preachers recruited in Germany.

The beginnings of Methodism in Scandinavia were similar to those in Germany—the result of the growth of the church among Scandinavians in the United States. Beginning among the sailors in New York, work among Swedish, Danish and Norwegian people has spread to all parts of the United States. The first Methodist churches in Norway and Sweden were planted before 1860. In all the Scandinavian countries a vigorous church has developed. These churches are now entirely led by men of their own nations.

In 1872 Italy was entered by Methodism, just two years after Victor Emanuel I took possession of Rome and the modern kingdom of Italy came into being. The effort has been made to bring forth an Italian church.

Though by a strict test of numbers the results in Italy would prove disappointing to one who measures all things by size, the Methodism of Italy has had large influence, and its testimony of religious experience has been of great value. Through educational institutions a far-reaching influence has been exerted. In addition, the Methodist Church in Italy has had a helpful influence on the work of the church among Italian-speaking people in the United States.

Two great fields remain to be mentioned, in which the be-

ginnings of Methodist mission work have already been traced—
South America and Africa.

§ 9. SOUTH AMERICA AND AFRICA

Missions in South America, as we have seen, were long in getting a real start. Thirty years of marking time elapsed before direct missionary work—preaching in Spanish—was allowed in Argentina. Work along the west coast was planted and developed by William Taylor, in one of his characteristic campaigns of self-supporting missions. Heroism and self-sacrifice of the highest sort went into these undertakings. But the necessity of supporting themselves hindered missionaries in their evangelistic work, and in 1903 the self-support feature was abandoned and progress has been made at a faster rate since the change of plan. William Butler, who was the pioneer of Methodist missions in India, laid the foundations of still another mission, that in Mexico in 1873.

Africa also, as will be remembered from the chapter on William Taylor, was touched by that giant in his stride around the world. From 1833 until 1884 Liberia was the only spot in Africa which Methodism had attempted to reach and the work in Liberia had been a checkered history of indifferent success.

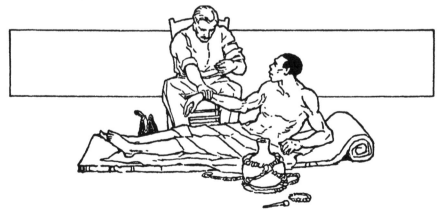

IN THE DARK CONTINENT

The annual appropriation for Liberia had declined to the insignificant figure of $2,500, where it remained for several years. In 1884 William Taylor opened several new stations on the self-supporting plan, in Angola, in the Congo and at Inhambane on the east coast. Some of Taylor's projects have developed into permanent work; others have been abandoned. In later years the work spread to many additional sections of Africa, including North Africa.

§ 10. The Woman's Foreign Missionary Society

No clear grasp of the foreign mission expansion of the Methodist Episcopal Church can be possible without the constant realization that in every continent the work has been supplemented and paralleled by the Woman's Foreign Missionary Society. It should not be forgotten that the very first steps in carrying the Christian message were taken by women: the announcement of the resurrection of Jesus on the first Easter morning. The first comment made regarding that proclamation was, "Certain women of our company amazed us." That comment holds good for the part played by women through all the Christian centuries. It has been a continual amazement. Certainly the story of the achievement of the Woman's Foreign Missionary Society is a chronicle of amazement.

The Society was organized March 23, 1869. But it should not be thought that this was the beginning of the participation of Methodist women in foreign missions. In the very first days of the missionary society women's auxiliaries were organized under the name (a queer-looking name to-day) of "Female Missionary Societies." The part played by women was confined to the collection of money and the development and sustaining of interest. After the Civil War the call for women missionaries for the women of India, and the success of women's mission boards in other denominations, aided also by the general enlargement of woman's place in the life of the world, which had been steadily progressing through a half century, led to the organization of a woman's society which should not only raise money to be handed over to men to spend and administer, but which should itself direct missionary work with independent and sole responsibility. It required some years of work in the non-Christian world to make irresistibly clear the absolute necessity for women's work in the mission field. The fact that "no nation can rise higher than the level it sets for its womanhood," gradually became the axiom of missionary philosophy which it is to-day.

The society has conducted its work, which now extends to nineteen foreign countries, with a gathering strength and efficiency which has been the marvel of church enterprises. Let two concrete illustrations of development shed a light on the characteristic working out of early beginnings.

When Isabella Thoburn went to India as the first missionary of the society her first project was a little bazaar school for the primary education of girls. Her effort met with active opposition which was the result of centuries of social tradition. The little school had to be guarded at the entrance by a boy armed with a club. That little school developed into the first Christian college for women in the Orient. It is now the woman's department of Lucknow University and enrolls students from all parts of India. In China more than fifty years ago Gertrude Howe "threw away her life on the Chinese." To-day as the result of her life's investment there are three high schools, three hospitals in charge of her former pupils, a home for cripples, four boarding schools, and seventy day schools with 2,000 pupils.

§ 11. FOREIGN MISSION CHANGES IN FIFTY YEARS

The foreign missionary work of the Methodist Episcopal Church, South, which has been a great part in the whole impact of Christianity on the modern non-Christian world, and one of the largest chapters of achievement of American Methodism, has been treated in another chapter.

There remain to be at least mentioned in the briefest form some of the changes and enlargements which have come to the missionary motive, aim, and method in the century which has passed since the beginning of Methodist missions. Of course, to treat this theme adequately would involve a good deal of the whole history of modern civilization in the nineteenth and twentieth centuries. All the changes in the political, social, economic, and religious thought and life have had large effects on the business of foreign missions. Just a few of the more obvious and important modifications can be listed here.

In the early years of the foreign movement it could not be foreseen that foreign missions would become one of the greatest civilizing forces of modern times and of all ages. The underlying motive of undertaking foreign missions was profoundly religious and for the most part centered on the evangelization of the individual, as evangelization had been carried on in the home land. The whole impact of this religious message on a non-Christian civilization could not be realized or provided for, except step by step as the experience of the mission forces grew and providential developments went on. "What the church people of those days saw was the picture of millions of 'heathen' perishing eternally without a saving knowledge of Jesus Christ, and in pity they were willing to give their lives to the work of rescue."

That motive has not passed out of foreign missions. When it does the history of missions will be closed. Indeed, it was never more deeply fixed or impelling than to-day. It has deepened. But it has also widened and been enriched with a new fullness coming from experience. The emphasis is not so much on saving "heathens" from the wrath of God and eternal destruction as it is to bring to God's children a knowledge of his love, the transforming power of the grace of God in their lives. The religious emphasis is laid on bringing abundant eternal life to men here, now, and hereafter.

A new emphasis which has steadily developed in foreign missions, especially in the last fifty years, has been on the social aspect of Christianity. This emphasis on the foreign field has been an accompaniment and result of the growing conviction on the part of the churches in Christian lands. The ideal and goal of Christian effort is not rescue by individual salvation only but the establishment of righteousness among men. In this view, it is the mission of Christianity to redeem the

INDIAN MOTHER AND CHILD

world—that is, its political, social, and economic institutions, its laws, its way of life, and make them true expressions of the spirit and ideal of Jesus. Thus, for instance, in India the ultimate goal is not merely the conversion of individuals out of a wicked environment, but the conversion of the environment itself. This means the abolition of child marriage, of caste, of poverty, of exploitation, of every injustice. In the working out of this ideal, educational, industrial, agricultural, and medical work has found place along with evangelistic effort. The result of missions, in this view, is never to be measured merely by the growth of the church but also by the moral and spiritual trends of the whole nation. A widening of the missionary purpose has come also with the undertaking to Christianize the whole impact of so-called Christian nations with non-Christian ones.

When foreign missions began, the missionary was frequently the chief, and often the only, person through whom the influences of the foreign nation were felt. Later came an extension of trade. To China, for instance, the Western nations sent gunboats as well as their Bibles, sabers as well as missionaries. The preaching of the missionary was discounted by the growling of the guns. The gospel of love was mocked by the employment of force to wrest unequal treaties from the Chinese, to exploit their labor. The result is that the connection of Christianity with Western civilization has often been a terrible handicap to the success of Christian missions. It would doubtless be true that it is just this connection in the minds of Oriental peoples which constitutes the most formidable obstacle to missions in the Orient to-day. It is seen to-day that the church will not be able to make her mission fully effective until the entire impact, commercial and political, of the West upon the East, of the strong races upon the weaker, shall be Christianized, and thus strengthen and not impair the message of the missionary enterprise.

A tremendously important change in foreign missions has been the growth of the national churches. This growth, as it goes on, will make the foreign missionary no longer necessary. Only as he makes himself unnecessary, does the missionary truly succeed. There were some men of keen vision among the first missionaries who looked with hope for the day when the national churches would be self-directing and independent. But that has not been always, or perhaps even frequently, a controlling idea. There has been a widespread reluctance to turn over authority and responsibility to the church on the foreign field. In the last ten years, however, the increase of initiative and self-control and self-support in the national churches, particularly in the Orient, has been rapid. The development of nationalistic feeling during and after the World War has contributed to this development. This will unquestionably be the outstanding movement of the next generation and will bring in what will be in many respects a new era in world Christianity.

A new emphasis in missions has come through a new feeling in regard to race relations. There was always in the true missionary a vivid sense of Christian brotherhood, of sympathy, of pity, and love. For this reason missions have been a force of large influence in creating interracial and international good will. Nevertheless, there is an entirely different feeling abroad, among thoughtful Christians, regarding questions such as the superiority of the white race, than there was fifty years ago. There has been an assumption on the part of large sections of the white race that it is superior to the colored races, a tone of snobbish arrogance that made itself felt in a thousand ways, little and big. The colored races have found this increasingly irksome and have come more and more to challenge it and resent it. Race prejudice has no place whatever in the mind of genuine Christianity. Present-day foreign missions are and will be increasingly characterized by respect for all races. This is evidenced in the outlawing of the word "native" in the missionary vocabulary because it seemed to have a lingering tone of condescension about it. The newer word "national" has taken its place.

A new respect also for the religions of non-Christian lands has marked foreign missions of the present day, in contrast to that of earlier times. The religions of India and China, such as Buddhism, Hinduism, Confucianism, were generally regarded as a wholly bad mixture of superstition, unmorality, and ignorance. Those who followed these non-Christian faiths were called "heathen." That word "heathen" is no longer good usage. That does not mean that there has been any diminution of the sense of the necessity of Jesus Christ to the world or of the universal mission of Christianity. It does mean that there has been a new understanding of non-Christian religions, a new

reverence for the elements of good in them and for what in them
has genuine spiritual value. It means also a deepened appreciation of and respect for the people who have followed these
faiths. In other words, the missionary takes as his purpose
the words of Jesus, "I come not to destroy but to fulfill."

CHAPTER XXIV

HIGH HOURS IN A CHURCH'S HISTORY

§ 1. AFTER THE CIVIL WAR

IN TRACING the beginnings of the Methodist Episcopal Church in America, a parallel was drawn between the new nation which had just come into being and the church which started its existence at the same time. The conditions and problems of the nation and the church were found to have many resemblances.

A similar parallel might with real truth be drawn between the situation of the United States and the Methodist Church in the generation following the Civil War. For, again, in what might truly be called the second birth of the nation, when the peril of disunion had been successfully overcome and a permanence guaranteed, the problems and conditions of the nation and the church, which had begun their corporate existence in practically the same hour, were remarkably similar.

When we consider the years from 1865 to about 1900, which is roughly the period with which the present chapter deals, we may say that in national life it was a period in which the ideals and institutions of government had been firmly established. But it was necessary to apply them to new conditions. For many, if not most, of the problems of American life were new, of a different sort than before the war. It is no exaggeration to say that the changes which came in the lifetime of this generation were greater in some ways than those which had taken place since the Roman Empire. In these years a whole new economic and social system came into existence and the problem was, in the large, one of adjusting the established institutions to these new systems.

It was politically a period of strengthening the national government. A study of the activities of the local, State, and national government will reveal a distinct and continuous movement in the direction of the enlargement of the sphere and function of the federal government. Many things which were formerly left to the initiative of the States, such as interstate commerce, for instance, were by the necessities of new conditions transferred to the federal government, strengthening and solidifying it.

"A PERIOD OF BUILDING"

It was a generation of building—stupendous building compared to that of earlier periods. It was a building era which used tools and power and materials which had been undreamed of before. Within these thirty-four years came the great railroad expansion, which swiftly spread a network of rails over the continent. Toward the end of the period came the trolley car, which made possible the modern city. Steel construction changed the face and enlarged the size of the cities. The energies which had been engaged in war and territorial expansion were turned into material construction of an amazing variety.

The exhaustion of free land made a profound change in the conditions of life in the United States. With a prodigality unknown in history, free farming land had been available for anyone who would take it and live on it. But by 1890 the last frontier had been reached and the country woke up to the fact that its supply of free, or almost free, virgin land was exhausted. During the nineties the last important opening of Indian reservations to settlement occurred. For more than a generation Horace Greeley's slogan, "Go west, young man," had practically been a national motto. This reaching the end of the desirable free land for distribution had important economic and social effects. It meant that a man no longer had the opportunity to create new wealth for himself by the simple expedient of migrating west. This had its effect on wages, on employment and on the general spirit of the country. The days of "the covered wagon," and all the romance and adventure which it represented, were definitely over.

The democratic movement in the nation gained large headway during the years 1865-1900. The rise of the frontier West to political power in the thirties, symbolized by the election of Andrew Jackson to the Presidency, had been the first great expression of the democratic revolt from the more or less aristocratic tendencies and traditions of the early years of the republic. During the period now under consideration, insistence on rights of the people as against privilege of every sort was active and growing, stimulated by the rise of new forces which jeopardized those rights. Some characteristic expressions of this movement, such as the popular election of United States senators, anti-trust laws, and the granting of suffrage to women, did not come until the twentieth century.

Foreign relations assumed a larger place of importance. This was natural as the population, wealth and world trade of the country increased, and as immigration increased. The largest leap of all in the importance of our relations with the outside world came as a result of the Spanish-American War of 1898 with the acquisition of the Philippines and Porto Rico.

A postwar interest which has bulked large in national affairs ever since 1865 is the Negro.

These seven different aspects of the conditions and problems of the United States are but a few among many. But they are all important and represent some of the outstanding characteristics of the history of the United States in the last third of the nineteenth century. And they are all very closely paralleled in the life and history of the Methodist Episcopal Church. A hasty glimpse at the similarities of situation and task will set out some characteristics of the history of Methodism in this period.

The church, just as the nation, was faced with the necessity of applying its institutions and organization to new problems. The first century of Methodism on the continent had established its polity, its inner spirit, its organization. The application of these to new conditions, to the whole new social order which was developing, was the task of the church for well over a generation and still is its great task. One illustration of this was the lengthening of the time limit of pastoral service, and its final abolition, due largely to the growth of cities. This will be discussed more in detail later. Another adaptation to new conditions, which came at a later period (1912), was the area system of episcopal administration.

The period was one of strengthening the general organization of the church. This was a process very closely resembling that of the strengthening of the federal government and the extension of its jurisdiction and function. In an earlier day, for instance, the expansion of the church in this country was very largely—for the most part, wholly—the work of local initiative. The Boards of Home Missions and of Education, had not come into existence. The denomination, as a whole, up to 1870 had done very little in shaping and carrying through policies dealing with nation-wide needs. Now pressure of new conditions imposed tasks too great to be met by sporadic, local efforts. New agencies created by and acting for the whole church were required.

Beginning with the Centenary celebration of 1866, already described, and continuing for more than a generation, the church was occupied with the most extensive building enterprises of its history. Those were carried forward both by local congregations and with the assistance, in many places, of the Church Extension Society. This building era in the church reflected the spirit and activity of the times throughout the nation. But this was more than the mere contagion of a building era. It was due evidence of both a real revival of interest in the church, marked and stimulated by the Centenary movement, and an enlarging conception of what constituted an adequate church plant under the new conditions.

The end of the so-called "free land" in the nation also had its parallel in the history of the church. The church, like the nation, reached a new era when it reached the last frontier. It is, of course, true that, up until the nineties and beyond, large portions of Western States, including Montana, Wyoming, Utah, Idaho, Nevada, and the Southwest, were still frontier territory, sparsely settled and very inadequately occupied by the church. Nevertheless, by 1890 the years of extensive expansion in this country were largely replaced by those of intensive effort. The church's "covered wagon" days were over. This meant that one of the most characteristic activities of Methodism, from the earliest itinerant pioneering of Francis Asbury, its continual pushing out into unoccupied territory, had come to a close. And the church turned back, as it were, to intensified efforts on older and changing fields. By the early years of the twentieth century a "new frontier," that of cities and industrial regions, filled with a new, foreign-born population, had developed as the place of greatest stress and need.

Again, as in the national development, the years were characterized by an increase of democracy. This was marked, for one thing, by the admission of laymen to the General Conference in 1872. The admission of women as delegates to the same body in 1904 was another expression of the same tendency. The increased participation of laymen in general in the work and responsibility of the church was a development of the period.

Again, foreign relations bulked increasingly large in the thought of the church, just as in the history of the government. The foreign-missionary work of Methodism first began to assume large proportions during this period. A new foreign-missionary interest, finding expression in such developments as the Student Volunteer Movement, began to stir all the churches, and the Methodists experienced their share of this.

Finally, as one of the most immediate results of the Civil War, the Negro received a new measure of attention and aid from the church. In particular the task of Negro education enlisted the sympathies and the energies of large numbers. To that undertaking, which makes such bright and stirring pages of Methodist history, we now turn our attention.

§ 2. THE FREEDMEN'S AID SOCIETY

Let us look first at one life, the romantic life of a boy born into slavery.

In 1833 there was a little building erected in Morristown, Tennessee, known as the Bethel Church. That building bears a strange and close relationship to the life of one man, A. F. Fulton. In that building he was sold as a slave. When the future of the Negro race seemed to be hopelessly dismal, his mother and four members of the family were auctioned off there on the slave block. The little boy was only four years of age but brought a good price for that time, $1,166. A few years later, in that same building, he was converted at a church service and joined the church. In that same room he also spent the greater part of his school days. After preparing himself to be a teacher he came back and taught here for more than a generation after the building had passed into the hands of the Freedmen's Aid Society and was operated by them as a Negro school. This school became the Morristown Normal and Industrial College, and the former slave boy became one of its able and honored teachers.

With the ratification of the Fourteenth Amendment to the Constitution of the United States in December, 1865, slavery was gone forever. Four million slaves were set free, constituting just about one third of the population of the whole South. This emancipation created one of the most formidable problems ever faced by any nation. The dimensions of the problem have only been clearly seen with the passage of the years. These four million Negroes, hastily thrust into the responsibilities of citizenship, were almost entirely illiterate. Education of the barest sort had been pretty largely taboo, since it was regarded as inimical to the institution of slavery. A vivid picture of the illiteracy of the freed men was presented at the organization of the Mississippi Mission Conference, one of the first Negro Conferences of the Methodist Episcopal Church, on Christmas Day, 1865. The presiding bishop called for the election of a secretary, on which it was revealed that not a single one of the Negro ministers could read!

The so-called "Reconstruction" years (though there is much bitter irony in the word) which followed the Civil War in the South were marked by two invasions from the North. One was the invasion of the "carpetbaggers." The Southern name for these gentlemen (only too appropriate in many instances) was "scalawags." These were men who went South to exploit the country politically and economically in the days of confusion following the war.

The activities of the "carpetbaggers," the corruption and the evil uses to which they put their political power, form one of the unlovely pages of American history. But fortunately there was another invasion from the North of a vastly different character. This was an invasion of teachers, of many educated young men and women who went into the South to make a sacrificial investment of themselves in the task of educating the Negroes. This urgent and enormous need also reached the hearts of many citizens in the North of large means. In about twenty years following the Civil War more than $20,000,000 had b e e n given by philanthropists of the North for Negro education.

"AN INVASION OF TEACHERS"

The M e t h o d i s t Episcopal Church w a s quick to see the need and respond to it. The command to "cease firing" had hardly been given when steps were taken to provide a beginning in the establishment of schools for Negro education. On August 7, 1866, a meeting of laymen and ministers in Cincinnati, Ohio, called to consider "the work of relief and education required in behalf of the freedman" resulted in the organization of the Freedmen's Aid Society. For sixty years this organization, now the Department of Education for Negroes of the Board of Education, has been the agency through which the Methodist Episcopal Church has carried on a far-reaching work of education among Negroes. With a swiftness worthy of the pioneer circuit riders in occupying new territory, the new Society was at work in the South three months after organization. By the end of the first year it had 52 teachers, conducting 59 schools with more than 5,000 pupils.

The first schools were primitive. An early visitor has

given this description of one of them: "On rough benches sat rougher people—youths, children, men, and women—in rags of linsey-woolsey, and jeans, patched like Joseph's coat, not through pride and plenty but through poverty; bootless, shoeless and stockingless, certainly knowledgeless—most would have said brainless. . . . There they sat crouching over their primers, spelling with difficulty the easiest words, answering stammeringly the simplest questions, strong only in the gift of song and the faith of their teachers."

From such rude beginnings the development and extension of schools went on.   Gradually they became of higher grade.   Colleges were built and professional schools for theology and medicine and dentistry were established. The early days were marked, as those to-day are marked, by remarkable devotion to securing an education on the part of many of the students.   One has described some characteristic efforts as follows:

One student walked two hundred miles across the country in order to be on hand for the opening day of school; another walked fifteen miles carrying the box with his books, clothing, and other necessities on his shoulder; one sat down every morning to a breakfast made up of a piece of rough bread and a cup of cold water for the sake of an education; one took a pig, his sole property, under his arm and started for "college"; two girls aged fourteen and sixteen walked nine miles a day, to and from school, through heat and rain and sometimes with blistering feet, in order to attend school.

Principles for the conduct of the work began to evolve.   It was seen after a few years that the effective method of education lay in the training of teachers.   It also became a policy to include industrial training in the curriculum.   Foundries, blacksmith shops, machine shops, printing plants, carpenter, plumbing and tailor shops, were placed in some schools. The chief emphasis of the Methodist educational policy for Negroes, however, has not been in the direction of teaching trades, but in general secondary and college education.

In sixty years more than 200,000 pupils have received instruction in these schools for Negroes. These students have gone out into all walks of life. More than 15,000 leaders in the public schools of the South have come from these Methodist institutions. There are now 19 schools located in 12 different States of the South.

§ 3. "BUILDING TWO A DAY"

A picture which abides in the memory of many people still living is that of a crowded church and a man on the platform singing. He was a man of commanding presence, never to be forgotten by those who saw and heard him. He was not a professional singer, though he sang practically all of his life and was known and loved throughout the entire country for his singing. There was a charm in his voice which went beyond the technique of training. It was a baritone voice of strange, plaintive sweetness; it had a thrilling magnetic power, a moving spiritual quality of a rare sort. Here are the words of the song:

"The infidels, a motley band,
    In council met and said:
'The churches die all through the land,
    The last will soon be dead.'
When suddenly a message came,
    It filled them with dismay:
'All hail the power of Jesus' name!
    We're building two a day.'

" 'Extend,' along the line is heard,
    'Thy walls, O Zion fair!'
And Methodism heeds the word,
    And answers everywhere.
A new church greets the morning's flame,
    Another evening's ray.
'All hail the power of Jesus' name—
    We're building two a day.' "

The singer was "Chaplain" Charles C. McCabe, for sixteen years—from 1868 to 1884—assistant secretary of the Church Extension Society of the Methodist Episcopal Church. The scene, the man, the song, well serve as a characteristic picture of a notable period in the life of the church and a chapter of prodigious achievement in church building and extension.

Behind the song lies a characteristic story. One day while traveling on his unending itinerary raising money for church

"BUILDING TWO A DAY!"

extension, "Chaplain" McCabe, reading a newspaper on a railway train, noticed a report of a "freethinkers' " convention at which Robert G. Ingersoll, the famous orator, then in the height of his militant opposition to the churches, had spoken. Mr. Ingersoll said in his address, "The churches are dying out all over the land; they are struck with death." At the next station McCabe got off the train and sent to Ingersoll this telegram:

DEAR ROBERT:

"All hail the power of Jesus' name"—we are building more than one Methodist Church for every day in the year, and propose to make it two a day! C. C. McCABE.

The incident stirred the church greatly and called forth the song of which two verses are quoted above. "Chaplain" McCabe literally sang the song from ocean to ocean and used it to give a new impulse to the building of churches.

"Building one a day" and "Building two a day"—the

phrases express the very spirit of an era. And "Chaplain" McCabe was both a characteristic product and leader of the church in that era, the last thirty years of the nineteenth century. He was the most irresistible "money-raiser" of his generation. Indeed, in all the history of American Methodism he was unique in his capacity to raise funds for church enterprises, both home and foreign. For thirty years, from 1866 till 1896, when he was elected bishop, he labored incessantly and furnished a new impulse and strength to the work of the church. Yet the term "money-raiser" can be in no sense a measure of the man. He quickened the work itself as well as raised money to support it.

We have already seen that the Centenary celebration of 1866, following on the close of the war, resulted in a renewal of energy and activity throughout the church. The westward movement of population was resumed with freshened vigor. Two new causes contributed to increase the volume of this westward migration—the railroad and the steamship. The transcontinental railroads were building. The Central and Union Pacific Railroad from Omaha to San Francisco was completed in 1869. By 1885 the Northern Pacific, the Southern Pacific, and the Atchison, Topeka, and Santa Fe Railroads were extended to the Western coast. The days of the "covered wagon" had been followed by those of "the iron horse." This meant that the Western States filled up with a volume of settlers and with a rapidity never possible before. Between 1864 and 1890 nine new States were admitted to the Union. Contributing to this result was the enormous increase of immigration from Europe which took place in these years. Not nearly as large a percentage of the immigrants in these years remained in the cities as was the case after 1890. Immigrants from Scandinavia poured into the Northwest. New settlers from northern Europe helped to swell the population of Western States.

This created a new problem in church extension. It was evident that the religious influences in this developing country must be supplied by the localities themselves. The task of erecting new churches was too great for the resources of the Missionary Society, which at this time had charge of missionary work in the United States as well as in foreign countries. It was in response to the urgency of this need that the Church Extension Society was organized by the General Conference of 1864. The first years were ones of stress and uncertainty, as discouraging and difficult as the first years of the Missionary Society forty years earlier. The second year of the Board's existence an appeal for $250,000 was made; less than $19,000 was received. At the General Conference of 1872 the organization was changed, the Society being superseded by the Board of Church Extension. From this time on the ship was righted and went forward on a remarkable career of service in aiding in the erection of churches in all parts of the country, but particularly in the West.

The present generation of Methodists are familiar with the home-missionary work of the denomination being conducted by a separate Board of Home Missions. But up until 1907 there was no Board of Home Missions. All the missionary work of the church, home and foreign, was administered by the one Missionary Society. Some of the home-missionary work was administered directly by the Society, and some by the different Conferences with the financial aid of the Society. It is interesting to note that the first missionary of the Society, sent out in 1819 to labor among the French in New Orleans, lived until 1889. During his lifetime he saw the receipts of the Society increase from a few dollars a year to over a million a year.

The outstanding contribution of the Board of Church Extension was in the Loan Fund which it projected and by means of which the erection of thousands of churches was aided.

Many churches were helped by an outright gift. Others were helped by a timely loan, which could not be secured in any other quarter, and which in time was paid back and was loaned again to other churches. Thus the fund was to a large extent a self-replenishing reservoir. The churches whose existence and growth had been made possible, as they grew in strength, became themselves contributors to the fund, from which other churches in turn were aided. By 1890 more than 7,000 churches had been aided by the fund. By 1926 the number had increased to more than twenty thousand.

But no manipulation of the adding machine can give any fair idea of what this farsighted activity in church extension has meant. It has been a great adventure in life, not in figures, and only as the imagination clothes the figures with life can the range of the work be realized. Churches of all sorts were erected, many of them extremely simple and plain wooden buildings in frontier towns, others more elaborate and costly. The loans were seldom higher than $500 and in nearly every case were contingent upon larger amounts being raised locally. Many churches were aided under a scheme by which Methodist churches were encouraged to make a gift to the building of some definite church in the West. By the donation of $250 the erection of many a church building was made possible. Subscriptions of $250 were solicited from individuals and societies, and each subscription insured the building of a church somewhere in the Western States. Hundreds of responses were made. Churches with a value of $1,250 to $10,000 sprang up with remarkable rapidity under this plan which had so much concrete appeal.

It will help to understand some of the spirit of this great endeavor in church extension to read one of the characteristically enthusiastic appeals to the church written by "Chaplain" McCabe:

M. De Lesseps wants 350 millions to carry out a commercial enterprise. He will get it too. The Board of Church Extension asks for one million in its loan fund, to secure the erection of 1,000 churches every five years. Can we have it? Of course we can. Give it to us and we will set a thousand bells ringing all along the frontier line. Give it to us and we will add 300,000 people to your great Methodist army every time the financial wheel makes a revolution, and it will make a revolution every five years. Lesseps wants to connect the stormy Gulf with the Pacific Ocean. Give us the money to build the churches, to create the pulpit, to organize Sabbath schools, to inspire the erection of the family altars, and who doubts but that we shall open the way before myriads of sin-wrecked souls into the Pacific Ocean of God's everlasting love?

If you are trying to get the better of your love of money, and want a little help in your tug with "Old Natur'," send for me. I would love to help you. Let us sing a little now:

> "Salvation! let the echo fly
> The spacious earth around,
> Till all the armies of the sky
> Conspire to raise the sound."

The story of the home missions of Methodism includes the vast achievement of the Woman's Home Missionary Society, organized eleven years after the Woman's Foreign Missionary Society, in 1880. This society came into being primarily to aid the Freedman's Aid Society in its work. But from the very first the broadest field of service was contemplated, the design being announced "to enlist and organize the efforts of Christian women in behalf of the needy and destitute women of all sections of the country." That is a large enough charter to engage the energies of Olympians, but that has been the sort of energy which the women have brought to the work. An extensive variety of institutions and agencies of work have been conducted: industrial training schools in the South, schools for foreign-speaking peoples, hospitals, training schools, deaconess schools, settlements, immigrant Homes, clinics, and orphanages. In 1926 there were 179 different institutions supported either by the National Society or Conference Woman's

Home Missionary Society, with 1,400 workers employed and more than 5,000 students. In 1925 almost $1,750,000 was received and disbursed through the National Society.

§ 4. THE REDISCOVERY OF YOUTH

If an ecclesiastical Rip Van Winkle who had been hibernating since about 1870 were to emerge from seclusion and descend upon the church of to-day, he would be amazed and bewildered at many things. But probably nothing would be more surprising to him than the place which childhood and youth occupy in the life and activity of the church, for the half century which has elapsed has been distinguished by nothing more far-reaching than the churches' rediscovery of youth. Just as the original Rip Van Winkle discovered on his descent from the Catskill Mountains that he had stepped into an entirely new order of things, so our imaginary Rip Van Winkle stepping from 1870 into the present day would find himself in the midst of a new order, a new emphasis and range of activity in the church. The rediscovery of youth has brought about a new geography in both the church building and its program.

In the last fifty years the church has come far nearer than ever before to following the example of Jesus when he set a child in the midst. Youth has moved from the fringe of the church's interest and attention to a place much nearer the center.

This does not mean, of course, that there were no Sunday schools before 1870 or thereabouts, or that children and young people were absent from the church—far from it. But about that time there began a period when a new understanding of childhood and youth developed, and a new valuation was placed on the teaching task of the church. This is true to a much greater degree of the quarter century from 1900 to 1925 than it was in the years from 1870 to 1900. While children and young people were in the church they had a place of great subordination. They were rigidly drilled in the catechism and to some extent in the Bible; much debate over the polemics of infant baptism was held. They were the objects of much prayer and counsel. And Sunday schools were very generally organized. But, as a rule, the principle, so satisfying to maturity and age, that "children should be seen and not heard," had the authority of a veritable Scripture text. Youth was expected to walk humbly in the sanctuary.

The rediscovery of youth was manifested first in the development and change in the Sunday school and later in the rise of the young people's societies, which in the Methodist Church became the Epworth League. The effects of these activities were felt throughout the entire church life.

The new educational conception and emphasis was not by any means a movement peculiar to the church. In large part it was a manifestation in the church of a general renaissance and transformation which marked the educational world during the period. Conventional and traditional methods of teaching, the subject matter of instruction, standards and objects of education were undergoing a new scrutiny. The sciences of pedagogy and psychology were struggling for recognition and beginning to be felt. The work of Froebel and Pestalozzi in the field of child nurture was revolutionizing, in many places, primary and elementary teaching. In general, the emphasis in education was changing from the effort to put something into the child's mind to the effort to make something happen there. The end of the frontier period meant the advent of an era when the necessity and worth of education were seen and stressed in a greatly increasing degree. In 1867, for instance, there were less than seventy free public high schools in the United States. Now there are more than fifteen thousand. From 1889 to 1925 the population of the United States just about doubled, but the number of students in high schools increased sixteen times.

The modern impetus in the Sunday-school movement dates

from about 1870. It was the first great interdenominational movement in the United States and, as such, has made an enormous contribution to the whole church life of the country. The Sunday school, both as a denominational enterprise and as an interdenominational interest, dates back far earlier than 1870 of course, but many developments of large importance, among which was the adoption of the Uniform Lesson system, mark that approximate date as a new starting point in the work of the church with childhood and youth.

The history of the whole Sunday-school movement in Methodism cannot be told here even in the briefest form. It is important to note, however, that Methodism has been very closely related to the Sunday school from its earliest birthday and has had all through its history a great influence in it. In 1748, a little less than forty years before Robert Raikes began his Sunday school in Gloucester, England, the Methodist Conference voted for the organization of children's societies for religious instruction and John Wesley wrote special rules for that instruction. It is very easy to find in early Methodist records evidences of blunders in child training which would not be tolerated by modern religious educators. John Wesley never understood children very well although he was profoundly interested in them and concerned for them. Yet the Methodists made a great contribution to the whole cause of religious education in their emphasis on child religion and their insistence that the child born in a Christian home belongs by birth to the kingdom of God, that he is entitled to and can respond to divine influences from the beginning.

Meeting the children for religious instruction both on Sundays and week days was a constant feature of the Methodist societies for a generation before Raikes' Sunday school of 1780. The Sunday school, which, in a loosely organized state, had been transplanted to America, was an increasing activity of the Methodist societies and churches from the organization of the church in 1784. In 1827 the Methodist Sunday School Union was formed for the promotion of Sunday-school interest throughout the church, and three years later more than 2,400 schools and 158,000 scholars were reported. A distinct stage in progress was the reorganization of the Sunday School Union. A growing literature was created although separate lesson leaves did not make their appearance until 1865.

With the election of John H. Vincent in 1868 as secretary of the Sunday School Union and editor of Sunday-school literature a period of new departures and advances was entered upon. Doctor Vincent held this office for twenty years and deeply influenced the development of religious education in many ways and throughout all the denominations. He was unique, a genius in the field of popular education with a sum total of achievement in that field unmatched in his time. He did much to revolutionize and rejuvenate the whole enterprise of Sunday-school teaching. He was the prophet of teacher training, and by means of normal classes, teachers' institutes, and training courses he did much to establish the idea that the Sunday-school teacher should be trained for his work. Bishop Vincent is perhaps best remembered to-day as one of the founders of Chautauqua Assembly, from which the Chautauqua movement spread throughout the country. But it should be remembered that the assembly at Chautauqua began as a Sunday-school teacher's assembly, a culmination of the institutes which Doctor Vincent had so assiduously promoted.

One of the outstanding advances about this time was the adoption of the Uniform Sunday School Lesson system, by means of which the same Scripture selection was studied on the same Sunday by the Sunday schools of all the churches. In bringing about this result Doctor Vincent played an indispensable part. The system of printing the selection of Scripture to be studied as the lesson had come into general use between 1865 and 1870, but there were many different series of lessons in use and no uniformity even within a particular denomination. Doctor Vincent was one of the first to see the many advantages of a Uniform Lesson in use in all Sunday schools. The consummation of this plan was delayed for several years by different publishing interests which were reluctant to risk the money the churches had invested in a particular set of lessons. But at the International Sunday School Convention in 1872 the Uniform Lessons were adopted, and for over thirty years were the principal, almost the sole, curriculum for the Sunday school. The lessons ran in a seven-year cycle and during that period covered a considerable section of the Bible, alternating semiannually or quarterly between the Old and New Testaments.

It is easy to look back from the vantage ground of to-day and note the deficiencies of the Uniform Lesson system as a means of teaching either the Bible or as training for Christian character. It is not nearly so easy to realize what a great step forward the system was. The Uniform Lessons popularized Bible study. As never before in Christian history the study of selections from the Bible, at least, was engaged in. The lessons, with the large variety of teaching aids provided by the denominations, marked a real educational advance. Not the least advantage was the making possible larger cooperation between churches, due to a common course of study. This not only led to union conventions and institutes but also emphasized the common faith of the various churches.

The next important step in the Sunday-school advance was the introduction of a system of graded lessons. Here, again, a long and difficult battle was fought before the idea was adopted by the International Sunday School Convention in 1908. The Sunday-school authorities of the Methodist Episcopal Church played a decisive part in bringing about this result, serving notice that unless completely graded courses were prepared, the Methodist Church would prepare its own. The purpose of the graded lessons was to provide continuous courses, suited to different age groups. The Sunday school thus becomes a real school and less of a religious mass meeting.

The year 1908 was also marked by the formation of the Board of Sunday Schools in the Methodist Episcopal Church. The years which followed were marked by conspicuous advance along many lines, in higher standards, in improved methods, in the development of teacher training, and the expansion and enrichment of the curriculum.

Another phase of this new valuation and recognition of youth is represented by the Epworth League, the young people's society of Methodism which was organized at Cleveland, Ohio, in May, 1889. This organization came about as the consolidation of various organizations which had sprung up to meet the same need of furnishing to the young people of the church a means of expressing and developing their social and religious life. This demand was an inevitable one, a fruit of the times, the desire of young people for responsibility, the right of initiative and recognition. The young people were growing tired of merely being heard. The General Conference of 1880 made provision for young people's "Lyceums," but the word and the idea had little thrill for youth. It was too formal, artificial, and literary. Several different young people's societies had sprung up in different parts of the church by 1888, all following the general model of the Christian Endeavor Societies, and these were consolidated in one organization. The Epworth League had an unexpected growth from the very beginning and was soon a vigorous part of the church's life everywhere. The Sunday evening devotional meeting was a central feature of the organization. Social, literary, missionary and charitable departments were also organized.

The Epworth League brought a great impetus to the church and proved to be both stimulus and training agency for multitudes of young people.

In 1890 the Epworth League of the Methodist Episcopal Church, South, was organized and proved to be as popular as in the Methodist Episcopal Church. The League's presence in both churches has been a strong influence for fellowship and has contributed largely to the movement for unification.

§ 5. How Methodism Was Saved From Heresy Trials

With the turn of the century, Methodism faced and answered another great question—that was as to whether its ministers were to be judged by the theological opinions which they held or by the spirit and results of their work for the kingdom. In view of all that has been said about the liberality of John Wesley's views, and his pride in having founded a society in which a man's opinions had nothing to do with his acceptability, it may seem strange that this issue ever came to plague the Methodists. But it happened that the closing years of the last century saw an astonishing amount of heresy-hunting in other churches. One has only to mention the Andover case among the Congregationalists, the Briggs case among the Presbyterians, the attacks on Phillips Brooks among the Episcopalians, the charges against President William Rainey Harper among the Baptists, to recall how general was the tendency to challenge the right to preach of men who in the slightest particular deviated from the dogmas of the past. Perhaps it was too much to expect that Methodism should have escaped a touch of the same thing.

The case which brought the matter to a head in the Methodist Episcopal Church was that of Professor H. G. Mitchell of the Boston University School of Theology. Doctor Mitchell was accused of teaching contrary to the standards of Methodism. In those days it was necessary for theological professors in that institution to be confirmed by the Board of Bishops, and in 1905 the bishops refused their indorsement. Professor Mitchell insisted on having a trial in his own Conference, the Central New York, but instead of giving him a trial the Conference administered a reprimand. This case was carried to the General Conference of 1908, which not only ruled that the Central New York Conference had been out of order in reprimanding the teacher without giving him a trial, but also inserted a clause in the *Discipline* saying, "Bishops are relieved from the duty of investigating and reporting upon charges of erroneous teaching in our theological schools." And that was really the end of the danger that Methodism might become a heresy-hunting church. There was, it is true, a later trial of one of Doctor Mitchell's colleagues on the Boston faculty, the great philosopher, Dr. Borden P. Bowne. But that trial was an utter fizzle. There may be other attempts at such trials in the future, but they have almost no hope of success. For the same reason that there was no chance, by the disciplinary methods, to convict Doctor Mitchell because of his opinions, the freedom to "think and let think" is established for Methodists. On all these mooted questions of interpretations and doctrine, that great word of Wesley's will abide: "Is thy heart as my heart? Then give me thy hand."

§ 6. Varied Pictures

The limits of this story prevent the detailing of many of the vital forces which acted upon the church during the period from 1870 down to the present time. Particularly is it impossible to sketch the background of church life, the things which remain vividly in the memory of multitudes still living. A random list of some things which ought to be pictured in any history of the period will suggest how varied and full such a history would be. Just a few of these things are here enumerated:

The creation of the order of Deaconesses by the General Conference of 1888 and the deaconess movement and work which has followed; the mammoth Epworth League conventions in Toronto, Chattanooga, Indianapolis, and San Francisco; the

Ecumenical Conferences of World Methodism at London in
1881, Washington in 1891, at London in 1901, Toronto in 1911,
London in 1921; the Moody and Sankey evangelistic meetings
which quickened the life of the church in many parts of the
country; the popular song books such as *Gospel Hymns* and
the *Epworth Hymnal;* Chautauqua Literary and Scientific
circles in hundreds of churches; the Akron Sunday School plan
of building—a feature, now sadly outgrown, of thousands of
churches erected in these years; the rise of the Student Volunteer Movement, its fruitful effect on missions, directing hundreds and thousands of young people to foreign missionary service; the slogan, "A Million for Missions" sounded by C. C.
McCabe when secretary of the Missionary Society in 1884,
with the goal reached in 1887.

At the organization of the church in America there was
no time limit for pastoral service. However, in a few years
the tendency grew up on the part of some ministers to cease
from traveling continuously and extensively and settle down
to a ministry in one locality. In order to prevent this and
keep an itinerant ministry, a time limit of one year was set.
Perhaps the outstanding change of church polity was the
lengthening of the time limit of pastoral service and finally its
total abandonment. In 1804 it was made two years; in 1864
it was extended to three years, and in 1888 to five. In 1900 the
limit was removed altogether, so that under the present rule a
minister can be appointed to a church indefinitely. These
changes came as a result of the growth of the church and of the
country. An incessant itineracy suited to the conditions of
pioneer days was not so uniformly efficient in a settled community, particularly in cities. The trolley car, which made
rapid transportation possible in cities and suburban communities, brought about great shifts in population. With the increased flow and movement it became necessary more and more
to have continuous pastoral leadership, making it necessary for

the pastor to be a reasonably fixed point, if there was to be any leadership at all.

A theme which would require the limits of a separate volume is the Episcopal leadership of the church during the half century 1875-1925. The bishops have been a vital and indispensable part of the progress of the church. Earlier in this story, when an estimate of the causes of the achievements of Methodism in the first half of the nineteenth century was attempted, a large place was given to the episcopacy as an institution and to the vigor, wisdom, and effectiveness of the men who served the church in the office of bishop. Since 1872 there have been seventy-six bishops elected. The office has never been confined to men of one type of ability or personality. Men of the very highest type of many sorts of ability have labored in the office. Some bishops have been distinguished primarily as preachers, some as administrators, some as ecclesiastical statesmen, some as scholars. They have been elected to the episcopacy from every type of ministerial service. Pastors, college presidents, editors, district superintendents, Board secretaries, missionaries. Between 1872 and 1916 nine missionary bishops were elected. These men were not elected as general superintendents but were elected to administer a particular section of the foreign-missionary field.

The episcopacy has always been a life office. At the General Conference of 1912 legislation was passed under which a bishop retires from active service at the General Conference nearest his seventy-third birthday. In 1912 also the "area system" of episcopal administration came into effect. Up until that time no particular territory was designated to a bishop for continuous responsibility and supervision. Certain cities over the country were designated as Episcopal Residences, but no particular local responsibility was placed upon the bishop. With the purpose of securing more continuity of administration and program and intensified and more effective leadership the church was divided in 1912 into a number of areas, for residential supervision. This legislation did not confine a bishop exclusively to one area, and bishops continued to preside at times over Conferences far removed from their residences. But the authority and responsibility of administration in the specified area remained with the designated bishop for the quadrennium.

In 1920 the General Conference did not abolish the missionary episcopacy but adopted the policy of sending general superintendents to the foreign fields, electing the effective missionary bishops at that time to the office of general superintendents. The future method of supervision in foreign fields in this day of the growing spirit of nationalism is one of the urgent problems of church polity.

The Methodist Episcopal Church, South, has elected thirty-five bishops between the years 1870 and 1922 and there, too, the leadership of the bishops has been an inseparable part of the achievement and success of the church.

CHAPTER XXV

THE BATTLEFIELDS OF REFORM

§ 1. Militant Methodism

METHODISM was born in a prayer meeting, but it learned to walk on a battlefield. Brickbats were a constant and enlivening feature of its early history. Nor were all its battles those of defense. The Methodist movement did not grow up in a theological vacuum, but was inextricably in the midst of life. The social evils of the time engaged the attention and energies of John Wesley and many of his followers, and the militant character of Methodism was firmly established. None of his sayings is more characteristic of the man than the one quoted so often as to become a bit threadbare: "I desire a league offensive and defensive with every soldier of Jesus Christ."

In launching some of his attacks on such intrenched evils as slavery and liquor John Wesley showed a foolhardy courage worthy of Jack the Giant Killer. He well merited the name. The struggles of the early Methodists against social evils cannot here be told again. They are recalled merely to establish the descent of a militant Methodism, active in warfare in the two centuries following, from the militant fathers of the eighteenth century. Two of the evils which Wesley and his followers attacked, slavery and alcoholic liquor, were the same evils against which raged the outstanding attacks of the churches in the nineteenth century in America. The exception must be made in the case of slavery, of course, since after the invention of the cotton gin in 1792, the anti-slavery sentiment, which had been steadily growing in the South, died down till Southern opposition to slavery almost totally disappeared.

The attitude toward slavery was determined by economic considerations. When the cotton gin made slavery economically profitable it gave that institution a new lease of life, to be ended only with the Civil War. Consequently, the story of the fight of the churches against slavery is the story of the churches in the North.

It is well worth noting that in the Methodist Church the attitude toward both of these evils followed the same course. There was a drop from the standards first adopted in the United States, standards which were the positions taken by John Wesley, and a long, slow, painful process during the years of coming back to the original position. In both cases the record is far from glorious. The church does not play the part of a pioneer, pushing far ahead of the practice and standards of the time. That is a picture which we would like to hold of the church as a whole, but the facts do not bear it out. Of course there were intrepid pioneer spirits who were scouts far out in advance of the social conscience of the majority. And it is due in large part to their vision, and to their irritating exhortation (which must often have felt like the stinging of a gadfly), that the main column of the army has advanced and occupied new positions. But there have been many times when the march of that main army has been very slow.

The story of the slavery question and Methodism has already been told in this volume. Other battles must occupy this short chapter. The slavery struggle is recalled, however, because of the parallel which it affords with the relation of Methodism to the liquor question. John Wesley referred to slavery as "the sum of all villainies." This was pitching the note too high for all of his Methodist descendants in the United States to carry the tune forward in that key. The fathers made a brave beginning. The earliest Methodist Conferences declared slavery to be contrary to all law and conscience and harmful to human society. But after the first few years following **1800,** the testimony of the church against slavery became vague and compromised, a constant receding going on both in declared testimony and general practice. Taking part in anti-slavery meetings and agitation, and other "abolitionist" leanings by ministers were frequently made the occasion of persecution. During the years, however, a counter movement was going on within the Methodist Episcopal Church, gaining much headway in the years between 1844 and 1860—a movement of uncompromising opposition to slavery.

§ 2. THE WAR AGAINST THE LIQUOR TRAFFIC

The same high beginning and the same befuddled compromise extending over half a century marked the warfare of Methodism against the liquor evil. It should be remembered, however, that though its official voice was blurred and often weak in the first half of the century, the church recovered its moral insight and courage and force in the long battle for the prohibition of the liquor traffic which extended from 1850 till the present day—a stretch of seventy-five years of incessant fighting, marked by growing conviction and aggressive effort on the part of Methodism in all its branches. It is not too much to say that the temperance movement was in many respects the *characteristic* Methodist battle of the century, the one which most fully enlisted the interest and enthusiasm of the church and the one in which Methodism rendered one of its largest services to the nation.

The story of one of the most stirring and notable exploits of Methodism in America cannot be told as a separate story. It was not a lone charge on the part of one denomination. There were plenty of Pickett's charges up high and bitterly defended hills occupied by the liquor forces. But the battle for temperance and prohibition was won by a great army, and the only true record must be that of the whole army. It is enough glory for any church to say, pointing to the achievements of the whole body, "We were a part of that." It is from that general standpoint that the part of Methodism in the fight against liquor must be suggested.

As has been indicated, the start of Methodism in its earliest days as a church was superb. When we consider that society was practically submerged in a bath of alcohol, the testimony of early Methodism was a striking example of social conscience in advance of the age. An idea of the general tolerance with which the drinking of liquor was held may be gleaned from the fact that the second and third Methodist churches in New York City had rooms for storing liquor in the basement. The fumes of alcohol cast an aroma over many church functions in America. "Rum and true religion" were boon companions. On occasions such as church dedications, pastoral installations, weddings, quarterly meetings, the flow of soul was accelerated by liquor, no matter what the consequences to the feast of reason might be. The Friends in Pennsylvania made quite an ecclesiastical innovation when they prohibited the use of strong drink at funerals, where it had been customary to serve it with sorry results. In 1820 over seven gallons per capita of distilled spirits were consumed.

The General Rules of the Methodist Societies, drawn up by Wesley, had an emphatic clause against "drunkenness, buying and selling spiritous liquors, or drinking them except in cases of extreme necessity." If the Methodist Church in America had been able to stick to this standard, its history in relation to liquor would have been a matter for far greater pride than it is at present. The early Conferences indeed made a gratifying start. In the Conference of 1780 at Baltimore the following official records were found:

Question 23: Do we disapprove of the practice of distilling grain into liquor? Shall we disown our friends who will not renounce the practice?

Answer: Yes.

In 1783, the year before the formal organization of the church, an even stronger position was taken:

Question 11: Should our friends be permitted to make spiritous liquors, sell, and drink them in drams?

Answer: By no means. We think it wrong in its nature and consequences; and desire all our preachers to teach the people by precept and example.

But in 1786 this declaration was sponged out and in 1790 Wesley's flag was hauled down ignominiously. The part of his rule forbidding the "buying and selling of spiritous liquors" was left out, thus removing the ban on the liquor business, and Wesley's words forbidding drinking "except in cases of extreme necessity" was changed to "cases of necessity." This left an easy excuse for a dram!

Wesley's rule was not restored to its place in the *Discipline* until fifty-eight years later. During all that time temperance sentiment within the church went forward and back, but with a general quickening of conscience on the matter. Leaders with decided convictions, among them Wilbur Fisk, added to the growing sentiment against liquor. It seems incredible to us in this day that the General Conference of 1812 defeated a motion making the penalty for a minister who sold alcoholic liquor the forfeiting of his ministerial character! But against the tremendous inertia of social custom progress continued to be made until, as

"THE FIGHT AGAINST DRINK"

recorded above, the clear cut rule of Wesley's went back into the *Discipline* in 1848. From this time forward the testimony of Methodism has been unwavering, and in practical effort in the fight against drink the church has not been surpassed by any group in the nation.

The restoration of the original position in regard to liquor in the Methodist Episcopal Church in 1848 coincided with the beginning of the first of three great waves of the temperance and prohibition movement in the United States. The first was in the fifties, one fruit of which was the enactment of the State prohibition law of Maine in 1850. The second was in the late eighties and early nineties. The third was the movement for national prohibition from 1910 on, culminating in the enactment of the prohibition amendment to the Constitution, the Eighteenth Amendment, in 1918. During these sixty years the official pronouncements of Methodism, both North and South, have steadily advanced. In 1872 the General Conference of the Methodist Episcopal Church expressed its conviction of "the absolute need of total legal prohibition."

The first active form of the temperance movement was the agitation of total abstinence. Many different temperance societies arose with hundreds of thousands of pledge-takers. These societies contributed mightily to the strength of the movement against the consumption of liquor. But it became increasingly evident that more than mere abstinence from the use of liquor would be required to rid the country of the evil. The prohibition of the traffic in liquor began to be recognized more and more widely as the indispensable adjunct to temperance.

Beginning with the early fifties in many States there were efforts to adopt State prohibition laws. These efforts were successful in several States. Between 1851 and 1856 the Legislatures of practically all the States were compelled to wrestle with prohibition. In many States prohibition laws were enacted, only to be declared unconstitutional. This happened in Rhode Island, Illinois, Indiana, Pennsylvania, and many other States. In some States prohibition laws were passed and later repealed. The results of this era of State prohibition efforts were, on the whole, discouraging. There were three chief factors in the nonsuccess of these efforts. One was the fact that the slavery issue became so acute just before the Civil War as to overshadow prohibition. A second reason was the partisan character of the support of prohibition measures. A third was the failure properly to follow up the victory. The educational value of these campaigns, however, was enormous.

A new form of the fight for the outlawry of the liquor traffic was the organization of the Prohibition Party, which became a national partisan political party in 1869, although in truth it was always more of a crusade than a political party. The first campaign in which there was a Prohibition candidate was 1872. The largest prohibition vote ever polled was in 1892—270,710 votes. But this, of course, was a mere drop in the political bucket. It was made clearly evident that no hope of prohibition was to be had through a separate party. The Prohibition Party, however, did valuable service in pioneering the path of political activity and helped to clear the way for the nonpartisan political activity which was to reap such sweeping victories in later years. In addition the Prohibition Party sounded the alarm against the growing liquor traffic. Many Methodists were among the Prohibition Party candidates both for the Presidency and governorship of various States.

The most spectacular, as well as one of the most influential features of the growing temperance movement was the advent of women into the story. Then the plot thickens, as usual. With the beginning of the so-called "Women's Crusade" in Ohio in 1873, on through the organization and achievement of the Woman's Christian Temperance Union, the fight against liquor took on a fervor and passion and "drive" which it had never known before.

A good many stories have started in this manner: "It was Christmas eve and the snow was falling." That is the way the story of woman's part in the prohibition struggle begins. We are not quite sure of the snow, but will put it in for appropriate

Christmas decoration. The Christmas Eve part is historical enough. On December 24, 1873, in the little town of Hillsboro, Ohio, a lecturer addressed some women of the town on the project of getting rid of the saloon in their community by

"IT WAS CHRISTMAS EVE AND THE SNOW WAS FALLING"

prayer and visitation. They decided to make such an attempt, and the following day they celebrated Christmas by beginning what was destined to sweep the country as a great moral crusade and out of which was to spring in the following year the Woman's Christian Temperance Union.

The method of the women may be said to have been "biblical" in that it followed very closely the tactics of the importunate widow in the Gospel story. It was a campaign of persistent and eventually irresistible irritation and agitation. It forms one of the most thrilling stories of all reform history. When the method assumed the form of women kneeling in the snow in the streets in front of saloons in Ohio towns, it was considered a theme for boundless ridicule and derision. But it did not take long for the saloon-keepers and the public to realize that ridicule was no weapon for this kind of an attack. Here was strategy of a new sort, force with an unknown X to it. Call it wild, as many did, yet it was the wildness of a hurricane. The year 1874 was memorable for the Woman's Crusade which swelled the ranks of total abstainers and put hundreds of saloons out of business. These women circulated pledges, appealed personally to druggists, physicians, real-estate owners and lawyers for cooperation. They visited saloons in companies, frequently praying with the proprietors and bartenders. They stood at the doors of saloons and took down the names of all who entered, thus bringing into action an effective form of social pressure.

Hundreds of these women were Methodists. Their names are not known to history, but they contributed mightily to the history of the church and deserve a notable place in its record. They helped forward one of the largest social movements in modern history. Their entrance into the active temperance fight did much to make it a passionate crusade.

Among this host of Methodist women unknown to fame, one stands out with an international reputation, one of the notable figures of her time—Frances E. Willard. She was a woman who does not readily fit into a pigeonhole. She compelled a classification for herself. She was a woman of a wide variety of abilities and found a superb field for them in the leadership of the women, first of the United States and later of the world, in the temperance cause. She was elected president of the National Woman's Christian Temperance Union in 1879 and of the World's Union when it was founded in 1883. She retained these positions until the time of her death in 1898. Her great contribution was made both as an orator and an executive. Her influence extended far beyond the limits of her organization or even the one cause of temperance. She helped forward greatly the cause of woman suffrage through her effective advocacy. Indeed, the Woman's Christian Tem-

perance Union did much to pioneer the cause of woman suffrage, which was destined to play so great a part in numerous
State and local prohibition campaigns.

An indispensable part of the story of the outlawing of
the saloon was played by the Anti-Saloon League. In this
organization the churches found for the first time an effective
political instrument against the saloon. By 1890 it had become evident that the partisan onslaught against liquor through a separate political party was doomed to failure. A new method was demanded and was brought into action by the Anti-Saloon
League which aimed to bring temperance forces into cooperative
action, regardless of all other alliances. It also supplied

FRANCES E. WILLARD

a new strategy in attacking the liquor traffic first at points of
least resistance, namely in small centers, towns and rural districts. The Anti-Saloon League was organized in 1893 in Ohio
and rapidly spread over the country. Many of the strong
leaders of this organization were Methodists, including national
directors, and two bishops who served as national president.

From 1895 the growth of dry territory was steady and
rapid. The outstanding feature of these years was an awakening to the curse of the saloon and a growingly irresistible determination to crush it. From State prohibition the demand for

national prohibition grew rapidly and steadily after 1900, till on July 1, 1918, a prohibition law was enacted as a war measure. The Eighteenth Amendment to the Constitution, making prohibition the law of the land, went into effect January 16, 1920.

That date is a great landmark. But it did not mark the end of the modern fight against liquor in the United States. It merely opened a new chapter. It was not to be expected that so great a social experiment as prohibition, involving such far-reaching changes as it did, could be established without a long and tense period of adjustment and effort at enforcement. The most formidable and violent assault against the prohibition law did not develop until 1925-26. The country is still in the midst of crucial and testing days. The danger is not that the Eighteenth Amendment will be repealed but that it may be nullified in many quarters. One of the great battles of the Methodist and all the churches for years to come will be fought on this battlefield.

§ 3. THE BATTLE FOR A CHRISTIAN SOCIAL ORDER

The battlefield of reform on which the supreme struggle of the present generation, and doubtless of this century, is being waged is that of the struggle to make the whole social order Christian, to apply the principles of Jesus to all institutions of society. This is an inclusive struggle which takes in the whole frontage of human life. The battlefield is not like a particular engagement which has often been the turning point in some notable conflict. It is, rather, like the battle line in the World War which stretched clear across the whole continent of Europe. This massive struggle extends all along the whole of civilization.

Of course it is true that in all ages there has been effort on the part of the Christian Church and individual Christians to better the conditions of human life. The Christian religion has always had beneficial social effects wherever it has gone. We have already glimpsed, for instance, some of the far-reaching social effects of the Evangelical Revival of the eighteenth century in which Methodism had its birth. Yet what is commonly called "the social gospel," as we know it to-day—which is the application of the teaching of Jesus and the total Christian message to the economic, political, and social life of mankind—is in the main, an emphasis which has characterized only the last fifty years. Indeed, the period of the social movement among the churches of the United States begins as recently as about thirty-five years ago, in 1890. It remains for us here to trace briefly the part which Methodism has played and is at present playing in this outstanding development in the Christianity of our time.

The recovery of the social gospel of Christianity has not been the achievement of any one denomination or group. It is not to be confined to any one nation. It is the result of a large number and variety of causes, some of which will be later mentioned. It is important to hold in mind, that the so-called "social gospel" is not a modern invention but a recovery of an emphasis on elements in the teaching of Jesus which were largely neglected and lost for centuries. Its recovery in our time has been a veritable Christian renaissance. It involves no risky venture in prophecy to hazard the prediction that the recovery of the social implications of Jesus' teaching will prove a renaissance much more far-reaching than that which marked the end of the Middle Ages. The social application of Christianity is the recovery of the main emphasis of the preaching of Jesus—the kingdom of God. Jesus promised membership in a social order—the kingdom of God. Before one could join this kingdom he must have the social attitude of love. As Christianity developed, however (and this seems the supreme tragedy of Christian history), this thought, so central in the teaching of Jesus, was not followed or stressed. The emphasis was placed, for the most part, either on ecclesiasticism in this world or on a future heaven. From this came the almost exclusively individual character of the gospel preached down until the latter part of the nineteenth century.

In truth, of course, there is only one Christian gospel of salvation. But its application can be both to individuals and social groups. The individual application occupied almost the entire emphasis through Christian history. The effort was largely to save individuals *out of* the world, with little idea of saving the world itself and making its institutions, its laws, its industry, government, and social agencies expressions of the principles of Jesus. A comprehensive Christianity will do both. It will lift men out of the gutter but will not stop there. It must destroy the gutter. The modern social conception of Christianity is a recognition that the gospel is for the redemption of the total life of man.

There were many causes contributing to the recovery of this enlarged conception of the gospel of Jesus. The last decade of the nineteenth century saw a rapidly growing interest in the social significance of Christianity. It came in part from a new emphasis laid on the central teaching *of* Jesus, in distinction from the biblical teaching *about* Jesus. The historical study of the Bible and Christianity contributed greatly. So did the rapid spread of interest in sociology. It became more and more recognized that man cannot be dissociated from his social surroundings and their influence, that economic welfare has inescapable bearing on spiritual welfare. The very development of industrial conditions forced these truths on the attention of thinking Christian people. Unrestricted individualism in industry had resulted in the exploitation of labor. Slums increased in the cities. Economic problems were more and more seen to be moral problems. In general, human values were being subordinated to property values, a state of affairs that was gradually recognized as utterly unchristian. Here and there ministers began to preach the social teachings of Jesus and the Hebrew prophets as they discovered them anew and cried out for the ethics of a Christian society.

Among this number were many Methodists. To the Methodist Episcopal Church belongs the honor of making the first ringing declaration on social questions in a national church convention. This was in the General Conference in 1908. This action was a landmark of the progress of social feeling and thinking in the church and had effects on the whole body of Protestant churches in North America. That General Conference adopted a report of the Committee on the State of the Church in which was embedded a bill of human rights, a declaration of social ideals which the church declared that it stood for. This became known as "The Social Creed of the Methodist Episcopal Church." Immediately after the General Conference, in December, 1908, the Federal Council of the Churches of Christ in America was organized, representing thirty-three Protestant denominations. This organization, as one of its first actions, adopted in an expanded form the social creed of the Methodists and it became known as "The Social Creed of the Churches." It was adopted later by many other denominations.

This pronouncement on social questions marked such an important step in the history of Methodism, and of the other churches, that it should be outlined in some detail. The Creed declares that the churches stand for equal rights and complete justice to all men; for the protection of the family, the abolition of child labor, and the regulation of work for women; for the abatement of poverty and the liquor traffic; for a living wage and the right of workers to unite; for the most equitable division of the product of industry that can ultimately be devised and for a new emphasis on the application of Christian principles to the acquisition and use of property.

Of course this creed represented a goal, an ideal. But as such it has been of large service in quickening the social thinking of the church and helping to bring actual practices up to the ideal.

It will not, of course, be imagined that the attempt to project Christian principles into industry and economic relations met with unanimous enthusiasm on the part of all church members. Far from it. For one thing there was the inertia of traditional conceptions to be overcome. There were those who insisted that the church should keep itself wholly aloof from social and economic questions and stick to preaching abstract virtue and individual morality. There was another group which held that any attempt to Christianize the social order is contrary to the belief in the second coming of Christ. Then it must be confessed that there has been still another group whose

"THE CHURCH STANDS FOR THE ABOLITION OF CHILD LABOR"

violent opposition to the application of the teachings of Jesus
has been due to interested motives. Their cry has been the old
one, "Let us alone." For the abolition of social injustice
strikes at unjust profits; it interferes with vested interests
based on the exploitation of labor. In the name of the brotherhood of Christ the aroused Christian social conscience thunders
into the ears of the modern taskmasters of industry, the command which Moses thundered into the ears of Pharaoh, "Let
my people go!"

In spite of opposition, however, the realization of the social
task of Christianity has taken steadily increasing hold on the
churches. In the Methodist Episcopal Church there has been
a continual advance both in formal authoritative statement of
the Church's position and conviction on social questions and
in the practical effort to apply Christian ideals in the economic
and industrial world. Every General Conference from 1908
to 1924 has made passionate and courageous concrete declaration on the social implications of the gospel of Jesus. Two
samples out of a large number of such authoritative utterances
may be given to indicate the trend. The first is from the Episcopal address to the General Conference of 1916:

We call upon our members as employers, investors, or wage-earn-
ers to do everything in their power to further measures such as trade
agreements between employers and organized workers, minimum wage
adjustments, profit sharing cooperative plans, which look to the main-
tenance of a living wage, the correction of unjust equalities in the distribution of wealth, the increasing democratization of industry, the
Christianization of the world's work in the name of that abundant life
which our Master came to promote.

The other is the action of the General Conference of 1924:

The fact that Christ died for all men is a sufficient warrant for
our deep concern with all social forces which touch the welfare of men.
The historic notes of emphasis in Methodism have been on conversion,
on entire sanctification, on the capture of the child life from earliest
infancy for the Kingdom of heaven, on the right of way of the spiritual

interests over all ecclesiastical organization. If these high religious values stand enthroned at the center of historic Methodism, we cannot stop short of the advocacy of such reconstruction of society in its industrial, agricultural, commercial, and political aspects, as will tend to the spread of scriptural holiness. We must stand for such social

"INDUSTRY SHALL LEAD A NEW LIFE"

measures as will give the inner personal life its chance. Our call for the evangelization of men rightly does not stop merely with the proclamation of free grace. We must preach the duty of the conversion and sanctification of men in their wider institutional relationships. We cannot do our full duty to Methodism if we do not insist that industry and commerce and politics shall henceforth lead a new life following the commandments of God and walking in his holy ways.

Industry should be made the instrument for aiding men to find that abundant life for which Christianity stands. We call once again not merely for the physical conditions which will make for the Christianization of industry—for a living wage and for all possible safeguards for health and security—but for the higher prerequisites for sound human existence, for the recognition of labor's right to organize, for the laborer's right to be heard through representatives of his own choosing, for an increasing share of responsibility by labor in the control of industry. We believe that the time has come for the serious trying out of plans aiming at doing away with unemployment.

The same emphasis on the social conception of the Christian gospel has been made in the Methodist Episcopal Church, South. The following declaration made in the Episcopal Address to the General Conference of the Methodist Episcopal Church, South, in 1926, fairly represents the ideal and standard of that church:

An outstanding fact in the life and work of the world to-day is the steady, irresistible translation into the life of individuals and of organized society of the teaching of Jesus Christ concerning the vital central truth of human brotherhood, of the obligation of neighborly love, including willing self-denial, and the implication and practical results which necessarily follow a sincere recognition of that fact.

Herein is implied the right of all men and women to a living wage, to limited hours of service, proper restrictions on child labor, a larger participation in the fruits of industry, better medical care, more parks and playgrounds, opportunity for self-culture and development—in short, whatever makes for a richer, fuller life.

This social movement in Methodism looks both toward the past and the future. It looks to the past, for it is the expression of an interest in social welfare which characterized Methodism in its earliest days. It is true, of course, that the preaching of Wesley and early Methodists was primarily directed to individual salvation. But the early leaders were not indifferent to the social consequences which followed their preaching. John Richard Green in his history of England has strongly emphasized this in a single sentence. "The noblest result of the Methodist revival," he says, "was the steady attempt, which has never ceased from that day to this, to remedy the guilt, the ignorance, the physical suffering, the social degradation of the profligate and the poor."

This social interest looks also to the far future, for the line of march of Christianity in this century will be on the increasing embodiment of the principles of Jesus into the fabric of civilization, into its institutions and human relationship, its whole varied life. Christ cannot be kept in any separate corner of life any more than he could be kept in the tomb on the resurrection morning. He must be Lord of all.

CHAPTER XXVI

A LIVING CHURCH IN A BROKEN WORLD

§ 1. WHEN THE WORLD EXPLODED

ONE of the most colorful conferences which the world has ever seen met in Edinburgh, Scotland, in 1910. To it came men from every continent. In it arose prayers in scores of tongues. Compared with it the councils which the church has called ecumenical—such as that of Nicea, sixteen hundred years ago—were mere local gatherings, for the Edinburgh conference of 1910 represented the missionary work of the Protestant Church, and that is the most far-flung, the most inclusive enterprise the world has ever known.

The delegates who came to Edinburgh had a right to feel some complacency. On all the continents they had seen the seed which had first been sown not much more than a hundred years before spring into great churches, numbering their adherents by the hundreds of thousands, and giving promise of the day when they should even outstrip in size the churches of Western lands. No one would have been surprised had the conference spoken as though it were celebrating what it believed must be forever the most remarkable period in the tale of the expansion of the church. But it did not do so. Instead, it listened to reports as they came in from all the continents, and then made the prophecy that "the next ten years will undoubtedly prove a turning point in human history."

If ever a prophecy was fulfilled beyond the furthest dreams of those who made it, that one was. For in the ten years that followed 1910 there burst upon the world a war which extended over four continents and involved twenty-three nations; which destroyed in one conflagration one half of the accumulated wealth of the world; which sent ancient empires crashing to doom and raised new republics to the family of nations; which fostered a new national and a new racial consciousness in every part of the earth; which speeded such social, mechanical, and scientific changes as have resulted in the development of the woman's movement and of the prohibition movement in one realm, the development of the aeroplane and the radio in a second, and the development of an almost new physics and chemistry in still a third.

Many of the nations have already bound themselves, in an effort to pay for their share in the World War, by debt settlements which have more than sixty years to run. But even if these agreements are carried out to the letter, and our grandchildren or our great-grandchildren see the last of the war debts paid, no one will then be able to say that the world has recovered from the madness of 1914-18. The world can never recover from the war. And the church, as an institution in the world, must from now on direct most of its energies to the discovery of a ministry which meets the needs of nations which have been torn and broken and embittered, and now come groping, stumbling, seeking some sure light. "When God rubs out," says Bossuet, "it is because he is beginning to write." The church must be quick to recognize the new writing, and the Methodist Church with all the rest.

§ 2. THE WAR

The coming of the war to America found the Methodist Church in a period of great prosperity. During the first quarter of a century the denomination had maintained its place as the largest, in point of membership, in the United States, and had taken its part in the various advance movements which were engaging the attention of American Protestantism. The war itself caught the church practically unprepared, as it caught the entire nation. The conflict which had been in progress for

more than two years on the other side of the Atlantic had not
seemed to apply to America. It had been regarded as a huge
piece of European insanity, the result of an outworn statecraft.
And then, suddenly, the Methodist Church found itself a part
of a nation in arms.

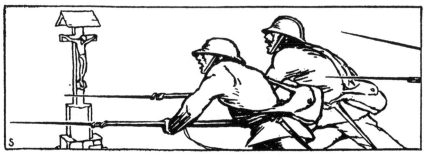

"FOR THE SPIRITUAL LIBERATION OF MANKIND"

For years there had been a movement toward world peace
within the churches. This movement had received encouragement from Methodist sources; many Methodists were conspicuous in its leadership. But with the outbreak of the war
the entire power of the church was mobilized in support of the
government. The American nation was being guided by a
President who, more than any other man in the world, was
able to interpret the conflict in terms of moral issues. Wood-
row Wilson's interpretation, of course, became the interpretation of the nation. And as it reached its mightiest expression in that great speech in which the President dedicated the
arms of America to "a war to end war" and to a crusade "to
make the world safe for democracy," the church felt its last
hesitation vanish, and rushed to pledge its support to such a
cause. Later, when these general phrases found specific application in the President's announcement of his "Fourteen
Points," the church again found basis for its faith that the war
was, at bottom, a venture for the spiritual liberation of mankind.

The war is still so fresh in our thought that it is not necessary to recall in detail the ways in which the church sought to aid the government. In every campaign for funds, both for the government itself and for such supplementary bodies as the Red Cross and the Y. M. C. A., and in the attempts to show to the public the necessity for conserving food and carrying on those other services so necessary behind the lines, the church played a conspicuous part. Nor was it content to confine its interest to the backing of the fighting forces. At the first possible moment the Methodist Church in both its branches rushed into Europe with relief work, which called for the expenditure of millions of dollars, but which showed without delay the interest which the church had in seeking to heal the wounds of the conflict.

§ 3. THE CENTENARY

The characteristic answer of Methodism to the war was the Centenary. Long before the United States entered the war the church had planned to celebrate with a program of missionary expansion the hundred years which had passed since John Stewart began to preach among the Wyandott Indians. At first this program was conceived as exclusively foreign missionary. Then, as the extent of the needs became more clear, home missions was included, and later the war relief work to which reference has already been made. Finally, practically all the work which the Methodists of America, both north and south, planned to do outside their local congregations during the five years following 1919 was made a part of the Centenary's interest. The cost of this five years of work was fixed at more than one hundred million dollars. It is to the lasting credit of Methodism that in the midst of a great national preoccupation, such as the war was, it could lift its eyes to prevision and provide on this scale for the needs of the non-Christian world.

Sometimes there has been hasty speech suggesting that the Centenary was merely an attempt to take advantage of the peculiar psychology evoked in the public by the war to finance a vast denominational program. It was much more than that. It was a recognition, even while the world was filled with battle-smoke, that the old world had passed, and that a new world must be built. "Jesus Christ alone can save the world," said a call issued to the church while the fighting was still in progress. "Guns cannot. They leave but a desert waste. The upbuilding of the world begins when war has spit its last bomb and thrust its last bayonet. Governments and armies can never accomplish the results necessary to the establishment of the kingdom of God. There is but one institution in the world that has such a program; that institution is the Church of Jesus Christ."

With world conditions what they were from 1916, when the Centenary was authorized, to the beginning of 1919, it is amazing that the church was able to discover as well as it did the needs of the fields. The way in which the surveys were made; the way in which the results of the surveys were carried to the churches; the way in which practically all the members of the churches were brought to feel that they had an individual responsibility for this next forward step—all this and much more that had to do with the mechanics of the enterprise is still so fresh in our minds that it needs no recounting here. It is enough to suggest the efficiency of the campaign, perhaps, to say that, with the Methodist Centenary under way, several other churches launched similar movements closely patterned after the model set by the Methodist leaders.

It is still too early to judge the Centenary fully. Like all great efforts, the perspective of many years will be required to show clearly what its effects on the life of the church and of the world have been. But it is possible to see that some things were accomplished. In the first place, American Methodists were helped to think of their religious enterprise in world terms at precisely the same time that Americans were being called on to think of all their other enterprises in those terms. There came a realization of the immense areas, both in terms of geography and of human living, into which the gospel has not yet entered, and of the size of the task which thus remains before the church. Standards of giving were raised. Young life was called to the service of the church with much the same enthusiasm which had recently been employed in recruiting for the nation's service. New buildings were erected, new enterprises begun, both in America and on the other continents.

That the Centenary was not all permanent advance will be admitted. There was, it is probable, too much use of the war psychology. How that might have been escaped in the atmosphere of 1917-1919 it is hard to see, but because it was not escaped, when the reaction struck the country at large it struck the church as well. Much that had been projected, and even pledged, under the enthusiastic spell of the days just after the armistice, was found impossible of fulfillment in the cold gray light of the postwar depression. Moreover, the Centenary did, by certain of its promotional methods, tend to make shoddy thinkers believe that the task of building the kingdom

THE CIRCUIT-RIDER OF THIS CENTURY

of God is simply a task of perfecting a high-pressure organization of churches and ministers for the raising of certain definitely ascertainable sums of money. In these, and perhaps some other ways, an atmosphere of false excitement and achievement was created, which could not be kept up. Gradually this promotional fever evaporated. With its passing there were left certain problems of adjustment which have perplexed many leaders, and many whom the church had commissioned for work in various difficult fields. The solution of these problems is a matter of time and hard thinking. When the readjustments are completed, the permanent benefit which has grown out of the Centenary will be clear.

§ 4. Problems on a World Scale

A church that would live powerfully in a broken world must grapple with problems which are world-wide in their bearing. Any consideration of the sort of issues which challenge the church to-day will suggest at once their international aspect. What are these issues?

First of all, there is the thing which has brought the world to ruin—war. War is seen to-day for what, with the aid of modern science, it has become, not a means of settling vital questions between nations, but an intricate system which often reduces those who are enmeshed within it to poverty, both of soul and of goods. The churches of the earth are arousing to fight the war system, and in conference after conference have given notice of their determination to wipe it off the earth. Methodism is sharing in this movement, and has contributed much to it. Here are some of the planks in the Methodist program against war, as adopted by the General Conference in 1924:

War is not inevitable. It is the supreme enemy of mankind. Its futility is beyond question. Its continuance is the suicide of civilization. We are determined to outlaw the whole war system. . . .

We set ourselves to create the will to peace. . . . We set ourselves to create the conditions for peace. . . . We set ourselves to
create organization for peace. . . .

The principles of brotherhood are plainly challenged.   The
progress of the kingdom of Jesus Christ is clearly at stake.   The issues
are so momentous, the opportunity for leadership is so great, that we
here and now call upon all people to avoid divisive and fruitless discussions and unite their energies in this great movement for a warless
world.

Then there is the race question.   Growing directly out of
the disillusionments of the war and of the peace which followed it, there has been the world around a great outburst of
racial consciousness and assertiveness.   The claim of the white
man to an inherent superiority, or to any right to rule over the
men of other nations because of the pigment of his skin, is
rejected, utterly and with scorn, by the peoples of the tinted
races.   Treatment of the racial issue, whether in the United
States, in Japan, in China, in India, or in Africa, has become
the touchstone by which the multiplied millions of the non-
Christian world are judging our right to act as missionaries of
Jesus of Nazareth.   There is no question which is more likely

to bring the whole
world to the verge of
another conflict than
this.   It is pre-emi-
nently the question
which is to prove the
ultimate test by which
a church will be
measured to ascer-
tain its fitness for a
world task.   The
Methodist Church
spoke thus on race
in 1924:

"TO CREATE THE WILL TO PEACE"

We repudiate as unchristian and untrue the idea that certain races are born to inherent and fixed superiority and rulership, while others are born to inherent and fixed inferiority and subordination. We stand for the life of open opportunity for all.

The same pronouncement declared against the present immigration policy of the United States, with its exclusion of Orientals on the racial basis, and spoke out in the strongest possible terms against the lynching horror.

Finally, there is the problem raised by modern industry. The industrial revolution, insofar as the Western World is concerned, is completed, and even Asia and Africa will to-morrow be industrialized. But industry can be a ferocious master. Inspired by the profit motive, it has not hesitated again and again to turn the days of childhood into hours of torture, and to deprive womanhood and manhood of their gentleness and their strength. The Methodist position on industrial questions has already been stated in the preceding chapter.

When you take documents such as these, and see not only what they say but also what thoughts lie behind them, you can easily understand in what a favorable position the Methodist Church is as it enters the second quarter of this twentieth century. Here are three overwhelming world questions. Yet on every one the church has already spoken officially, and in a way to hearten all those whose faces are turned toward the future. The only question is whether or not the church means what she has said. We have already seen, sadly, how boldly the church spoke out on slavery, and again on temperance, and how she temporarily retreated from her first fine stand on those great issues when the fire became too hot for comfort. Will she repeat that course on war, on race, and on industry? Or will she, having taken her stand, refuse to budge an inch, except it be to go forward? Will she, having put her hand to the plow, drive the furrow straight through to the end, however long it may be?

§ 5. METHODISM'S FUTURE

There are, of course, other issues than these which the church must face. War, race, industry—these are problems which confront all men. Methodism has some problems which are peculiarly her own. Most pressing, probably, are the ones which grow out of the missionary expansion of recent years, of which we have already written.

It is a curious fact that while the Methodist Church came into existence without its founder ever planning that it should be a church, it has spread as has no other Protestant body, and it has become the most closely organized religious group in the world, with the single exception of the Roman Catholic communion. This is particularly true of the two Methodist Episcopal Churches. Attend a General Conference of either of these bodies and you will be struck by the presence of delegates from all the continents except Australia, sitting with the same legal powers as the delegates from the Conferences of the United States. These men and women in Methodist General Conferences do not come from India, from China, from Rhodesia, as representatives of *missions*. That is the status with which Christian workers from those lands come to the national assemblies of many other denominations. But in the case of the Methodists, they come as members of Annual Conferences. And those Conferences are represented on exactly the same terms as the Conferences of New York, or Indiana, or California.

This is what men have in mind when they talk about the world-wide organization of Methodism. In these days when such a struggle is in process to set up means of tying the world together in interests which transcend national boundaries, such an organization as the Methodist Episcopal Churches have might seem to be a providential one. But it brings its difficulties as well as its promises. If the Methodist Church is to be one body on all the continents, that may be a source of power. But it may equally be a source of discord, unless the church chooses its path with great care.

It has already been said that the years following the war have witnessed an amazing growth of racial and nationalistic spirit among the nonwhite peoples of the earth. If, now, the Methodist Church, with its roots so largely in a white land, should persist in conducting its work in Asia and in Africa, and even in the Latin countries, in a way which showed that— whatever its protestations—it really thought of those lands as fields for the building of an ecclesiastical empire, to be controlled by the white ecclesiast, just as political empires have been controlled by white colonial administrators, there would come inevitably an uprising that would bring the whole structure down in ruin. If the world-wide conception of the Methodist Church is to persist, it can only be on a basis of mutual recognition between the parts in the East and the West which shall give to all those parts virtual self-control.

The church already recognizes something of the demands of this situation. Its first impulse, following the war, when it saw the new fields of opportunity standing wide open, was to reach those fields as they had been reached in the past. The years of the Centenary saw more than six hundred and fifty new missionaries go out from the United States, and a group of more than a dozen new American bishops to lead the new campaigns thus made possible. But, as the changed situation on the other continents has been more clearly seen, it has become clear that just sending out Americans is not the answer to the new needs. Accordingly, the church has begun to rewrite its *Discipline* covering the control of its work overseas. By actions taken in 1924, the Methodists of the other continents now have the right very largely to set up the disciplinary standards which shall control their life. Within a very few years they will be asking that the final means of control be placed in their hands, and that they shall have likewise the power to select their own leaders. All this is now seen as the inevitable course of a church which is no longer an "infant," but on every continent a lusty youngster, rapidly reaching full manhood.

The other pressing problem before the church grows out of the same condition. On all these other continents, the yeast of new ideas, new self-consciousness, is affecting not only the Methodists, but the members of all churches. And, as these Christians look about and see themselves surrounded by the millions of other faiths, they instinctively draw closer and closer together. So the day has come when they have begun to ask why they should not, in many lands, make of the Protestant Christians one united body. What difference does it make to the Christians of China whether the Anglican Church in the eighteenth century was not wise enough to make a place for Wesley's societies, or whether the American Methodists of the nineteenth century could not withstand the disruption of a Civil War, or whether the Scotch Presbyterians of the twentieth century could not agree on the details of church government? Come together these Oriental Christians eventually will, for the Western denominational lines which now divide them are too shadowy, too artificial long to hold. The problem that the Methodists must solve, if they are to preserve their message around the world, is as to how they can join in this growing movement toward unity and at the same time hold what they now have. Perhaps they can't. Perhaps it is not God's will that they should. Perhaps the next great step in the path which God would have them walk is a step toward the sinking of their denominational name and individuality in something greater.

§ 6. Conclusion

When the world has been rent, as it has been during the first quarter of the present century, no man is wise enough to say what the future is to be. So any prophecy as to the exact ways in which the Methodists will play their part in the building of a new world on the shattered foundations of the old would be a waste of time. There are two things which we have seen, however, as this record of the past has unfolded, both of which should have some significance for the future. The first was the promise which John Wesley made to those who listened to him, and on which the structure of Methodism has been reared. The second is the spirit in which the advances of the past have been accomplished.

Expressed in the simplest words, the promise of John Wesley was that men might experience the power of religion to help them in such a way that they would be willing to rely on its reality. Wesley came to people in a befuddled time, when a lifeless, academic doctrinal preaching had left the masses a fair mark for the ridicule of all the doubters. Wesley said: "The way out from all that is to let God work *in* you. What happens there, you will know has happened." This has been called the Methodist emphasis on experience. It is still a valid emphasis. The world badly needs a good deal of it just now.

The spirit in which Methodism has made its real advances, as this story has tried to show, has been in its readiness to adventure in unaccustomed ways. Methodism really began when a handful of college students defied the conventions of their campus; it spread over England when a handful of daring young ministers defied the conventions of their church; it has reached the world in those hours when its heroes have defied the conventions of their times. Methodism has had its hours of regularity, of conformity, of walking in the well-marked roads. But those have not been the high hours. A conforming Methodism is just one among many denominations—a healthy influence in the life of the community, of course, but not to be distinguished by much from the other healthy religious influences there. But whenever the moment comes that Methodism is ready to break the trammels of convention, to forget the trodden paths, to mount again for a new circuit through some new wilderness or along some new border, then Methodism becomes a-flame once more, and there burns again before the eyes of men that pillar of fire which John Wesley dreamed that the movement which he founded should ever be.

INDEX

LaVergne, TN USA
01 September 2009
156546LV00003B/7/A

9 780687 063871

Made in the USA
Lexington, KY
10 May 2019